ELEMENTARY NUMERICAL COMPUTING WITH
MATHEMATICA®

ELEMENTARY NUMERICAL COMPUTING WITH
MATHEMATICA®

ROBERT D. SKEEL

University of Illinois at Urbana-Champaign

JERRY B. KEIPER

Wolfram Research Inc.

McGraw-Hill, Inc.

New York   St. Louis   San Francisco   Auckland   Bogotá   Caracas   Lisbon
London   Madrid   Mexico   Milan   Montreal   New Delhi   Paris   San Juan
Singapore   Sydney   Tokyo   Toronto

ELEMENTARY NUMERICAL COMPUTING WITH *MATHEMATICA*®

2 3 4 5 6 7 8 9 0   DOH DOH   9 0 9 8 7 6 5 4 3

ISBN 0-07-057820-6

The editor was Eric M. Munson;
the designer was Jared Schneidman;
the production supervisor was Paula Keller.
R. R. Donnelley & Sons Company was printer and binder.

Mathematica is a registered trademark of Wolfram Research Inc.

Figure 1.3 is courtesy of Helmut Heller. Figure 2.2 is courtesy of W. Kahan.

Library of Congress Cataloging-in-Publication Data

Skeel, Robert D.
    Elementary numerical computing with Mathematica / Robert D. Skeel,
  Jerry B. Keiper. — 1st ed.
        p.   cm. — (McGraw-Hill computer science series)
    Includes bibliographical references and index.
    ISBN 0-07-057820-6
      1. Numerical analysis — Data processing.   2. Mathematica (Computer
file)   I. Keiper, Jerry B.   II. Title.   III. Series.
QA297.S545   1993
519.4'0285'5369 — dc20   92-44410

About the Authors

Robert D. Skeel is professor of Computer Science at the University of Illinois at Urbana-Champaign, where he has taught and performed research since 1973. He received his Ph.D. in computer science from the University of Alberta. He has written numerous articles in journals and elsewhere on numerical methods for ordinary and partial differential equations and linear algebra, and he serves on the editorial board of the *SIAM Journal of Scientific and Statistical Computing*. He is now involved in research at University of Illinois Beckman Institute on computational methods for the dynamics and modeling of biological molecules.

Jerry B. Keiper is one of the original eight co-developers of *Mathematica* and continues to work on its further development. His contribution to *Mathematica* includes much of the code for evaluation of elementary and special mathematical functions as well as many of the numerical algorithms. He received his Ph.D. in computer science in the area of numerical analysis from the University of Illinois in 1989. He has taught mathematics and computer science in various capacities in Nigeria and the United States for over 15 years. Besides mathematics and numerical analysis his interests include bicycling and pipe organ building.

to Marjorie
and
to Susan

Contents

Preface

This book offers a practical, up-to-date, technically sound introduction to numerical methods at an elementary level. Numerical analysis is a subject whose content is shaped by progress in computer science and in hardware and software technology. Much of what should be included in a timely numerical methods textbook cannot be readily found in existing books. For example, the subject of floating-point arithmetic, which is the one numerical tool most often encountered by a computer user, is in need of a correct and practical treatment, especially now that standardized floating-point arithmetic is becoming universal. Another example is adaptive quadrature, which should be done using the *robust* global strategy. Also, our thinking about how to solve problems numerically should not be constrained by the limitations of a language like Fortran (which is nonetheless extremely useful for specialists in scientific computing). For example, with traditional programming languages it is not possible to write a simple program for Newton's method, which is a fundamental tool of numerical analysis. Rather, we should expose students to the greatest range of possibilities for scientific computing—future progress is stimulated by heightened expectations, not by coping with the limitations of the past. More specifically, students should be employing computer algebra and good, easy-to-use graphics. In this regard there is no system currently available that is as advanced in its design and as comprehensive as *Mathematica*. It is a powerful programming language that knows a lot of mathematics, and it is gaining wide acceptance. The usefulness of *Mathematica* and the importance of symbolic computation warrant a place for them in the curriculum.

This is a sophomore/junior level book for students of computer science, mathematics, and engineering. The exposition and written exercises do not require a knowledge of *Mathematica*. Also, many of the computer problems can be adapted to certain other languages. The book contains lessons on *Mathematica* but also assumes reasonable access to the *Mathematica* manual [Wolfram (1991)].

The student is assumed to know a procedural programming language like Pascal or Fortran and elementary calculus and linear algebra. This book is unique in that it does not rely on partial derivatives, which many students study but fail to master. At the same time it covers systems of ordinary differential equations in order to give the student an accurate picture of scientific computing. Since we do not assume a differential equations course, we introduce this topic in Section 8.1. An introduction to differential equations in a numerical methods book is appropriate because numerical techniques have greater intuitive appeal than analytical methods. Also, we assume almost no knowledge of physics or other applications; anything more than superficial contact with applications would be an obstacle for unprepared students.

Above all, the goal of this book is to teach the principles of numerical analysis—to teach concepts that will be remembered after many of the details are forgotten. Other major goals are to teach some simple and useful numerical methods, to indicate the sort of techniques that are used in actual numerical software and thereby suggest what kind of performance might be expected and when it might fail with or without informing the user, to give practical advice on the assessment and enhancement of accuracy, and to show how problems requiring numerical computation arise in applications.

A one-semester course would probably omit some sections. Starred sections are particularly good candidates for omission. Ideally the chapters should be covered in order. However, there are only a few strong dependencies:

- Sections 1.2–1.4 and 2.1–2.4 are needed throughout.
- Sections 1.5 and 2.5 are needed in Chapter 4.
- Sections 5.1–5.3 are needed in Chapter 7.
- Sections 5.1 and 7.2 are needed in Chapter 8.

Starred problems explore topics not fully developed in the text.

For testing the book in class and making valuable suggestions, we wish to thank Professor Paul Saylor and Dr. Lisa Goldberg. We appreciate the forbearance of five classes of CS/Math 257 and one of CS 290. For their assistance we thank the following reviewers: Michael Albertson, Smith College; Renato Deleone, University of Wisconsin; Nessan Fitzmaurice, Case Western Reserve University; George Fix, University of Texas; Elgin Johnston, Iowa State University; Baker Kearfott, University of Southwestern Louisiana; Edward Lumsdaine, University of Toledo; Haesun Park, University of Minnesota; George Polyzos, University of California, San Diego; Kris Stewart, San Diego University; Jennifer Voitle, University of Toledo; Stan Wagon, Macalester College. We also thank the staff of McGraw-Hill, and the compositor, Glenn Scholebo. For their help, we thank Michelle Wilson, who prepared LaTeX for overhead transparencies that formed the nucleus of the first draft; Becky Green, who prepared LaTeX for some later additions; and Christian Erickson, who helped with some figures.

1. Introduction

This book is about
     applying
           the power of mathematics
     and
           the power of the computer
    to solving quantitative problems in
        science and engineering.
This book is about *numerical analysis*.

The *Oxford English Dictionary* (second edition) has the entry

numerical analysis the branch of mathematics that deals with the development and use of numerical methods for solving problems (usually ones too complicated for analytical methods); so numerical analyst.

The use of the term dates back to 1946 at the dawn of the computer era. Although numerical analysis is most often regarded as a branch of mathematics, it is strongly dependent on developments in computer science and technology, and on the needs of applications.

Three attractions of numerical analysis can be mentioned. One is the joy of doing mathematics—working on puzzles having lasting significance. Another is the satisfaction of developing useful software. A third is the excitement of solving interesting applications problems. For a down-to-earth example, consider the problem of determining the effective rate of interest on a home mortgage with "points" as a function of how long one keeps the home.

Applications make numerical analysis a useful tool. Even when numerical methods are embedded in applications software, an acquaintance with numerical computing is needed to understand the limitations of the software. Also, designing computer systems that support such applications requires some familiarity with numerical computing. A most dramatic example occurred during the 1991 Gulf War, when tiny errors in numerical computations compromised the accuracy of a Patriot defense missile and an Iraqi Scud missile slipped through and hit the Army barracks in Dhahran.[1]

---

[1] Even without these errors serious doubts have been expressed about the Patriot's ability to intercept Scuds.

This chapter contains the following sections:

1.1 Applications

Computers have many applications. To many people, especially those in universities, the most exciting application is the advancement of knowledge. And in this arena numerical computation plays a much bigger part than nonnumerical computation. Moreover, crunching numbers is what computers do best. The 1990 winner of the Gordon Bell Prize in the raw computing performance category, a seismic modeling application on a Connection Machine, achieved a computing rate of 14 billion arithmetic operations per second.

How numerical computing is used might be classified as follows:

1. Foremost is simulation. This can have various objectives. Computer simulation is often a key part of the design cycle as in computer-aided design (CAD). Or it can be used strictly for purposes of prediction. Or it can be used in training people in some task, such as how to fly an airplane. In some simulations such as those in computer games, a knowledge of numerical analysis may not matter. But if *realism* is important, then numerical analysis is needed.

2. Also there is data analysis. This includes statistical analysis as well as signal processing and computer vision.

3. Numerical computations occur in real-time applications such as control systems and robotics.

4. Numerical computations are important in computer graphics.

A most important application is **fluid dynamics**. In fact, computational fluid dynamics, widely known by the acronym CFD, is a well-established area of its own. There are computers known as numerical wind tunnels, which are dedicated to modeling flow around aircraft. For the proposed National Aerospace Plane there do not exist physical wind tunnels that can simulate the Mach 25 speeds that are desired, so its design is strongly dependent on numerical simulation. Often fluid flow includes chemical reactions, as in the internal combustion engine.

Another application of great importance is **biology and medicine**. Examples include the analysis of CAT scans and the modeling of blood flow, cell physiology, nerve impulses, and biomolecules. The last of these are not only of scientific interest but are also among the

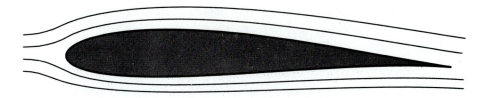

Figure 1.1: Flow around an airfoil

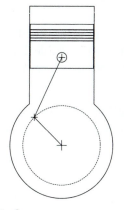

Figure 1.2: Piston in cylinder

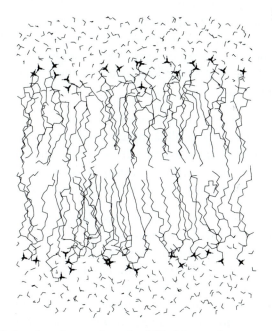

Figure 1.3: Molecular dynamics of a bilipid membrane patch in water

intended products of computer-aided molecular design. More specifically, there are efforts to create proteins, drugs, vaccines, and agrochemicals; of special interest are treatments for cancer and AIDS.

Computational questions of interest in **astronomy** include the formation of stars and the large-scale structure of the universe. Related is the design of flight paths of spacecraft to minimize power requirements. The $902 million spacecraft *Galileo* will reach Jupiter in December 1995 after traversing a path that includes a visit to Venus and two returns to the vicinity of the earth.

These are only three of a broad range of applications dependent on numerical methods. These and others are listed with examples in Table 1.1. It is these applications that were the driving force behind the invention of computers, and today they are the driving force behind advances in supercomputers.

So important is the role of computing that there are many who assert that in addition to experimental science and theoretical science there is now a third mode, computational science, or more broadly, *computational science and engineering*. It is useful for us to distinguish three steps in computational science:

mathematical modeling To solve a scientific or engineering problem on the computer, we need a precise and complete specification; that is, we need a *mathematical* description. The description of some reality by mathematics is called a *model*, and its formulation is called modeling. Models are appearing in an ever-expanding diversity of disciplines, increasing the mathematization of knowledge. However, modeling is not an exact science. Moreover, some models do not give useful answers, but even these can be useful because they force us to clarify our ideas, to put them out in the open, unobscured by ambiguities of natural language.

numerical analysis To make use of most mathematical models, they must be transformed into computer programs, so that all steps are specified in terms of operations executable on a computer. Approximations are usually needed, which implies the use of numerical analysis. Also important are symbolic techniques, which involve the use of nonnumerical data as well as exact integers (and rational numbers).

software development A software interface must be developed so that the modeling program interacts in a friendly way with the user. In particular, there is the need to present the results of the computation to the user. This can be in the form of formulas, tables, and graphics. The question of how to render data as graphical images has attracted a lot of attention under the banner *scientific visualization*. More recently, *virtual reality*, in which the viewer wears a head-mounted stereo display and a data glove, has been proposed as a way to see and interact with data, for example, positioning a drug molecule in the vicinity of DNA.

Application	Example(s)
fluid dynamics	flow around an aircraft, chemically reacting flows such as in an internal-combustion engine
structural and solid mechanics	analysis of a vehicle crash, which in 1990 took 36 hours of Cray time; a bird striking the transparency (windshield) of a fighter jet
materials science	analysis and synthesis of metals, ceramics, polymers, and electronic materials
electrical engineering	modeling electromagnetics, electric circuits, and semiconductor devices; signal processing; control systems
geophysics	seismic data analysis; oil reservoir simulation, which accounts for 10% of supercomputer purchases; and groundwater-management studies. Numerical simulation of fluid flow in porous media dates back to the late 1950s.
meteorology	weather forecasting; global climate modeling—in particular, there is much concern about global warming
physics	plasma physics, where there is the pursuit of controlled nuclear fusion; particle physics, which studies elementary particles; condensed-matter physics, which, for example, attempts to deduce the properties of matter from forces between molecules
astronomy	formation of stars and the large-scale structure of the universe; design of flight paths for spacecraft
chemistry	quantum mechanics calculations for molecules
biology and medicine	analysis of CAT scans; modeling of blood flow, cell physiology, nerve impulses, and biomolecules
economics and finance	computer models to aid decision making and financial planning. The discoveries by L. Khachian and N. Karmarkar of polynomial-time algorithms for linear programming were important science news stories in the 1980s.

Table 1.1: Applications of numerical computing

An example of a model is the diagram of a circuit in Figure 1.4. This is not a real circuit but only a model of the circuit; the matrix equation represents exactly the same model. The diagram is a more understandable representation. Good applications software allows us to construct such diagrams via interactive graphics. Without such tools it can be challenging to set up the model or the problem. In this book we consider only the comparatively easier task of solving the problem.

We use the word "problem" in a technical sense. By a (mathematical) problem we mean a specification of the data (the input), the solution (the output), and the functional relationship

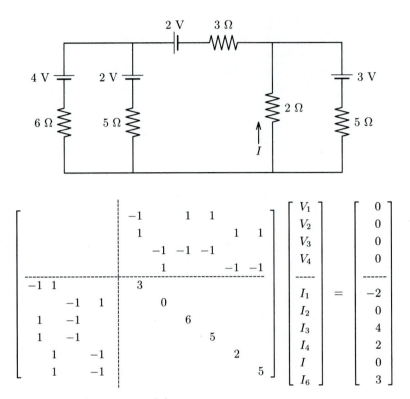

Figure 1.4: This is a model.

between the data and the solution. The objective of numerical analysis is to create reasonably general algorithms for the numerical solution of problems in continuum mathematics.

A simple example of a problem is this: Given real numbers a, b, c, find all real numbers x such that $ax^2 + bx + c = 0$. The answer depends on the sign of the discriminant $b^2 - 4ac$. If it is negative, there is no such x. If it is zero, $x = -b/(2a)$. If it is positive, there are two such x's: $(-b + \sqrt{b^2 - 4ac})/(2a)$ and $(-b - \sqrt{b^2 - 4ac})/(2a)$.

Other kinds of problems are

- evaluating expressions, elementary and special functions, and infinite sums,
- evaluating derivatives and integrals,
- finding eigenvalues, eigenvectors, and roots of polynomials,
- solving systems of equations,
- finding the minimum value of a function, and
- solving differential and integral equations.

The circuit diagram of Figure 1.4 requires the solution of a system of equations in order to find the branch current I.

Historically, numerical methods were regarded as an alternative to *analytical methods*, particularly for those problems for which analytical techniques fail. However, if you want to see the solution of a problem graphically, then numbers will be needed before the graph is plotted—a graph is numbers, sometimes millions of numbers. In such a case there is no special need for analytical methods. Only if we want the answer as a formula are numerical methods inadequate.

In addition to the use of numbers, *numerical* implies the use of approximate operations on numbers. The use of *exact* operations on numbers is normally grouped with symbolic rather than numerical methods. Approximate operations on numbers are very common. If you have ever borrowed money you know that federal Truth in Lending rules require that the Annual Percentage Rate of interest be disclosed to all borrowers. Computing such rates of interest is a nontrivial calculation, and approximations must be used. Even summations are often computed approximately, and such a problem is in the domain of numerical analysis. Much can be said that is interesting about summations (most of which is known only to a few specialists).

The necessity of approximation is the topic of the next section.

Supplementary notes

For a definitive survey of numerical analysis, see the article by C.W. Gear in *The New Encyclopædia Britannica*, 15th ed., Vol. 25, Chicago, 1988, pp. 37–48.

Over the years there has been a trend among specialists to narrow the meaning of the term "numerical analysis" to include only the "analysis of numerical methods," and to use terms like "scientific computing" for the more practical side of the subject. In choosing the title of this book we have somewhat yielded to this trend. At the same time, we believe this development is unhealthy. It is better to retain the dictionary meaning of the term and keep together theory and practice.

1.2   Computational Errors

"Generally the numerical analyst does not strive for exactness."—F.B. Hildebrand, *Introduction to Numerical Analysis*, McGraw-Hill, 1956

Usually we want the solution of a mathematical problem to be available as a finite string of decimal digits, but the exact solution almost always has a nonterminating decimal expansion.

Therefore, errors are unavoidable. Such errors are not mistakes; they are made deliberately. This is what distinguishes numerical computing from symbolic computing. In fact, numerical analysis is a response to the challenge of coping with computational error. If there were no computational error, there would be little left of numerical analysis (and what was left could be absorbed by algebraic and combinatorial computing).

There are two kinds of computational errors:

1. **Roundoff error.** Suppose that a and b are numbers having at most four significant digits. Then the sum $a + b$ might have many more digits; for example, $9.999 \times 10^9 + 9.999 \times 10^{-9}$ has 22 digits. The product $a \times b$ has up to eight digits. The quotient a/b might have an infinite number of digits.

2. **Truncation error.** An infinite process is truncated to produce a finite process; for example,

$$e^x \approx \sum_{n=0}^{100} \frac{x^n}{n!} \quad \text{and} \quad f'(a) \approx \frac{f(a+h) - f(a-h)}{2h}$$

See also Figure 1.5.

Should we then ask for only the first k correct digits of a numerical result? We answer with an example.

Suppose we want the first 18 *correct* digits of $\exp(\pi\sqrt{163})$. Suppose we calculate that

$$\exp(\pi\sqrt{163}) = 262\ 537\ 412\ 640\ 768\ 744.00000$$
$$\pm\ 0.00001.$$

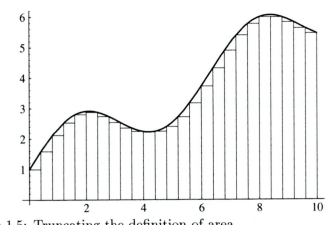

Figure 1.5: Truncating the definition of area

Can we be sure that the units digit (the digit just before the decimal point) is 4? No. Suppose we calculate that

$$\exp(\pi\sqrt{163}) = 262\ 537\ 412\ 640\ 768\ 744.0000000000$$
$$\pm\ 0.0000000001.$$

Can we be sure that the units digit is 4? No! Suppose we calculate that

$$\exp(\pi\sqrt{163}) = 262\ 537\ 412\ 640\ 768\ 743.999999999999250$$
$$\pm\ 0.000000000000001.$$

Can we be sure now that the units digit is 3? Yes, finally we can resolve the identity of the units digit. This illustrates that the quest for correct digits can take us further afield than we might have bargained for. In this example we need about 31 "accurate" digits to get 18 *correct* digits.

In general, there is no telling how much accuracy might be needed to resolve the identity of a given digit. In most cases, not too much accuracy will be needed; in the example just given, tremendous accuracy was needed. The same difficulty arises for a correctly *rounded* result.

So then what should be done? To begin with, the purpose of computing a number is not to determine what its digits happen to be (in base 10) but rather to find its *value.* Thus for almost all practical purposes it is sufficient to determine an approximate value that is within a prescribed **error tolerance** of the exact value. We say that a solution is *acceptable* or *correct* if it differs from the exact solution by no more than the tolerance. Thus there are usually many correct solutions. Error tolerances should be part of the specifications of an algorithm. Often these are fixed. For example, programs for the elementary functions might be written that deliver results with errors less than one unit in the eighth significant digit. In such a case both 2.7182818 and 2.7182819 would be correct values for exp(1.). For longer calculations it is more usual to have the user specify how much accuracy he or she wants. For example, 0.000005 might be specified as the error tolerance.

Of course, the cost of doing the calculation will depend on the desired accuracy. This is a major theme of numerical analysis—the trade-off between accuracy and cost; see Figure 1.6.

The practical necessity of computing answers not all of whose digits are correct is virtually unknown to educated (and even technically educated) people. For example, the September 1982 issue of *Consumer Reports* evaluates calculators without ever raising the question of accuracy or precision. It states, "Basic calculators have room for eight digits in their display." The implication is that all you get to see are the first eight (correct) digits of the answer. Also, in publicity given to computational science there is almost never mention of errors. (It is not good public relations!) For example, a publication of the National Center for Supercomputing Applications defines numerical relativity as "a means of constructing solutions to Einstein's

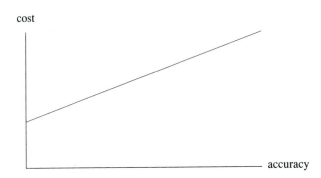

Figure 1.6: Cost vs. accuracy

equations by *translating* [emphasis added] analytical and theoretical expressions in numerical form, and solving those equations with the use of supercomputers."[2] No mention of grievous translation errors.

The most important idea in this section *and in this book* is that *the exact answer* for most problems is either impossible or impractical to get. *Computational error* is a necessary evil. However, the evil lies not so much in the presence of error as in the complications that ensue. A small enough error is not usually of practical concern, and it is enough that

$$|\text{computed answer} - \text{exact answer}| \leq \text{some tolerance.}$$

Any computed answer that is within these bounds (what bounds?) is *a correct answer*. Note here the absolute-value operation and the inequality. These pervade numerical analysis, and an intimate familiarity with them is essential. To work with these concepts *and to succeed in this subject*, you are encouraged to visualize a number not as a string of digits punctuated by a decimal point but as a point on "the real line." Then the absolute value and inequalities become geometric concepts. You need both geometric and algebraic reasoning skills. This is a good place to warn against carelessness with absolute values; in a computer program it could be literally disastrous.

Summarizing, it is impossible to compute exact answers numerically. It is impractical to compute a specified number of correct digits or even correctly rounded digits. For practical purposes a correct answer is one that is within the error tolerance.

Supplementary note

The question of computing correct digits is taken up in
    O. Aberth, *Precise Numerical Analysis*, W. C. Brown, 1988.

---

[2]R. Graham, "General relativity at NCSA," *Access*, March–April 1991, pp. 4–5.

Exercises

1. Give an example of two numbers x and $\hat{x}$ such that they differ by less than 10^{-4} and yet their digits are different starting from the hundredths position.

2. Answer the question "what bounds?" in the text, which follows the inequality

$$|\text{computed answer} - \text{exact answer}| \leq \text{some tolerance}.$$

3. Let $-4 \leq a \leq 4$, $-6 \leq b \leq 8$, $6 \leq c \leq 10$. Determine the minimum value of $|ab| - |bc|$. Explain your reasoning.

4. Let x, y, z be (real) numbers. Write down a mathematical relation that says that x is closer to y than it is to z.

5. True or false?

    (a) $\max\{x, 0\} + \min\{x, 0\} = x$ for all real x.

    (b) $\dfrac{|x| + x}{2} = \max\{x, 0\}$ for all real x.

    (c) $\dfrac{|x| - x}{2} = \min\{x, 0\}$ for all real x.

6. Let a and b be real numbers.

    (a) Prove that $\max\{a, b\} = (a + b)/2 + |b - a|/2$ algebraically.

    (b) Also motivate it geometrically by drawing a picture, labeling points a, b, $(a + b)/2$, and distances $|b - a|$, $|b - a|/2$.

7. Using the triangle inequality and other properties of the absolute value, prove that $|b + a| - |b - a| \leq 2|a|$.

8. If $0.1 \leq t \leq 1$, find a reasonable upper bound for $|f''(t)|$ where

$$f(t) = e^{1/t} \cos(1/t).$$

Be sure to justify your bound rigorously.

Computer problems

1. What is the smallest precision p such that one gets the units digit of
`N[Exp[Pi Sqrt[163]], p]` correct?

2. Solve the following problems using sufficiently high precision to convince yourself of the correctness of your answers.

(a) Find the integer that is nearest to the number $\pi + 203454624397/567663097408$.

(b) Is the number $3764847038432651e - 3257556411651706\pi$ positive or negative?

1.3 Algorithms

The *goal* of numerical analysis, as a discipline, is not to solve specific problems, for example, compute $\sqrt{3}$ to six-digit accuracy, but *to construct algorithms* for solving classes of problems, for example, compute $\sqrt{x}$ to six-digit accuracy, and *to find general principles* that are useful for constructing algorithms.

One can, of course, and often does use numerical techniques to do a "one-time" calculation. We shall, however, focus on the task of writing algorithms that work for a variety of inputs. One begins, in theory anyway, with a specification of the relationship of output values to input values and develops this into a procedure of steps that are executable on the computer. Numerical computing is particularly rich in algorithms because a given problem can have many correct answers.

Mathematical algorithms are used with varying degrees of user involvement. At one extreme they are embedded in applications software, and the user is only vaguely aware of their presence. Such software has become a large-scale enterprise. One example is NASTRAN, used in structural engineering and developed at a cost of $10 million. It consists of 300,000 Fortran statements and has a 2000-page reference manual. Another example is that of a complete system, software and hardware, for linear-programming problems that was marketed for over $8 million.

Mathematical algorithms are also available as subroutines. The most basic ones are built into programming languages: Fortran, C, Matlab, *Mathematica*, Maple. Others are available in libraries: IMSL, NAG. Still others are to be found only in packages: LAPACK, ODEPACK, MINPACK, to name just three.

Because there is such a diversity of problems, it is often hard to find software well suited to a given problem, and algorithms must be programmed by the user. Even when an applicable routine can be located, it may not exploit special properties of the problem and thus may be grossly inefficient.

But learning to program your own algorithms is not the only reason, and may not be the main reason, to learn numerical analysis. First, it takes a rudimentary knowledge of algorithms to understand how to use packaged software. Second, numerical software sometimes fails without warning. Normally this might be regarded as a bug, but for numerical software it is a feature—in order to be reasonably efficient, the software is deliberately designed not to perform correctly in all situations. To get a sense of the risks, some knowledge of numerical analysis is needed. This is true even in the simplest situations. For example, during a period of 22 months in the early 1980s the Vancouver Stock Exchange index steadily declined due to unnoticed compounding of errors in the calculation. After discovery it took 3 weeks to correct the errors, after which the index bolted from 574.081 to 1098.982.

An example from LAPACK of the header of a "canned" program is given below:

```
SUBROUTINE SGETRF(M, N, A, LDA, IPIV, INFO)
INTEGER INFO, LDA, M, N, IPIV(*)
REAL A(LDA, *)
```

The name of the routine is SGETRF, and it is followed by a list of its parameters. The parameters M, N, A, and LDA are inputs, meaning that their initial values affect the computation. However, M, N, and LDA are there solely to specify the location of the values of A. The parameters A, IPIV, and INFO are outputs, meaning that their final values are affected by the computation. At an abstract level this program is a mapping from a set of input values to a set of output values.

We mention Fortran in this book because it is part of the culture of numerical computing. Also it is well suited to numerical computing and has a number of useful features unavailable in other programming languages. However, Fortran is not an easy language for programming.

We conclude with an example of an algorithm, one for computing the square root known to the Old Babylonians nearly 4000 years ago. Suppose we have some approximation x to $\sqrt{c}$ where c is the (nonnegative) number whose square root we seek. Actually x can be any positive number. Then $x \cdot (c/x) = \sqrt{c} \cdot \sqrt{c}$, suggesting that c/x is another equally good (or equally poor) approximation to $\sqrt{c}$ *except* that if x is too small then c/x will be too large and vice versa. (Note that $\sqrt{c}$ is the geometric mean of x and c/x.) In either case the actual root must lie between x and c/x. This suggests that the two approximations be averaged to yield a new and better approximation. The process can be repeated again and again; if it converges, then we can narrow down the search as close as we like.

> **procedure** square root of c with error $\leq \varepsilon$
> **begin**
> $x := 1.;\ y := c/x;\quad (*\ \sqrt{c}\ \text{between}\ x\ \text{and}\ y\ *)$
>   **while** $|x - y| > 2. * \varepsilon$ **do**
> $x := 0.5 * (x + y);\ y := c/x\quad (*\ \sqrt{c}\ \text{between}\ x\ \text{and}\ y\ *)$
>   **end while;**
>   **return** $0.5 * (x + y)$
> **end**

With data $c = \mathbf{2.000}$ and $\varepsilon = \mathbf{0.005}$, the algorithm generates values

x	y
1.000	2.000
1.500	1.333
1.417	1.413

before returning the result **1.415**.

The algorithm given above would need modifications before it could become good software. First, it is probably an unnecessary inconvenience to insist that the user provide some error tolerance ε. Second, provision must be made in case c is not a nonnegative number. Third, provision must be made for the limitations of computer arithmetic. Fourth, steps must be taken to ensure that there are always a reasonable number of iterations. Attending to all these details is for the most part beyond the scope of this book; instead, we shall tend to focus on only some issues at any one time.

Supplementary note

The contributions of the Old Babylonians to mathematics are described in
   Carl D. Boyer, *A History of Mathematics*, Wiley, New York, 1968.

Exercises

1. Let c and x be positive numbers, let $y = c/x$, and let $x' = (x + y)/2$.

   (a) Show that

   $$x' = \sqrt{c} + \frac{1}{2x}(x - \sqrt{c})^2.$$

   (b) What, if anything, can we conclude about the relative ordering (less than, less than or equal to, etc.) of x' and $\sqrt{c}$? Explain.

2. Let c and x be positive numbers such that $x \neq \sqrt{c}$. Prove that $\sqrt{c}$ lies between x and c/x. Your logic must be clear and impeccable.

3. Let $c > 0$. Let I be the interval with endpoints x and y where $x \neq c$, $x > 0$, and $y = c/x$. Do *not* assume that $x < y$. Let I' be the interval with endpoints x' and y' where x' is the midpoint of I and $y' = c/x'$.

   (a) Show that

   $$\frac{y' - x'}{y - x} = \frac{x^2 - c}{2(x^2 + c)}.$$

   (b) Use this to prove that the length of I' is less than half the length of I. Pay attention to signs.

Computer problems

1. We can store code in a variable by using := as in

```
it := ( x = (x + c/x)/2 )
```

Do this and then check by entering ?it . Once x has an initial value, you can execute this by simply typing it . With $c = 2.$ and $x = 1.$ execute it five times. To save space, put all five "commands" into a list. Using %, take the resulting list, square it, and subtract 2.

1.4 Error

The goal of this section is to make absolutely precise the meaning of "error." Errors arise from approximations, and approximations are ubiquitous. An ancient example of approximation is $\pi \approx 3$ implied by I Kings 7:23 and II Chronicles 4:2. A more modern example is the use of $2^{7/12}$ (?!) to approximate $\frac{3}{2}$ in the even-tempered musical scale.

1.4.1 Definitions

We present a number of different measures of error. Particularly important is the idea of relative error and the use of logarithmic measures.

We use as our definition

$$\textbf{error} \overset{\text{def}}{=} \text{approximate value} - \text{true value}$$

This definition is not universal, but it is consistent with popular, nontechnical usage. It agrees with the notions that an approximate value is the result of adding error to the true value and that the true value can be recovered from an approximate value by subtracting out the error. In some situations it is convenient to have a name for the negative of the error:

$$\text{true value} \overset{\text{def}}{=} \text{approximate value} + \textbf{remainder}.$$

Often, if not usually, it is only the magnitude of the error, |error|, which is of interest. At times people are loose with terminology and call this simply "the error." However, there are many situations where the sign is significant.

We would like our errors to be small, but what does "small" mean? Is 100 femtoseconds small? It depends; in particular, it depends on how small the values are that we are approximating. What we want is the error to be *relatively* small. For this purpose it is helpful to use the concept

$$\boxed{\textbf{relative error} \overset{\text{def}}{=} \frac{\text{error}}{\text{true value}}}$$

Often the term "relative error" will refer only to its magnitude; we should choose the more sensible interpretation in each context. When we want to refer to the error (as defined in the first box) and emphasize that we do not mean "relative error," we use the term **absolute error**. A useful consequence of the definitions that is worth remembering is the relation

$$\text{approximate value} = (\text{true value})\,(1 + \text{relative error}). \tag{1.1}$$

A convenient measure of accuracy akin to relative error is to measure the error relative to 1 *ulp* (*u*nit in the *l*ast *p*lace). It requires, though, an explicit representation of the approximate value. We define one unit in the last place to be the positive value obtained by replacing all the digits of the approximate value by zeros except for the last, which is replaced by a 1. Dividing the error by 1 ulp gives the error in ulps. For example, for $\pi \approx 3.14160$, 1 ulp = 0.00001 and the magnitude of the error, $0.000007346\cdots$, is $0.7346\cdots$ ulp. An error no greater than 0.5 ulp is always possible, but, as stated in Section 1.2, it is not always practical.

Because errors are often very small, we introduce for convenience logarithmic measures of absolute and relative error. Suppose that the

$$|\text{error}| = 10^{-d}.$$

If we solve for d, we get what we call

$$\boxed{\textbf{decimal places of accuracy} \overset{\text{def}}{=} -\log_{10}|\text{error}|}$$

If d is an integer, what this means is that the dth digit *to the right of the decimal point* is off by one unit, i.e., that the approximation has d accurate decimal places. If d is not an integer, we can still make sense of its meaning. Next suppose

$$|\text{relative error}| = 10^{-\delta}.$$

Solving for δ gives what we call

$$\boxed{\textbf{digits of accuracy} \overset{\text{def}}{=} -\log_{10}|\text{relative error}|}$$

If δ is an integer, this means *roughly* that the δth digit *counting from the first nonzero digit* is off by one unit, i.e., that the approximation has δ accurate digits. Again, δ need not be an integer.

The terms "decimal places of accuracy" and "digits of accuracy" have no standard definitions; ours are simple and consistent with current usage. To illustrate these ideas, let us consider

$$\text{true value} \quad = \quad 2718.281828\cdots$$
$$\text{approximate value} \quad = \quad 2718.282137.$$

A simple calculation shows that the accuracy is 3.5 decimal places and also 6.9 digits. This agrees with the observation that there are, say, 3 accurate digits after the decimal point and 7 accurate digits. Another illustration is

$$\text{true value} \quad = \quad .00299823\cdots$$
$$\text{approximate value} \quad = \quad .00300000.$$

A calculation shows that the accuracy is 5.8 decimal places and also 3.2 digits. Observation indicates that there are 5 accurate digits after the decimal point and 3 accurate digits (not counting leading zeros).

1.4.2 Sources of error

It is usual for there to be error in the results of a numerical calculation. As depicted in Figure 1.7, there are two sources of error: **data error** already present in the input data before the computation begins and **computational error** introduced by the computational procedure itself.

Data error may be the result of *measurement* or of *previous computation*. It may also be the result of *modeling* errors such as ignoring the viscosity[3] or compressibility of a fluid or using classical mechanics rather than quantum mechanics to model molecular forces or assuming the independence of a set of random variables. This means that the "wrong" equations are used. Because such an effect may be difficult to discuss, we shall in this book tend to overlook modeling errors.

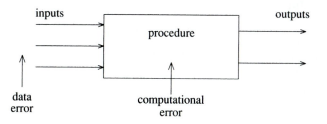

Figure 1.7: Sources of error

---

[3]Technical term meaning friction in fluids.

Recall that computational error is classified into *roundoff error* due to the finite precision of computer numbers and *truncation error* due to the truncation of some infinite limiting process. These errors are deliberate. But errors may also be introduced unintentionally by program *bugs* and *hardware errors*. Because these cannot be analyzed by normal means, we will not consider them.

Why is this distinction between data error and computational error important? Because, if we get answers of unacceptable accuracy, we want to know why. We want to know whether the errors are due to the data or the computation. For example, in order to improve weather forecasts should one collect more data, or should one build faster computers and improve numerical methods?

The likely occurrence of data error should not be used as an excuse to do inaccurate computation. An extreme form of such an attitude is the claim that because the data are accurate to only three digits (say), every computation can be done to just three digits. There are two reasons why this idea is mistaken. First of all, the buildup of computational error is difficult to predict, and errors that we think are no worse than data errors could be much worse. Second, the user may want to redo the computation with slightly perturbed data in order to see what effect this has on the results. With inaccurate computation these effects might well be swamped by the effects of computational error, and the user may be misled. It is best to treat the input values as exact and not make judgments about their accuracy or the morality of computing accurate answers to inaccurate problems.

It is possible to make a sharp distinction between the respective contributions of data error and computational error. Let a be the true value and $\tilde{a}$ a given value tainted with data error. Let $f(x)$ denote the desired mapping from input datum to output datum. Then $f(a)$ is the true value of the result and $f(\tilde{a})$ is the best we can do with the given datum. We shall let

$$f(\tilde{a}) - f(a) \stackrel{\text{def}}{=} \textbf{propagated data error}$$

because it is due to the data error $\tilde{a} - a$. This effect is called **error propagation**. In practice the exact $f(x)$ may not be computationally feasible, so a computable approximation $\hat{f}(x)$ is used instead and the computed result is $\hat{f}(\tilde{a})$. The difference

$$\hat{f}(\tilde{a}) - f(\tilde{a}) = \text{computational error.}$$

These relationships are graphed in Figure 1.8. Note that the relationship between the propagated data error and the data error depends on the slope of $f(x)$ and that *the choice of algorithm has absolutely no effect on the propagation of data error*.

1.4.3 Specifying uncertain quantities

Suppose a measurement of some quantity is repeated five times and the results are

$$1.423, \quad 1.399, \quad 1.491, \quad 1.449, \quad 1.480.$$

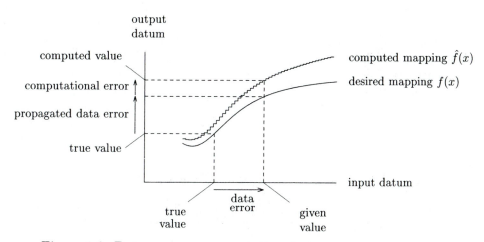

Figure 1.8: Data error vs. computational error

How should we interpret this information? Assuming certain random distributions of the measurement error, we could use statistical techniques. However, let us take a simpler approach: let us assume that the true value lies between, or is equal to one of, the least and the greatest of these five values. If so, we can use the closed *interval* [1.399, 1.491] to denote the set of possible values, sometimes written $1.^{491}_{399}$ or, equivalently, 1.445 ± 0.046 .

Greater brevity is possible if we use a notion of *significant digits*. There is no consensus on what this means. Suppose, though, that we make this idea precise and adopt the convention suggested by one book, which is that the least significant digit given in a measured quantity should be in error by at most *five* units. In the example we are considering, this would mean using 1.4 to represent our data; see Figure 1.9 for the explanation. Unfortunately, this representation discards a lot of information—the implied width of the interval of un-

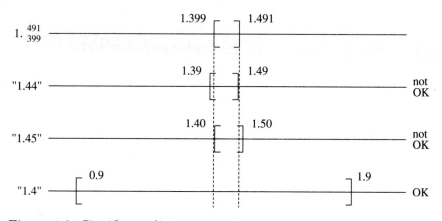

Figure 1.9: Significant-digits convention

certainty is exaggerated by a factor of 11. Such loss of information might be tolerable for *displaying* approximate values. However, this convention is utterly unsuitable for *recording* such values, because it would accelerate error accumulation. In this book we do not attach a precise meaning to the number of digits given. We regard each number as representing a single point on the real line rather than a range of values, and we regard the accuracy of a value to be related only in some vague way to the number of digits used. When we wish to represent an interval, we do so explicitly and do not use the notion of significant digits.

Review questions

1. List the basic facts about the logarithm. (Consult Appendix B.)

2. Give the formula for the power function x^y in terms of the natural logarithm ln and the exponential exp functions.

Exercises

1. Let $\tilde{x} = 2.62$ approximate $x = 2.615$. What is the relative error in $\tilde{x}$? in $\exp(\tilde{x})$? Give numerical answers.

2. If the true value of some quantity is known to lie in the closed interval $[1.3, 1.5]$ and we take 1.4 as our approximation, what is the range of possible values for the relative error? Give the *exact* answer to this problem.

3. Let x be a nonzero real number and let u denote one unit in the first nonzero digit of x.

   (a) If $x = 17.5$, what is u? What if $x = -0.0235$?

   (b) What is the most specific assertion that can be made about u without any reference to the values of x? For example, you might say that u is positive, but a more specific statement can be made.

   (c) Give a formula for u in terms of x by using the logarithm and the ceiling or floor function. Note: The ceiling $\lceil x \rceil$ of x is that integer n such that $x \le n < x+1$, and the floor $\lfloor x \rfloor$ is that integer m such that $x - 1 < m \le x$.

4. Derive the formula for $\log_b t$ in terms of natural logarithms. Assume that $\log_b t$ is defined by the equation $b^{\log_b t} = t$.

5. (a) Given a numerical value w such that $1024 \approx 10^w$, determine an approximate value of $\log_{10} 2$.

   (b) What is this approximation if we use 3 for w?

6. Suppose an approximation y_1 has one-third as much relative error as another approximation y_2. How many more (decimal) digits of accuracy does y_1 have than y_2? Reminder: The answer need not be an integer.

7. Consider the problem of computing $1/(1-h)$ for small h. Suppose we use $1+h(1+h)$ with exact arithmetic as an algorithm to compute an approximate solution to the problem. Suppose we are given the value 0.2 for h but the true value is 0.21. Express the total error in the computed result as the sum of the computational error plus the propagated data error.

Computer problems

1. `Solve` the equation $|\text{error}| = 10^{-d}$ for d. (Equations are formed using the `Equal` operator `==`.)

2. `Solve` the first two framed equations in Section 1.4.1 for the "approximate value" eliminating the "error." To be used with `Solve[ ]`, a system of equations must be enclosed in braces and separated by commas.

3. The value $2.^{5/12}$ is used by the even-tempered scale to approximate a perfect fourth. Determine its value and use a *Mathematica* comment to state what simple ratio it is supposed to approximate.

4. Define a function

$$\texttt{accdec[xa\_, xt\_] := ...}$$

that for two `Real` values `xa` and `xt` computes the decimals of accuracy of the first as an approximation to the second, using the definition on page 16. Create a list

$$\texttt{pilist = \{3., 3.1, 3.14, 3.142, 3.1416, 3.14159, 3.141592\}}$$

and then compute `accdec[pilist, N[Pi]]`. This will return a list, assuming your definition of `accdec` uses only `Listable` functions.

5. Define a function

$$\texttt{accdig[xa\_, xt\_] := ...}$$

that for two `Real` values `xa` and `xt` computes the digits of accuracy of the first as an approximation to the second, using the definition on page 16. Compute `accdig[pilist, N[Pi]]` with the `pilist` defined in the previous problem.

1.5 Error Propagation

The vice president of a large engineering company has said

> Engineers applying theoretical ideas may not realize the importance of the buildup
> of mechanical or electrical tolerances, margins of error, and margins of safety
> because they usually do not learn about those concepts in school.[4]

An important aspect of this matter is the question of propagation of errors in the data of a
problem, whether the errors are due to measurement or are previous computational errors.
Let us assume here that solution of the problem introduces no additional error, that the exact
solution *for the given data* is obtained. What is important to realize is that small relative
errors in data do not imply equally small errors in the results (assuming exact computation)—
propagated errors can be relatively much larger. The impact of this on numerical computing
is the subject of Section 2.5.

Example 1.1 Suppose you want to compute the distance c between two very distant points
and you know the distances $a = 100$ and $b = 101$ to each of the points as well as the
angle $\gamma = 1°$ between the two points, as shown in Figure 1.10. From first principles we get
$c = \sqrt{(b\cos\gamma - a)^2 + (b\sin\gamma)^2}$. Rearrangement yields the more elegant formula

$$c = \sqrt{(b-a)^2 + 4ab\sin^2\frac{\gamma}{2}} = 2.0190\cdots.$$

Now suppose that a were in error, that we use the erroneous value 100.1 for a. Then the error
0.1 would propagate through the computation as shown in the table on page 23.

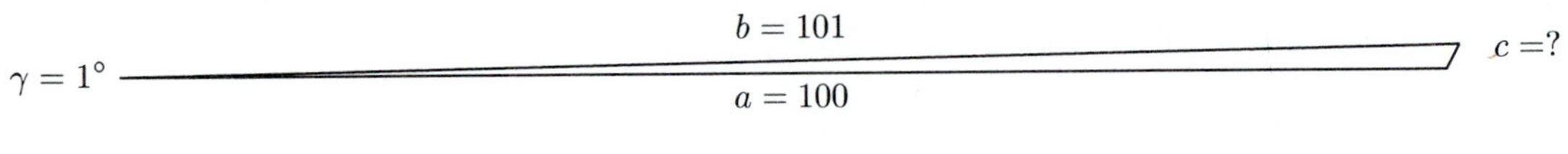

Figure 1.10: The third side of a triangle

---

[4]G.A. Paulikas of Aerospace Corporation in the Spring 1990 *Engineering Outlook*, University of
Illinois, Urbana.

	True value	Approx value	Rel error
a	100	100.1	0.1%
$b - a$	1	0.9	-10%
$(b - a)^2$	1	0.81	-19%
$4ab\sin^2\dfrac{\gamma}{2}$	$3.0765\cdots$	$3.0796\cdots$	0.1%
$(b - a)^2 + 4ab\sin^2\dfrac{\gamma}{2}$	$4.0765\cdots$	$3.8896\cdots$	-4.6%
c	$2.0190\cdots$	$1.9722\cdots$	-2.3%

What you notice is that the relative error can vary a great deal as the error propagates through the computation and that a 0.1% error in the data gives rise to an error of magnitude 2.3% in the result. In case this table suggests otherwise, we wish to emphasize that propagated data error in the final result c does not depend on how c is computed, as long as we do not introduce any computational errors along the way. We would have obtained the same final error if we had used the original, less elegant formula for c. After all, if two formulas are identically equal, they both define the same function, and it is this function that defines the propagated data error.

Example 1.2 Wilkinson's polynomial given by

$$p(z) = (z - 1)(z - 2)\cdots(z - 20) = z^{20} - 210z^{19} + \cdots + 20!$$

is very sensitive to changes in its coefficients. If you change -210 to $-210 + 10^{-7}$, then the roots $1, 2, \ldots, 20$ of $p(z)$ change dramatically, as shown in Figure 1.11.

Example 1.3 The problem of predicting weather is a standard example of a physical problem having sensitive dependence on data. It is said that if there were two identical planets with identical atmospheric conditions except for the presence of a butterfly on one of the planets, then after a couple of months the two atmospheres would be as dissimilar as two random

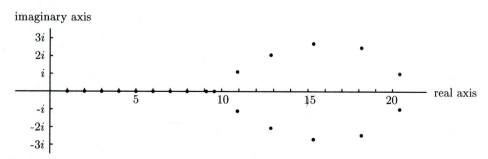

Figure 1.11: Effect of a perturbation on roots of a polynomial

states of the atmosphere of one of the planets. This is an example of *chaos*, which means *extremely sensitive dependence on initial conditions*. In the case of weather, this results in a "finite limit to predictability" of roughly 15 days.

This idea of being sensitive can be quantified:

$$\text{sensitive} \quad \overset{\text{def}}{\Longleftrightarrow} \quad \frac{|\text{rel. error in results}|}{|\text{rel. error in data}|} \gg 1.$$

(Note: "$\gg$" means "much greater than" and "$\ll$" means "much less than.") Again we are assuming exact computation. In numerical analysis jargon, the ratio above is called the **condition number**. Similarly, **ill-conditioned** means sensitive, and **well-conditioned** means insensitive.

We see from these examples that data of, say, six-digit accuracy does not imply (even with exact computation) answers of six-digit accuracy; we could be solving a problem whose solution has no accurate digits. Consequently, we might want to assess the effect of data uncertainty. In rare cases this information is provided by the routine that we are using to solve the problem. Otherwise, we can try re-solving the problem with the data perturbed. A much more thorough approach is **interval analysis**. The idea is that we specify the problem data as intervals that we believe contain the true values. Suppose in Example 1.1 we have the following values:

$$a \in [99.9, 100.1], \quad b \in [100.9, 101.1], \quad \gamma \in [0.99°, 1.01°].$$

Then for c we would like to get the interval of possible values

$$c \in [1.9119, 2.1397].$$

In simple situations of sufficient importance it is worth doing an analytical *sensitivity analysis*. The question we ask is the following: How is the relative error in the result related to the relative errors in the data? We look first at the sensitivity of arithmetic operations (assuming exact computation, of course) and then at general unary operations, also known as functions of one variable.

We start with addition of two true values $a + b$. Suppose we introduce a relative error ε_a into a and ε_b into b. Let ε_{a+b} be the relative error in the sum of the two approximate values. Then with the help of (1.1), the equation "worth remembering," we can write an equation expressing the approximate sum as the approximate a plus the approximate b:

$$(a + b)(1 + \varepsilon_{a+b}) = a(1 + \varepsilon_a) + b(1 + \varepsilon_b).$$

Solving for the relative error in the sum, we get

$$\varepsilon_{a+b} = \frac{a}{a+b}\varepsilon_a + \frac{b}{a+b}\varepsilon_b.$$

This expresses the relative error in the result as a linear combination of relative errors in the operands. The coefficients multiplying the relative errors are large if (and only if) $a \approx -b$. Large coefficients mean that small relative errors in the operands of addition (or subtraction) can become a large relative error in the result. As an example consider

$$\begin{array}{r} 80.0499 \\ -80.0000 \\ \hline 0.0499 \end{array}$$

If the operands are accurate to within one unit in the *sixth* digit each (relative errors of about 10^{-6}), the result will be accurate to within two units in the *third* digit (a relative error of about 10^{-3}). The three leading digits have canceled each other. We call this *catastrophic cancellation*. The catastrophe is evident only because we are looking at the relative errors.

Consider now the product $a \cdot b$. If we analyze this as we did the sum, we get

$$\varepsilon_{a \cdot b} = \varepsilon_a + \varepsilon_b + \varepsilon_a \varepsilon_b.$$

Assuming small relative errors, we can neglect the last term and say that for multiplication relative errors add. So there is no problem with relative error amplification; multiplication is not a sensitive operation.

For the quotient a/b you get

$$\varepsilon_{a/b} = \frac{\varepsilon_a - \varepsilon_b}{1 + \varepsilon_b}.$$

We can say that, "to a first approximation," the relative errors subtract. Again there is no problem; division is not a sensitive operation.

⋆ 1.5.1 Condition number of a unary operation

Finally, we consider the sensitivity of unary operations and other functions $f(x)$ of one variable (still assuming exact computation). Let us define the approximate result of $f(a)$ to be the result of using an approximate a. Then we use (1.1) twice to get

$$f(a)(1 + \varepsilon_{f(a)}) = f(a(1 + \varepsilon_a)).$$

The ratio of the relative error in $f(a)$ to that in a is

$$\frac{\varepsilon_{f(a)}}{\varepsilon_a} = \frac{f(a + a\varepsilon_a) - f(a)}{f(a)\varepsilon_a}.$$

If $f(x)$ has a derivative at a, then

$$\frac{f(a + a\varepsilon_a) - f(a)}{a\varepsilon_a} \to f'(a) \qquad \text{as } \varepsilon_a \to 0.$$

Hence,

$$\frac{\varepsilon_{f(a)}}{\varepsilon_a} \to \frac{af'(a)}{f(a)} \qquad \text{as } \varepsilon_a \to 0.$$

This ratio is called the *relative derivative* of $f(x)$, and it measures in a relative sense the sensitivity of $f(a)$ to small changes in a. The absolute value of the relative derivative is called the **condition number** of $f(x)$ at a. For example, the relative derivative of e^x is x and the condition number is $|x|$. The exponential function is sensitive (in a relative error sense) for $|x| \gg 1$ and insensitive for $|x| \ll 1$. The natural logarithm $\ln x$ has a condition number of $1/|\ln x|$, so it is sensitive for $x \approx 1$.

1.5.2 Interval analysis

In the preceding section we briefly mentioned the use of intervals as a means of expressing the uncertainty in a value. Here we show how intervals can be used in a systematic way to analyze the effects of errors by computing bounds on the worst-case behavior of errors. Interval analysis depends on the ability to minimize and maximize and a knowledge of those functions that are monotonic. It can be implemented on the computer, making possible an automated error analysis.

The idea is to perform operations with intervals with the understanding that they represent sets of possible values for the operands and that the result should be an interval containing the set of all possible values for the result of the operation. We illustrate this with $\bar{x} = [-1.02, -1.01]$ and $\bar{y} = [2.01, 2.02]$ where bars have been used to distinguish variables that represent intervals. The sum of these two is

$$\begin{aligned}
\bar{x} + \bar{y} &\overset{\text{def}}{=} \{x + y \mid x \in \bar{x}, y \in \bar{y}\} \\
&= \{-1.011 + 2.017, -1.016 + 2.0105, -1.0199 + 2.02, \dots\} \\
&= [0.99, 1.01].
\end{aligned}$$

The result was computed by taking the least of $\bar{x}$ plus the least of $\bar{y}$ as the left endpoint and the greatest of $\bar{x}$ plus the greatest of $\bar{y}$ as the right endpoint. The set of all possible products $\bar{x}\bar{y} = [-2.0604, -2.0301]$. Arithmetic defined on intervals in this way is called **interval arithmetic**. For the exponential function we get

$$\begin{aligned}
\exp \bar{x} &= \{\exp x \mid x \in \bar{x}\} \\
&= [\exp(-1.02), \exp(-1.01)]
\end{aligned}$$

where we use the fact that $\exp(x)$ is strictly increasing.

In general, for a function $f(x)$ of one variable, $f(\bar{x})$ is a set; and if $f(x)$ is continuous, $f(\bar{x})$ is an interval. Similarly for $g(\bar{x}, \bar{y})$ where $g(x, y)$ is a function of two variables.

Therefore, we see that we can systematically extend operations defined for single values (points) to sets of values. However, *a word of caution*: If two expressions in some variable are equal for point values (numbers), it does not follow that they will be equal when an interval is substituted for the variable. For example, two formulas for the effective resistance of two resistors in parallel are

$$R = \frac{1}{1/R_1 + 1/R_2} = \frac{R_1 R_2}{R_1 + R_2}.$$

Suppose the two resistances are known to lie in intervals

$$\bar{R}_1 = \left[\tfrac{4}{5}, 1\right], \quad \bar{R}_2 = \left[2, \tfrac{5}{2}\right].$$

The first formula gives

$$R \in \frac{1}{1/\left[\tfrac{4}{5}, 1\right] + 1/\left[2, \tfrac{5}{2}\right]} = \frac{1}{\left[1, \tfrac{5}{4}\right] + \left[\tfrac{2}{5}, \tfrac{1}{2}\right]} = \frac{1}{\left[\tfrac{7}{5}, \tfrac{7}{4}\right]} = \left[\tfrac{4}{7}, \tfrac{5}{7}\right],$$

and the second formula gives

$$R \in \frac{\left[\tfrac{4}{5}, 1\right]\left[2, \tfrac{5}{2}\right]}{\left[\tfrac{4}{5}, 1\right] + \left[2, \tfrac{5}{2}\right]} = \frac{\left[\tfrac{8}{5}, \tfrac{5}{2}\right]}{\left[\tfrac{14}{5}, \tfrac{7}{2}\right]} = \left[\tfrac{16}{35}, \tfrac{25}{28}\right] = \left[\tfrac{3.2}{7}, \tfrac{6.25}{7}\right].$$

The first formula gives a narrower interval and hence a more precise result. Note that in the first case the upper bound on R is determined by the upper bounds on R_1 and R_2, but in the second case the upper bounds are used in one occurrence and lower bounds in the other occurrence of these variables. This suggests that the multiple occurrence of some set representing the same uncertain value can lead to unnecessarily wide intervals because the rules of interval analysis will treat such sets as each representing a different uncertain value. *Nonetheless*, we can be confident that the true value lies in the resulting set; and if this set is small enough, it does not matter that it is not the smallest possible set.

Review question

1. Give an exact expression for the relative propagated error in $f(x)$ due to a relative error ε_a introduced into $x = a$.

Exercises

1. Construct a table like that in Example 1.1 for the algorithm $c = \sqrt{(b\cos\gamma - a)^2 + (b\sin\gamma)^2}$. Use as row labels a, $b\cos\gamma - a$, $(b\cos\gamma - a)^2$, $(b\cos\gamma - a)^2 + (b\sin\gamma)^2$, c.

2. The Patriot missile defense system would track potential targets by dividing elapsed time by the speed of the target. As originally programmed the elapsed time was calculated as

$$t_1 := \widetilde{0.1} \times n_1; \quad \ldots; \quad t_2 := \widetilde{0.1} \times n_2; \quad \ldots; \quad \Delta t := t_2 - t_1$$

where $\widetilde{0.1} = 0.1(1 - 2^{-20})$ and n_1, n_2 were obtained from the computer's clock in units of tenths of seconds. (The reason for the approximation $\widetilde{0.1}$ is explored in Exercise 5 of Section 2.1.)

   (a) What is the relative error in $\widetilde{0.1}$?

   (b) Suppose after initialization at zero the clock had run for 8 hours when n_1 was determined and an additional 2 seconds, say, when n_2 was determined. What is the error in Δt due to the use of $\widetilde{0.1}$ instead of 0.1? What is the relative error?

   (c) Answer part (b) with 8 hours replaced by 100 hours.

   (d) During the 1990–91 Gulf conflict the Patriot system software was modified to cope with the high speed of Scud ballistic missiles. More accurate code for calculating the clock time in seconds was inserted into the software but not at every point where it was needed. (It was easy to make such a mistake because the software was complex and was written in assembly language twenty years earlier.) In any case the calculation of t_2 was made much more accurate but not the calculation of t_1. Answer part (b) assuming that the calculation of t_2 but not t_1 was performed with 0.1 instead of $\widetilde{0.1}$.

   (e) Answer part (c) under the assumptions of part (d). (This scenario represents the situation when the Patriot failed to attack the Scud that hit the army barracks in Dhahran.)

3. Prove the formulas given for $\varepsilon_{x \cdot y}$ and $\varepsilon_{x/y}$.

4. Let x be some exact value and $\tilde{x}$ an erroneous value. Define $y = \exp x$ and $\tilde{y} = \exp \tilde{x}$. Obtain an expression for the relative error in $\tilde{y}$ in terms of the following two quantities only: x and the relative error in $\tilde{x}$.

5. Consider the product (in exact arithmetic) of two numbers, one having a relative error of at most 1% in magnitude and the other having a relative error of at most 2% in magnitude. Determine the *greatest possible* magnitude of the resulting relative error in the product.

6. Determine the maximum magnitude of the relative error in determining p_1 from the relation $p_1 v_1^{1.4} = p_2 v_2^{1.4}$ where the maximum magnitudes of the relative errors of v_1, v_2, and p_2 are 0.5%, 0.5%, and 0.6%, respectively.

7. Show that $\sqrt{\tilde{x}}$ has $0.30103 \cdots$ more digits of accuracy than does $\tilde{x}$. Use $\sqrt{1 + \delta} \approx 1 + \frac{1}{2}\delta$ for $|\delta| \ll 1$.

8. Assume that the cosine function can be evaluated exactly. Let b be in the open interval $]0, \pi/2[$.

   (a) There is almost always some error e in b, and, hence, $\cos(b+e)$ is evaluated instead of $\cos b$. But the magnitude of the absolute error $|\cos(b+e) - \cos b|$ is never greater than $|e|$. Why?

   (b) Nevertheless, $\cos(b + e)$ may be a disastrous approximation to $\cos b$. Why?

9. Compute each of the following using interval operations:

   (a) $[3.4, 3.5] - [3.4, 3.5]$

   (b) $|[-4, \ 4] \ [-6, \ 8]| \ - \ |[-6, \ 8] \ [6, \ 10]|$

   (c) $[-12, 6]/[-3, -2]$

   (d) $\sin[1, 4]$ and then $(\sin[1, 4])^2$ (The argument is assumed to be in radians.)

   (e) $[-1, 1]^2$

10. Show that $\bar{x}^2 \neq \bar{x} \cdot \bar{x}$. (Hint: Begin with the definition of each side.)

11. For $-4 \le b \le 8$ find the maximum and the minimum of

$$2|b| - |b + 6|.$$

(Show how you arrived at your answer.) Compare your answer to

$$2|\bar{b}| - |\bar{b} + 6|$$

where $\bar{b} = [-4, \ 8]$.

12. Let $\bar{x}$ be an interval of positive numbers. Which is narrower,

$$\frac{\bar{x}}{\bar{x} + 1} \quad \text{or} \quad \frac{1}{1 + 1/\bar{x}}?$$

Check your answer using $\bar{x} = [1, 2]$.

13. Let $\bar{x}$, $\bar{y}$, and $\bar{z}$ denote intervals.

   (a) Does
$$\bar{x}(\bar{y} + \bar{z}) \subseteq \bar{x}\bar{y} + \bar{x}\bar{z}$$
   always hold? If not, give a counterexample.

   (b) Does
$$\bar{x}(\bar{y} + \bar{z}) \supseteq \bar{x}\bar{y} + \bar{x}\bar{z}$$
   always hold? If not, give a counterexample.

(c) Does the distributive law hold for interval arithmetic?

⋆14. For which values of $x > -1$ do tiny relative changes in x produce

(a) relative changes in $\ln(1 + x)$ much larger in magnitude?

(b) relative changes in $\ln(1 + x)$ much smaller in magnitude?

Show how you obtain your answer.

Mathematica notes

We will have occasion to discuss most of the control constructs in *Mathematica* in detail in a later lesson of Appendix A, but we need to understand `While[ ]` for Computer Problem 1 below. The `While[ ]` construct takes two arguments, the first being the condition under which the second argument gets executed and the second being the iterative computation to be done. Of course, the second argument had better affect the variables in the first argument in some way or the condition will never change. As an example let us look at a *Mathematica* implementation of the square-root procedure presented on page 13.

Define the function. The `Print` statements are only there to monitor the values of x and y. They should be commented out or removed once the function seems to be working properly.

```
In[1]:= sqrt[c_, epsilon_] :=
            Module[{x = 1., y = c},
              While[Abs[x-y] > 2. epsilon,
                Print[{x, y}];
                x = 0.5 (x+y);
                y = c/x
              ];
              Print[{x, y}];
              0.5 (x+y)
            ]
```

An approximation to $\sqrt{2}$.

```
In[2]:= sqrt[2, 0.005]

{1., 2}
{1.5, 1.33333}
{1.41667, 1.41176}

Out[2]= 1.41422
```

A better approximation to $\sqrt{2}$.

```
In[3]:= sqrt[2, 0.0001]

{1., 2}
{1.5, 1.33333}
{1.41667, 1.41176}
{1.41422, 1.41421}

Out[3]= 1.41421
```

An interval is represented in *Mathematica* as `Interval[{a, b}]`.

You can do basic arithmetic with intervals.	*In[4]:=* **Interval[{1, 3}] Interval[{12, 13}]**
	Out[4]= Interval[{12, 39}]
Let x be the interval from -2 to 3.	*In[5]:=* **x = Interval[{-2, 3}]**
	Out[5]= Interval[{-2, 3}]
Multiplying an interval by itself is different from squaring it. The reciprocal of an interval containing 0 gets split into two pieces.	*In[6]:=* **{x^2, x x, 1/x}**
	Out[6]= {Interval[{0, 9}], Interval[{-6, 9}], Interval[{-Infinity, -1/2}, {1/3, Infinity}]}
Define the function f[ ].	*In[7]:=* **f[x_] := (2x+3)/(x^2+1)**
f[ ] works with numbers.	*In[8]:=* **f[4.3]**
	Out[8]= 0.595177
f[ ] also works with intervals.	*In[9]:=* **f[Interval[{4.29999, 4.30001}]]**
	Out[9]= Interval[{0.595173, 0.595181}]

With floating-point numbers the arithmetic is such that the endpoints of the intervals are rounded outward. This allows rigorous computation to be done with floating-point numbers.

In versions 2.1 and earlier of *Mathematica*, Interval[ ] was defined in the package NumericalMath`IntervalAnalysis`. To use this package you need to issue the command << NumericalMath`IntervalAnalysis` . Also, the syntax was slightly different: The interval from 1 to 3 was represented by Interval[1, 3] rather than Interval[{1, 3}].

Computer problems

1. In Appendix A we mention that N[*expr*, *n*] often does not deliver *n* digits of accuracy, because errors change as they propagate through the computation. Define a function nn[expr_, n_] that delivers a result whose Precision is n by invoking N[,] repeatedly with increasing precision. For the first attempt use n. Base future attempts on the hypothesis that n and Precision[N[*expr*, n]] differ by some constant that depends on expr. Assume that expr does not contain any Reals. For interest's sake have the Precision printed out after every unsuccessful attempt. Test nn[ ] with a precision of 40 on

$$\pi - \frac{245850922}{78256779}$$

and on

$$\sqrt{(b\cos\gamma - a)^2 + (b\sin\gamma)^2}$$

and

$$\sqrt{(b-a)^2 + 4ab\sin^2\frac{\gamma}{2}}$$

with $a = 100$, $b = 101$, $\gamma = 1°$ (`1 Degree` in *Mathematica*).

2. In this problem we experimentally find the condition number of the 15th root of Wilkinson's polynomial with respect to the coefficient of x^{19}.

   (a) Use `Expand[Product[x-i, {i, 20}]]` to find Wilkinson's polynomial. Use the function `NRoots[`*poly* `== 0, x, 40]` to find the roots of Wilkinson's polynomial starting with 40 digits of accuracy. Take the second part (the right-hand side of the equation) of the 15th part of the solution. This is the 15th root of the polynomial.

   (b) Perturb the original polynomial by adding $210 \cdot 10^{-15}x^{19}$ (i.e., one part in 10^{15}). Consider this perturbation to be data error.

   (c) Find the 15th root of the perturbed polynomial. What is the relative error in this result? Find the condition number of the 15th root with respect to the coefficient of x^{19}, i.e., the ratio of the relative errors.

3. The lengths of intervals tend to grow in many calculations using interval arithmetic. We will examine that growth in this problem.

   (a) Start with the interval `x = 10.^-5 Interval[{-1,1}] + 1`. Perform the iteration `x = 2x - x` 30 times. How much does the interval grow with each iteration?

   (b) Start with the interval `x = 10.^-5 Interval[{-1,1}] + 1`. Perform the iteration `x = (2/x+x)/2` 10 times. What is the relative error?

   (c) Start with the interval `x = 10.^-5 Interval[{-1,1}] + 1`. Perform the iteration `x = (2+x^2)/(2x)` 10 times. Note that these last two iterations are algebraically equivalent. Which is the better form for using interval computations to evaluate the square root of 2?

2. Floating-Point Computation

For good practical reasons almost all numerical computation is performed with numbers having a limited number of (significant) digits. As a consequence there are roundoff errors. Rounding is the most important approximation in numerical computing. Without it we could take only a few steps before drowning in digits. The error due to rounding is minuscule *relative to the number that is rounded*. Nonetheless, such errors can become a problem, and we want to know how to avoid such problems. This book says more than most books about rounding errors. Of all topics in this book this is the one you are most likely to encounter in your use of computers.

One of several themes in this chapter is that floating-point arithmetic does not behave in some vague, obscure manner, but rather in a precisely defined way. The idea that floating-point numbers are fuzzy is fiction—bad fiction. The actual facts are not complicated. Without knowing these facts the behavior of computer floating-point number operations can appear bizarre. The main idea is that the computer works with a finite subset of the reals known as *machine numbers*. An operation with machine numbers may or may not yield a result that is exactly equal to a machine number; if not, it is rounded to the nearest machine number.

This chapter contains the following sections:

2.1 Positional Number Systems
2.2 Floating-Point Numbers
2.3 Rounding
2.4 Basic Operations
2.5 Numerical Instability

2.1 Positional Number Systems

Below is a *Mathematica* While loop:

```
x = 1.0;
While[ x != 0.0,
    Print[ x ];
    x = x - 0.1
]
```

What happens? On most computers this loop never terminates. Why? If you respond "roundoff error," your answer is inadequate. On any *calculator* the loop executes correctly. All that is needed is one digit of precision and there will be no roundoff error. The reason the loop fails on most computers is that they do not use *decimal* digits and cannot exactly represent most decimal fractions. For reasons of performance other number systems are used. This is appropriate for large-scale scientific computing, and specialists in this area should learn about non-decimal number systems. But for the majority of users who do not need massive number-crunching capabilities, it would be better if their computers were more friendly and used base 10. At present this is not the case, so you should learn how other number systems work.

To minimize the effects of using computer number systems the loop above might be written

```
x = 10.;
While[ x != 0.,
    Print[ x/10. ];
    x = x - 1.
]
```

Our decimal system of representing numbers is called *positional* because the value of a digit in a number depends on its position and each position corresponds to some integer power of 10. The choice of 10 is a consequence of human anatomy. There is a duodecimal society that advocates base 12. The Old Babylonians, who invented positional notation 4000 years ago, used base 60. We still use their system for measuring time and angles.

Example 2.1 According to the May/June 1977 issue of *Mother Earth News*, base 3 is used to assign numbers to swine. Five positions on an ear are identified, each position weighted with a power of 3: $1, 3, 9, 27, 81$. The first four positions have room for up to two notches each, and the last position has room for one notch. See Figure 2.1. The number represented in the figure is

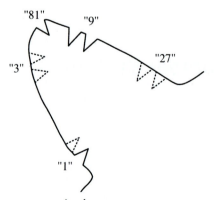

Figure 2.1: Number on a swine's ear

$$1 \times 81 + 0 \times 27 + 2 \times 9 + 0 \times 3 + 1 \times 1 \;=\; 10201_3$$
$$=\; 100.$$

Also there has been a Soviet computer that uses base 3. More common have been computers that use octal, with digits $0, 1, \ldots, 7$, or hexadecimal, with digits $0, 1, \ldots, 9, A, B, \ldots, F$. Most common are computers that use binary, with digits 0, 1. Calculators and a few computers use decimal; some microcomputers have used base 100.

Conversion to decimal from some other base is straightforward.

Example 2.2

$$1010.11_2 \;=\; 8 + 2 + \tfrac{1}{2} + \tfrac{1}{4} = 10.75$$

Example 2.3

$$177.6_8 \;=\; 1 \times 64 + 7 \times 8 + 7 \times 1 + 6 \times \tfrac{1}{8} = 127.75$$

What about conversion in the opposite direction, from decimal to something else? A naive approach for binary is to subtract decreasing powers of 2, for example,

$$
\begin{aligned}
5.2 \;&=\; 100_2 + 1.2 \\
&=\; 101_2 + 0.2 \\
&=\; 101.001_2 + 0.075 \\
&=\; 101.0011_2 + 0.0125 \quad \textit{ad infinitum!}
\end{aligned}
$$

The process never stops because 5.2 does not have a terminating binary expansion. In fact, most numbers with terminating decimal expansions are nonterminating in base 2, including the number 0.1 used in the `While` loop example at the beginning of this section. The tiny error that compromised the Patriot missile defense system can be traced to a truncated binary expansion of 0.1. See Exercise 5.

Supplementary note

More sophisticated methods for conversions between bases can be found, for example, in Atkinson (1985).

Exercises

1. What is the advantage of base 12 over base 10?

2. The Patriot missile defense system kept time in units of one-tenth of a second. When the fatal Scud (that hit Dhahran) was detected, the Patriot clock had been running for

100 hours. How many bits in base 2 are required to represent 100 hours in units of one-tenth of a second?

3. Do numbers with terminating binary expansions always have terminating decimal expansions? Either explain why this is true or give a counterexample.

4. Give an example of a binary number with four bits that cannot be exactly represented as a hexadecimal number with one hexadecimal digit.

5. The original version of the software in the Patriot missile defense system used for one-tenth a base 2 representation consisting of the first 23 bits after the binary point.

   (a) What is this value in base 2?

   (b) Precisely what is the error in this truncated representation of 0.1? Express your answer in base 2.

   (c) Show that your answer to part (b) is (exactly) equal to -0.1×2^{-20}.

6. Precisely how many bits are required to represent $1 - 2^{-53}$ exactly in binary? How many decimal places are required to represent the same number exactly in base 10?

7. Convert $\frac{1}{7}$ to an octal fraction without first converting it to a decimal fraction.

8. Express $(0.666\cdots)_8$ as a ratio of two decimal integers.

9. Given that $3.14 \le x \le 3.15$, find as many *correct* digits as possible for the binary form of x.

Mathematica notes

Mathematica provides for input (`^^`) and output (`BaseForm[ ]`) in bases other than base 10. To gain a better understanding of positional number systems, let us consider how we might program base conversion.

Define a function that gives a number from a list of digits representing the integer part and a list of digits representing the fractional part. The digits are understood to be base `base` digits.

```
In[1]:= number[int_List, frac_List, base_Integer] :=
          Sum[int[[-i]] base^(i-1), {i, Length[int]}] +
          Sum[frac[[i]] base^(-i), {i, Length[frac]}]
```

The digits in the integer part represent coefficients of nonnegative powers of the base.

```
In[2]:= number[{a,b,c,d}, {}, 3]
```
$$Out[2]= 27\ a + 9\ b + 3\ c + d$$

The digits in the fractional part represent coefficients of negative powers of the base.

```
In[3]:= number[{}, {a,b,c,d}, 3]
```
$$Out[3] = \frac{a}{3} + \frac{b}{9} + \frac{c}{27} + \frac{d}{81}$$

Mathematica finds the rational equivalent of the number represented.

$In[4]:=$ **number[{3}, {1,4,1,5,9,2,6,5,3,5,8,9,7,9}, 11]**

$$Out[4]= \frac{1186762701790147}{379749833583241}$$

N[ ] gives the decimal fraction approximation.

$In[5]:=$ **N[%, 15]**

$Out[5]=$ 3.12511710826072

The same result using ∧∧.

$In[6]:=$ **11∧∧3.14159265358979**

$Out[6]=$ 3.125117108260718

BaseForm[ ] provides the inverse operation.

$In[7]:=$ **BaseForm[%, 11]**

$Out[7]//BaseForm=$ 3.14159265358979
                                  11

Computer problem

1. In the solution to this problem you will write a procedure for converting a number to its binary representation.

    (a) Define a function ibinary[i_Integer] that gives a list of the bits for the binary representation of the integer i. Use IntegerDigits[ ] to check your function.

    (b) Define a function fbinary[f_Real] that gives a list of the first 20 bits in the binary representation of the fractional number f. You may assume that $0 \le f < 1$. Use RealDigits[ ] to check your function.

    (c) Combine the two functions ibinary[ ] and fbinary[ ] to define a function tobinary[x_] that gives a pair of lists of bits representing the integer and fractional parts of the number x in binary.

    (d) Modify the function tobinary[ ] to return its result as a String of characters in Mathematica input format; e.g., tobinary[2.375] should return the string "2∧∧10.01100000000000000000" (the quotes will not be displayed.) Note: Map[ToString, *digitlist*] will convert each 0 and 1 in the list *digitlist* into the characters "0" and "1", respectively, and return the list of those characters. StringJoin[ ] and Apply[ ] are other Mathematica functions that will be useful.

2.2 Floating-Point Numbers

Two computer representations of real numbers have been in common use. One is **fixed point** in which the sign and the digits are stored with an assumed fixed location for the radix point (which is a name given to the decimal point when the discussion is not limited to base 10).

sign	d i g i t s

All numbers in a given computation are uniformly scaled by the program as often as necessary so that there is enough room to the left of the radix point for the leading digits of the largest number. This means that leading zeros will be stored for most numbers. These days, except in special situations, fixed point is used only to represent integer values. For non-integer values general-purpose computation is done exclusively with **floating point**. Storage is provided not only for the sign and digits but also for the location of the radix point.

sign	position of radix point	d i g i t s

These two representations are given, respectively, the names `INTEGER` and `REAL` in Fortran, `int` and `float` in C, and `Integer` and `Real` in *Mathematica*. It is good programming practice to keep the two data types separate: to use `Integer`s for counting (and that includes most exponents) and `Real`s for measuring. Computers have separate operations for the two types of numbers. If an operation involving two different types of numbers is wanted, this usually requires conversion from one type to another. We recommend that type conversions be explicit, using, for example, `FLOAT( )` in Fortran, `(float)` in C, and `N[ ]` in *Mathematica* to convert an integer to a floating-point number. This serves as an acknowledgment that computing time is being expended to do the conversion, and it helps to document the types of the variables. Mixing number types is a common cause of program bugs in a language like Fortran and to a lesser extent in *Mathematica*.

Following are some examples of floating-point representations of four-decimal-digit numbers in which the position of the decimal point is specified relative to the position after the first digit:

$$+(1)5047 \longrightarrow 50.47,$$
$$+(5)1860 \longrightarrow 186000.,$$
$$-(1)1270 \longrightarrow -12.70,$$
$$+(-4)5024 \longrightarrow 0.0005024.$$

You see here the advantage of floating point: it is unnecessary to store leading and trailing zeros. More generally,

$$\pm(e)d_1d_2d_3d_4 \longrightarrow \pm10^e \times d_1.d_2d_3d_4.$$

Figure 2.2: A floating point (W. Kahan, 1981)

Note that multiplication by 10^e has the effect of moving the decimal point e places to the right. The value of e is known as the **exponent**, and the digits are called the **mantissa** or **significand**. The use of a power of 10 in the display of a numerical value is not a necessary feature of floating-point representation. There are some floating-point calculators that do not use *scientific notation* but simply allow the position of the decimal point to vary. Of course, this limits significantly the possible positions of the decimal point. Even with scientific notation there will be a limited exponent range; for demonstration purposes take this to be $-9 \le e \le 9$.

We will make frequent references to numbers that are exactly representable as n-digit floating-point numbers, and for convenience we call these simply n-digit numbers. To alert you to our rather special use of this language, we formalize this as follows:

Definition 2.1 *A real number is said to be an* n-**digit number** *if it can be expressed as* $\pm 10^e \times d_1.d_2 \cdots d_n$.

That is, we need only n digits to represent the number, excluding leading and trailing zeros. What is an n-bit number?

Note that some numbers have multiple representations as floating-point numbers, for example,

$$10^2 \times 0.012 = 10^1 \times 0.120 = 10^0 \times 1.200.$$

For some purposes, like comparisons, it is convenient to have a unique representation for each value. It is customary to use a **normalization** in which the first digit of the mantissa is nonzero except that zero $= +10^{-9} \times 0.000$.

Actually, the details of *how* numbers are represented do not concern us in numerical analysis; rather, our concern is *whether* a number is representable. A real number that is exactly representable as a floating-point number is said to be a **machine number**. Examples for our "demonstration" floating-point-number system are

$$10 = +10^{+1} \times 1.000,$$
$$\frac{1}{5} = +10^{-1} \times 2.000,$$
$$\sin \frac{\pi}{6} = +10^{-1} \times 5.000.$$

Thus the term "machine number" refers only to the *value* of a number and not its representation.

The set of machine numbers is finite:

$$0,$$
$$\pm 10^{-9} \times 1.000, \quad \pm 10^{-9} \times 1.001, \quad \ldots, \quad \pm 10^{-9} \times 9.999,$$

$$\pm 10^{-8} \times 1.000, \ \pm 10^{-8} \times 1.001, \ \ldots, \ \pm 10^{-8} \times 9.999,$$

$$\cdots$$

$$\pm 10^{9} \times 1.000, \ \pm 10^{9} \times 1.001, \ \ldots, \ \pm 10^{9} \times 9.999.$$

Although decimal numbers are used by calculators, they are not used by most computers. Many computers have floating-point chips that adhere more or less to the IEEE standard for binary floating-point arithmetic. Their machine numbers are

$$\pm 2^{e} \times (b_1.b_2 \cdots b_{24})_2 \qquad \text{where } -126 \le e \le 127,$$
$$\pm \infty,$$
NaN (not-a-number).

The set of machine numbers for binary floating-point numbers is easy to describe *without* using binary representation of numbers. For IEEE standard binary floating-point arithmetic the machine numbers consist of zero and all those values that can be expressed as

$$\pm 2^{e-23} \times (1b_2 \cdots b_{24})_2,$$

or equivalently as

$$\pm 2^p \times m$$

where $2^{23} \le m \le 2^{24} - 1$ and $-149 \le p \le 104$. We can omit the lower bound on m because the magnitude of m can easily be boosted by transferring factors of 2 from 2^p, provided that p does not go below -149. Restated, the machine numbers consist of any value of the form

$$\pm 2^p \times m$$

where $0 \le m \le 2^{24} - 1 = 16777215$ and $-149 \le p \le 104$ *excluding* those numbers for which $0 < 2^p \times m < 2^{-126}$. (These excluded numbers are known as denormalized numbers.)

Example 2.4 Thus $10^{10}, 2\frac{7}{8}, -\frac{1}{64}$ are machine numbers but $10^{11}, 0.1, 2^{128}$ are not. The number 10^{11} can be expressed as $2^{11} \times 5^{11}$ but $5^{11} > 2^{24} - 1$, the number 0.1 cannot be represented as an integer power of 2 times some integer, and the number 2^{128} requires an exponent that is too great.

It is an important fact that most decimal fractions are *not* representable.

There are three basic parameters of a floating-point number system:

- the **base** β,

- the **precision** n, which is the number of digits in the mantissa, and

- the **exponent range**.

For IEEE single precision, $\beta = 2$, $n = 24$, and the exponent range is $[-126 : 127]$. In **double precision**, $\beta = 2$, $n = 53$, and the exponent range is $[-1022 : 1023]$.

This is a good place to mention the difference between precision and accuracy. If we say $\pi \approx 3.142857142857$, we are being very precise but not very accurate! Precision is a capacity for accuracy: using many digits to approximate a number, using a polynomial of high degree to approximate a function. (In *Mathematica* the words "precision" and "accuracy" have different, specialized meanings.)

In order to underscore the granularity of a set of machine numbers, we have shown in Figure 2.3 the set of numbers

$$\pm 2^e \times (b_1.b_2b_3)_2, \qquad -2 \leq e \leq 1.$$

Note that they are evenly spaced, but only between powers of 2. With one exception every machine number has a **predecessor**, and with one exception every machine number has a **successor**.

The closeness of the spacing is a measure of the precision. By this measure 24-bit numbers are as closely spaced as are n-decimal-digit numbers where n ranges from about 6.9 to 8.2, depending on what part of the number line we are on.

Supplementary notes

Figure 2.3 is an example from G.E. Forsythe and C.B. Moler, *Computer Solution of Linear Algebraic Systems*, Prentice-Hall, Englewood Cliffs, N.J., 1967. The hole near zero in this figure is not really there, *if* we do not require numbers with the minimum exponent to be normalized. If such were the case, there would be three equally spaced machine numbers on each side of zero. These are called **denormalized** numbers, and they are part of the IEEE standard. For the demonstration number system, denormalized numbers would have the form

$$\pm 10^{-9} \times 0.d_2d_3d_4$$

Figure 2.3: Machine numbers on a toy binary computer

where $d_2d_3d_4 \neq 000$. We do not regard these as full-fledged machine numbers because they all have fewer than four digits of precision.

A reference for the IEEE standard and related information is

> D. Goldberg, "What every computer scientist should know about floating-point arithmetic," *ACM Computing Surveys 23*, 1991, pp. 5–48.

Exercises

1. Any nonzero real number x can be uniquely expressed as $10^e \cdot s$ where e is an integer and $1 \leq |s| < 10$. Express e in terms of x by using the logarithm and the ceiling or floor function. Note: The ceiling $\lceil x \rceil$ of x is that integer n such that $x \leq n < x + 1$, and the floor $\lfloor x \rfloor$ is that integer m such that $x - 1 < m \leq x$.

2. (a) If x is exactly representable as a 53-bit number and $\frac{1}{2} \leq x < 1$, what is the maximum number of digits that might be needed to represent x in decimal? Give an example of a number x that requires the maximum number of digits.

   (b) If x is exactly representable as a 53-bit number and $\frac{1}{2} \leq x < 1$, what is the minimum number of digits that might be needed to represent x in decimal? Give an example of a number x that requires the minimum number of digits.

   (c) Repeat parts (a) and (b) for $\frac{1}{4} \leq x < \frac{1}{2}$.

   (d) Repeat parts (a) and (b) for $2 \leq x < 4$.

3. Which of the values $0.01, 0.02, \ldots, 1.00$ are machine numbers assuming base 2 floating-point arithmetic?

4. Which of the following are machine numbers for (single-precision) IEEE binary floating-point arithmetic?

   (a) $\tan \frac{\pi}{4}$, (b) $\sin \frac{\pi}{4}$, (c) 0.5625, (d) 0.2, (e) $10^{10} - 1$, (f) 12^{12}, (g) 20×10^9, (h) 3×2^{126}.

5. What is the smallest positive *integer* that is not a machine number for (single-precision) IEEE binary floating-point arithmetic?

6. Below is a very tiny piece of the real line with *consecutive* eight-digit precision base 10 floating-point numbers marked below the line and *consecutive* 24-bit precision base 2 floating-point numbers marked above the line.

Given that $1 \leq X \leq 10$, determine what X must be.

Computer problem

1. Use the function `Table[ ]` to form a list of all of the positive (normalized) machine numbers on a three-digit, base 4 computer with exponents in the range −2 to 2. How many numbers are there in the list? What are the smallest and largest numbers in the list? `ListPlot` the `Log` of the `Sorted`, `Flattened` list of numbers. Why do the points tend to lie in a straight line? Why is the "line" scalloped? Would the scallops be more or less pronounced in base 16?

2.3 Rounding

The purpose of rounding in computation is to turn any real number into a machine number, preferably the nearest one.

For rounding to n digits (*reminder*: we disregard leading zeros) the following rule is good:

> If the digits following the nth digit are
> > less than $50000\cdots$
> > > then discard these digits
> > greater than $50000\cdots$
> > > then discard these digits and add 1 to the nth digit
> > exactly equal to $50000\cdots$
> > > then discard these digits and add 1 to the nth digit if it is odd.

In other words, we round to the nearest n-digit number, and in a *perfect* tie we round up or down equally often.

Here are some examples, where fl denotes rounding to four digits:

$$
\begin{aligned}
fl(999.94999) &= 999.9, \\
fl(999.95) &= 1000., \\
fl(-999.95) &= -1000., \\
fl(999.85) &= 999.8, \\
fl(999.8500001) &= 999.9.
\end{aligned}
$$

Note that in the rare case where rounding causes a carry to propagate beyond the leading digit, the rounded digit is always a zero, so no further rounding is needed due to the carry.

Let us call this rounding rule

RULE I "round-to-even" $\stackrel{\text{def}}{=}$ "Round to nearest, with round to even in case of a tie."

There is no standard name for this rule; the name "round-to-even" has been used before. One way to picture this rule is to associate with every machine number the set of all numbers that get rounded to it. Suppose the use of four-decimal-digit numbers. With the number 2.000 we associate the closed interval [1.9995, 2.0005], and with 2.001 we associate the open interval]2.0005, 2.0015[. Whether the interval is closed or open depends on the parity of the last digit of the particular machine number.

There are two other rounding rules that should be mentioned. One is

RULE II "rounding" $\stackrel{\text{def}}{=}$ "Round to nearest, with round away from zero in case of a tie."

In terms of digits the rule is the following: If the $(n + 1)$th digit ≥ 5 then round up the nth digit; otherwise round down the nth digit. If applied to the examples given before for round-to-even, the only difference is that

$$fl(999.85) = 999.9.$$

This is the popular way to do rounding that you probably learned in school. It is simpler than round-to-even and good for displaying values but slightly inferior for computation. Supposing the use of four-decimal-digit numbers, let us consider the set of those real numbers that get rounded to each of the machine numbers. For 2.000 the half-open interval [1.9995, 2.0005[is the set of such numbers. For every other machine number, except zero, it is also a half-open set that gets rounded to it.

The third rule worth mentioning here is

RULE III "chopping" $\stackrel{\text{def}}{=}$ "Round toward zero."

In other words, the rule is to drop the excess (significant) digits as shown in the example

$$fl(999.999999) = 999.9.$$

This is sometimes called "truncation."

Note: The word "rounding" has two meanings for us. It has a generic sense, meaning any rounding rule, and a specific sense, meaning rounding rule II.

There are **exceptions** to these rules due to the limited exponent range of most floating-point-number systems. We illustrate this with our demonstration floating-point-number system: four decimal digits of precision, an exponent range from -9 to 9, round-to-even rounding. When the exponent would be too great, the number is "rounded" to infinity: $fl(10^{10} \times 1.000) = +\infty$. Sometimes the exponent would be too great only after rounding to four digits: $fl(10^9 \times 9.9995) = +\infty$. This never happens for a smaller positive number. In

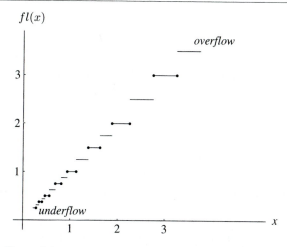

Figure 2.4: Round-to-even

both cases an **overflow** flag is raised and the computation may be interrupted. When the exponent would be too little, the number is rounded to an unnormalized number, or to zero: $fl(10^{-10} \times 9.99949)$ = something tiny. The **underflow** flag is raised and the computation may be interrupted. However, $fl(10^{-10} \times 9.9995) = 10^{-9} \times 1.000$. The precise details of what happens when the exponent is too little are too technical to be included here. They are given in the "Supplementary notes" of the preceding section and of this section. If rounding a real number x causes neither underflow nor overflow, we say that x is **representable**.

Rounding is a function $fl(x)$ that maps reals to nearby machine numbers. It approximates the function x that maps a real to itself. This approximation is illustrated for round-to-even in Figure 2.4. We consider now the accuracy of rounding.

The error = $fl(x) - x$ for chopping is graphed in Figure 2.5(a).

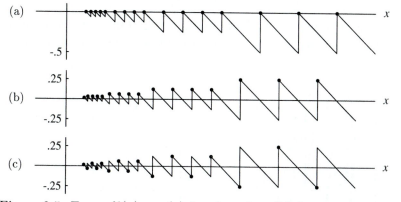

Figure 2.5: Error $fl(x) - x$ (a) for chopping, (b) for rounding, and (c) for round-to-even

The error for rounding is shown in Figure 2.5(b). We note that the error for rounding is on the average half as large as it is for chopping. Also the error for rounding is positive and negative almost equally often, and as a consequence rounding errors tend to cancel in a computation that generates a number of roundoff errors. Chopping errors, on the other hand, are extremely biased and as a consequence tend to accumulate much more rapidly than rounding errors.

The error for round-to-even is shown by the graph of Figure 2.5(c). Comparing this to the graph in Figure 2.5(b), we may notice a slight bias in simple rounding due to its error always being positive at the jumps in its graph. In practice this case occurs with probability greater than zero.

In the plots of the various roundoff errors we note that their magnitudes increase linearly with x if small-scale oscillations are overlooked. Given in Figure 2.6 is a plot of the *relative* error in round-to-even. Its magnitude stays constant as x varies if small-scale variations are neglected.

We have been promoting the idea of a machine number as a point on the real line. Another view is that each machine number represents all numbers that would be rounded to it; in other words, each machine number is regarded as a very narrow range of points. This idea, that a floating-point value is smeared out, is counterproductive. Often a value is exact, and often it has an error that far exceeds the representation error. Not knowing the actual error, the best course is to treat the value as though it were exact. Thus, for example, programming languages should have relational operations that are executed exactly without any error tolerances. In particular, an equality between two floating-point values should succeed only if they are exactly equal. If equality and the other relational operations are fuzzy, it makes them more complicated to define, it frustrates and inconveniences knowledgeable programmers, and it destroys the familiar properties of these operators. When it is desirable to work with ranges of values, explicit intervals, as discussed in Section 2.4.2, should be used.

The base, precision (number of available digits), and rounding rule of a floating-point-number system have a direct bearing on how accurately we represent arbitrary real numbers.

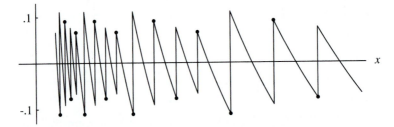

Figure 2.6: Relative error $(fl(x) - x)/x$ in round-to-even

By definition the relative representation error for a number x is

$$\frac{fl(x) - x}{x} \stackrel{\text{def}}{=} \delta_x$$

where we usually just write δ instead of δ_x. Rearranging, we can write the result of rounding as $fl(x) = x(1 + \delta)$.

Our goal is to obtain an upper bound on the magnitude of the relative error δ that is at most slightly greater than the maximum possible $|\delta|$ for any x. Before giving a general bound, let us do its derivation for the demonstration case $\beta = 10$, $n = 4$ with $fl =$ round or round-to-even. Suppose we are dealing with a representable real number $x = \pm 10^e \times d_1.d_2d_3d_4d_5d_6 \cdots$ where $d_1 \neq 0$. The absolute rounding error will be greatest in magnitude for x halfway between two four-digit numbers. Such a number has the form $\pm 10^e \times d_1.d_2d_3d_45$ where $d_1 \neq 0$, and it has an absolute rounding error of magnitude $10^e \times 0.0005$. Therefore, the absolute rounding error for x has a magnitude

$$|fl(x) - x| \leq 10^e \times 0.0005,$$

and the *relative* error for x has a magnitude

$$\left| \frac{fl(x) - x}{x} \right| \leq \frac{10^e \times 0.0005}{10^e \times d_1.d_2d_3d_4d_5d_6 \cdots} = \frac{0.0005}{d_1.d_2d_3d_4d_5d_6 \cdots}$$
$$\leq \frac{0.0005}{1.000}.$$

(Why is the minimum value of the denominator 1.000?) So the worst-case relative roundoff error has magnitude $\leq \frac{1}{2} \times 10^{-3}$. If we generalize from base 10 to β and from precision 4 to n, we obtain (Exercise 7) the bound $\frac{1}{2}\beta^{1-n}$ on the magnitude of the relative error.

The convenient and usual way of stating the accuracy of rounding is to write

$$fl(x) = x(1 + \delta)$$

where

$$\boxed{|\delta| < \tfrac{1}{2}\beta^{1-n} \stackrel{\text{def}}{=} \text{unit roundoff error}}$$

This is normally a very small quantity. The most important thing to know about roundoff errors is that they are tiny relative to the computed results. For this reason rounding error is often not a problem in practice.

For base 2 the unit roundoff error is simply 2^{-n}. For IEEE single precision this is $2^{-24} \approx 10^{-7}$, and for double precision $2^{-53} \approx 10^{-16}$.

Operations analogous to rounding, but more complex, occur in the display on computer graphics devices of objects such as points, lines, and surfaces. There are interesting algorithms for drawing correctly quantized straight lines and circles.

Supplementary note

We have been vague about the result of an operation that underflows. In the case of the demonstration number system the result would be rounded to the appropriate number of the form

$$\pm 10^{-9} \times 0.d_2 d_3 d_4.$$

Note that this rounding is to 12 decimal places and not to four (significant) digits. These numbers, with the exception of zero, are the denormalized numbers discussed in the "Supplementary notes" of the preceding section. The relative rounding error in this case will generally *not* satisfy the bounds that we obtained earlier. However, that result is true *as stated* because we defined the set of *representable reals* to exclude those that underflow when rounded. Anyway, the underflow flag signals the possibility that the relative rounding error is not tiny. (However, this last statement is not quite correct because in the IEEE standard the precise definition of underflow is an "implementor's option.")

Review question

1. What do we call those points in Figure 2.5 where the error is zero?

Exercises

1. Let fl denote round-to-even rounding to four decimal digits with an exponent range $[-9:9]$. Evaluate each of the following:

   (a) $fl(12.345)$,   (b) $fl(-12.345)$,   (c) $fl(12354)$,
   (d) $fl(12.34500001)$,   (e) $fl(9.9994 \times 10^9)$,   (f) $fl(9.9994 \times 10^{-10})$.

2. Let fl denote the operation of rounding a number to five decimal digits using the round-to-even rule. If $fl(x) = 100$, what can one say about x? (This means determine the set of all reals x such that $fl(x) = 100$.)

3. On November 22, 1981, a sign on Green Street displayed the temperatures 1°C and 35°F. Is it possible that each of these is a correctly rounded value, and if so, what can we say about the temperature?

4. Write $74\frac{4}{7}$ as a normalized six-digit base 8 floating-point number. Use rounding rather than chopping.

5. Suppose you are given a function *nint* that rounds to the nearest integer (using simple rounding, say). How can you use this to round to n decimal places?

6. Show how the function *nint* in the preceding exercise can be defined in terms of the floor function $\lfloor y \rfloor$ (which denotes the greatest integer $\leq y$). Your definition should work for negative arguments as well.

7. Extend the derivation of the roundoff error bound given for $\beta = 10$ and $n = 4$ to general β and n.

8. Let $x = 10^e \cdot s$ where $1 \leq s < 10$, and let $fl(x)$ be the value of x rounded to n base 10 *digits*.

   (a) Give an expression for $fl(x)$ in terms of e, s, and n by making use of a function *nint* that rounds to the nearest integer (using simple rounding, say).

   (b) Suppose $fl(x) = 10^{\bar{e}} \cdot \bar{s}$ where $1 \leq \bar{s} < 10$. Precisely when will it be the case that $\bar{e} \neq e$?

9. For base 10,

$$\frac{\frac{1}{2} \times 10^{1-n}}{1 + \frac{1}{2} \times 10^{1-n}}$$

   is an upper bound on the magnitude of the relative rounding error.

   (a) How does this compare to the bound given in the text?

   (b) Give an example for which the bound is realized.

Mathematica notes

It is easy to define a function that does limited decimal rounding.

Define $fl(x)$ for n-digit decimal rounding.

```
In[1]:= fl[x_, n_] :=
          Module[{nx = N[x], s},
            s = 10.^(Floor[Log[10., Abs[nx]]]+1-n);
            N[Round[nx/s]s, n]]
```

fl[ ] rounds results to the specified number of digits.

```
In[2]:= fl[Pi, 8]

Out[2]= 3.1415927
```

You should make fl[ ] Listable to use it extensively. Note that there is a problem with fl[ ]: because it represents rounded decimal numbers as machine numbers, rounding occurs twice and correct round-to-even rounding cannot work. An alternative is to use NumericalMath`ComputerArithmetic`.

The package NumericalMath`ComputerArithmetic` provides facilities for learning about arithmetic in any base from 2 to 16 with any of several rounding schemes. There are parameters that define the arithmetic being used. These parameters can be examined with Arithmetic[ ] and changed with SetArithmetic[ ].

Read in the package.

```
In[1]:= << NumericalMath`ComputerArithmetic`
```

The default arithmetic is 4 digits in base 10 with an exponent range of −50 to 50 and round-to-even rounding.

```
In[2]:= Arithmetic[ ]
Out[2]= {4, 10, RoundingRule -> RoundToEven,
    ExponentRange -> {-50, 50}, MixedMode -> False,
    IdealDivide -> False}
```

Change the arithmetic to be 2 digits in base 3 with round-to-infinity rounding. This is our rounding rule II.

```
In[3]:= SetArithmetic[2, 3, RoundingRule ->
RoundToInfinity]
Out[3]= {2, 3, RoundingRule -> RoundToInfinity,
    ExponentRange -> {-50, 50}, MixedMode -> False,
    IdealDivide -> False}
```

Find the closest `ComputerNumber` to the real number π.

```
In[4]:= ComputerNumber[Pi]
Out[4]= 10.
          3
```

The function `Normal[ ]` converts a `ComputerNumber` to its rational equivalent.

```
In[5]:= Normal[%]
Out[5]= 3
```

Define a function that gives the absolute error in the computer representation of a number.

```
In[6]:= f[x_] := Normal[ComputerNumber[x]] - x
```

Plot the absolute error for all numbers between 1/9 and 3.

```
In[7]:= Plot[f[x], {x, 1/9, 3}, PlotPoints -> 121]
```

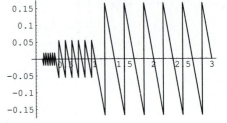

Plot the relative error for the same numbers.

```
In[8]:= Plot[f[x]/x, {x, 1/9, 3}, PlotPoints -> 121]
```

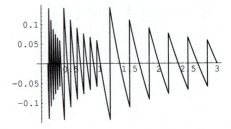

Computer problems

1. This problem examines the error in the representation of numbers on the toy computer described in this section. The approach here is rather inefficient but has the advantage of being rather straightforward.

   (a) Let `machnos` be a sorted list of the 17 nonnegative machine numbers that the toy computer can represent. A simple way to get this list is to `Flatten` the result of `Table[i 2^j, {i, 4, 7}, {j, -4, -1}]` and `Append` to this the number 0. Let `machnos` be the result of `Sorting` this list.

   (b) Define a function `pos[x_]` that gives the position of the machine number in the list `machnos` that is closest to `x`. A simple way to find this position is to first find the list of differences `Abs[machnos - x]`. Then find the position of the minimum value in this list. Useful *Mathematica* functions: `Min[ ]` and `Position[ ]`.

   (c) Plot the absolute error due to rounding for the toy floating-point-number system. Restrict the range to those positive numbers whose rounded value does not overflow or underflow. It is not necessary to remove the vertical lines that appear where the error switches from being negative to being positive. You may have to use a larger value than the default for the option `PlotPoints` to get a nice-looking graph.

   (d) Plot the relative error due to rounding.

2. The magnitude of the error in the machine representation of numbers increases suddenly at integer powers of the base used. With `NumericalMath`ComputerArithmetic``, exhibit this behavior by plotting the error. How is the size of this increase related to the base?

2.4 Basic Operations

We consider in this section the question of performing operations on *machine numbers* so that the result is still a machine number. Just as machine floating-point numbers approximate real numbers, machine floating-point *operations* approximate their mathematical counterparts.

2.4.1 Correctly rounded arithmetic

Let a and b be machine numbers. Let $\circ$ be one of $+$, $-$, $*$, $/$. Then the floating-point operation $\hat{\circ}$ is defined by

$$a \mathbin{\hat{\circ}} b \overset{\text{def}}{=} fl(a \circ b).$$

In other words, you first compute $a \circ b$ to infinite precision and then round the result. This result depends only on the true result $a \circ b$, not on how this result is obtained, not on the operation and operands. Here are two examples:

$$99.98 \; \hat{-} \; 0.005010 = fl(99.98 - 0.00501) = fl(99.97499) = 99.97,$$
$$2.000 \hat{/} 3.000 = fl(2/3) = fl(0.6666\tfrac{2}{3}) = 0.6667.$$

Note that in the second example even though the true result has an infinite decimal expansion it is not necessary to do the expansion beyond the fourth digit if the remainder is retained. Therefore, a practical computer implementation of correctly rounded arithmetic is possible even though we may visualize the process as using an infinite decimal expansion. Another important point to remember is that machine arithmetic is defined only for operands that are machine numbers.

Let us examine the error that arises from a single arithmetic operation. Using the result that we obtained for the relative error in fl, we have

$$a \; \hat{\circ} \; b = (a \circ b)(1 + \delta) \quad \text{where } |\delta| < \tfrac{1}{2}\beta^{1-n}.$$

Thus the relative error δ in the floating-point operation is just the representation error for the exact result $a \circ b$. Accordingly we can say that the relative roundoff error from a single operation is *minuscule*.

2.4.2 Rounded interval arithmetic

The purpose of interval analysis is to produce intervals that are certain to contain the true result. If machine floating-point numbers are used to represent the endpoints of the intervals, then computational errors will be introduced. This may be all right as long as allowances are made for such errors when forming the intervals, so that the true value does not escape the containment. We illustrate with an example. If $\bar{x} = [1.001, 1.002]$ and $\bar{y} = [2.001, 2.002]$, the exact product is $\bar{x} * \bar{y} = [2.003001, 2.006004]$. In finite-precision interval arithmetic, assuming four digits, we should get

$$\bar{x} \; \hat{*} \; \bar{y} = fl(\bar{x} * \bar{y}) \quad = \quad fl([2.003001, 2.006004])$$
$$= \quad [2.003, 2.007].$$

Note that the interval was rounded outward in order to produce the smallest possible machine-representable interval that still contains the unrounded interval. To do this efficiently requires hardware for *directed rounding*, which is part of the IEEE binary floating-point standard.

The most effective use of interval computation is not to use it alone but to use it for validating results obtained by ordinary floating-point computation with "point" values. This combination is known as *self-validating* scientific computation.

2.4.3 Elementary functions—exp, sin, tan, arctan,...

In Section 1.2 we asserted that for some types of computations it is impractical to compute the first n correct digits of the result and also impractical to compute the result correctly rounded to n digits. Such a limitation applies to most elementary functions including $\exp(x)$ (but not the square root). Consequently, we might ask instead that the magnitude of the error be strictly less than 1 ulp (unit in the last place). This is feasible; in fact, there exists a practical program for computing the exponential with error ≤ 0.54 ulp. The requirement that the error be strictly less than 1 ulp is not entirely arbitrary: it ensures that if the exact result is a machine number, the exact result will be computed.

2.4.4 Input/output

Input/output is of concern to us because of the need to convert between base 10 and the number system used by the computer. We illustrate using *Mathematica* on a computer with 53-bit-precision floating-point arithmetic.

The value of x is the machine number nearest to the entered decimal number. For nice-looking output, the value of x is first rounded to the nearest 6-digit number, but x itself is not affected.

```
In[1]:= x = 1. * 123.456789
Out[1]= 123.457
```

The actual value of x.

```
In[2]:= SetPrecision[x, 60]
Out[2]= 123.456789000000000555701262783259153366088671875
```

This *Mathematica* example is one of many apparent mysteries that can be explained if you realize that

$$\boxed{\text{what you see is } \underline{\text{not}} \text{ what you have}}$$

The occurrence of I/O error can be overstated. As a rule the algorithms we study do not do much decimal/binary conversion and so I/O roundoff error is usually *not* present. (Otherwise we would be spending a lot of time typing in numbers.) For example, the assignment "a = b + c;" in *Mathematica* or any other programming language involves at most one rounding error due to the addition. (Loading from and storing to memory normally produces no error.)

Input errors can usually be avoided by expressing non-machine numbers in terms of machine numbers, for example, 1./3. instead of 0.3333333 and 4.*arctan(1.) instead of 3.141593. This has two benefits: we avoid the rounding error in the decimal representation and we avoid the question of how many decimal places to use.

2.4.5 Multiple operations

For several floating-point operations, the result of each operation is subject to a possible rounding. For example, the expression `0.1 - x * y` has the value $fl(fl(0.1) - fl(xy))$, and the *Mathematica* expression `1.38 10^-23` has the (internal) value $fl(\,fl(1.38)\,fl(1/fl(10^{23}))\,)$.

Actually the result of evaluating an expression may not be so predictable. First, the interpreter or compiler for the programming language may rearrange an expression before it is evaluated. This can sometimes be prevented by inserting parentheses. Second, evaluation of intermediate results in an expression may be performed with additional precision. In the case of C it is standard to do calculations in double precision even if operands and the stored result are single precision.

Bounds on the roundoff error due to multiple operations are not easy to determine. One way to get bounds is to use intervals and interval operations. However, there are few programming-language interpreters or compilers that provide this facility. Also, the use of intervals does increase program execution time. Furthermore, the error bounds returned by the simple substitution of intervals for numbers are very often much larger than the actual errors. Special algorithms and higher precision are needed to obtain good error bounds. For these reasons it is almost universal practice *not* to keep track of roundoff errors. Rather we rely on experience in making judgments about the probable effects of roundoff errors. Under these conditions we can, of course, say *nothing for certain* about the accuracy of our results. They *could* be in error by 100%!

A simple and usually dependable way to estimate the effect of roundoff error for a computation is to redo it all in higher precision. For Fortran and C this is practical only if the original computation uses single-precision values; no such restriction applies to languages like *Mathematica*, which provide, via software, arithmetic of arbitrary precision.

It is to be hoped that in the future we will see systems for doing numerical calculations that automatically ensure that all answers are "correct":

- every printed numerical value not off by more than 1 ulp,

- every plotted graph not off by more than 1 pixel.

The technology exists to build such a system for *small-scale computation.*

Exercises

1. Assuming four-digit decimal floating-point arithmetic with round-to-even rounding, perform the following computations:

   (a) $0.6668 + 0.3334$,   (b) $1000. - 0.05001$,

   (c) $2.000 * 0.6667$,   (d) $25.00/16.00$.

2. Assuming n-digit decimal floating-point arithmetic with round-to-even rounding, what are the values of the expressions that follow?

   (a) $1\hat{+}10^{-n-1}$, (b) $1\hat{+}10^{-n}$, (c) $1\hat{+}10^{-n+1}$,
   (d) $1\hat{-}10^{-n-1}$, (e) $1\hat{-}10^{-n}$, (f) $1\hat{-}10^{-n+1}$.

   You may write your answer using the exact arithmetic operations "+" and "−."

3. Consider a normalized floating-point-number system with base 2, precision 24, and exponent range $[-126 : 127]$.

   (a) Let x and y be floating-point numbers, and let $x + y$ be the floating-point sum attained by round-to-even arithmetic. Determine the set of possible values for the exponent of $x + y$ if x has an exponent of 0 and y has an exponent of (i) 0, (ii) 1, (iii) 2, (iv) 23, (v) 24, (vi) 48.

   (b) Repeat (a) for $x * y$ and x/y where both x and y have exponents of 0.

4. If we wish to approximate a given quantity x by a machine number y with an error of less than 1 ulp, how many possible correct answers y are there?

5. Assume four-digit decimal floating-point arithmetic with round-to-even rounding.

   (a) Find a machine number x such that $1.001 \hat{*} x$ is the (first) successor of x and another y such that $1.001 \hat{*} y$ is the tenth successor of y.

   (b) Find a machine number z such that $0.9995 \hat{*} z$ is the (first) predecessor of z and another w such that $0.9995 \hat{*} w$ is the fifth predecessor of w.

6. Discuss the pros and cons of having $\widehat{\sin}(fl(\pi)) = 0$.

7. Using *Mathematica* on a certain machine, if you enter 1122334455.667 - 1122334455.666 you get 0.00100017. Furthermore, if you enter 112233445566.7 - 112233445566.6 you get 0.0999908. Clearly the correct differences are 0.001 and 0.1, respectively. What is the most plausible explanation for these results? (Please do not do any calculations.)

8. Below is a microscopic look at the real line in a neighborhood of the point 2. The ticks rising above the line represent 24-bit numbers and those below the line represent eight-digit numbers.

   spacing $= 2^{-23} \approx 1.2 \times 10^{-7}$ spacing $= 2^{-22} \approx 2.4 \times 10^{-7}$

                                        2

   spacing $= 10^{-7}$

   Consider a computer that uses 24-bit numbers, i.e., base $= 2$, precision $= 24$.

(a) On this computer the following happened:
    The value 2.0000003 was read into X and then
    the value 2.0000002 was written from X.
    Using the diagram, explain what happened.

(b) What should happen if we read 1.9999999 into X and then write X?

(c) What should happen if we read 2.0000001 into X and then write X?

9. In the first example in Section 2.4.5 of multiple operations, why is it sufficient to write $fl(fl(0.1) - fl(xy))$ rather than $fl(fl(0.1) - fl(fl(x)fl(y)))$?

10. Assuming four-decimal-digit floating-point arithmetic with round-to-even rounding, execute the following:

$$s := 1.; \; c := 0.; \; t1 := 0.3333; \; t2 := 0.3333;$$
$$sold := s; \; s := s + t1;$$
$$c := c + (t1 - (s - sold));$$
$$sold := s; \; s := s + t2;$$
$$c := c + (t2 - (s - sold));$$
$$\text{print}(s + c)$$

11. Consider the floating-point number system with a precision of three decimal digits, an exponent range of -9 to 9, and round-to-even rounding. If $\circ$ denotes an arithmetic operation, then let $\hat{\circ}$ denote the corresponding floating-point operation.

(a) Give an example of machine numbers a, b, and c for which

$$(a \; \hat{+} \; b) \; \hat{+} \; c \neq a \; \hat{+} \; (b \; \hat{+} \; c).$$

(b) Give an example of machine numbers a and b for which $a \neq b$ and yet

$$1 \hat{/} a = 1 \hat{/} b.$$

(c) Give an example of machine numbers a, b, and c for which

$$a \; \hat{\times} \; (b \; \hat{+} \; c) \neq (a \; \hat{\times} \; b) \; \hat{+} \; (a \; \hat{\times} \; c).$$

12. Assuming four-digit decimal floating-point arithmetic with round-to-even rounding, find all machine numbers x that satisfy

$$(x \; \hat{+} \; x) \; \hat{+} \; x = 1.000.$$

Mathematica **notes**

Correct understanding of the "numerical" function `N[ ]` is based on the realization that like everything in *Mathematica* its behavior is based on rules. In particular, the arguments of `N` are evaluated *before* the application of `N`. If `N` encounters a nonnumerical value, it has rules that it can apply. For example, `N[Sin[2]]` is transformed to `N[Sin[N[2]]]` because `Sin[2]` does not evaluate to a number.

`SetPrecision[ ]` can be used to define a function that converts machine numbers to arbitrary-precision numbers with twice the precision.

Define the function `dble[ ]` that turns numbers into arbitrary-precision numbers with precision 2 `$MachinePrecision`.

```
In[1]:= dble[x_] := SetPrecision[x, 2 $MachinePrecision]
```

This example shows how to compute the roundoff error in 1./3.. The assumption is that errors in operations where *both* operands have doubled precision are (hopefully) negligible compared to the errors in a hardware floating-point operation.

```
In[2]:= dble[1./3.] - dble[1.]/dble[3.]
```
$$Out[2]= -1.850371707708594\ 10^{-17}$$

Remember that the displayed value of a `Real` number is often just a good approximation to its actual (internal) value. The reason for not displaying the exact internal value is to improve readability in the case of machine numbers and to indicate those digits that are thought to be correct in the case of arbitrary-precision numbers. If you want to see exactly what is stored internally (e.g., for purposes of comparing two numbers), you can use the function `$NumberBits[ ]`, which gives the individual bits of a number. This may not be as useful as `SetPrecision[ ]`, which delivers the exact value in decimal if sufficiently high precision is requested.

By default *Mathematica* normally displays only six digits of a machine number, and trailing zeros are suppressed so you may get even fewer digits. You can, however, change the default behavior.

Start with a number known to be a machine number. Note that only a few digits are displayed.

```
In[1]:= a = N[Pi]
Out[1]= 3.14159
```

`NumberForm[ ]` gives more of the digits.

```
In[2]:= NumberForm[a, 16]
Out[2]//NumberForm= 3.141592653589793
```

`$Post[ ]` is a function that gets applied at the very end of every `Out[ ]` .

```
In[3]:= $Post := NumberForm[#, Precision[#]]&
Out[3]//NumberForm= Null
```

Now the default behavior is to print all "significant" digits.

In[4]:= **a**

Out[4]//NumberForm= 3.141592653589793

Following is an example of how you can exploit the granularity of machine numbers. It also illustrates procedural programming in *Mathematica*.

```
sqrt[c_] := Module[ {x, y, x1},
          x = Max[c, 1.];
          y = c/x;
          x1 = y + 0.5(x-y);
          While[ y - x1 < 0  &&  x1 - x < 0,
             x = x1;
             y = c/x;
             x1 = y + 0.5(x-y)
          ];
          x1
       ]
```

The test y - x1 < 0 && x1 - x < 0 is used in the While loop rather than y < x1 && x1 < x because < is slightly "fuzzy" in *Mathematica*. For the same reason you should use x - y == 0. instead of x == y to test for equality between two Real numbers. In fact, all of the comparisons <, <=, ==, !=, ===, =!=, >, and >= are "fuzzy" when comparing floating-point numbers.

Several interesting functions are defined in the package NumericalMath`Microscope`. These functions can be used to examine the total accumulated rounding error in evaluation of an expression as well as look at the granularity of machine arithmetic.

Read in the package.

In[1]:= **<< NumericalMath`Microscope`**

The behavior of the logarithm function for machine numbers near x == 7 on this computer.

In[2]:= **Microscope[Log[x], {x, 7}]**

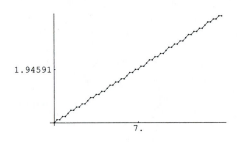

The scale on the vertical axis is in ulps. The error is smaller than 1 ulp for machine numbers near 1.

In[3]:= `MicroscopicError[(x-1.1)^3, {x, 1}]`

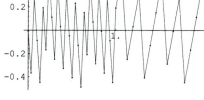

If you expand the expression, the errors are several thousands of ulps!

In[4]:= `MicroscopicError[Expand[(x-1.1)^3], {x, 1}]`

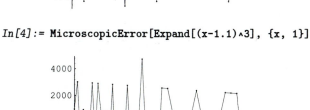

The absolute size of an ulp in the previous problem.

In[5]:= `Ulp[(0.1)^3]`

Out[5]= $2.1684\ 10^{-19}$

The error at a particular point.

In[6]:= `MachineError[Expand[(x-1.1)^3], x -> 1.]`

Out[6]= `2048. Ulps`

Computer problems

1. Enter the following sequence of expressions, omitting the comments:

   ```
   x = 123.456789
   1. x
   (1. x) - x  (* use subtraction not == to test equality between reals *)
   Clear[x, y]  (* clear them of their values, a good habit to develop *)
   ```

2. The function `Round[ ]` in *Mathematica* rounds numbers to integers. By considering what `Round[ ]` does to `Range[0, 5, 1/4]`, describe what sort of rounding scheme it apparently uses for rational numbers.

3. The machine parameter `$MachineEpsilon` is the difference between 1. and the next larger machine number. Consider the list of numbers

$$\text{xlist} = 1. + \$MachineEpsilon\ Range[0.,4.,0.25].$$

By examining (xlist-1.)/$MachineEpsilon, decide whether your computer conforms to the IEEE standard with respect to the rounding in this example.

4. Write a function rat[ ] that converts a Real value x to its *exact* rational equivalent. The method is to multiply x by 2 repeatedly until it is (exactly) an integer and then divide by the appropriate power of 2 (without a decimal point). The test

$$x \ - \ \text{Round}[x] \ == \ 0$$

should be foolproof. Try out rat[ ] on $fl(0.1)$ (which you enter into the computer by typing "0.1"). Then use N[ ] to display the first 200 digits of this number. For comparison use Rationalize[SetPrecision[0.1, 100]].

5. Set x = 1.000000123 and determine which of the values x∧4, (x x)∧2, (x x) (x x), and x x x x are equal to which. (One way to do this is to form a list of the four values and make a table of comparisons Table[...{i, 4}, {j, 4}] by taking individual elements of the list. The actual pairwise comparison can use either subtraction or equality of $NumberBits[ ]. An alternative would be to use Outer[Subtract, *list*, *list*] which forms the table of all differences of two numbers from *list*. In either case use MatrixForm[ ] to display the result in 4×4 format.)

6. Use MicroscopicError[ ] to examine the error in the function Sin[x] near x == Pi/2. Notice that the labels on the vertical axis are all zeros. Use MachineError[ ] to examine what the error really is at several of these points. (Look at 0.5 N[Pi] + 16. $MachineEpsilon, for example.)

7. With the help of dble[ ] (see page 57), determine the accumulated roundoff error for

$$\underbrace{0.1 + 0.1 + \cdots + 0.1}_{J \text{ times}}$$

computed with Sum for $J = 5, 10, 20$. Give the errors in base 2 using BaseForm[ ] or $NumberBits[ ].

8. Repeat Computer Problem 7 using ComputerArithmetic` with six-bit binary arithmetic, but use Do instead of Sum. Using Normal[ ], give the exact rational numbers that approximate the sums.

9. Let

$$H_n := \sum_{j=1}^{n} fl(\frac{1}{j}).$$

Assume that floating-point division is done correctly and use 1./N[j] to evaluate $fl(1/j)$. Define two functions hf and hb each having a parameter n_, the first to compute H_n by a forward summation starting with $j = 1$ and the second by a backward summation starting with $j = n$. Also define h[n_] for calculating the "true" result by summing the terms `dble[1./N[j]]` (see page 57). Generate results[1] for $n = 1000, 2000, 4000$, and calculate the errors. (Use `dble[ ]` to convert the machine-precision result to doubled precision before subtracting to find the error.) Do not use `Sum` for the two low-precision summations, because for technical reasons it reorders the terms. Use `Do` instead.

10. Compute the rounding error in each of the "low-precision" additions of `hf` and `hb` of Computer Problem 9 and form a list of these errors for each of `hf` and `hb`. To compute the roundoff error in an addition, use

$$dble[s + t] - (dble[s] + dble[t]).$$

ListPlot these long lists of errors scaled by `10^$MachinePrecision` for $n = 1000$.

2.5 Numerical Instability

It can happen that a few computations, each one done very accurately, can nonetheless yield an answer that has no accuracy whatever. With more than one floating-point arithmetic operation the relative error in the result can be 100%. For example, in four-digit arithmetic,

$$(100.0 \mathrel{\hat{+}} 0.04000) \mathrel{\hat{-}} 100.0 = 0..$$

With more than two arithmetic operations the relative error can be infinite:

$$((100.0 \mathrel{\hat{+}} 0.04000) \mathrel{\hat{-}} 100.0) \mathrel{\hat{-}} 0.04000 = -0.04000.$$

The choice of algorithm has an important effect on computational error. Algorithms that are equivalent in exact arithmetic are quite different in finite-precision floating-point arithmetic owing to roundoff error. Although a roundoff error is relatively very small, it can alter the subsequent computation. This alteration is the propagated roundoff error, which can be very large. How big it is depends on the organization of the computation. However, recall that the choice of algorithm has *no* effect on propagation of data error. (Why? Because the propagated data error is the difference between exactly solving the problem with the given data and exactly solving it with the true data.)

The construction of an algorithm involves breaking a problem into smaller units,

problem $\longrightarrow$ subproblem; subproblem,

---

[1]Probability theory (the law of large numbers) suggests that `hf` will be worse than `hb` by a factor of $(\log n)/\sqrt{2}$.

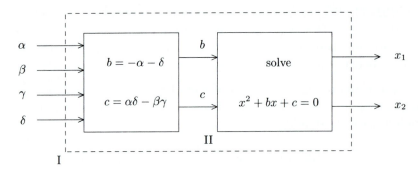

Figure 2.7: Refinement of a problem into two subproblems

and doing this again and again until all the units are "indivisible" operations. There are usually many ways to do this, but in floating-point arithmetic they are usually not equivalent. Figure 2.7 portrays an algorithm consisting of two subalgorithms. The first subalgorithm introduces rounding errors into its outputs b and c. These errors are regarded as computational errors with respect to the algorithm as a whole but as data errors with respect to the second subalgorithm. (Recall that data error was defined to include *previous* computational error.) Thus, the distinction between data error and computational error depends on context.

As an example of numerical stability that is easy to picture, we look at two algorithms for computing $z = 1.000 - 1.208/x$. The first and obvious one is

ALGORITHM 1 $y := 1.208/x;\ z := 1.000 - y$

Below we illustrate the computation for $x = 1.209$. Horizontal arrows denote exact computation and slanted arrows the result of computing with four digits.

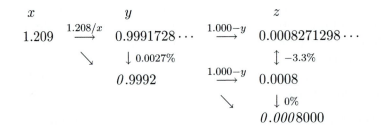

Note how we have isolated the effects of the computational errors generated by each of the two steps. The second algorithm is

ALGORITHM 2 $y := x - 1.208;\ z := y/x$

For the same value of x the computation is

$$
\begin{array}{cccc}
x & & y & z \\
1.209 & \xrightarrow{\;x-1.208\;} & 0.001 & \xrightarrow{\;y/x\;} & 0.0008271298\cdots \\
& \searrow & \downarrow 0\% & & \updownarrow 0\% \\
& & \mathit{0.00}1000 & \xrightarrow{\;y/x\;} & 0.0008271298\cdots \\
& & & \searrow & \downarrow -0.0036\% \\
& & & & \mathit{0.000}8271
\end{array}
$$

We see that the second algorithm returns a result that is off by less than 1 ulp, whereas the first returns a result that is off by 271 ulps. Altogether in both diagrams there are four computational errors represented by downward arrows, and they are in the range 0% to 0.0036%. There are two vertical double arrows representing the propagation of an error introduced previously. What should stand out is that the addition error in Algorithm 1 has grown in magnitude from 0.0027% to 3.3%. Subtraction is sensitive for arguments that are nearly equal. The error generated in computing the solution of the first subproblem $y := 1.208/x$ has been amplified by the second subproblem $z := 1.000 - y$.

The principle that this illustrates is that the decomposition

$$\text{problem} \longrightarrow \text{subproblem; sensitive subproblem}$$

is *bad*, because computational errors from the first subproblem feed into the second subproblem where they are amplified. On the other hand, the decomposition

$$\text{problem} \longrightarrow \text{subproblem; insensitive subproblem}$$

is *good*. This is our explanation of **numerical instability**, which we define to be *unacceptably large amplification of computational errors in an algorithm*. What is "unacceptable" depends partly on what is possible in practice. If the given problem is itself sensitive, there is often no efficient algorithm that does not amplify computational errors, in which case we might accept some amplification.

Examples we have seen of sensitivity are computing $\ln x$ for $x \approx 1$ (in Section 1.5.1) and subtracting two nearly equal operands. With these examples in mind we might restate the principle above as

> If possible, avoid sensitive operations with operands contaminated by *computational* error.

In particular, one should organize computations (i.e., design algorithms) so that cancellation does not occur unless neither operand is contaminated by computational error. Keep in mind that computational error excludes *all* errors introduced into the data before the data are given to us. The choice of algorithm has no effect on such errors; we might as well ignore such errors when organizing the calculation.

Here is another example showing how cancellation creates instability by amplifying computational error. We also use it to illustrate a concrete error analysis. Suppose we are given an algorithm broken into a sequence of steps. In order to study the effect of the error introduced in the kth step, we do two computations. In the first computation, we switch to higher precision just *before* the kth step, and in the second we switch to higher precision just *after* the kth step. The errors introduced by the higher precision are assumed to be negligible, so the difference we see between the two computations after the kth step is the effect of the error generated by the kth step of the first computation. This is what we did to analyze Algorithms 1 and 2 for computing $1 - 1.208/x$. Here we are suggesting that as a practical matter we use higher precision to approximate exact computation.

Example 2.5 Assume, as usual, that we are using four-digit decimal arithmetic with round-to-even rounding. The table appearing below shows the effects of rounding errors in the computation of $\sqrt{10000. + 65.00} - 100.0$. Each column of the table represents a computational sequence in which the precision increases from single to double at some point in the computation; for example, the column with heading "1st" is a sequence in which the computation of v_1 is performed in single precision and the computation of v_2 and v_3 in double precision.

Single-precision steps	None	1st	1st, 2nd	1st, 2nd, 3rd
$v_1 = 10000. + 65.00$	10065.000	10060.	10060.	10060.
$v_2 = \sqrt{v_1}$	100.32447	100.29955	100.3	100.3
$v_3 = v_2 - 100.0$	0.32447000	0.29955000	0.30000000	0.3000

The differences between the first two columns represent effects of the floating-point-addition error. The error begins as a 0.05% error in 10065, becomes a 0.025% error in 100.32447, and is amplified 300-fold by the subtraction to become a 7.7% error in 0.32447. The error due to the square root happens to be much smaller, and there is no error introduced by the subtraction. Note that the error introduced by the addition is equivalent to changing 65.00 to 60.00, quite a substantial change!

The numerical instability of the preceding example can be remedied by rearranging the expression (Exercise 8). We demonstrate such a rearrangement for the particularly important problem of finding the roots of a quadratic,

$$ax^2 + bx + c = 0,$$

for which the standard formula is

$$x_{1,2} = \frac{-b \pm \sqrt{b^2 - 4ac}}{2a}. \tag{2.1}$$

The remedy for the cancellation between $-b$ and the square root uses a standard trick. Multiply numerator and denominator of formula (2.1) by $-b \mp \sqrt{b^2 - 4ac}$. We get

$$x_1 = \frac{-b + \sqrt{b^2 - 4ac}}{2a} = \frac{2c}{-b - \sqrt{b^2 - 4ac}},$$

$$x_2 = \frac{-b - \sqrt{b^2 - 4ac}}{2a} = \frac{2c}{-b + \sqrt{b^2 - 4ac}}.$$

If b is positive, use the second formula for x_1 and the first for x_2; if b is negative, use the first formula for x_1 and the second for x_2. The cancellation inside the radical is not easily avoided, so we live with it or use double precision inside the radical.

The following expressions have cancellation problems when $x \approx y$. Rearrangements that avoid harmful cancellation are given to the right of each arrow.

$$x^2 - y^2 \qquad \longrightarrow \qquad (x - y)(x + y)$$

$$\sin x - \sin y \qquad \longrightarrow \qquad 2 \sin \frac{x - y}{2} \cos \frac{x + y}{2}$$

$$\left. \begin{array}{c} \ln x - \ln y \\ \ln(x/y) \end{array} \right\} \qquad \longrightarrow \qquad 2 \tanh^{-1}\left(\frac{x - y}{x + y}\right)$$

$$e^x - e^y \qquad \longrightarrow \qquad 2 \sinh \frac{x - y}{2} \exp \frac{x + y}{2}$$

The first thing you notice is that in each case the cancellation has not been eliminated—it has been pushed down to the lowest level, where it is no longer harmful. When both operands are input parameters to the algorithm and/or representable real constants, they have no computational error to be amplified by the cancellation. (If we are given an expression to compute without its context, then as far as we are concerned all variables are "input parameters.") You might also have noticed that $\ln(x/y)$ has no cancellation. This was included for the purpose of indicating that this rearrangement is *not* a solution to the cancellation problem in $\ln x - \ln y$; the logarithm itself is sensitive for $x/y \approx 1$. You might also wonder whether we seriously expect everyone to know all these tricks. We do not; at least one of them is little more than a curiosity. Nonetheless, they do demonstrate that there are ways of solving problems that we might never imagine. Also, it might be pointed out that these identities are simply the rules of the calculus of finite differences, from which one derives differential calculus. Finally, there is a message here concerning built-in functions for programming languages. In Pascal only a rudimentary set of elementary functions is a standard part of the language on the theory that the others can be constructed from these. For example, $\sinh x$ can be constructed as $(\exp(x) - \exp(-x))/2$. This would be true only if the computation were exact; in practice, cancellation can do damage to the accuracy. It is important, for accuracy, to have an extensive collection of elementary functions.

The classic example of cancellation difficulties is the calculation of the variance. The maximum-likelihood estimate of the mean of a set of observations $\{y_i\}$ is given by

$$\bar{y} = \frac{1}{N} \sum_{i=1}^{N} y_i$$

and that of the variance is given by

$$\frac{1}{N-1} \sum_{i=1}^{N} (y_i - \bar{y})^2 = \frac{1}{N-1} \left(\sum_{i=1}^{N} y_i^2 - N\bar{y}^2 \right),$$

where the equality is a consequence of the equation for $\bar{y}$. Although mathematically equal, there can be a dramatic difference numerically. The left-hand-side formula produces cancellations at intermediate stages in the overall calculation; the right-hand-side formula produces a cancellation at the very end. The result from this latter formula can be so bad that it is negative! We have seen a widely distributed applications program that uses the bad method and has patches to avoid square roots of negative numbers.

Even if we are clever, there are situations where rearrangement is not possible. An alternative remedy for many difficulties is to use a truncated Taylor series expansion, which is discussed further in Section 5.1.

There is a third remedy, which is the most obvious one, and that is to use higher precision for delicate computations. More precisely, you begin by extending all values to higher precision, you then compute in the higher precision, and you finish by rounding the results back to the original precision. Because this is simple and general, it is for most purposes the best tactic.

We have now seen many examples that show that

$$\boxed{\text{cancellation can be bad.}}$$

This is because cancellation amplifies computational errors already present in the operands. Put in a different way, errors that are minuscule relative to the operands can be significant relative to the result. The actual *origin* of the damaging roundoff error precedes the subtractive cancellation. Often it is in the addition of a small number to a large number, in which the lower order bits of the smaller number are obliterated even though they might have made a significant difference to the final result.

However, cancellation is a two-edged sword, and in floating-point arithmetic

$$\boxed{\text{cancellation can be good.}}$$

Cancellation implies that the add/subtract was performed exactly. This is because cancellation means that the result has fewer digits than the operands, and because the operands are machine numbers the result must be a machine number. More precisely, the result of a subtraction is exact whenever the operands differ by no more than a factor of 2.

Proposition 2.2 *If x and y are machine numbers, $\frac{1}{2} \le x/y \le 2$, then*

$$fl(x - y) = x - y \text{ (exactly)}.$$

There are calculations that exploit this fact. One example is the formula for $\ln(x/y)$ given earlier; another is the Gill-Moller "magic adding" algorithm, in which two single-precision variables are used to accumulate a sum. (See "Supplementary note" for references.) Two other examples follow.

Example 2.6 The calculation of $y_3 - 2y_2 + y_1$ where $y_3 \approx y_2 \approx y_1$ is typical of what might be encountered in solving differential equations. If computed as is, there is a good chance of a roundoff error being generated by $y_3 - 2y_2$, which would then be amplified by the cancellation that occurs when y_1 is added. Instead use

$$(y_3 - y_2) - (y_2 - y_1),$$

which introduces *no* roundoff error (provided that the approximations above hold in a relative sense).

Example 2.7 The calculation of $x - \pi$ is typical of what must be done to compute trigonometric functions. Assume the use of four-decimal-digit numbers. If you use $x - 3.142$, you will get a completely wrong answer for $x = 3.142$ and poor accuracy for nearby values. However, $(x - 3.141) - 0.0005927$ produces results correctly rounded to four significant digits for all x. Note, though, that a carefully crafted expression like this can be undone by an optimizing compiler that assumes that the associative law holds for floating-point addition.

Supplementary note

Two steps of magic adding are given in Exercise 10 of Section 2.4. A fuller description is in Dahlquist and Björck (1974, p. 49) and in

A.I. Forsythe, T.A. Keenan, E.I. Organick, and W. Stenberg, *Computer Science: A First Course*, 2nd ed., Wiley, New York, 1975, pp. 598–601.

Exercises

1. Consider a digital thermometer that measures approximate temperature in both Celsius and Fahrenheit, giving values rounded to the nearest integer.

   (a) If the temperature is correctly measured in Fahrenheit and rounded, and that rounded value is converted to Celsius and rounded, what is the maximum possible error in the Celsius value?

   (b) If the temperature is correctly measured in Celsius and rounded, and that rounded value is converted to Fahrenheit and rounded, what is the maximum possible error in the Fahrenheit value?

   (c) Which of these two possibilities gives the greater error in measurement of the temperature? (You cannot simply compare numerical values to answer this.)

2. Using two-digit decimal floating-point arithmetic with round-to-even rounding, give an example to show that
$$fl(fl(x + y) + z),$$
   where x, y, and z are machine numbers, can have a relative error $\geq 100\%$.

3. Consider the following calculation performed in round-to-even four-digit arithmetic:
$$\begin{aligned}(1234. \,\hat{+}\, 123.4) \,\hat{\times}\, 1.100 \;&=\; 1357. \,\hat{\times}\, 1.100 \\ &=\; 1493.\end{aligned}$$

   Express the (accumulated) error in the result as a sum of the error due to multiplication plus the propagated error due to addition.

4. Assuming eight-decimal-digit round-to-even floating-point arithmetic, compare the floating-point result of $x^2 - y^2$ to that of $(x-y)(x+y)$ for $x = 1.0002000$, $y = 1.0000000$. Compute the relative error in the result of each.

5. Let a, b, and c be *nonnegative* numbers having at most four significant decimal digits, and let fl denote the round-to-even rounding of a number to four significant digits. For which of the following expressions is it *not* always *true* that the result has a *relative* error of less than 10^{-3}?
   (a) $fl(a - fl(b \times c))$,   (b) $fl(fl(a - b) \times c)$,
   (c) $fl(fl(a + b) \times c)$,   (d) $fl(fl(a \times b) + c)$.

   Support your answer with an example.

6. One can calculate $z = e^{-4.7}$ either by

   (a) $z = 1 + x + \dfrac{x^2}{2!} + \dfrac{x^3}{3!} + \cdots$ or

(b) $z = 1 \left/ \left(1 - x + \dfrac{x^2}{2!} - \dfrac{x^3}{3!} + \cdots \right) \right.$

where $x = -4.7$. Which method yields a more accurate result? Explain.

7. (a) Apply Equation (2.1) to $x^2 + 800x + 1 = 0$ using four-digit arithmetic.

   (b) Check the accuracy of the computed roots by using them to reconstruct the polynomial.

   (c) What rounding errors occurred in the computation in part (a)?

   (d) Redo part (a) using the recommended algorithm.

8. Rearrange to avoid cancellation.

   (a) $\sqrt{1 + x} - 1$. Hint: Use the same standard trick as for the roots of a quadratic.

   (b) The expression in Example 2.5.

   (c) $1 - \cos x$. Hint: Use a trigonometric identity.

   (d) $\tan x - \sin x$.

9. Mathematically,

$$\sqrt{(b\cos\gamma - a)^2 + (b\sin\gamma)^2} \;=\; \sqrt{(b-a)^2 + 4ab\sin^2\frac{\gamma}{2}}.$$

   Which is less accurate with floating-point arithmetic assuming that both a and b are positive? Explain.

10. The manual for one calculator suggests using the INV $\ln x$ capability (the exponential function) to compute $\sinh(x)$. Briefly explain when and why this will sometimes yield poor accuracy.

11. Write an algorithm that computes both roots r_1 and r_2 of $x^2 + 2bx + c = 0$ as accurately as possible in single precision assuming that $b^2 - c$ is positive. Reuse common subexpressions to minimize arithmetic.

12. Show how one can rearrange the expressions below so as to avoid large roundoff errors when $|\delta| \ll x$:

   (a) $\sqrt{x + \delta} - \sqrt{x}$

   (b) $\cos(x + \delta) - \cos\ x$ (Hint: Try various trigonometric identities.)

13. For which of the following two computations is there the possibility of a large relative roundoff error?

   (a) $x \,\hat{\times}\, (y \,\hat{+}\, z)$

(b) $x \mathbin{\hat{\times}} y \mathbin{\hat{+}} x \mathbin{\hat{\times}} z$

For which values of x, y, and z is the error relatively large? Why is one arrangement much better than the other in this case?

14. Let x and y be nonzero floating-point numbers, and for any arithmetic operation $\circ$ let $\hat{\circ}$ denote the corresponding (rounded) floating-point operation. Also assume that no underflow or overflow occurs as the result of any operation in this problem.

   (a) For what (exactly representable) values of x and y would the value of $1\mathbin{\hat{/}}x \mathbin{\hat{+}} 1\mathbin{\hat{/}}y$ be a *relatively* poor approximation to $1/x + 1/y$? Expected is an answer of the form "for values such that $\cdots \approx \cdots$." or of the form "for values such that $\cdots \ll \cdots$."

   (b) For "round-to-even" four-digit base 10 floating-point arithmetic give an example for which the relative error in $1\mathbin{\hat{/}}x \mathbin{\hat{+}} 1\mathbin{\hat{/}}y$ is at least 100%.

   (c) Rearrange the computation so that it is always accurate and explain why it is always accurate.

15. Let x be a machine number.

   (a) For what values of x is the error in $(x \mathbin{\hat{+}} 2) \mathbin{\hat{\times}} x \mathbin{\hat{+}} 1$ due to finite-precision floating-point arithmetic relatively large?

   (b) Why?

   (c) Rearrange this expression to avoid relatively large roundoff error effects.

16. Do the preceding exercise for the expression $1\mathbin{\hat{/}}(x \mathbin{\hat{-}} 1) \mathbin{\hat{-}} 1\mathbin{\hat{/}}(x \mathbin{\hat{+}} 1)$.

17. Let
$$f(x) = \frac{x - 3 + \sqrt{x(x - 1)}}{5x - 9}, \quad x \geq 1.$$

(This arose in practice.) How should you program $f(x)$ to avoid bad cancellation and division by zero? Note: There are two possibilities for bad cancellation in the expression as it stands: "$\cdots + \sqrt{\cdots}$" and "$\cdots - 9$." The other possible cancellations "$x - 3$" and "$x - 1$" are good because their operands are uncontaminated by *computational* error.

18. If the designer of a language decides not to include the functions sinh, cosh, and tanh, why would it be better to provide expm1 where $\mathrm{expm1}(x) \overset{\text{def}}{=} \exp(x) - 1$ rather than exp? Note that $\exp(-x) = 1/\exp(x)$.

19. Let $u_0 \approx u_1 \approx u_2$ be exactly representable floating-point numbers. Assuming correctly rounded floating-point arithmetic, which of the following arrangements is likely to be most accurate?
$$(u_2 + u_0) - 2 \times u_1,$$
$$(u_2 - 2 \times u_1) + u_0,$$
$$(u_2 - u_1) - (u_1 - u_0)$$

For the two that you did not choose, explain why they are likely to be less accurate.

$\star$20. Rearrange $\ln(1 + x)$ so that it can be computed accurately for $|x| \ll 1$.

$\star$21. Find a cancellation-safe formula for

$$y^{\alpha} \; - \; x^{\alpha}$$

where α is a real number and x and y are positive. Hint: Use $t^{\alpha} = \exp(\alpha \; \log \; t)$.

Mathematica notes

As we said earlier, the most general way to deal with cancellation problems is to evaluate an expression using higher precision, but it is awkward to have to retype an expression using high-precision numbers everywhere. Here we see how to let *Mathematica* do the work for us.

Define the function `hpeval[ ]`.

```
In[1]:= (
    SetAttributes[hpeval, HoldFirst];
    hpeval[expr_, prec_] :=
        Module[{h = Hold[expr]},
            h = h /. x_Real :> SetPrecision[x,prec];
            ReleaseHold[h]
        ]
)
```

Notice that we have to make an effort to prevent *Mathematica* from evaluating things until we get them changed to high precision: the function needs to have the attribute `HoldFirst`, and the first argument must be wrapped in `Hold` to prevent evaluation when it is assigned to h. Also, because `SetPrecision[x,prec]` would evaluate to x itself if x were a symbol, we must use ":>" (`RuleDelayed`) rather than "->" (`Rule`) to prevent evaluation until x is actually a real number. The "`x_Real`" represents any expression with a head of `Real`.

At machine precision a lot of cancellation occurs.

```
In[2]:= Sin[355./226.] - Sin[52174./33215.]
                       -15
Out[2]= -8.88178 10
```

Using high-precision evaluation, cancellation still occurs, but there are more digits to start with.

```
In[3]:= hpeval[Sin[355./226.] - Sin[52174./33215.], 30]
                                              -15
Out[3]= -8.895377823641226873309 10
```

This is nearly the same result.

```
In[4]:= Sin[SetPrecision[355/226, 30]] -
            Sin[SetPrecision[52174/33215, 30]]
                                              -15
Out[4]= -8.895377823641226873309 10
```

In the *Mathematica* notes in Section 2.3 we introduced the package `NumericalMath`ComputerArithmetic`, which implements computer arithmetic using various bases, precisions, exponent ranges, and rounding rules.

Read in the package.   *In[1]:=* << NumericalMath`ComputerArithmetic`

The default format for printing a decimal   *In[2]:=* ComputerNumber[Pi]
ComputerNumber is just the ordinary
decimal expansion. The default arithmetic   *Out[2]=* 3.142
is decimal, with four digits.

Start with a list of computer numbers   *In[3]:=* x = Table[ComputerNumber[t/1000],
called x.   {t, 1090, 1110}]

                                                  Out[3]= {1.09, 1.091, 1.092, 1.093, 1.094, 1.095, 1.096,

                                                     1.097, 1.098, 1.099, 1.1, 1.101, 1.102, 1.103, 1.104,

                                                     1.105, 1.106, 1.107, 1.108, 1.109, 1.11}

Define the computer numbers one and   *In[4]:=* {one,three} = ComputerNumber /@ {1,3}
three.
                                                  Out[4]= {1., 3.}

One way to compute $(x-1)^3$.   *In[5]:=* z1 = (x-one)^3

                                                  Out[5]= {0.000729, 0.0007536, 0.0007787, 0.0008044,

                                                     0.0008306, 0.0008574, 0.0008847, 0.0009127, 0.0009412,

                                                     0.0009703, 0.001, 0.00103, 0.001061, 0.001093,

                                                     0.001125, 0.001158, 0.001191, 0.001225, 0.00126,

                                                     0.001295, 0.001331}

An alternative way to compute what   *In[6]:=* z2 = x^3 - three x^2 + three x - one
should be the same as $(x-1)^3$.
                                                  Out[6]= {0.001, 0.002, 0.002, 0, 0, 0.001, 0.002, 0.002,

                                                     0, 0, 0.001, 0.002, 0.002, 0, 0.001, 0.001, 0.002,

                                                     0.003, 0, 0.001, 0.002}

The FullForm of a ComputerNumber contains a lot of information, and we can use that information to examine roundoff error. In particular, as we saw in the *Mathematica* notes in Section 2.3, Normal[ ] gives the value of a ComputerNumber as an Integer or Rational. Also, Last[ ] gives a high-precision approximation to the real number to which that computer number ideally corresponds. Thus, the total propagated error in a ComputerNumber x can be evaluated as Normal[x]-Last[x].

Define a function that finds the error for us.   *In[7]:=* cnerr[x_ComputerNumber] := Normal[x]-Last[x]

This gives the errors in $(x-1)^3$.

In[8]:= `ListPlot[Map[cnerr, z1], PlotJoined -> True]`

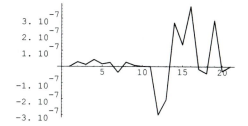

This gives the errors in $x^3 - 3x^2 + 3x - 1$. This is several orders of magnitude worse.

In[9]:= `ListPlot[Map[cnerr, z2], PlotJoined -> True]`

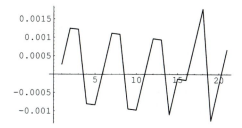

The plotting commands `Microscope[ ]` and `MicroscopicError[ ]` defined in the package `NumericalMath`Microscope`` can be controlled to include any number of machine numbers near the point of examination.

Read in the package.

In[1]:= `<< NumericalMath`Microscope``

Examine `Sin[x]` at the machine numbers within 5 ulps of 1.5.

In[2]:= `Microscope[Sin[x], {x, 1.5, 5}]`

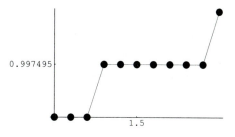

Examine the error (in ulps) in `Sin[x]` at
the machine numbers within 50 ulps of 1.5.

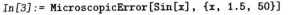

`In[3]:= MicroscopicError[Sin[x], {x, 1.5, 50}]`

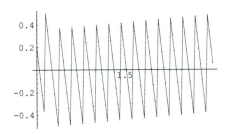

Computer problems

1. Define the two functions `f[x_] = Product[x-i, {i, 0, 30}];` and `g[x_] = Expand[f[x]];`. Plot `f[x]` and `g[x]` on the interval `{x, 10, 20}`. Explain the results.

2. In this problem we want to compare errors on plots, and it is important that the plots use the same scale. Issue the command `SetOptions[Plot, PlotRange -> {-5. $MachineEpsilon, 5. $MachineEpsilon}]` to do this. Plot $x^3 - 3.x^2 + 3.x - 1$. for $0.999999 \leq x \leq 1.000001$ with the option `PlotLabel -> "Standard Form"`. Plot $-1. + x(3. + x(-3. + x))$ for the same values of x with the option `PlotLabel -> "Nested Form"`. Finally, plot $(x - 1.)^3$ for the same values of x with the option `PlotLabel -> "Factored Form"`.

3. Use `MicroscopicError[ ]` to examine the difference between the two algorithms $z := \exp(10.0 + x)$ and $z := \exp(10.0) \exp(x)$ for x within 70 ulps of 0.1. `Show` both plots on the same graph. Which algorithm is more stable?

4. Use `Microscope[ ]` to examine the difference between the two algorithms $z := \sqrt{10000. + x} - 100.$ and $z := x/(\sqrt{10000. + x} + 100.)$ for x within 70 ulps of 65. `Show` both plots on the same graph. Which algorithm is more stable?

5. Verify that `hpeval[ ]` works properly on the expression `Sin[72. + 207653./809150.]`.

6. Use `NumericalMath`ComputerArithmetic`` to verify that the four-digit arithmetic in Example 2.5 is correct.

7. Use `NumericalMath`ComputerArithmetic`` to verify that the arithmetic in the examples evaluating $z = 1.000 - 1.208/x$ on page 62 is correct. Note: `x/y` gets evaluated as `Times[x, Power[y, -1]]`. This involves two rounding operations. Use `IdealDivide[x,y]` to do division with a single rounding operation.

8. Why is `MachineError[Sqrt[x]-1., x -> 1.+5.$MachineEpsilon]` so large?

3.   Rootfinding

We consider the solution of a single equation in a single unknown. Several equations in several unknowns are more difficult to solve numerically and are not considered in this book.

This chapter contains the following sections:

3.1 Roots

Consider a mortgage loan for 15 years at 10.25% interest plus 2.5 points. What this means for a nominally $90,000 loan is that you get to borrow only $87,750 but you make payments as though you had borrowed $90,000. Hence, the effective rate of interest is greater than 10.25%. How much greater depends on whether you take the full 180 months to pay off the mortgage or whether you sell the house and pay it off early. (Which of these gives a higher effective rate of interest?) However, to keep the problem simple let us assume no early payoff of the loan. The amount you get to borrow is $p = 87,750$. Your monthly payments, based on a principal of $90,000, are given by the formula

$$m = \frac{(0.1025/12)(90000)}{1 - (1 + 0.1025/12)^{-180}} = 980.96.$$

The effective monthly rate of interest r, based on a principal of $87,750, is the solution to

$$\frac{(r/12)(87750)}{1 - (1 + r/12)^{-180}} = 980.96.$$

Equivalently, the unknown interest rate r is the root of the function

$$f(r) \stackrel{\text{def}}{=} \frac{(r/12)(87750)}{1 - (1 + r/12)^{-180}} - 980.96.$$

75

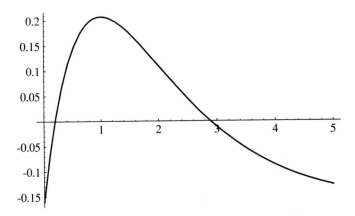

Figure 3.1: Set of points satisfying $y = xe^{-x} - 0.16064$

Because the first term denotes the monthly payment as a function of r, we expect $f(0.1025)$ to be negative and $f(r)$ to be strictly increasing without bound as r increases. In other words, there should be exactly one root.

More generally, the problem of solving an equation we write as $f(x) = 0$ where $f(x)$ denotes some given expression in the unknown x. A value r such that $f(r) = 0$ we call a **root** or a **zero** of $f(x)$. Unless $f(x) = ax + b$ for constants a and b, we call $f(r) = 0$ a *nonlinear equation*, for example,

$$xe^{-x} - 0.16064 = 0,$$

which is shown in Figure 3.1. A nonlinear equation cannot normally be solved exactly using just the four basic arithmetic operations in a finite number of steps.

Most numerical methods for solving $f(x) = 0$, or equivalently finding a root of $f(x)$, require only the ability to evaluate $f(x)$ for any x. We need only write a procedure like

```
f[x_] := x*Exp[-x] - 0.16064
```

and by judicious sampling of values of $f(x)$ the numerical method calculates an estimate of a root, if it can find one. In particular, the numerical method does not "see" a graph of the function, such as Figure 3.1. Constructing a graph requires more computation than what merely finding a root requires. As an example,

```
FindRoot[f[x] == 0, {x, {a, b}}, AccuracyGoal -> decimals]
```

uses four input parameters: a function $f(x)$, values a and b that define an interval, and an optional value *decimals*. For the parameters a and b the user should try to choose values so that $f(a)$ and $f(b)$ have opposite signs. Then the intermediate-value theorem ensures the existence of a root r provided that $f(x)$ is continuous. The computed root $\hat{r}$ satisfies

$$|f(\hat{r})| \leq 10^{-decimals}.$$

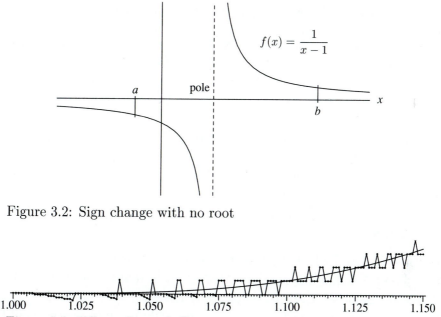

Figure 3.2: Sign change with no root

Figure 3.3: Effect of roundoff near a triple root

Complications can occur. It may happen that that even though $f(x)$ has a sign change, it has no root because it is discontinuous. The example $f(x) = 1/(x-1)$ is given in Figure 3.2. That this happens may not always be obvious from the formula for the function. Another difficulty is that the function values may be noisy, which may result in spurious roots. This is illustrated by Figure 3.3 for the effect of roundoff error in the evaluation, by Horner's rule, of

$$f(x) = ((x-3)x+3)x - 1$$

with four-digit arithmetic using the round-to-even rule. The computed $f(x)$ has numerous roots although the original $f(x)$ has just a triple root at $x = 1$.

Exercise

1. Plot $\tan x$ and $\tanh x$ on the same graph. Let r_m denote the mth positive root of $\tan x - \tanh x$. Determine an interval $[a_m, b_m]$ that contains r_m and on which $\tan x$ is bounded.

Mathematica notes

The function FindRoot[ ] has several options. Two of them are WorkingPrecision and AccuracyGoal. WorkingPrecision controls the precision of the arithmetic used in finding the root. `AccuracyGoal` controls the tolerance for error in the result. In particular, an `AccuracyGoal` of n will cause `FindRoot[ ]` to attempt to find a solution accurate enough to satisfy the defining equation or function within 10^{-n}. Note that this is quite different from giving a result that is correct to within 10^{-n}. If you enter

$$\text{FindRoot[x\textasciicircum2 == Pi, \{x, \{1, 2\}\}, AccuracyGoal -> 300],}$$

Mathematica will fail to give a satisfactory result: the default is to use machine numbers to do the arithmetic, and there are no machine numbers that satisfy the equation `x^2 == Pi` with an error less than 10^{-300}. The default for `AccuracyGoal` is `Automatic`, which means 10 less than the value given for `WorkingPrecision`.

Computer problems

1. Use `FindRoot[ ]` to find the root near 3 of $xe^{-x} - 0.16064$.

2. Use `FindRoot[ ]` to find the root near 3 of $xe^{-x} - 0.16064$ such that $|xe^{-x} - 0.16064| \leq 10^{-70}$. (Note: `SetPrecision[0.16064, 80]` does *not* give an 80-digit approximation to the number 0.16064. It instead gives an exact 80-digit representation of the machine number closest to 0.16064.)

3. What happens if you enter the following?

$$\text{FindRoot[x\textasciicircum2 == Pi, \{x, \{1, 2\}\}, AccuracyGoal -> 300]}$$

What needs to be done to make it work correctly?

3.2 Bisection Method

The bisection method is a natural and effective way to find zeros. The basic idea of this method is often applied to nonnumerical searching, where it is known as a *binary search*. In the numerical case we are searching for a value of x such that $f(x) = 0$.

3.2.1 Algorithm

As an example consider $f(x) = x^2 - 3$. We know there is a root between $a = 1$ and $b = 2$ because $f(1) = -2$ and $f(2) = 1$. We can reduce the uncertainty by evaluating $f(x)$ at the midpoint $x = 1.5$. Doing this shows that $f(1.5) < 0$, so we conclude that the root lies between 1.5 and 2. This and two subsequent steps of the **bisection method** are depicted in Figure 3.4. We continue the bisection until the endpoints of the bracketing interval are within a factor of 2 of the error tolerance. At this stage the midpoint will be within the error tolerance of the root.

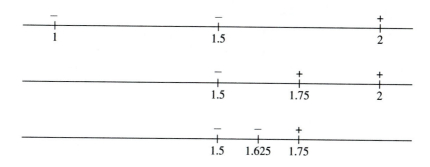

Figure 3.4: Bisection method

Following is an algorithm for bisection. The need for an error tolerance is avoided by iterating until an answer of machine precision is obtained. This will happen when the bracketing interval is so tiny that its endpoints consist of consecutive machine numbers, in which case averaging the endpoints in floating-point arithmetic does not produce an in-between number.

$$fa := f(a); fb := f(b);$$
$$c := a + 0.5 * (b - a);$$
while $a < c < b$ **do**
   $fc := f(c);$
   if sign(fc) = sign(fa) **then**
      $a := c; fa := fc$
   else
      $b := c; fb := fc$
   end if;
   $c := a + 0.5 * (b - a)$
end while

It may be worth noting that (except in base 2) $0.5 * (a + b)$ is not as accurate as $a + 0.5 * (b - a)$. For example, in four-digit floating-point arithmetic with the round-to-even rule we have $0.5 * (5.001 + 5.003) = 5.000$ but $5.001 + 0.5 * (5.003 - 5.001) = 5.002$. This illustrates a general principle for the accurate arrangement of iterative computations:

> new approximation = current approximation + correction

If one wants to find all the roots on a given interval, a preliminary search is needed to isolate all the roots. An adaptive algorithm in the same spirit as that described for plotting in Section 5.5.2 is appropriate. With interval analysis it is possible to do a rigorous and exhaustive search.

3.2.2 Advantages and disadvantages

The advantage of bisection is that it always works, provided you can find a sign change (and the function is continuous). The need to have $\text{sign}(f(a)) \neq \text{sign}(f(b))$ could be a disadvantage. Also it turns out that bisection is slow compared to what is possible with other methods. Each iteration reduces uncertainty by $\frac{1}{2}$, so 10 iterations are needed for every additional three decimal digits of accuracy (because $2^{-10} \approx 10^{-3}$).

Exercises

1. Given that $a < r < b$ and $|b - a| \leq 2\varepsilon$, show that $|r - (a + b)/2| < \varepsilon$. Show each logical step, and do not use geometric arguments.

2. Write a complete algorithm for computing the reciprocal of a real number $c > 0$ without doing divisions.

Computer problems

1. Define a function `bis1[f_, a_?NumberQ, b_?NumberQ]` that uses the bisection method to find a root of the function f between a and b. Use the algorithm given in this section. Test your solution with `bis1[(Cos[#] - #)&, 0., 1.]`. Also, make it do something sensible (i.e., issue a message and exit or proceed as appropriate) if the endpoints are 1. and 2. instead.

2. Define a function `bis2[fx_, x_Symbol, a_?NumberQ, b_?NumberQ]` that uses the bisection method to find a value of x between a and b that is a root of the expression fx. Use the algorithm given in this section. Test your solution with `bis2[Cos[x] - x, x, 0., 1.]`. Useful *Mathematica* functions: `Rule[ ]` (i.e., ->) and `ReplaceAll[ ]` (i.e., /.). Also, make it do something sensible (i.e., issue a message and exit or proceed as appropriate) if the endpoints are 1. and 2. instead.

3. Using a bisection-like search, find two consecutive double-precision machine numbers (single precision is not used by *Mathematica*) a and b such that in floating-point arithmetic 1. + a == 1. and 1. + b > 1.. To do this correctly, we need *exact* relational operators for Reals. (The operators ==, >, and others in *Mathematica* are "fuzzy" and will not work properly for comparing two nonzero numbers in this problem.) We can get what we need by comparing the *difference* between the numbers to zero, but we need to force the operations to be done in a specified order because computer arithmetic is not associative. In particular, we want `Evaluate[1. + a] - 1. == 0.` and `Evaluate[1. + b] - 1. > 0..` When you have found the values for a and b, print their exact values using `BaseForm[SetPrecision[{a, b},100],2]`. Finally, using a *Mathematica* comment, state what the value of a should be if the arithmetic conformed to the IEEE standard.

3.3 Newton's Method

This method is also called Newton-Raphson, which is a useful label because it helps to distinguish this idea from the many others that also bear Newton's name. However, the credit for the idea belongs to Newton alone.

3.3.1 Algorithm

Newton's method computes not a sequence of nested intervals that bracket the root but rather a sequence of points that, with some luck, converge to the root. One begins with an initial guess x_0. In general, it is difficult to give advice on how this should be chosen; in specific cases there is usually some indication of what to do. Anyway, at the point x_0 we compute not only the value $f(x_0)$ but also the derivative $f'(x_0)$. This information is enough to determine the straight line that is tangent to the graph of $f(x)$ at $x = x_0$ as shown in Figure 3.5(a). Where this line cuts the x axis is an approximation to the root that we hope is better than x_0, and thus we label it x_1. For the new point $x = x_1$ we repeat the process by constructing a tangent to the graph of $f(x)$. This step and the next are shown in Figures 3.5(b) and 3.5(c). The basis of Newton's method is thus a sequence of straight-line approximations to $f(x)$.

There is, of course, a formula for Newton's method that relates the approximation $x_k \approx r$ to the normally better approximation x_{k+1}. We give a geometric derivation of this formula. Looking at Figure 3.6, we see that there are two expressions

$$\frac{f(x_k) - 0}{x_k - x_{k+1}} = f'(x_k)$$

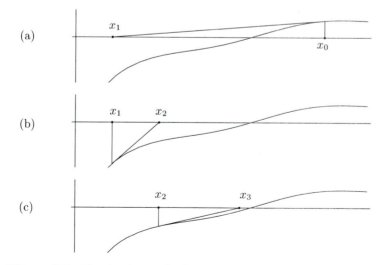

Figure 3.5: Newton's method

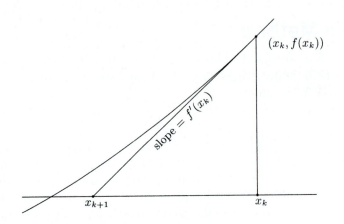

Figure 3.6: Formula for Newton's method

for the slope of the straight line. Solving this equality for x_{k+1} yields the formula

$$x_{k+1} = x_k - \frac{f(x_k)}{f'(x_k)}$$

This is *well worth remembering*. Many iterative methods can be viewed as approximations to Newton's method.

Example 3.1 The square root of a positive number a solves the equation $x^2 - a = 0$. Hence, $f(x) = x^2 - a$ is the function whose root we seek and $f'(x) = 2x$ is its derivative. The Newton iteration is

$$
\begin{aligned}
x_{k+1} &= x_k - \frac{x_k^2 - a}{2x_k} \\
&= \frac{1}{2}\left(x_k + \frac{a}{x_k}\right).
\end{aligned}
$$

Recall that this is the Old Babylonian method for finding square roots, in which one averages two approximations that are known to bracket the true root. Following is an example for $a = 4$ with initial guess $x_0 = 1$:

$$
\begin{aligned}
x_0 &= 1, \\
x_1 &= 2.5, \\
x_2 &= 2.05, \\
x_3 &= 2.000609756097560975609756097560975609756097560975609756097560975609756,
\end{aligned}
$$

$$x_4 = 2.00000009292229466031325963975884806089755502858289783751235866518 9822,$$
$$x_5 = 2.0000000000000021586381109417172262212869091611099918033920872653 75484,$$
$$x_6 = 2.0000000000000000000000000000000116492962350250511457334751247336 1407373,$$
$$x_7 = 2.0000000000000000000000000000000000000000000000000000000000000000339265257.$$

Note how rapidly the iteration converges. Each iteration doubles the number of accurate digits. This is an excellent way to compute roots on a four-function calculator.

Example 3.2 Newton's method can be applied to determine the reciprocal of a number. This is useful on computers without division hardware. The trick is to express the equation as

$$\frac{1}{x} - a = 0.$$

Hence, $f(x) = 1/x - a$, $f'(x) = -1/x^2$, and the iteration is

$$x_{k+1} = x_k - \frac{1/x_k - a}{-1/x_k^2} = (2 - a\,x_k)x_k.$$

Following is an example for $a = 3$ with initial guess $x_0 = 0.5$:

$$x_0 = 0.5,$$
$$x_1 = 0.25,$$
$$x_2 = 0.3125,$$
$$x_3 = 0.33203125,$$
$$x_4 = 0.3333282470703125,$$
$$x_5 = 0.3333333332557231187820434570 3125,$$
$$x_6 = 0.3333333333333333333315263297125241592766542453318834304809570 3125,$$
$$x_7 = 0.33333333333333333333333333333333333333333333332353754707648093743 3593862189815,$$
$$x_8 = 0.33333333333333333333333333333333333333333333333333333333333333333333333333333333333.$$

3.3.2 Convergence and nonconvergence

We have not said whether it matters how the initial guess is chosen. It is usually quite important.

Example 3.3 Consider again the application of Newton's method to $f(x) = 1/x - a$. As suggested by Figure 3.7, convergence $x_k \to 1/a$ occurs if $0 < x_0 < \bar{x}$. Otherwise, if $x_0 = 0$ or $\bar{x}$, then $x_k = 0$ for all $k \geq 1$; else, $x_k \to -\infty$. How do we find $\bar{x}$? Set $x_0 = \bar{x}$ and $x_1 = 0$ in the equation, $x_1 = (2 - ax_0)x_0$, that gives the iteration, and solve for $\bar{x}$. We obtain $\bar{x} = 2/a$.

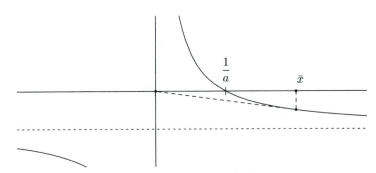

Figure 3.7: Convergence of Newton's method

A complete convergence analysis such as this is not usually possible nor would it be practical unless, as in this situation, one is developing an algorithm dedicated to solving a particular type of problem again and again.

More generally the following is true:

Theorem 3.1 *If $f(r) = 0$, $f'(r) \neq 0$, and $f'(x)$ is continuous, then there is an open interval $N(r)$ containing r such that $x_0 \in N(r) \Rightarrow x_k \to r$ as $k \to \infty$ where the sequence x_k is defined by Newton's method.*

It is some comfort to know that if the initial guess is close enough to a root, Newton's method does converge to that root. It may or may not be easy to know whether or not x_0 is close enough.

Example 3.4 For Newton's method applied to $f(x) = x/|x|^{1/2}$ we have, as shown in Figure 3.8, a cycle that never converges, whatever the initial guess. Theorem 3.1 is not violated because one of its hypotheses is not satisfied: the function has an infinite derivative at $x = 0$ (so $f'(x)$ does not exist there).

Example 3.5 Newton's method for $f(x) = x/(1 + x^2)$ converges, as shown in Figure 3.9, for x_0 in an open interval $]-\bar{x}, \bar{x}[$ where $\bar{x}$ is some positive number. Exactly at the endpoints of this open interval the iteration cycles between two values, and exterior to the interval there is "divergence" to $+\infty$ or $-\infty$, as shown in Figure 3.10. These observations use the fact that the "left half" of $f(x)$ is the inverted mirror image of its "right half." As an exercise let us determine $\bar{x}$. We set $x_0 = \bar{x}$ and $x_1 = -\bar{x}$ in the Newton iteration, that is,

$$-\bar{x} = \bar{x} - \frac{f(\bar{x})}{f'(\bar{x})}.$$

Solving, we get $\bar{x} = \sqrt{\frac{1}{3}}$.

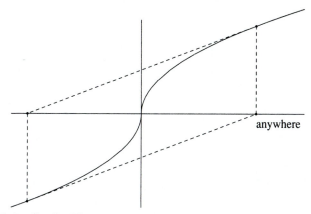

Figure 3.8: Cyclic Newton iteration

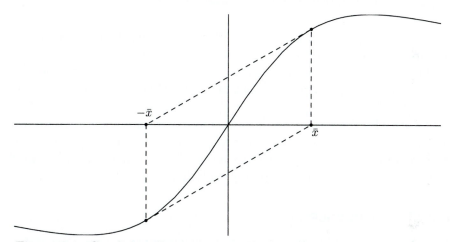

Figure 3.9: Conditionally convergent Newton iteration

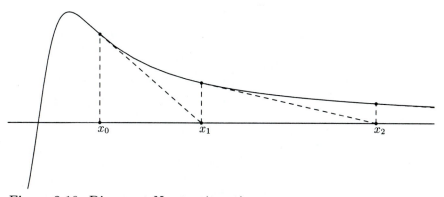

Figure 3.10: Divergent Newton iteration

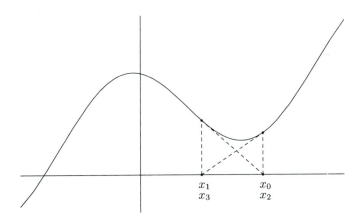

Figure 3.11: Trapped in a local minimum

Example 3.6 There is another possible behavior of Newton's method. As shown in Figure 3.11 the iteration can be trapped in a local minimum if conditions are fairly special. (One way to interpret this behavior is that Newton's method is "trying" to converge to one of two complex conjugate pairs of roots but cannot break out of the real line.)

Although Newton-Raphson does not always converge, there is a variant known as *damped Newton* that always converges either to a root or to a local minimum of a function. The idea is to accept the correction given by Newton's method only if it results in a smaller value of $f(x)$; otherwise, we try again with a correction only half as great.

3.3.3 Order of convergence

It is important to know not only whether an iteration converges but also how fast it converges. The following theorem gives a relationship between the errors of successive iterations that holds in the limit.

Theorem 3.2 *If $f(r) = 0, f'(r) \neq 0$, and $f''(x)$ is continuous, then for x_0 close enough to r,*

$$\lim_{k \to \infty} \frac{e_{k+1}}{e_k^2} = \frac{f''(r)}{2f'(r)}$$

where $e_k \stackrel{\text{def}}{=} x_k - r$.

For practical purposes we can think of this result as stating

$$e_{k+1} \approx \frac{f''(r)}{2f'(r)} e_k^2.$$

If e_k is small, e_{k+1} is much smaller.

The rapid convergence of Newton's method can be best appreciated by using a logarithmic measure of accuracy:

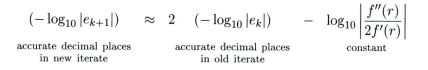

$$\underbrace{(-\log_{10}|e_{k+1}|)}_{\substack{\text{accurate decimal places} \\ \text{in new iterate}}} \quad \approx \quad 2 \quad \underbrace{(-\log_{10}|e_k|)}_{\substack{\text{accurate decimal places} \\ \text{in old iterate}}} \quad - \quad \underbrace{\log_{10}\left|\frac{f''(r)}{2f'(r)}\right|}_{\text{constant}}$$

Each iteration doubles the number of accurate decimal places (or digits) if we neglect the constant term, which we can do for larger k.

Not all iterations converge at the same rate as Newton-Raphson. There are other rates of convergence as suggested by the following definition.

Definition 3.3 Let $x_0, x_1, x_2, \ldots$ be a sequence converging to a limit r and set $e_k = x_k - r$. If for some $p \geq 1$ and $C > 0$,

$$\lim_{k \to \infty} \frac{|e_{k+1}|}{|e_k|^p} = C,$$

then we call p the *order of convergence* and C the *asymptotic error constant*.

The practical interpretation of this definition is that $|e_{k+1}| \approx C|e_k|^p$, with the approximation getting better as $k \to \infty$. It is crucial that $0 < C < +\infty$, because this makes p unique if it exists. (Any power less than p would give a limit of 0; any power greater, a limit of ∞.) The special case $p = 1$ is called **linear convergence**, and $p = 2$, **quadratic convergence**.

Using a logarithmic measure of the accuracy, we have for pth-order convergence that

$$(-\log_{10}|e_{k+1}|) \approx p(-\log_{10}|e_k|) + (-\log_{10}C).$$

If $p = 1$ so that convergence is linear, then $|e_{k+1}| \approx C|e_k|$. For the new error to be smaller than the old error we want $C < 1$. Each iteration is then good for an additional $-\log_{10}C$ digits. The number of accurate digits grows arithmetically with the number of iterations. If $p > 1$, we have **superlinear convergence**. Each iteration is good for p times as many digits as before, neglecting the constant term. Digits of accuracy grow geometrically with the number of iterations.

3.3.4   Advantages and disadvantages

The big advantage of Newton's method is that it normally converges very fast. The fact that an initial bracketing interval is not needed is a plus, but the failure to bracket the result is a minus. A much more serious drawback of Newton-Raphson is that it does not converge if the initial guess is not good enough. Also, the need for an analytical derivative can be a disadvantage. Analytical differentiation by the user is error-prone and tedious. This can be true even for a relatively simple formula such as the monthly payment formula given at the beginning of this chapter. Fortunately, symbolic differentiation is a possibility. For example, *Mathematica* can produce symbolic derivatives,

```
In[1]:= f[r_] := r/12. 87750./(1.-(1.+r/12.)^(-180))-980.96; InputForm[f'[r]]
```

```
Out[1]//InputForm=
   7312.5/(1. - (1. + 0.0833333333333333*r)^(-180)) -
   (109687.5*r)/
    ((1. - (1. + 0.0833333333333333*r)^(-180))^2*
     (1. + 0.0833333333333333*r)^181)
```

to be used within *Mathematica*. Alternatively, such expressions can be formatted in Fortran (or in C),

```
In[2]:= FortranForm[f'[r]]
```

```
Out[2]//FortranForm=
   -   7312.5/(1. - (1. + 0.0833333333333333*r)**-180) -
   -     109687.5*r/
   -      ((1. - (1. + 0.0833333333333333*r)**-180)**2*
   -       (1. + 0.0833333333333333*r)**181)
```

for insertion into a program written in that language. More efficient Fortran code than this can be obtained by use of specially designed *automatic differentiation* routines. Unfortunately, automatic and symbolic differentiation software is not always conveniently available.

What we have not yet mentioned is that convergence of Newton-Raphson can be slower than bisection. Let r be a root of $f(x)$ of multiplicity $m \geq 2$:

$$f(r) = f'(r) = \cdots = f^{(m-1)}(r) = 0$$

(see Figure 3.12). Then it can be shown that convergence is linear with asymptotic error constant $(m-1)/m$.

Exercises

1. Find a root of $x^3 - 2x - 5 = 0$ using the Newton-Raphson method with $x_0 = 2$ until "convergence" on your calculator or computer, showing the result of each iteration. Also write down the "program" you used.

2. Construct a quadratic polynomial with integer coefficients such that the golden ratio $(1 + \sqrt{5})/2$ is one of its roots. Apply the Newton-Raphson method with initial guess $x_0 = 1$ to this quadratic in order to determine the golden ratio to four significant digits.

Mathematica notes

The *Mathematica* function FindRoot[ ] offers a variety of algorithms to find the root of an equation or function. In particular, if you specify a single starting point, it tries to find an expression for the derivative and then proceeds with an algorithm based on Newton's method.

Computer problems

1. Use FindRoot[ ] with Newton's method to find the root of $x - \sin x$ starting at $x = 1$. Why is the result such a poor approximation to the true solution?

2. In this problem you are to use Newton's method to solve for the rate of interest as described at the beginning of Section 3.1. However, we generalize the problem to include the case where the balance of the loan is paid off after n months. This balance would be

$$\left(1 + \frac{0.1025}{12}\right)^n 90000 - \frac{(1 + 0.1025/12)^n - 1}{0.1025/12}\, 980.96.$$

If r were the effective interest rate, the balance would be

$$\left(1 + \frac{r}{12}\right)^n 87750 - \frac{(1 + r/12)^n - 1}{r/12}\, 980.96.$$

Thus for a given number of months the effective rate of interest is the positive root of the function formed by subtracting the first expression from the second.

(a) Write a program that, for given n and initial guess 0.1025, returns the interest rate as its value. The differentiation must be done by *Mathematica*. Iterate as long as $|f(r_k)|$ decreases. Calculate the effective interest rate assuming the loan is paid back after 1 month, after 2 months, after 6 months, after 1 year, after 2 years, after 5 years, and after 15 years. Thus there are seven different cases to do.

(b) In the program for part (a), insert a Print statement that, for each iterate beginning with the initial guess, prints the number of *decimal places* of accuracy. This assumes that you have already run the program once to determine the "true" answer. Run this for the cases of 1 year and 15 years.

(c) Following are the decimal places of accuracy for a sequence of Newton iterates from part (b) on a particular computer: 2.34573, 3.64775, 6.27204, 11.5196, 15.7785, 16.0126, 16.1587, 16.2556, 16.3806, Infinity. Explain why the doubling of the number of accurate decimal places stops after four iterations. Explain why the last iterate has infinite decimal places of accuracy.

3.4 Functional Iteration

Here we discuss a *type* of method for solving equations rather than a particular method. The Newton-Raphson method is included as well as less systematic ways. The Newton-Raphson iteration can be expressed as

$$x_{k+1} = g(x_k) \quad \text{where } g(x) = x - \frac{f(x)}{f'(x)}.$$

For a root r of $f(x)$ we have $g(r) = r$. Such a value r we call a *fixed point* of the mapping $g(x)$. As we have said, a drawback of Newton's method is that the formation of $f'(x)$ can be complicated (and this is even more the case for the generalization of Newton's method to a system of nonlinear equations, for which the division by $f'(x)$ is also an inconvenience). As an example, recall the equation

$$\frac{(r/12)87750}{1 - (1 + (r/12))^{-180}} - 980.96 = 0.$$

Here we develop for this equation another, simpler iteration. The expression raised to the power -180 might be regarded as a correction that accounts for the amortization of the loan; if the principal were never repaid, this term would be absent and the monthly payment would be somewhat smaller. With this in mind let us solve the equation for the first occurrence of r in terms of the second, and presumably less significant, occurrence of r:

$$r = g(r) \qquad \text{where } g(r) \stackrel{\text{def}}{=} \frac{12}{87750} \left(1 - \left(1 + \frac{r}{12}\right)^{-180}\right) 980.96.$$

We could try iterating this equation with some initial guess; an example is

0.1025, 0.105129, 0.106241, 0.106699, 0.106885, 0.106961, 0.106991, 0.107003, 0.107008, 0.107010, 0.107011, 0.107011, 0.107012, 0.107012, 0.107012, ...

This iteration seems to be converging. It has a particularly instructive graphical construction. Assume we have a plot of the curve $y = g(x)$ and the straight line $y = x$. We begin with the point (x_0, x_0) on the straight line $y = x$ and move vertically to the graph of $g(x)$, reaching the point $(x_0, g(x_0)) = (x_0, x_1)$. A horizontal move to the line $y = x$ takes us to (x_1, x_1). Thus each iteration is a vertical move from $y = x$ to $y = g(x)$ and a horizontal move back to $y = x$, and a sequence of iterations is a zigzag path between $y = x$ and $y = g(x)$. See Figure 3.13.

Let us try this idea on another example. The golden ratio is the positive root of $x + 1 = x^2$. This can be rearranged as $x = g(x)$ where $g(x) \stackrel{\text{def}}{=} x^2 - 1$. When applied with an initial guess other than a fixed point of $g(x)$, what happens is that either the iteration "converges" to $+\infty$ or it ultimately reaches a *limit cycle* of period 2 with values that alternate between 0 and -1, as in the following example:

0.5, -0.75, -0.43750, -0.80859, -0.34618, -0.88016, -0.22531, -0.94923, -0.09896, -0.99021, -0.01949, -0.99962, -0.00076, $-1, 0, -1, 0, -1, 0, \ldots$.

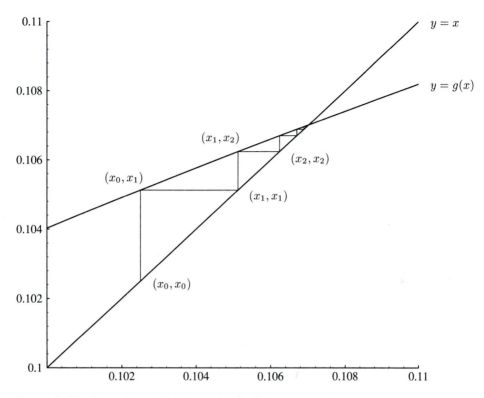

Figure 3.13: Functional iteration to find interest rate

Graphically the situation is as shown in Figure 3.14. You can see that neither root is an *attractor*. What you need for r to be an attractor is that $|g'(r)| < 1$. Compare this to the previous example.

There exist possibilities other than a limit point (finite or infinite) or a limit cycle. A famous iteration, given by

$$x_{k+1} = ax_k(1 - x_k),$$

exhibits a variety of behaviors depending on the value of the parameter a. With $a = 3.6$ and an arbitrary initial guess, we have

> 0.300000, 0.756000, 0.664070, 0.803091, 0.569288, 0.882717, 0.372700, ... ,

and after 1981 iterations,

> 0.871321, 0.403635, 0.866569, 0.416257, 0.874754, 0.394415, 0.859867,
> 0.433786, 0.884216, 0.368560, 0.837805, 0.489197, 0.899580, 0.325209,
> 0.790014, 0.597212, 0.865980, 0.417812, 0.875683, 0.391906, ...

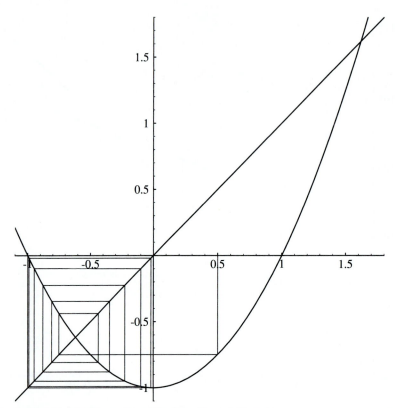

Figure 3.14: Limit cycle with functional iteration

Iterates bounce around forever in some subset of $[0,1]$. This is a model of seemingly random, and yet deterministic, unstable behavior known as *chaos*.

Exercises

1. The equation

$$\frac{x(0.50 + x)}{0.10 - x} = 1.8 \times 10^{-5}$$

arises in chemistry where x is known to be very small. Set up a convergent iteration for solving this equation that is simpler than Newton's method and that requires no square root.

2. The equation $\lambda^3 + 4\lambda^2 + 6\lambda + 4 = 0$ can be rearranged as

$$\lambda = g(\lambda) \quad \text{where } g(\lambda) \stackrel{\text{def}}{=} -\frac{4(\lambda^2 + 1)}{\lambda^2 + 6}.$$

Show that $|g'(\lambda)| < 1$ for all λ. How many fixed points does the iteration $\lambda_{k+1} = g(\lambda_k)$ have? How do you know? For what starting values do we have convergence to each fixed point?

3. It is desired to compute the positive root of the quadratic $bx^2 + x - c = 0$ where $b, c > 0$ by using the iteration scheme $x_{k+1} = c - bx_k^2$. What is the condition that b and c should satisfy so as to ensure convergence for an initial guess in some neighborhood of the fixed point?

4. The even-numbered iterates of the iteration

$$x_{k+1} = g(x_k) \overset{\text{def}}{=} x_k^2 - 1$$

satisfy an iteration of the form

$$x_{k+2} = G(x_k).$$

We can find limit cycles of period 2, and fixed points, of $g(x)$ by determining the fixed points of $G(x)$.

(a) What is $G(x)$?

(b) What are the fixed points of $G(x)$?

(c) Which of the fixed points of $G(x)$ are fixed points of $g(x)$, and which are part of limit cycles of period 2?

(d) Which of the fixed points of $G(x)$ are attractors?

(e) Use the result of (c) to predict the behavior of the original iteration.

(f) For each of the attractors of $\bar{r}$ of $G(x)$, determine the precise relationship between two successive "errors" e_{k+1} and e_k where $e_k \overset{\text{def}}{=} x_k - \bar{r}$. What is the order of convergence in each case?

Mathematica notes

It is quite easy to execute functional iteration in *Mathematica*. The functions Nest[ ] and NestList[ ] do it all for you.

Define a function to be iterated.   In[1]:= g[x_] := 3.6 x (1 - x)

Form a list of the first 10 iterates of g
starting with 0.271. (Note that the list
includes the zeroth iterate and contains 11
values!)

In[2]:= data = NestList[g, 0.271, 10]

Out[2]= {0.271, 0.711212, 0.739402, 0.693673, 0.764967,

0.647253, 0.82194, 0.526877, 0.897399, 0.331465,

0.797746}

Return the 10th iterate of **g** starting with 0.271.	*In[3]:=* **Nest[g, 0.271, 10]** *Out[3]=* 0.797746

It is also possible to draw nice graphs with the iterates clearly shown.

Form a doubled list of the iterates.	*In[4]:=* **data2 = Flatten[Table[{data[[i]], data[[i]]}, {i, Length[data]}]];**

Partition the data into pairs, advancing one element for each pair.	*In[5]:=* **data2 = Partition[data2, 2, 1]**
	Out[5]= {{0.271, 0.271}, {0.271, 0.711212},
	    {0.711212, 0.711212}, {0.711212, 0.739402},
	    {0.739402, 0.739402}, {0.739402, 0.693673},
	    {0.693673, 0.693673}, {0.693673, 0.764967},
	    {0.764967, 0.764967}, {0.764967, 0.647253},
	    {0.647253, 0.647253}, {0.647253, 0.82194},
	    {0.82194, 0.82194}, {0.82194, 0.526877},
	    {0.526877, 0.526877}, {0.526877, 0.897399},
	    {0.897399, 0.897399}, {0.897399, 0.331465},
	    {0.331465, 0.331465}, {0.331465, 0.797746},
	    {0.797746, 0.797746}}

Reset the first point to be on the x axis.	*In[6]:=* **data2[[1, 2]] = 0** *Out[6]=* 0

Form the graphics object that traces out the iterates.	*In[7]:=* **p1 = Graphics[Line[data2]]** *Out[7]=* -Graphics-

Draw the plot of the line $y = x$ and the curve $y = g(x)$.	*In[8]:=* **Plot[{x, g[x]}, {x, 0, 1}]**

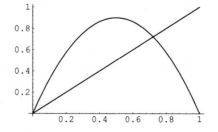

Show both graphs together using thin lines.   *In[9]:=* **Show[{%, p1}, Prolog -> Thickness[.001]]**

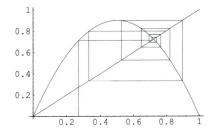

Computer problems

1. Define a function dfi[g_, x0_, n_] that takes the name of a function, a starting value, and the number of iterations and draws a graph of the functional iterates like the graphs in this section. The domain of the graph should be chosen automatically and should extend over slightly more than the range of the iterates.

2. Use dfi[ ] from the previous problem to examine the limit cycles of $x_{k+1} = ax_k(1-x_k)$ with the following values of a: 2.8, 3.2, 3.5, 3.55, 3.566, 3.83, 3.843, and 3.849. Use Nest[ ] with a large number of iterations to get a starting value that lies on the limit cycle. This will eliminate a lot of confused lines that occur prior to convergence to the limit cycle. How are the lengths or periods of the limit cycles related?

3. Use dfi[ ] to examine the limit cycles of $x_{k+1} = r \sin \pi x_k$ with the following values of r: 0.7, 0.75, 0.85, and 0.86. How are the lengths or periods of the limit cycles related?

4. Consider the function f[x_] := Nest[g, x, 50] where g[x_] := 4. x (1.-x). This is an example of a chaotic iteration. Determine experimentally using small perturbations whether f[ ] is well-conditioned or ill-conditioned.

3.5   Secant Method

The principal motivation for this method is to overcome one of the drawbacks of Newton-Raphson by using numerical differentiation to approximate the first derivative. The method we get turns out to be more efficient than Newton-Raphson in most cases.

3.5.1   Algorithm

We give two derivations. The first one is the simplest, assuming you know the formula for Newton's method. The Newton-Raphson iteration

$$x_{k+1} = x_k - \frac{f(x_k)}{f'(x_k)}$$

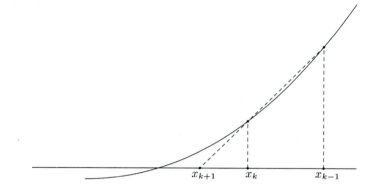

Figure 3.15: One secant iteration

has an analytical derivative in the denominator. Suppose we know not only x_k but also x_{k-1} (in other words, that $k \geq 1$). With $f(x_{k-1})$ and $f(x_k)$ we can approximate $f'(x_k)$ by the slope of the line that cuts $f(x)$ at $x = x_{k-1}$ and x_k:

$$f'(x_k) \approx \frac{f(x_k) - f(x_{k-1})}{x_k - x_{k-1}} \stackrel{\text{def}}{=} f[x_k, x_{k-1}].$$

This approximation yields the **secant method**,

$$x_{k+1} = x_k - \frac{f(x_k)}{f[x_k, x_{k-1}]}.$$

The quantity $f[x_k, x_{k-1}]$ is called a **divided difference**. (It is also known as a *difference quotient*.) Note that this method needs two initial guesses x_0 and x_1.

The second derivation is entirely geometric. Looking at Figure 3.15, we note the two formulas for the slope

$$\frac{f(x_k)}{x_k - x_{k+1}} = \frac{f(x_{k-1}) - f(x_k)}{x_{k-1} - x_k}.$$

We solve for x_{k+1} and get the formula given previously.

A third derivation for the secant method based on *linear interpolation* is given in the introduction to Chapter 5. Also introduced there is a rootfinder based on quadratic interpolation called **Muller's method** and later, in Section 5.7, a related method based on **inverse quadratic interpolation**.

Example 3.7 The secant method applied to $f(x) = x^2 - 3$ with starting values $x_0 = 1$ and $x_1 = 2$ generates the following values:

k	x_k	$f(x_k)$	$f[x_k, x_{k-1}]$	$-f(x_k)/f[x_k, x_{k-1}]$
0	1.000000000	−2.000000000		
1	2.000000000	1.000000000	3.000000000	−0.333333333
2	1.666666667	−0.222222222	3.666666667	0.060606061
3	1.727272727	−0.016528926	3.393939394	0.004870130
4	1.732142857	0.000318878	3.459415584	−0.000092180
5	1.732050680	−0.000000440	3.464193538	0.000000127
6	1.732050808			

The true value is $\sqrt{3} = 1.7320508575\cdots$. Note that iterates 2 and 3 do not bracket the root. It is normal for the secant method that some fraction of the iterates will fall on the same side of the root as their predecessors.

3.5.2 Convergence and nonconvergence

The secant method shares with Newton's method the property of always converging for a close enough initial guess.

Theorem 3.4 *If $f(r) = 0, f'(r) \neq 0$, and $f'(x)$ is continuous, then there is an open interval $N(r)$ containing r such that $x_0, x_1 \in N(r) \Rightarrow x_k \to r$ as $k \to \infty$ where the sequence x_k is defined by the secant method.*

As with Newton's method, continuity of the first derivative is important for convergence, even though it is not explicitly needed to use the method.

Example 3.8 An example of failure to converge is not so easy to construct because the secant method is not so simple. For the example plotted in Figure 3.16 you see that for starting values far from the root $r = 0$, the iterates go off to $+\infty$.

3.5.3 Order of convergence

Following is a precise statement of the rate of convergence for the secant method under normal circumstances.

Theorem 3.5 *If $f(r) = 0, f'(r) \neq 0$, and $f''(x)$ is continuous, then for x_0, x_1 close enough to r,*

$$\lim_{k \to \infty} \frac{|e_{k+1}|}{|e_k|^\phi} = \left| \frac{f''(r)}{2f'(r)} \right|^{\phi-1}$$

where $e_k \overset{\text{def}}{=} x_k - r$ is the error in the secant iteration and $\phi = (\sqrt{5} + 1)/2 = 1.618034\cdots$.

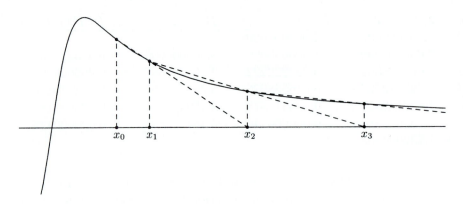

Figure 3.16: Divergence of secant method

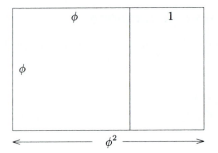

Figure 3.17: Golden ratio

Thus, the order of convergence is the *golden ratio* ϕ, which satisfies $\phi^2 = \phi + 1$. (A special property of the golden ratio is shown in Figure 3.17. If a square is removed from one end of a rectangle that has a ratio of length to width of ϕ, the smaller rectangle that remains also has a ratio of ϕ. The golden ratio is sometimes touted as the most aesthetically pleasing shape for windows on buildings.) The practical meaning of this theorem is that

$$|e_{k+1}| \approx \left| \frac{f''(r)}{2f'(r)} \right|^{\phi-1} \cdot |e_k|^{\phi}.$$

An intermediate step in the proof of the theorem is to show that if x_0 and x_1 are close enough to r, then

$$\frac{e_{k+1}}{e_k e_{k-1}} \rightarrow \frac{f''(r)}{2f'(r)} \quad \text{as} \quad k \rightarrow \infty,$$

whose practical meaning is that

$$e_{k+1} \approx \frac{f''(r)}{2f'(r)} e_k e_{k-1}.$$

Compare this to Newton-Raphson, for which

$$e_{k+1} \approx \frac{f''(r)}{2f'(r)} e_k^2.$$

Because e_k is (expected to be) smaller than e_{k-1}, a Newton iteration is more powerful than a secant iteration.

3.5.4   Advantages and disadvantages

Compared to Newton-Raphson, the secant method has two advantages. One is that it requires no analytic derivatives. The other is that it is more efficient assuming that we measure cost as the sum of the number of evaluations of $f(x)$ plus the number of evaluations of $f'(x)$. We explain this in the next paragraph.

One Newton-Raphson iteration gives

$$|e_{k+1}| \approx \left| \frac{f''(r)}{2f'(r)} \right| |e_k|^2.$$

This has a cost equal to that of two secant iterations, for which

$$|e_{k+2}| \quad \approx \quad \left| \frac{f''(r)}{2f'(r)} \right|^{\phi-1} |e_{k+1}|^\phi = \left| \frac{f''(r)}{2f'(r)} \right|^{\phi-1} \left(\left| \frac{f''(r)}{2f'(r)} \right|^{\phi-1} |e_k|^\phi \right)^\phi$$

$$= \left| \frac{f''(r)}{2f'(r)} \right|^\phi |e_k|^{\phi+1}.$$

The order of this doubled-up secant method is $\phi + 1 = 2.618034\cdots$, which is greater than that of Newton-Raphson.

Review questions

1. Derive the secant method.

2. Execute the secant method for $f(x) = x^2 - 3$ with starting values $x_0 = 1$ and $x_1 = 2$.

3. What is the order of convergence of the secant method?

4. Relate the secant method to Newton-Raphson.

Exercises

1. Use two iterations of the secant method to approximate a root of $p(x) = x^3 - 3x^2 - 2x + 4$. Start with $x_0 = 0, x_1 = 3$.

2. Following is the secant iteration for finding the root of some function:

$$x_{k+1} = \frac{x_k x_{k-1} + 1}{x_k + x_{k-1} - 1}.$$

   (a) What is the the Newton-Raphson iteration for the same function? (It is not necessary to determine the function.)

   (b) What is the root of the function? (Again, it is not necessary to determine the function.)

3. Consider the use of the secant method to find the root α of a function $f(x)$ where $f(x_0) < 0, f(x_1) > 0$, and $f''(x) > 0$ on the interval $[x_0, x_1]$. Describe the position of the iterates x_2, x_3, x_4, and x_5 relative to α:

Iterate	x_0	x_1	x_2	x_3	x_4	x_5
Position relative to α	left	right				

4. Consider the use of the secant method to find the root r of a function having a nonzero first derivative and a positive second derivative. If $f(x_1)$ and $f(x_2)$ are negative, what can we say about the signs of $f(x_{99})$ and $f(x_{100})$? (Assume exact arithmetic.)

5. Consider the secant method applied to $1/x - a = 0$.

   (a) Obtain an equation relating the relative error ε_{k+1} in x_{k+1} to the relative errors ε_k and ε_{k-1}, respectively. Your equation should not involve the approximate values x_{k-1}, x_k, x_{k+1}.

   (b) Prove that the secant method converges if $|\varepsilon_0| < 1$ and $|\varepsilon_1| < 1$.

6. Show that convergence of order ϕ for the secant method is consistent with the approximate equation

$$e_{k+1} \approx \frac{f''(r)}{2f'(r)} e_k e_{k-1}.$$

Computer problem

1. Using the function `accdig[ ]` defined in Computer Problem 4 of Section 1.4, examine the convergence rate of the secant method. Use $x^2 - 2$ and do the arithmetic to 500 decimal digits. How close is the ratio of accurate digits to `GoldenRatio`?

4. Systems of Linear Equations

It has been estimated that the solution of a linear system of equations enters in at some stage in about 75 percent of all scientific problems.

G. Dahlquist and Å. Björck (1974)

Solving systems of linear equations remains the most important problem of scientific computing. A simple example of such a problem is

$$
\begin{aligned}
3x + 5y - z &= 10, \\
7x - 2y + 3z &= 12, \\
x + 5y - 4z &= -1.
\end{aligned}
$$

A set of equations typically arises from some system of discrete components in equilibrium. Examples include structures and electric circuits. The steady-state behavior of an AC circuit (with passive, linear components) gives rise to a problem involving complex numbers, whereas a DC circuit involves just real numbers. Systems of linear equations also arise as subproblems in nonlinear, differential, and integral equations. In its most general form the problem is expressed as

$$
\begin{aligned}
a_{11}x_1 + a_{12}x_2 + \cdots + a_{1n}x_n &= b_1, \\
a_{21}x_1 + a_{22}x_2 + \cdots + a_{2n}x_n &= b_2, \\
\vdots \qquad\qquad \vdots \qquad\qquad \vdots \qquad \vdots \\
a_{n1}x_1 + a_{n2}x_2 + \cdots + a_{nn}x_n &= b_n,
\end{aligned}
$$

where a_{ij} is the coefficient in the ith equation of the jth variable x_j.

We begin with mathematical preliminaries. Then we study the Gaussian elimination algorithm, and a variant known as partial pivoting. We shall see that this algorithm computes what is known as an LU factorization.

This chapter contains the following sections:

4.1 Matrices

4.1.1 Definitions and properties

A **matrix** is a two-dimensional array of numbers with a certain number of rows and columns, for example,

$$A = \begin{bmatrix} 3 & 5 \\ 7 & -2 \\ 1 & 5 \end{bmatrix}.$$

A matrix is normally denoted by an uppercase letter and an element of it by the corresponding lowercase letter with subscripts indicating row and column. Thus, the element in the ith row (from the top) and the jth column (from the left) is denoted by a_{ij}. In the example above, $a_{31} = 1$. There are three kind of matrices of special importance. A matrix with just one row is called a **row vector**, for example,

$$\begin{bmatrix} 2 & 0 & -2 & 0 & 1 \end{bmatrix}.$$

A matrix of one column is a **column vector**, and a matrix having an equal number of rows and columns is a **square matrix**. Respective examples are

$$\begin{bmatrix} 3 \\ -1 \\ 0 \end{bmatrix} \quad \text{and} \quad \begin{bmatrix} 0.8 & 0.6 & 0 & 0 \\ -0.6 & 0.8 & 0 & 0 \\ 0 & 0 & 1 & 0 \\ 0 & 0.2 & 0.2 & 1 \end{bmatrix}.$$

Three operations are defined for matrices. One is **matrix addition**, in which corresponding elements of two matrices are added to get the corresponding element of the resulting matrix, for example,

$$\begin{bmatrix} 1 & 2 \\ 0 & 2 \end{bmatrix} + \begin{bmatrix} -1 & 1 \\ 1 & -1 \end{bmatrix} = \begin{bmatrix} 0 & 3 \\ 1 & 1 \end{bmatrix}.$$

A second is **scalar multiplication**, in which a scalar multiplies each element of a matrix, for example,

$$3 \begin{bmatrix} 1 & 2 \\ 0 & -1 \end{bmatrix} = \begin{bmatrix} 3 & 6 \\ 0 & -3 \end{bmatrix}.$$

The third is **matrix multiplication**, which is more complicated. This operation may at first seem artificial, but it arises naturally in many situations; an example is given at the end of this section. Also, the basic idea arises frequently in still other applications if we substitute different operations for addition and multiplication. Due to the relative complexity of matrix multiplication we begin with a special case. A row vector times a column vector of equal length is defined by

$$[a_1 \quad a_2 \quad \cdots \quad a_m] \begin{bmatrix} b_1 \\ b_2 \\ \vdots \\ b_m \end{bmatrix} \stackrel{\text{def}}{=} a_1 b_1 + a_2 b_2 + \cdots + a_m b_m.$$

This is called an **inner product** and gives a scalar result as depicted below:

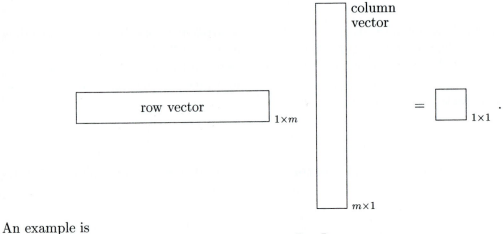

An example is

$$[1 \quad -2 \quad 1] \begin{bmatrix} 1 \\ 1 \\ 1 \end{bmatrix} = 0.$$

Now we define the general case in terms of the special case. The matrix product of two matrices is not defined unless they are *conformable*, meaning that the first matrix has as many columns as the second matrix has rows. If the first matrix is an $l \times m$ matrix A and the second is an $m \times n$ matrix B, then the product is defined to be some $l \times n$ matrix C. More specifically, C is formed by taking inner products between rows of A and columns of B. It is a "table" of all such products as pictured in Figure 4.1. Hence,

$$c_{ij} \quad = \quad [i\text{th row of } A] \begin{bmatrix} j\text{th} \\ \text{col} \\ \text{of} \\ B \end{bmatrix}$$

$$= \quad [a_{i1} \quad a_{i2} \quad \cdots \quad a_{im}] \begin{bmatrix} b_{1j} \\ b_{2j} \\ \vdots \\ b_{mj} \end{bmatrix}$$

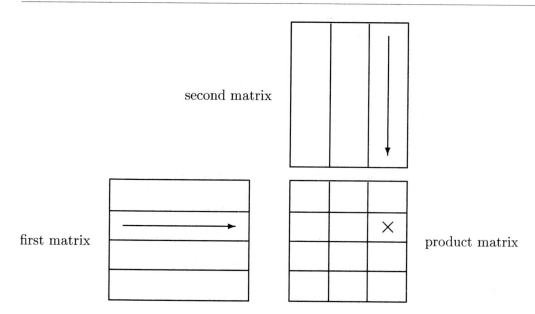

Figure 4.1: A table of inner products

$$= \quad a_{i1}b_{1j} + a_{i2}b_{2j} + \cdots + a_{im}b_{mj}$$

$$= \quad \sum_{k=1}^{m} a_{ik}\, b_{kj}.$$

Note that the matrix product is a summation over the two "inside" subscripts. Following is an example with one of the inner product operations highlighted:

$$\begin{bmatrix} 1 & -1 \\ 1 & -2 \end{bmatrix} \begin{bmatrix} 1 & 2 & -1 \\ 1 & 0 & 3 \end{bmatrix} = \begin{bmatrix} 0 & 2 & -4 \\ -1 & 2 & -7 \end{bmatrix}.$$

Another special case of the matrix product is when the first matrix has one column and the second has (necessarily) one row. This is the product of a column vector times a row vector and is known as an **outer product**. The result is a table of products as suggested by Figure 4.2.

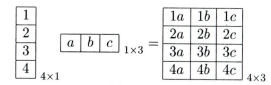

Figure 4.2: An outer product

Matrix multiplication has many of the properties of multiplication of two scalars. There is an **identity matrix**

$$I_n = \begin{bmatrix} 1 & & & \\ & 1 & & \\ & & \ddots & \\ & & & 1 \end{bmatrix};$$

so if A is $l \times m$, then $I_l A = A$ and $A I_m = A$.

The matrix product is **associative**, meaning that if A is $l \times m$, B is $m \times n$, and C is $n \times p$, then

$$(AB)C = A(BC).$$

This implies that the product of any number of matrices can be grouped in any way. This has important practical consequences.

Is matrix multiplication commutative? Products AB and BA are not both defined unless A is $l \times m$ and B is $m \times l$ for some l and m. So we ask, is

$$\underbrace{AB}_{l \times l} = \underbrace{BA}_{m \times m}?$$

Clearly this is possible only if $l = m$. Even then the answer is *generally no*. This fact makes matrices interesting objects. Here is an example:

$$\begin{bmatrix} 1 & 1 \\ -1 & -1 \end{bmatrix}\begin{bmatrix} 1 & -1 \\ -1 & 1 \end{bmatrix} = \begin{bmatrix} 0 & 0 \\ 0 & 0 \end{bmatrix}, \quad \begin{bmatrix} 1 & -1 \\ -1 & 1 \end{bmatrix}\begin{bmatrix} 1 & 1 \\ -1 & -1 \end{bmatrix} = \begin{bmatrix} 2 & 2 \\ -2 & -2 \end{bmatrix}.$$

Note that the product of two nonzero matrices can be the zero matrix.

Do square matrices have multiplicative **inverses**? For a matrix

$$A = \begin{bmatrix} 1 & 2 \\ 0 & 0 \end{bmatrix}$$

to have an inverse X means that $AX = I_2$ and $XA = I_2$. If we express X in terms of its elements x_{ij} and write out the first of these two equations, we get

$$\begin{bmatrix} x_{11} + 2x_{21} & x_{12} + 2x_{22} \\ 0 & 0 \end{bmatrix} = \begin{bmatrix} 1 & 0 \\ 0 & 1 \end{bmatrix}.$$

Clearly A has no inverse.

The situation with respect to inverses is fortunately quite tidy. There are only two kinds of square matrices A, *singular* and *nonsingular*. If A is **singular**, then there exists no X such that $AX = I$ nor does there exist an X such that $XA = I$. If A is **nonsingular**, then there exists a unique X such that $AX = I$ and $XA = I$, in which case we denote X by A^{-1}. If you have studied determinants, the following fact will be helpful: A matrix is singular if and only if its determinant is zero. However, for the most part we do not assume a knowledge of determinants (nor do we have much use for them in numerical methods). An example of an inverse is

$$\begin{bmatrix} 1 & 2 \\ 3 & 4 \end{bmatrix}^{-1} = \begin{bmatrix} -2 & 1 \\ \frac{3}{2} & -\frac{1}{2} \end{bmatrix}.$$

There is a thin line between being singular and nonsingular. The matrix

$$\begin{bmatrix} 1 & 1 \\ 1 & 1 + \varepsilon \end{bmatrix}$$

is nonsingular if and only if $\varepsilon \neq 0$. There is a formula for the inverse of a matrix product: If A and B are nonsingular, then

$$(AB)^{-1} = B^{-1}A^{-1}.$$

To prove this, one needs to show only that $(AB)(B^{-1}A^{-1}) = I$, which is an immediate consequence of basic properties. Note how the order of the product is reversed when taking the inverse. We will give an example at the end of this section that shows why this is sensible.

It is useful to mention the **transpose** A^{T} of a matrix A. It is formed by interchanging the rows with the columns as in the example

$$\begin{bmatrix} 1 & 2 \\ -1 & 0 \\ 3 & 2 \end{bmatrix}^{\mathrm{T}} = \begin{bmatrix} 1 & -1 & 3 \\ 2 & 0 & 2 \end{bmatrix}.$$

The transpose satisfies $(AB)^{\mathrm{T}} = B^{\mathrm{T}}A^{\mathrm{T}}$, with an order reversal like the inverse. This chapter uses the transpose only to construct column vectors from row vectors and to denote row vectors in terms of column vectors. It is customary to use lowercase boldface letters for column vectors and to use the transpose of such a symbol for a row vector. With this convention, inner and outer products are easy to identify: An inner product $\boldsymbol{u}^{\mathrm{T}}\boldsymbol{v}$ has the transpose symbol on the inside, and an outer product $\boldsymbol{u}\boldsymbol{v}^{\mathrm{T}}$ has the transpose symbol on the outside.

4.1.2 Relevance to linear equations

We now explain the relevance of matrix algebra to systems of linear equations like

$$\begin{aligned} 3x + 5y - z &= 10, \\ 7x - 2y + 3z &= 12, \\ x + 5y - 4z &= -1. \end{aligned}$$

These three scalar equations can be written as the single vector equation

$$\begin{bmatrix} 3x + 5y - z \\ 7x - 2y + 3z \\ x + 5y - 4z \end{bmatrix} = \begin{bmatrix} 10 \\ 12 \\ -1 \end{bmatrix}.$$

Please be aware that this vector is a mathematical convenience; it is usually not a physically meaningful vector. At the same time, this use of geometric language suggests mental images that guide our algebra. The left-hand side of the vector equation happens to be the product of a matrix times a column vector:

$$\begin{bmatrix} 3 & 5 & -1 \\ 7 & -2 & 3 \\ 1 & 5 & -4 \end{bmatrix} \begin{bmatrix} x \\ y \\ z \end{bmatrix} = \begin{bmatrix} 10 \\ 12 \\ -1 \end{bmatrix}.$$

A general linear system of n equations in n unknowns can be expressed $A\,\boldsymbol{x} = \boldsymbol{b}$ where A is an $n \times n$ matrix of coefficients, $\boldsymbol{x}$ a column vector of n unknowns, and $\boldsymbol{b}$ a column vector of n right-hand sides. If A is nonsingular, $\boldsymbol{x} = A^{-1}\,\boldsymbol{b}$. If A is singular, either there is no solution or there are infinitely many. At the start we may not know whether or not the matrix is singular. It is in the process of solving that we find out.

Let us take a close look at $A\,\boldsymbol{x} = \boldsymbol{b}$. It is useful to introduce

$$\boldsymbol{e}_j \stackrel{\text{def}}{=} j\text{th unit vector} \stackrel{\text{def}}{=} \begin{bmatrix} 0 \\ \vdots \\ 0 \\ 1 \\ 0 \\ \vdots \\ 0 \end{bmatrix} \leftarrow j\text{th element.}$$

Then $A\,\boldsymbol{e}_j$ is the jth column of A; for example,

$$\begin{bmatrix} 1 & 2 & 3 & 4 \\ 5 & 6 & 7 & 8 \\ 9 & 10 & 11 & 12 \\ 13 & 14 & 15 & 16 \end{bmatrix} \begin{bmatrix} 0 \\ 0 \\ 1 \\ 0 \end{bmatrix} = \begin{bmatrix} 3 \\ 7 \\ 11 \\ 15 \end{bmatrix},$$

and $\boldsymbol{e}_i^{\mathrm{T}} A$ is the ith row of A; for example,

$$\begin{bmatrix} 0 & 0 & 1 & 0 \end{bmatrix} \begin{bmatrix} 1 & 2 & 3 & 4 \\ 5 & 6 & 7 & 8 \\ 9 & 10 & 11 & 12 \\ 13 & 14 & 15 & 16 \end{bmatrix} = \begin{bmatrix} 9 & 10 & 11 & 12 \end{bmatrix}.$$

Note that the identity matrix is made up of these unit vectors, and it is the above property that allows multiplication by the identity matrix to replicate the matrix. With this notation for unit vectors we can write

$$A\boldsymbol{x} = A(x_1\boldsymbol{e}_1 + x_2\boldsymbol{e}_2 + \cdots + x_n\boldsymbol{e}_n).$$

Using the distributive law for matrix addition and multiplication and the fact that the x_i are scalars, we can rewrite the linear system as

$$x_1(A\boldsymbol{e}_1) + x_2(A\boldsymbol{e}_2) + \cdots + x_n(A\boldsymbol{e}_n) = \boldsymbol{b}.$$

Thus, the problem of solving for $\boldsymbol{x}$ is equivalent to that of expressing $\boldsymbol{b}$ as a linear combination of columns of A. In summary, we can look at $A\,\boldsymbol{x} = \boldsymbol{b}$ in two ways. In terms of the rows of A the problem is to find $\boldsymbol{x}$ given the value of its inner products with the n rows of A. In terms of columns of A the problem is to find a linear combination of the n columns of A that reproduces $\boldsymbol{b}$. The two points of view are depicted in Figure 4.3. This observation is useful both theoretically and computationally.

4.1.3   An application of the matrix product

We conclude this section with an example that illustrates the usefulness of the matrix product and motivates its lack of commutativity as well as the rule for the inverse of a product.

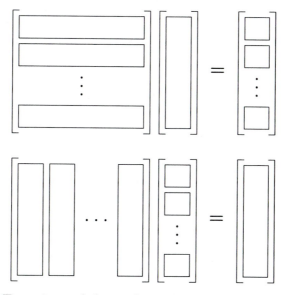

Figure 4.3: Two views of $A\,\boldsymbol{x} = \boldsymbol{b}$

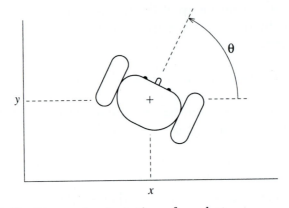

Figure 4.4: Position and orientation of a robot

Consider a robot that is capable of simple locomotion on a flat surface. The robot has a position that can be specified by coordinates x and y and an orientation, the direction in which it is pointed, specified by an angle θ (in radians) measured counterclockwise from the direction of the x axis; see Figure 4.4. The robot is able to move any distance d, positive or negative, in the direction in which it is pointed. It can also rotate by any angle ϕ, positive or negative, measured counterclockwise. Each of these two motions will change the position or orientation of the robot. We show how this can be computed by means of a matrix–vector multiplication. The *state* of the robot is specified by x, y, and θ. However, in order to be able to use matrices we will need a redundant state vector

$$\begin{bmatrix} x \\ y \\ \cos\theta \\ \sin\theta \end{bmatrix}.$$

Note that the state vector is composed of a pair of two-dimensional physical vectors. One is the position vector

$$\begin{bmatrix} x \\ y \end{bmatrix}$$

and the other is a direction vector

$$\begin{bmatrix} \cos\theta \\ \sin\theta \end{bmatrix},$$

of unit length. To move a distance d, *premultiply* the state vector by the matrix

$$\begin{bmatrix} 1 & 0 & d & 0 \\ 0 & 1 & 0 & d \\ 0 & 0 & 1 & 0 \\ 0 & 0 & 0 & 1 \end{bmatrix}.$$

To rotate through an angle ϕ, premultiply by

$$\begin{bmatrix} 1 & 0 & 0 & 0 \\ 0 & 1 & 0 & 0 \\ 0 & 0 & \cos\phi & -\sin\phi \\ 0 & 0 & \sin\phi & \cos\phi \end{bmatrix}.$$

(We leave the derivation of these two transformations as an exercise.)

To perform the sequence of motions

1. Move 10 units forward,
2. Turn left 90° $(\theta = \pi/2)$,
3. Move 5 units backward,

premultiply the state vector by

$$\begin{bmatrix} 1 & 0 & -5 & 0 \\ 0 & 1 & 0 & -5 \\ 0 & 0 & 1 & 0 \\ 0 & 0 & 0 & 1 \end{bmatrix} \begin{bmatrix} 1 & 0 & 0 & 0 \\ 0 & 1 & 0 & 0 \\ 0 & 0 & 0 & -1 \\ 0 & 0 & 1 & 0 \end{bmatrix} \begin{bmatrix} 1 & 0 & 10 & 0 \\ 0 & 1 & 0 & 10 \\ 0 & 0 & 1 & 0 \\ 0 & 0 & 0 & 1 \end{bmatrix} = \begin{bmatrix} 1 & 0 & 10 & 5 \\ 0 & 1 & -5 & 10 \\ 0 & 0 & 0 & -1 \\ 0 & 0 & 1 & 0 \end{bmatrix}.$$

Note that the ordering of operations is from right to left and that we can use associativity to combine these all into a single matrix (which is of immense benefit in computer graphics). To reverse this, perform the *inverse* of each of the operations *in reverse order*:

1. Move 5 units forward,
2. Turn right 90° $(\theta = -\pi/2)$,
3. Move 10 units backward.

In terms of matrices, premultiply the state vector by

$$\begin{bmatrix} 1 & 0 & -10 & 0 \\ 0 & 1 & 0 & -10 \\ 0 & 0 & 1 & 0 \\ 0 & 0 & 0 & 1 \end{bmatrix} \begin{bmatrix} 1 & 0 & 0 & 0 \\ 0 & 1 & 0 & 0 \\ 0 & 0 & 0 & 1 \\ 0 & 0 & -1 & 0 \end{bmatrix} \begin{bmatrix} 1 & 0 & 5 & 0 \\ 0 & 1 & 0 & 5 \\ 0 & 0 & 1 & 0 \\ 0 & 0 & 0 & 1 \end{bmatrix} = \begin{bmatrix} 1 & 0 & 5 & -10 \\ 0 & 1 & 10 & 5 \\ 0 & 0 & 0 & 1 \\ 0 & 0 & -1 & 0 \end{bmatrix}.$$

Note that the three matrices on the left are the inverses of those in the previous equation but in reverse order. The advantage of using matrices in a situation like this is that what is apparently complex gets reduced to matrix algebra, which is well understood.

4.1.4 Programming style

This is a good time to discuss programming style. We do not recommend excessive comments about what the program is doing (except in cases where the coding is excessively intricate because of performance or accuracy concerns). In most cases the code speaks for itself. Perhaps the greatest impediment to understanding are names. The programmer ought to keep the number of different names to a minimum. Names ought to be extremely well chosen and not too long. They should attempt to imitate mathematical language as well as English. For example, in the context of linear algebra, `a[[i,j]]` is preferable to `matrix[[row,column]]`— use `i` and `j` specifically if possible! As a rule of thumb, use English-like words only for the quantities that a mathematics book would not refer to with symbols. Programs are no place for creative names. In cases where it is not easy to guess the role of a variable there should be an in-line comment the first time it is assigned a value. Likewise, excessive numbers of short procedures are not good. Global names are an even bigger nuisance to remember than are local variables.

Exercises

1. Let A and B be $n \times n$ matrices, and let c be a column vector of n elements. Exactly how many additions and how many multiplications are needed

    (a) to compute $A(Bc)$?

    (b) to compute $(AB)c$?

2. Prove the associative law for matrix multiplication. I.e., show $(AB)C = A(BC)$.

3. If AB is nonsingular, show that A and B are also. Do not use determinants.

4. Determine the inverse of $I + u\,v^{\mathrm{T}}$ where I is the $n \times n$ identity matrix and u and v are n-component column vectors. What condition is necessary and sufficient for the existence of the inverse? Hint: Try $I + \alpha\,u\,v^{\mathrm{T}}$ where α is some scalar to be determined, and note that a 1×1 matrix can be treated as a scalar.

5. For a linear system $Ax = b$ of two equations, show that if $a_{11}a_{22} \neq a_{12}a_{21}$, then the system has exactly one solution.

6. Suppose that
$$Au = b, \ \ Av = b, \ \ u \neq v$$
where A is an $n \times n$ matrix and b, u, v are vectors of dimension n. By explicit construction show that
$$Ax = b$$
has an infinite number of different solutions x.

7. Recall that Ax can be expressed as a linear combination of the columns of A. Write an algorithm that uses this idea to compute the product of an $n \times n$ matrix A with a vector x of dimension n. (The elements of A should be used in the following order: $a_{11}, a_{21}, \ldots, a_{n1}; a_{12}, a_{22}, \ldots, a_{n2}; \ldots; a_{1n}, a_{2n}, \ldots, a_{nn}$.) The result should be stored in a vector y. Do not use operations on entire arrays or on "sections" of arrays.

8. Let A and B be square matrices. What is the (i,j)th element of $A\,e_p\,e_q^{\mathrm{T}}\,B$ where e_k denotes the kth unit vector?

9. Let A and B be $n \times n$ matrices.

   (a) Prove the identity

   $$AB = Ae_1e_1^{\mathrm{T}}B + Ae_2e_2^{\mathrm{T}}B + \cdots + Ae_ne_n^{\mathrm{T}}B.$$

   (b) Write an algorithm for multiplying two $n \times n$ matrices A and B *based* on the identity given in part (a). The result is to be stored in C. *Please note*: The algorithm should be such that after m executions of the outermost loop the array C contains the value

   $$Ae_1e_1^{\mathrm{T}}B + \cdots + Ae_me_m^{\mathrm{T}}B.$$

10. (a) For the example at the end of this section, verify the matrix transformation for moving a distance d and the matrix transformation for rotating through an angle ϕ.

   (b) How can the state of the robot and its motions be expressed in terms of matrix notation if *post*multiplication is used instead of premultiplication?

★11. Let us consider only matrices whose elements are either nonnegative or $+\infty$. For two $n \times n$ matrices A, B, define matrix "addition" and "multiplication" by

   $$\begin{aligned}(A + B)_{ij} &= \min\{a_{ij},\ b_{ij}\}, \\ (AB)_{ij} &= \min_{1 \leq k \leq n}(a_{ik} + b_{kj}).\end{aligned}$$

   (a) Verify distributivity $A(B + C) = AB + AC$.

   (b) What is the matrix I such that $IA = A$ for any A?

   (c) Suppose we have n cities labeled 1, 2, $\ldots$, n, and we have a set of one-way roads going from some cities to others. Define a matrix B such that b_{ij} is the length of the shortest road from i to j. (If there is no road, the length of the shortest road is $+\infty$.) Define a route to be a sequence of zero or more roads such that each successive road in the sequence begins where the previous one ends. Define the length of a route to be the sum of the lengths of the roads. (The length of a 0-road route is 0.) Obtain in terms of B and the special matrix operations an expression for the matrix whose (i, j)th entry gives the length of the shortest 2-road route from i to j.

(d) Generalize part (c) to k-road routes where k is some fixed nonnegative integer.

(e) Obtain in terms of B and the special matrix operations an expression for the matrix whose $(i,\ j)$th entry gives the length of the shortest route from i to j. Must we consider k-road routes for all possible nonnegative values of k?

Mathematica notes

Vectors and matrices in *Mathematica* are represented as lists and lists of lists, respectively. Note that a simple list of numbers is just a vector; there is no distinction between row vectors and column vectors. This is usually not a problem. If you do need to distinguish between row and column vectors, you can simply write a row vector as a matrix with one row and a column vector as a matrix with one column. A matrix is a list of vectors, all of which are the same length. The different parts of the matrix represent its various rows. This means that the notation a[[i, j]], i.e., the jth part of the ith part of a, represents the element a_{ij} of the matrix a. The matrix product is available in *Mathematica* under the name Dot or in infix form as ".". The transpose of a matrix is given by the function Transpose[ ]. Let

$$u = \begin{bmatrix} -3 \\ 4 \end{bmatrix}, \qquad v = \begin{bmatrix} -5 \\ 7 \end{bmatrix}, \qquad A = \begin{bmatrix} 1 & 2 \\ 3 & -2 \end{bmatrix}, \qquad B = \begin{bmatrix} -7 & 2 \\ 5 & 4 \end{bmatrix}.$$

The corresponding *Mathematica* syntax is

```
u = {-3, 4}
v = {-5, 7}
a = { {1, 2}, {3, -2} }
b = { {-7, 2}, {5, 4} }
```

The matrix products $u^\mathrm{T}v, AB, Au, v^\mathrm{T}B$ are represented, respectively, by u.v, a.b, a.u, and v.b.

An outer product of two vectors cannot be obtained with the *Mathematica* dot product unless the vectors are represented as an $n \times 1$ matrix and a $1 \times n$ matrix. Whenever outer products are involved, you should represent vectors as matrices or use the function Outer[ ], which is for generalized outer operations. For linear algebra, we can use it with the operation Times[ ] to get the outer product. For example, for uv^T one needs to use Outer[Times, u, v] if u and v are simple lists of numbers. This is a bit clumsy; however, some customization is possible. What one can do is define o[a_, b_] := Outer[Times, a, b] and then use the infix form u ~o~ v. (To carry this a step further, one might also define into = LinearSolve and write a ~into~ b as a computational realization of $A^{-1}b$.) Thus, $Au^\mathrm{T}vB$ could be evaluated as a.(u ~o~ v).b or (a.u) ~o~ (v.b). (Which of these is more efficient?)

It is awkward to have to look at lists and lists of lists and try to visualize the vectors and matrices that they represent. We can use MatrixForm[ ] to get them displayed in standard array format.

A 3×2 matrix.

```
In[1]:= a = {{1, 2}, {3, -2}, {4, 17}}
Out[1]= {{1, 2}, {3, -2}, {4, 17}}
```

The same matrix printed using `MatrixForm`.

```
In[2]:= MatrixForm[a]
Out[2]//MatrixForm= 1    2
                    3    -2
                    4    17
```

We can cause `MatrixForm[ ]` to be applied to every result after it gets evaluated in the normal way.

```
In[3]:= $Post = MatrixForm
Out[3]//MatrixForm= MatrixForm
```

Now `a` is printed in array form.

```
In[4]:= a
Out[4]//MatrixForm= 1    2
                    3    -2
                    4    17
```

The transpose of the matrix `a`.

```
In[5]:= Transpose[a]
Out[5]//MatrixForm= 1    3    4
                    2    -2   17
```

Get rid of the `MatrixForm[ ]` applied to every result.

```
In[6]:= $Post = .
```

This product collapses to a 1×1 matrix and is reduced to a scalar.

```
In[7]:= {1, 2, 3} . a . {1, 2}
Out[7]= 117
```

The functions `VectorQ[ ]` and `MatrixQ[ ]` return the values `True` or `False` and answer the question of whether their arguments are a vector or a matrix, respectively. Note that *Mathematica* considers $1 \times n$ and $n \times 1$ matrices to be matrices, not vectors. A vector is simply a one-dimensional list of expressions that are not themselves lists. Likewise a matrix is a two-dimensional list of nonlists. The function `Dimensions[ ]` will give you the dimensions of a vector or matrix.

This is a vector.

```
In[1]:= VectorQ[{1, 2, 3, a, x}]
Out[1]= True
```

This is a matrix, not a vector.

```
In[2]:= VectorQ[{{1, 2, 3, a, x}}]
Out[2]= False
```

| This is a vector, not a matrix. | `In[3]:= MatrixQ[{1, 2, 3, a, x}]` |
| | `Out[3]= False` |

This is not a matrix because the two rows are not the same length.

`In[4]:= MatrixQ[{{1, 2}, {3, a, x}}]`

`Out[4]= False`

This is a matrix.

`In[5]:= MatrixQ[{{Sin[z], 1, 2}, {3, a, x}}]`

`Out[5]= True`

`Dimensions[ ]` gives a list containing the length of a vector.

`In[6]:= Dimensions[{1, 2, 3, a, x}]`

`Out[6]= {5}`

`Dimensions[ ]` gives a list containing the dimensions of a matrix.

`In[7]:= Dimensions[{{Sin[z], 1, 2}, {3, a, x}}]`

`Out[7]= {2, 3}`

Computer problem

1. The function `Outer[ ]` can be used to generate operation tables for binary operations and many other things. For example, consider

        a = Range[0, 8]
        MatrixForm[Outer[Binomial, a, a]]

   Such a matrix is called lower triangular. What is the lower triangular part of this matrix usually referred to as? How would one use `Outer[ ]` to generate the operation table for the logical operator `And[ ]`?

4.2 Norms and Sensitivity

4.2.1 Vector and matrix norms

Suppose there are two approximations x_{I} and x_{II} to a set of values x where

$$x_{\mathrm{I}} = \begin{bmatrix} 1.01 \\ 1.01 \\ 1.01 \end{bmatrix}, \quad x_{\mathrm{II}} = \begin{bmatrix} 1 \\ 1.02 \\ 1 \end{bmatrix}, \quad \text{and} \quad x = \begin{bmatrix} 1 \\ 1 \\ 1 \end{bmatrix}.$$

Which is the better approximation? Which error is smaller,

$$\begin{bmatrix} 0.01 \\ 0.01 \\ 0.01 \end{bmatrix} \quad \text{or} \quad \begin{bmatrix} 0 \\ 0.02 \\ 0 \end{bmatrix} \; ?$$

This can be decided if we have a single number to measure the size of a vector of errors. Such a value is available with a **norm**. A norm is a mapping that assigns to each vector a nonnegative real number. It generalizes the notion of absolute value. For example, Euclidean length

$$\left(\sum_{i=1}^{n} |x_i|^2 \right)^{1/2}$$

is a norm. Our vectors may have no physical significance; they are merely ordered sets of numbers. Therefore, we need not feel constrained to use the Euclidean norm. More convenient computationally is the **maximum norm**:

$$\|x\| \overset{\text{def}}{=} \max_{1 \le i \le n} |x_i|$$

The symbol "∥ ∥" is used in this chapter exclusively for the maximum norm. Also convenient is the *1-norm*

$$\sum_{i=1}^{n} |x_i|$$

used in some programs for solving linear equations. Returning to the example of the two errors, we have

$$\left\| \begin{bmatrix} 0.01 \\ 0.01 \\ 0.01 \end{bmatrix} \right\| = 0.01, \qquad \left\| \begin{bmatrix} 0 \\ 0.02 \\ 0 \end{bmatrix} \right\| = 0.02,$$

so in the maximum norm x_{I} is the better approximation. (In the 1-norm it would be x_{II}.) Because our vector might be artificial, it may not be meaningful to compare magnitudes of its components and take the maximum. Therefore, we assume that the variables $x_1, x_2, \ldots, x_n$ have been appropriately scaled so that meaningful comparisons are possible and that $\|x_{\mathrm{I}} - x\| \ll \|x_{\mathrm{II}} - x\|$ implies that x_{I} is better than x_{II}.

Norms can also be defined for matrices. For an $n \times n$ matrix the maximum norm is given by

$$\|A\| = \max_{1 \le i \le n} \sum_{j=1}^{n} |a_{ij}|.$$

An example is

$$\left\| \begin{bmatrix} 1 & -2 \\ 0 & 1 \end{bmatrix} \right\| = \max\left\{ |1| + |-2|, |0| + |1| \right\} = \max\left\{ 3, 1 \right\} = 3.$$

As another example consider a **diagonal matrix**

$$D = \text{diag}\,(d_{11}, d_{22}, \ldots, d_{nn}) \overset{\text{def}}{=} \begin{bmatrix} d_{11} & & & 0 \\ & d_{22} & & \\ 0 & & \ddots & \\ & & & d_{nn} \end{bmatrix}.$$

A short calculation shows that

$$\|D\| = \max\,\{|d_{11}|, |d_{22}|, \ldots, |d_{nn}|\}.$$

The Euclidean norm and the 1-norm are also defined for a matrix. The motivation for the definitions of matrix norms is given in Section 4.2.4.

4.2.2 The residual and the error

We have introduced a norm as a single number to measure the accuracy of a set of approximate solution values $\hat{x}$ for a set of equations. However, the situation is not that simple. There are many reasons for solving equations. We consider two possibilities.

For some applications we desire the *residuals* $r \overset{\text{def}}{=} b - A\hat{x}$ to be small, e.g., $\|r\| \leq eps$, and the size of the errors $e \overset{\text{def}}{=} \hat{x} - x$ is of no consequence. For example, the problem of determining the coefficients of a polynomial $p(x) = c_0 + c_1 x + \cdots + c_n x^n$ that satisfy $p(x_0) = y_0$, $p(x_1) = y_1$, $\ldots$, $p(x_n) = y_n$ for given data x_i, y_i can be written as a linear system

$$\begin{bmatrix} 1 & x_0 & \cdots & x_0^n \\ 1 & x_1 & \cdots & x_1^n \\ \vdots & \vdots & & \vdots \\ 1 & x_n & \cdots & x_n^n \end{bmatrix} \begin{bmatrix} c_0 \\ c_1 \\ \vdots \\ c_n \end{bmatrix} = \begin{bmatrix} y_0 \\ y_1 \\ \vdots \\ y_n \end{bmatrix}.$$

We are not concerned about the accuracy of the computed coefficients $\hat{c}_j$ as long as the polynomial

$$\hat{c}_0 + \hat{c}_1 x + \cdots + \hat{c}_n x^n$$

comes sufficiently close to fitting the data. See Figure 4.5. For instance, we might want residuals not to exceed 10^{-3} in magnitude and not care about the coefficients.

For most applications we desire small errors $e = \hat{x} - x$ rather than small residuals. For example, in determining the currents in an electric circuit, it is the accuracy of the currents that is important and not how accurately we satisfy Ohm's law. Moreover, we may be interested in only some of the unknowns. Another example is that of determining forces in a framed structure, where it is the accuracy of the forces that matters—not the equilibrium of forces.

Figure 4.5: Residuals in polynomial interpolation

The relative error can be defined to be $\|e\|/\|x\|$ and the relative residual to be $\|r\|/\|b\|$. The latter is sensible for the example of polynomial interpolation. These two measures of accuracy might not be similar; they could be very different. Nonetheless, they are related via A: $r = b - A\hat{x} = A(x - \hat{x}) = -Ae$.

4.2.3 Sensitivity for systems of linear equations

The coefficient matrix and right-hand-side vector of a linear system are seldom known exactly because of measurement errors or errors made in calculating them. The effect of such errors depends on the sensitivity of the solution to changes in A or b. The relationship between the true values is

$$x = A^{-1}b.$$

This defines a mapping from $n^2 + n$ inputs to n outputs. If data errors ΔA and Δb are introduced, this causes errors Δx given by

$$x + \Delta x = (A + \Delta A)^{-1}(b + \Delta b).$$

What can be said about the size of the errors in the solution? The answer to this also has important implications for the roundoff error incurred in solving the linear system. It is known that roundoff errors can often be interpreted in terms of small changes to the original data of the problem.

This is the question: How does the relative error $\|\Delta x\|/\|x\|$ in the solution compare to the relative errors $\|\Delta A\|/\|A\|$ in the coefficient matrix and $\|\Delta b\|/\|b\|$ in the right-hand-side vector? The answer is that

$$\frac{\|\Delta x\|}{\|x\|} \leq \frac{1}{1-\varepsilon} \cdot \text{cond}(A) \cdot \left(\frac{\|\Delta A\|}{\|A\|} + \frac{\|\Delta b\|}{\|b\|} \right)$$

where $\varepsilon \overset{\text{def}}{=} \text{cond}(A)\|\Delta A\|/\|A\|$ is assumed to be < 1 and the **condition number** of a square matrix A is defined as

$$\text{cond}(A) \overset{\text{def}}{=} \begin{cases} \|A\| \, \|A^{-1}\|, & A \text{ nonsingular,} \\ +\infty, & A \text{ singular.} \end{cases}$$

The factor $\text{cond}(A)$ in this bound cannot be improved.[1] Hence, $\text{cond}(A)$ is approximately the maximum magnification factor for small relative errors in A and $\boldsymbol{b}$, and it is a measure of the sensitivity for the solution of a linear system. It is shown in Section 4.2.4 that a condition number is ≥ 1 and that $\text{cond}(I) = 1$. If the condition number of a matrix is much greater than 1, then the problem is ill-conditioned. Recall the discussion of Section 1.5.

Example 4.1 Suppose $\|\Delta A\|/\|A\| \approx 10^{-16}$ due to errors in computing A in double precision and that $\text{cond}(A) \approx 10^{11}$. Then the bound above indicates that

$$\frac{\|\Delta \boldsymbol{x}\|}{\|\boldsymbol{x}\|} \lesssim 10^{11} \cdot 10^{-16} = 10^{-5},$$

corresponding to five digits of accuracy.

Example 4.2 Let

$$A = \begin{bmatrix} 4.1 & 2.8 \\ 9.7 & 6.6 \end{bmatrix}.$$

Then

$$A^{-1} = \begin{bmatrix} -66 & 28 \\ 97 & -41 \end{bmatrix}, \quad \|A\| = 16.3, \quad \|A^{-1}\| = 138, \quad \text{and} \quad \text{cond}(A) = 2249.4.$$

Also let

$$\boldsymbol{b} = \begin{bmatrix} 6.9 \\ 16.3 \end{bmatrix}, \quad \boldsymbol{b} + \Delta \boldsymbol{b} = \begin{bmatrix} 6.91 \\ 16.29 \end{bmatrix}.$$

Then

$$\Delta \boldsymbol{b} = \begin{bmatrix} 0.01 \\ -0.01 \end{bmatrix} \quad \text{and} \quad \frac{\|\Delta \boldsymbol{b}\|}{\|\boldsymbol{b}\|} = \frac{0.01}{16.3} \approx 0.06\%.$$

Consequently,

$$\frac{\|\Delta \boldsymbol{x}\|}{\|\boldsymbol{x}\|} \leq (2249.4)\left(\frac{0.01}{16.3}\right) \approx 138\%.$$

Actually,

$$\boldsymbol{x} = \begin{bmatrix} 1 \\ 1 \end{bmatrix}, \quad \boldsymbol{x} + \Delta \boldsymbol{x} = \begin{bmatrix} 0.06 \\ 2.38 \end{bmatrix}, \quad \Delta \boldsymbol{x} = \begin{bmatrix} -0.94 \\ 1.38 \end{bmatrix},$$

and

$$\frac{\|\Delta \boldsymbol{x}\|}{\|\boldsymbol{x}\|} = \frac{1.38}{1} = 1.38,$$

showing that the error bound is attained for this example. But that is not typical; normally $\|\Delta \boldsymbol{x}\|/\|\boldsymbol{x}\|$ is smaller than the bound.

---

[1] In the sense that it cannot be replaced by some smaller quantity that depends only on A and $\boldsymbol{b}$.

The condition number has another, nice interpretation, which we give without proof (cf. Exercise 6). The reciprocal $1/\text{cond}(A)$ measures in a relative sense *how close A is to being singular*. More precisely, let $\tilde{A}$ be a singular matrix that is closest (in norm) to A. Then

$$\frac{\|\tilde{A} - A\|}{\|A\|} = \frac{1}{\text{cond}(A)}.$$

For example, a condition number of 100 means that the matrix is within 1% of being singular. The determinant is not a good measure of whether a matrix is relatively close to being singular. If an $n \times n$ matrix A is multiplied by a scalar α, its condition number is unchanged but its determinant is multiplied by a factor α^n.

Section 1.3 mentions LAPACK, which is a set of high-quality, public-domain Fortran subroutines for doing linear-algebra computations. In LAPACK is a routine `SGECON` that computes a value `RCOND` that estimates $1/\text{cond}(A)$. It is recommended[2] that

$$(1. \ + \ \text{RCOND}) \ \ .\text{EQ.} \ \ 1.$$

be executed to test whether the matrix is within a roundoff error (in each element) of being singular (where ".`EQ`." is Fortran for "="). This test succeeds only if $1/\text{cond}(A) \leq u$, implying that a relative change $\leq u$ in A (using the maximum norm) can make A singular. For example,

$$\begin{bmatrix} 1.000 & 0.3333 \\ 0.3333 & 0.1111 \end{bmatrix} = \begin{bmatrix} 1 & \frac{1}{3} \\ \frac{1}{3} & \frac{1}{9} \end{bmatrix} + \text{a roundoff error.}$$
$$\quad\ \text{nonsingular} \qquad\qquad \text{singular}$$

Ill-conditioning has a geometric interpretation that can be easily visualized for $n = 2$. Figure 4.6 shows two straight lines, each representing an equation. The point at which these two lines intersect is the solution. If these two lines are nearly parallel, then the location of the solution point will be sensitive to slight changes in the lines. A small change in one of the equations could cause a much greater change in the solution. (A slightly different way of stating this is that the uncertainty in the problem data imparts thickness to the lines; and if they are nearly parallel, the set of possible solutions formed by intersecting the two lines is highly elongated.) For $n = 3$ the geometric interpretation is that of three planes at least two of which are nearly parallel.

If instead of considering the relative error, we consider the relative residual $\|\boldsymbol{b} - A(\boldsymbol{x} + \Delta\boldsymbol{x})\|/\|\boldsymbol{b}\|$, it happens that relative changes ΔA in A are again amplified by as much as the

---

[2]On page 1.1 of the *LINPACK Users' Guide*, J.J. Dongarra, J.R. Bunch, C.B. Moler, and G.W. Stewart, SIAM, 1979.

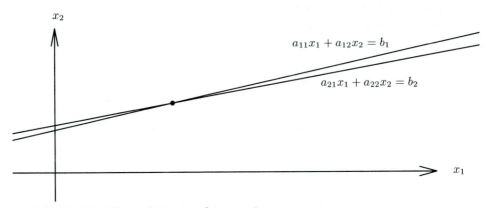

Figure 4.6: Ill-conditioning for $n = 2$

condition number of A but that changes Δb in b are not amplified at all. So it is always important to minimize the errors in forming an ill-conditioned matrix.

Our definition of relative error for vectors and matrices is not sacrosanct. In defining the relative error for the solution x we could instead compute the relative error for each component and then take the maximum of these as the relative error of the vector: $\max_i(|\Delta x_i|/|x_i|)$ instead of $(\max_i |\Delta x_i|)/(\max_i |x_i|)$. Or some other definition of relative error may be most appropriate. It will depend on the situation. Our use of norms to define relative error is the simplest approach.

⋆ 4.2.4 More about norms and condition numbers

The maximum norm, and (by definition) any other norm, has certain basic properties:

> fundamental vector norm properties
> $$x \neq 0 \;\Rightarrow\; \|x\| > 0,$$
> $$\|cx\| = |c|\,\|x\|,$$
> $$\|x + y\| \leq \|x\| + \|y\|.$$

An immediate consequence is that $\|0\| = 0$. (Why?) The first of the three properties is sometimes called *positivity*. The third is the well-known **triangle inequality**.

The norm of a matrix A is defined to be the maximum effect that multiplication of a vector by A can have on the norm of the vector. More precisely,

$$\|A\| \stackrel{\text{def}}{=} \max_{x \neq 0} \frac{\|Ax\|}{\|x\|}.$$

(It can be shown that there is an x for which the ratio is maximized.) For example, to get the norm of

$$A = \begin{bmatrix} 1 & 2 \\ 0 & 1 \end{bmatrix}$$

we can imagine an enormous, indeed infinite, table: The norm is the largest of all the values in the last column.

x	Ax	$\|x\|$	$\|Ax\|$	$\|Ax\|/\|x\|$
$\begin{bmatrix} 0 \\ 1 \end{bmatrix}$	$\begin{bmatrix} 2 \\ 1 \end{bmatrix}$	1	2	2
$\begin{bmatrix} 0 \\ 2 \end{bmatrix}$	$\begin{bmatrix} 4 \\ 2 \end{bmatrix}$	2	4	2
$\begin{bmatrix} 1 \\ -1 \end{bmatrix}$	$\begin{bmatrix} -1 \\ -1 \end{bmatrix}$	1	1	1
$\begin{bmatrix} 1 \\ 2 \end{bmatrix}$	$\begin{bmatrix} 5 \\ 2 \end{bmatrix}$	2	5	5/2
$\vdots$	$\vdots$	$\vdots$	$\vdots$	$\vdots$

$$\text{max} = 3$$

Fortunately, for the maximum norm there is an easy-to-compute formula. For any $n \times n$ matrix it can be shown that

$$\|A\| = \max_{1 \le i \le n} \sum_{j=1}^{n} |a_{ij}|,$$

the formula given previously.

The following two properties of the matrix norm are immediate consequences of its definition:

$$\|Ax\| \;\le\; \|A\|\,\|x\|,$$

$$\forall A \;\; \exists x \ne \mathbf{0}, \;\; \|Ax\| \;=\; \|A\|\,\|x\|.$$

Other basic properties are

$$A \ne 0 \Rightarrow \|A\| > 0,$$

$$\|cA\| = |c|\,\|A\|,$$

$$\|A + B\| \le \|A\| + \|B\|,$$

$$\|AB\| \le \|A\|\,\|B\|.$$

The first three of these four are properties possessed by vector norms. The fourth one is a triangle inequality for multiplication. Recall the example where $A \ne 0$ and $B \ne 0$ and yet

$AB = 0$. Note that in generalizing from absolute values of scalars to norms of matrices we lose the property $|\alpha\beta| = |\alpha|\,|\beta|$.

We defined the norm of a matrix to be the maximum factor by which it can magnify the norm of a vector. We can ask what the minimum factor is. The answer is given by the following theorem, which we do not prove.

Theorem 4.1

$$\min_{x \neq 0} \frac{\|Ax\|}{\|x\|} = \begin{cases} \|A^{-1}\|^{-1}, & A \ \textit{nonsingular,} \\ 0, & A \ \textit{singular.} \end{cases}$$

The effect that multiplication of vectors by a given matrix can have on their norms can range from none to great. The degree of variability turns out to play an important role in sensitivity analysis. The ratio

$$\frac{\max_{x \neq 0} \frac{\|Ax\|}{\|x\|}}{\min_{x \neq 0} \frac{\|Ax\|}{\|x\|}} = \begin{cases} \|A\|\,\|A^{-1}\|, & A \ \text{nonsingular,} \\ +\infty, & A \ \text{singular,} \end{cases}$$

which is the condition number $\text{cond}(A)$ of the matrix A.

The ratio given for $\text{cond}(A)$ implies that a condition number is ≥ 1. This is also easy to show from the second expression:

$$\text{cond}(A) \geq \|AA^{-1}\| = \|I\| = 1.$$

Exercises

1. Let

$$A = \begin{bmatrix} 1.0 & 0.99 \\ -2.0 & -1.1 \end{bmatrix}, \quad b = \begin{bmatrix} 1.1 \\ -2.8 \end{bmatrix}.$$

   Assume that $A = fl(M)$ and $b = fl(c)$ where fl means two-decimal-digit rounding. Determine tight upper and lower bounds on the residuals $r = c - M\hat{x}$ where

$$\hat{x} = \begin{bmatrix} 2.0 \\ -1.0 \end{bmatrix},$$

   and thus determine whether or not it is conceivable that $\hat{x}$ exactly solves $My = c$.

2. Calculate the condition number of

$$\begin{bmatrix} 1 & 0.3333 \\ 0.3333 & 0.1111 \end{bmatrix}.$$

3. Let $x = A^{-1}b$ where $b = [10 \quad 25 \quad -40 \quad 25]^{\mathrm{T}}$ and $\mathrm{cond}(A) = 60$ in the maximum norm. If we make a change $\Delta b = [0.04 \quad -0.05 \quad 0.16 \quad -0.05]^{\mathrm{T}}$ in b, what can we say about the corresponding change Δx in x?

4. Let $\tilde{x}$ solve the system $A\tilde{x} = \tilde{b}$ where $\tilde{b}$ has components $10, 40, -2,$ and 6. Suppose the first two components are in error by as much as 0.01% and the last two are in error by as much at 0.05%. Also, suppose that A has maximum norm ≤ 3 and A^{-1} has maximum norm ≤ 40. Obtain a good bound on the relative error $\|\tilde{x} - x\|/\|x\|$ where x solves the system with the correct value b on the right-hand side.

5. Suppose that it is known that $Ax_1 = y_1$ and $Ax_2 = y_2$ where

$$x_1 = \begin{bmatrix} 1 \\ -1 \\ 0 \\ 2 \end{bmatrix}, \quad y_1 = \begin{bmatrix} 0 \\ 1 \\ 7 \\ -4 \end{bmatrix}, \quad x_2 = \begin{bmatrix} 3 \\ 4 \\ 0 \\ -1 \end{bmatrix}, \quad y_2 = \begin{bmatrix} 5 \\ 4 \\ -5 \\ 2 \end{bmatrix}.$$

   (a) Show that $\|A\| \geq 7/2$.

   (b) Show that $\|A^{-1}\| \geq 4/5$.

   (c) What can we say about $\mathrm{cond}(A)$?

6. Let A be any $n \times n$ nonsingular matrix, and let k be such that

$$|\alpha_{k1}| + |\alpha_{k2}| + \cdots + |\alpha_{kn}| = \|A^{-1}\|$$

   where α_{ij} is the $(i, \ j)$th element of A^{-1}. Define a vector s of dimension n by $s_i = \mathrm{sign}\,\alpha_{ki}$, and define

$$\tilde{A} = A - \frac{s e_k^{\mathrm{T}}}{\|A^{-1}\|}.$$

   (a) By considering the product $\tilde{A}\,A^{-1}s$ show that $\tilde{A}$ is singular.

   (b) Show that $\|\tilde{A} - A\|/\|A\| = 1/\mathrm{cond}(A)$.

⋆7. Using only the fundamental vector norm properties, prove that $\|u+v\| \geq |\,\|u\| - \|v\|\,|$.

⋆8. Give rigorous proofs of the following two assertions:

   (a) For any nonsingular matrix B and any vector y,

$$\|By\| \geq \|B^{-1}\|^{-1}\,\|y\|.$$

   (b) For any nonsingular matrix B there exists a vector y (depending on B) such that

$$\|By\| = \|B^{-1}\|^{-1}\,\|y\|.$$

★9. Suppose that we can prove that

$$\frac{\|\hat{x} - x\|}{\|\hat{x}\|} \leq \mathrm{cond}(A)\ \phi(n)\beta^{-t} < 1$$

where $\phi(n)$ denotes some polynomial in n. Give a step-by-step proof that the relative error

$$\frac{\|\hat{x} - x\|}{\|x\|} \leq \frac{\mathrm{cond}(A)\ \phi(n)\beta^{-t}}{1 - \mathrm{cond}(A)\ \phi(n)\beta^{-t}}.$$

Hint: Express $\|\hat{x}\|$ in terms of $\|\hat{x} - x\|$ and $\|x\|$.

★10. For the maximum norm prove that

$$\|Ax\| \ \leq\ \left(\max_{1 \leq i \leq n} \sum_{j=1}^{n} |a_{ij}| \right) \|x\|.$$

Do not use any facts about *matrix* norms.

★11. (a) For

$$A = \begin{bmatrix} 1 & -5 \\ -2 & 3 \end{bmatrix}$$

show there exists $x \neq 0$ such that $\|Ax\| = \|A\|\ \|x\|$.

(b) Repeat part (a) for an arbitrary 2×2 matrix A.

(c) Repeat part (a) for an arbitrary $n \times n$ matrix A.

★12. Prove Theorem 4.1. Treat the two cases separately. For the first case do a change of variable.

Mathematica notes

It is quite easy to define functions in *Mathematica* that do different things for different types of arguments. For example, if we define a function `norm[ ]` that is supposed to work with both vectors and matrices, we need it to do different things for each. There are several ways to control the checking of rule applicability so that the appropriate rule will be used with any particular type of argument. The preferred way, if it can be made to work, is to use a restricted pattern.

Define a rule for the norm of a vector.   `In[1]:= norm[v_?VectorQ] := Max[Abs[v]]`

It gives the norm of the vector.   `In[2]:= norm[{1,-3,2}]`
                                             `Out[2]= 3`

The rule does not apply to matrices. $In[3]:=$ `norm[{{1,2},{3,4}}]`

$Out[3]=$ `norm[{{1, 2}, {3, 4}}]`

Note that if we had used the pattern `v_List`, the rule would have applied to both vectors and matrices as well as to other expressions with a head of `List`.

This rule also applies to vectors with $In[4]:=$ `norm[{a,b}]`
symbolic elements.

$Out[4]=$ `Max[{Abs[a], Abs[b]}]`

The predicate function `VectorQ[ ]` allows a second argument. If the expression in question is indeed a vector, the second argument is applied as a predicate function to each of the elements of the vector.

This is `True` because `{1,2,3}` is a vector $In[5]:=$ `VectorQ[{1,2,3}, NumberQ]`
and each of its elements is a number.

$Out[5]=$ `True`

This is `False` because one of the elements $In[6]:=$ `VectorQ[{1,2,3,x}, NumberQ]`
of the vector is not a number.

$Out[6]=$ `False`

Clear the old definition of `norm[ ]`. $In[7]:=$ `Clear[norm]`

The predicate `VectorQ[#, NumberQ]&` is a $In[8]:=$ `norm[v_?(VectorQ[#, NumberQ]&)]` `:= Max[Abs[v]]`
pure function that tests whether the formal
argument `v` is a vector of numbers.

It works for vectors of numbers. $In[9]:=$ `norm[{1, -2}]`

$Out[9]=$ `2`

If `v` had evaluated to a vector of numbers, $In[10]:=$ `norm[v]`
this would have evaluated its norm. Since `v`
evaluated to a symbol, `norm[ ]` did nothing $Out[10]=$ `norm[v]`
with it.

Computer problem

1. This problem illustrates the use of high-precision numbers to compute the errors and the residuals that arise from the use of low-precision numbers. We assume that we have solved the matrix equation $Ax = b$ for x. We have a representing A, x representing an approximation to the true solution x, and b representing b. It is assumed that a, x, and b are of the appropriate dimensions and that each is made up of machine numbers.

(a) Make another rule for `norm[ ]` with another restricted pattern so that it finds the (maximum) norm of matrices of numbers. Test it on the vector `v = {-3.`, `-1., 0., 2.}` and the matrix `m = {{3., -4.}, {1., 5.}}`.

(b) Define a function `relres[a_, x_, b_]` that computes the "normwise" relative residual (as given in this section) for `x` as a solution to `a x == b`. The very first thing you should do is to wrap `dble` (given on page 57) around the three arrays so that your computations are performed in doubled precision. Our application of this procedure will be to calculate the effects of machine-precision roundoff errors. We will not see those effects unless we do our calculation in higher precision. (Your `relres` function should not, however, change the values of its arguments.)

(c) Define a function `relerr[a_, x_, b_]` that computes the relative error in the approximation `x`. The very first thing you should do is to wrap `dble` around the three arrays so that your computations are performed in doubled precision. (Your `relerr` function should not, however, change the values of its arguments.) Use `LinearSolve[ ]`, not `Inverse[ ]`, for this part.

(d) Define a function `cond[a_]` for computing the condition number of a square matrix. You may use `Inverse` for this part.

(e) Define a matrix `a` having machine-precision values $a_{ij} = (5. + j)^{i-1}$, $1 \le i, j \le 7$, and a vector `b` having machine-precision values $b_i = (12.^i - 6.^i)/i$, $1 \le i \le 7$. Use `LinearSolve` to determine the solution of `a x == b`. (This problem arises from the method of undetermined coefficients applied to determining the weights of a seven-point closed Newton-Cotes formula for the interval $[6, 12]$, a topic discussed in Chapter 7.)

(f) Evaluate

```
relerr[a, x, b]
relres[a, x, b]
0.5 $MachineEpsilon cond[a]
```

Note: `$MachineEpsilon` is twice the unit roundoff error.

4.3 Gaussian Elimination

Recall that the general form of a system of linear equations is

$$
\begin{aligned}
a_{11}x_1 + a_{12}x_2 + \cdots + a_{1n}x_n &= b_1, \\
a_{21}x_1 + a_{22}x_2 + \cdots + a_{2n}x_n &= b_2, \\
\vdots \qquad \vdots \qquad\quad \vdots \qquad\; \vdots \\
a_{n1}x_1 + a_{n2}x_2 + \cdots + a_{nn}x_n &= b_n.
\end{aligned}
$$

4.3.1   How to solve linear systems

A method that many people learn in mathematics classes is *Cramer's rule*, which expresses each unknown as a ratio of two $n \times n$ determinants. This method is good for the theoretical insights it provides. It is also good for 2×2 and perhaps 3×3 systems, which often occur in geometric calculations. However, because the number of operations is of order $n!$, it is utterly impractical as a general method.

Writing the system as $A\boldsymbol{x} = \boldsymbol{b}$ suggests computing $\boldsymbol{x} = (A$ inverse) times $\boldsymbol{b}$. However, computing the inverse happens to require *three* times as many arithmetic operations as the most practical method for solving the linear system, and it is less accurate. If the coefficient matrix has many zero elements, the penalty can be much more severe. It is one of the really important messages of this chapter that one should

almost
NEVER COMPUTE AN INVERSE.

This is an example of an important principle in mathematical computing: it is often not a good idea to translate mathematical formulas literally into computer code. In that sense the name FORmula TRANslator is slightly misguided. It is common for applications people, notably physicists, to speak of "inverting matrices," but often they use this language to avoid the more clumsy "solving systems of linear equations," to which numerical analysts adhere. There is an example[3] that makes this point quite nicely. To solve the equation $7x = 21$, we compute

$$x = \frac{21}{7} = 3;$$

we do not compute

$$x = 7^{-1} \times 21 = 0.1429 \times 21 = 3.001.$$

The latter requires more work and introduces more roundoff errors.

As suggested by the toy example, the way to solve a system of linear equations is to

compute $A^{-1}\boldsymbol{b}$ as A divided into $\boldsymbol{b}$.

In other words, "divide" the vector $\boldsymbol{b}$ by the matrix A. The number of operations and the number of roundoff errors are fewer. A good method for "matrix division" is the main subject of this chapter. One method we will not say much about is **Gauss-Jordan**. This is typically taught in a linear algebra course as a practical method for solving linear systems. The method works by augmenting the coefficient matrix with the right-hand-side vector and then applying row operations to the augmented matrix so as to transform it column by column

---

[3]From Forsythe, Malcolm, and Moler (1977).

to an augmented identity matrix, whose last column is then the desired solution vector. Schematically,

$$\begin{bmatrix} a & a & a & | & b \\ a & a & a & | & b \\ a & a & a & | & b \end{bmatrix} \rightarrow \begin{bmatrix} 1 & a' & a' & | & b' \\ 0 & a' & a' & | & b' \\ 0 & a' & a' & | & b' \end{bmatrix} \rightarrow \begin{bmatrix} 1 & 0 & a'' & | & b'' \\ 0 & 1 & a'' & | & b'' \\ 0 & 0 & a'' & | & b'' \end{bmatrix} \rightarrow \begin{bmatrix} 1 & 0 & 0 & | & b''' \\ 0 & 1 & 0 & | & b''' \\ 0 & 0 & 1 & | & b''' \end{bmatrix}$$

where the lowercase letters are generic names for array elements. This method is elegant and relatively simple, but it requires 50% more floating-point operations and is less accurate than necessary. However, Gauss-Jordan has found favor for use on parallel computers, like the Connection Machine CM-2, because the simplicity of the method permits significantly more operations to be performed in parallel. The method we study for doing matrix division is **Gaussian elimination**.

4.3.2 Forward elimination and back substitution

We shall review Gaussian elimination, which you probably learned in high school, by doing the simple example

$$
\begin{array}{rrrrrrll}
2x & + & y & + & z & = & 7 & \{1\} \\
4x & + & 4y & + & 3z & = & 21 & \{2\} \\
6x & + & 7y & + & 4z & = & 32 & \{3\}
\end{array}
$$

The first of two parts of Gaussian elimination is **forward elimination**. To save writing, we shall use matrix notation:

$$
\begin{bmatrix} 2 & 1 & 1 \\ \boxed{4} & 4 & 3 \\ \boxed{6} & 7 & 4 \end{bmatrix}
\begin{bmatrix} x \\ y \\ z \end{bmatrix}
=
\begin{bmatrix} 7 \\ 21 \\ 32 \end{bmatrix}
\qquad
\begin{array}{l} \{1\} \\ \{2\} \\ \{3\} \end{array}
$$

Giving names to the matrices and vectors, we write this as $Ax = b$. The idea is to use the first equation to eliminate the first variable x from Equations $\{2\}$ and $\{3\}$, thus introducing zeros where there are the two boxed entries. A multiple of the first equation is subtracted from the second, and another multiple of the first is subtracted from the third. These **multipliers** are calculated by dividing the boxed entries by the entry just above them, which produces the desired effect as shown below.

$$
\begin{array}{l} \{1\} \\ \{2\} - 2 \times \{1\} \\ \{3\} - 3 \times \{1\} \end{array}
\qquad
\begin{bmatrix} 2 & 1 & 1 \\ 0 & 2 & 1 \\ 0 & \boxed{4} & 1 \end{bmatrix}
\begin{bmatrix} x \\ y \\ z \end{bmatrix}
=
\begin{bmatrix} 7 \\ 7 \\ 11 \end{bmatrix}
\qquad
\begin{array}{l} \{1\} \\ \{2'\} \\ \{3'\} \end{array}
$$

We now have a system whose last two equations involve only the last two variables. The procedure is repeated for these two equations. We eliminate the boxed entry by subtracting some multiple of Equation $\{2'\}$ from $\{3'\}$, this multiple being the boxed entry divided by the entry just above it:

$$\begin{matrix} \{1\} \\ \{2'\} \\ \{3'\} - 2 \times \{2'\} \end{matrix} \quad \begin{bmatrix} 2 & 1 & 1 \\ 0 & 2 & 1 \\ 0 & 0 & -1 \end{bmatrix} \begin{bmatrix} x \\ y \\ z \end{bmatrix} = \begin{bmatrix} 7 \\ 7 \\ -3 \end{bmatrix}.$$

The final result is a system whose coefficient matrix has a special structure. Because all of its nonzero elements are either on its diagonal or above the diagonal, we say that the matrix is **upper triangular**. We denote the final result of forward elimination by

$$U\boldsymbol{x} = \boldsymbol{c}.$$

It is important to note the reversible nature of row operations. We can recover the original equations by performing the inverse of each row operation in reverse order. This means that the two systems are equivalent and have the same solution.

The second part of Gaussian elimination is **back substitution**. If we revert from matrix notation, the reduced upper triangular system is

$$\begin{aligned} 2x + y + z &= 7, \\ 2y + z &= 7, \\ -z &= -3. \end{aligned}$$

We solve the last equation for z,

$$z = (-3)/(-1) = 3$$

and substitute this value into the second equation, which we solve for y,

$$y = (7 - z)/2 = \cdots = 2,$$

and substitute both found values into the first equation, which we solve for x,

$$x = (7 - y - z)/2 = \cdots = 1.$$

The basic idea of Gaussian elimination is to reduce a large problem to a smaller problem that is of the same type as the larger problem—a system of n equations in n unknowns is reduced to $n - 1$ equations in $n - 1$ unknowns. Hence, it is most natural to express the algorithm recursively:

$$\textbf{procedure } SOLVE \left\{ \begin{aligned} a_{11}x_1 + \cdots + a_{1n}x_n &= b_1 \\ \vdots \qquad\qquad \vdots \quad &\ \ \vdots \\ a_{n1}x_1 + \cdots + a_{nn}x_n &= b_n; \end{aligned} \right.$$

begin
   if $n > 1$ **then**
      use 1st equation to eliminate x_1 from
       remaining equations and obtain

$$\left\{ \begin{array}{l} a_{11}x_1 + a_{12}x_2 + \cdots + a_{1n}x_n = b_1 \\ \qquad a'_{22}x_2 + \cdots + a'_{2n}x_n = b'_2 \\ \qquad \vdots \qquad\qquad \vdots \qquad \vdots \\ \qquad a'_{n2}x_2 + \cdots + a'_{nn}x_n = b'_n \ ; \end{array} \right.$$

$$SOLVE \left\{ \begin{array}{l} a'_{22}x_2 + \cdots + a'_{2n}x_n = b'_2 \\ \quad \vdots \qquad\qquad \vdots \qquad \vdots \\ a'_{n2}x_2 + \cdots + a'_{nn}x_n = b'_n \end{array} \right.$$

   end if;
    $x_1 = (b_1 - a_{12}x_2 - \cdots - a_{1n}x_n)/a_{11}$
end

Because of performance considerations, it is better to use a nonrecursive algorithm instead. Beginning with a system

$$A\boldsymbol{x} = \boldsymbol{b},$$

forward elimination is applied to reduce it to a system

$$U\boldsymbol{x} = \boldsymbol{c}$$

where U is upper triangular, and back substitution is used to obtain the solution $\boldsymbol{x}$. The reduction to upper triangular form is achieved column by column, as depicted in Figure 4.7 in terms of arrays labeled A and B.

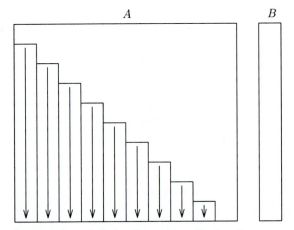

Figure 4.7: Arrays A and B in Gaussian elimination

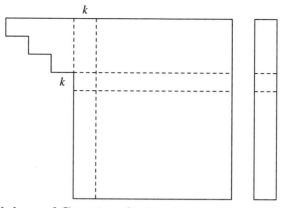

Figure 4.8: k loop of Gaussian elimination

At the highest level, forward elimination takes the form

for $k := 1$ **to** $n - 1$ **do**
    subtract multiples of kth equation from remaining equations to eliminate kth unknown
end for

The meaning of the k index is pictured in Figure 4.8. We can refine the body of the k loop by describing what happens for a particular value of k:

for $k := 1$ **to** $n - 1$ **do**
    for $i := k + 1$ **to** n **do**
        $m := A[i, k]/A[k, k]$; $(* \, A[i, k] - m * A[k, k] = 0 \, *)$
        subtract m times kth equation from ith equation
    end for
end for

The meaning of the i index is pictured in Figure 4.9. We can complete the refinement of the algorithm to get

for $k := 1$ **to** $n - 1$ **do**
    for $i := k + 1$ **to** n **do**
        $m := A[i, k]/A[k, k]$;
        for $j := k + 1$ **to** n **do**
            $A[i, j] := A[i, j] - m * A[k, j]$
        end for;
        $B[i] := B[i] - m * B[k]$
    end for
end for

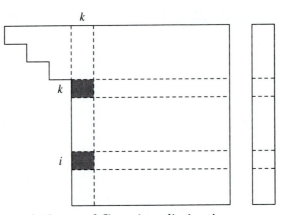

Figure 4.9: k and i loops of Gaussian elimination

which is a triply nested loop. The meaning of the j index is pictured in Figure 4.10. If we eliminate the temporary variable m from the algorithm and focus on what the kth step of forward elimination does to the coefficient matrix, we see striking symmetry and balance in the heart of the algorithm:

$$A[i,j] := A[i,j] - \frac{A[i,k] * A[k,j]}{A[k,k]}, \quad k+1 \leq i,j \leq n.$$

Let us do an operation count for forward elimination. A short calculation shows that the number of multiplications for each particular value of k is $(n-k)(n-k+1)$. These can be summed to get a total of

$$\underbrace{(n-1)n}_{k=1} + \underbrace{(n-2)(n-1)}_{k=2} + \cdots + \underbrace{1 \cdot 2}_{k=n-1} = \cdots = \frac{n^3 - n}{3} \approx \frac{n^3}{3}$$

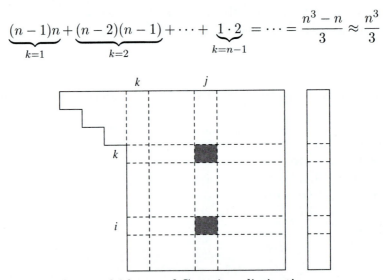

Figure 4.10: k, i, and j loops of Gaussian elimination

multiplications. There are an equal number of subtractions. The number of divisions is

$$(n - 1) + \cdots + 1 + 0 = \frac{n^2 - n}{2} \approx \frac{n^2}{2},$$

which is less significant. As an illustration suppose one innermost loop iteration takes 3 microseconds of CPU time. Then forward elimination for 100 equations in 100 unknowns would take 1 second of CPU time.

The result of forward elimination is an upper triangular matrix U, stored in part of the array $A[*, *]$, and a revised right-hand-side vector c, stored in $B[*]$, such that $U x = c$, or equivalently

$$
\begin{array}{rcl}
u_{11}x_1 \; + \; u_{12}x_2 \; + \; \cdots \; + \; u_{1n}x_n &=& c_1, \\
u_{22}x_2 \; + \; \cdots \; + \; u_{2n}x_n &=& c_2, \\
\ddots \qquad \vdots && \vdots \\
u_{nn}x_n &=& c_n.
\end{array}
$$

We now consider the second half of the algorithm. At the highest level, back substitution is

> **for** $i := n$ **down to** 1 **do** solve ith equation for $X[i]$ **end for**

Developing the details of the algorithm gives

> **for** $i := n$ **down to** 1 **do**
> $\quad X[i] := (B[i] - A[i, i+1] * X[i+1] - \cdots - A[i, n] * X[n])/A[i, i]$
> **end for**

and then

> **for** $i := n$ **down to** 1 **do**
> $\quad X[i] := B[i];$
> $\quad$ **for** $j := i+1$ **to** n **do**
> $\quad\quad X[i] := X[i] - A[i, j] * X[j]$
> $\quad$ **end for**;
> $\quad X[i] := X[i]/A[i, i]$
> **end for**

The number of multiplications is

$$\underbrace{0}_{i=n} + \underbrace{1}_{i=n-1} + \cdots + \underbrace{(n-1)}_{i=1} = \cdots = \frac{n^2 - n}{2} \approx \frac{n^2}{2}$$

and the number of divisions is n. Contrast this with the $n^3/3$ multiplications required by forward elimination. If each iteration of the inner loop requires 3 microseconds and there are 100 equations, the total time would be about 0.015 second, much less than the 1 second required by forward elimination. Thus we see—and this is important—that it is the *forward elimination that uses almost all the time* required to solve a linear system.

4.3.3 Mathematical pivoting

Can Gaussian elimination ever fail? (Let us put aside for now the limitations of floating-point arithmetic.) Since Gaussian elimination is nothing but arithmetic, the question boils down to: Can arithmetic ever fail? The answer to this is that failure occurs only if we attempt to divide by zero. In forward elimination, division occurs for each value of k when we form the multipliers $m := A[i,k]/A[k,k]$. We divide by the coefficient of the kth variable in the kth equation. This element remains unchanged for the rest of the elimination. Hence it is u_{kk}. See Figure 4.11. Also in back substitution, when solving for x_i, we divide by u_{ii} in the assignment $X[i] := X[i]/A[i,i]$. The value u_{kk}, which we call the kth **pivot**, is important to the success of the algorithm. Gaussian elimination fails if a pivot is zero.

A zero pivot does *not* mean that the problem does not have a unique solution. The system

$$\begin{bmatrix} 0 & 1 \\ 1 & 0 \end{bmatrix}\begin{bmatrix} x \\ y \end{bmatrix} = \begin{bmatrix} 2 \\ 3 \end{bmatrix}$$

has a zero pivot, but it has a unique solution.

There is a fix for this problem, called **mathematical pivoting**, that avoids zero pivots by interchanging rows. If one of the pivots would be zero, then the pivot row is interchanged

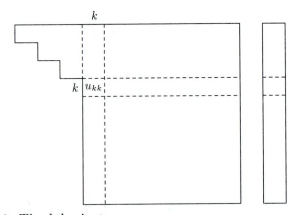

Figure 4.11: The kth pivot

with one of the remaining rows. This does not change the solution because it is merely the swapping of two equations. For example, one step of elimination applied to

$$\begin{bmatrix} 1 & 2 & 3 \\ 2 & 4 & -2 \\ 1 & 3 & -1 \end{bmatrix} \begin{bmatrix} x \\ y \\ z \end{bmatrix} = \begin{bmatrix} 13 \\ 3 \\ 2 \end{bmatrix}$$

yields

$$\begin{bmatrix} 1 & 2 & 3 \\ 0 & 0 & -8 \\ 0 & 1 & -4 \end{bmatrix} \begin{bmatrix} x \\ y \\ z \end{bmatrix} = \begin{bmatrix} 13 \\ -23 \\ -11 \end{bmatrix},$$

which has a zero in the (2, 2) pivot position. However, interchanging the second row with the third gives

$$\begin{bmatrix} 1 & 2 & 3 \\ 0 & 1 & -4 \\ 0 & 0 & -8 \end{bmatrix} \begin{bmatrix} x \\ y \\ z \end{bmatrix} = \begin{bmatrix} 13 \\ -11 \\ -23 \end{bmatrix},$$

for which elimination is complete. More generally, if the kth pivot would be zero, we interchange the kth row with one of the remaining rows whose kth coefficient is nonzero.

However, what if the kth coefficients of the remaining rows are all zero? See Figure 4.12. Then the matrix is singular, and either there is no solution or there are infinitely many solutions. (Nonetheless, reduction to upper triangular form can proceed and is useful for some applications, so this is done by LAPACK routines.)

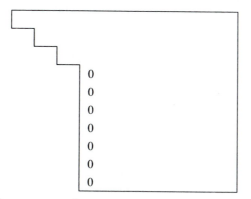

Figure 4.12: No nonzero pivot

Exercises

1. Solve $Ax = b$ by Gaussian elimination where

$$A = \begin{bmatrix} 6 & -2 & 2 & 4 \\ 12 & -8 & 6 & 10 \\ 3 & -13 & 9 & 3 \\ -6 & 4 & 1 & -18 \end{bmatrix}, \qquad b = \begin{bmatrix} 16 \\ 26 \\ -19 \\ -34 \end{bmatrix}.$$

2. Consider a *lower triangular* system of linear equations $Lx = b$, whose coefficients satisfy $l_{ij} = 0$ for $j > i$.

   (a) Write an algorithm for solving this system using *forward elimination*.

   (b) Write an algorithm for solving this system using *forward substitution*.

   Note: These algorithms differ in that the first processes the matrix column by column and the second row by row.

3. Write an algorithm for Gauss-Jordan to solve $Ax = b$. Obtain a precise count of the number of floating-point multiplications, divisions, and subtractions.

4. Consider a system of linear equations whose coefficients satisfy $a_{ij} = 0$ for $j < i - 1$. Modify the algorithm for forward elimination (with the triply nested loop) given on page 135 so that it takes advantage of the elements that are known to be zero. (This type of system is known as an upper Hessenberg system.)

5. If it takes 2 seconds for the computer to solve a system of 10 equations, about how long would it take to solve 50 equations?

6. Verify

$$(n - 1)n + (n - 2)(n - 1) + \cdots + 1 \cdot 2 = \frac{n^3 - n}{3}.$$

7. Using exact operations, how can one determine whether or not a matrix is singular?

8. Maybe in the case of Figure 4.12 if we had chosen different pivots, things would have worked out. Assuming exact arithmetic, either give an example of this or explain why it is impossible.

Mathematica notes

Many linear-algebra problems are very large, and it is important to be frugal with both memory and CPU time. In particular, one should never make a second copy of a matrix. For the same reason nearly all of the work of Gaussian elimination should be done within the memory allocated to the matrix. In *Mathematica*, copying an expression as in a = b is, in fact, just a matter of setting a pointer to the already existing data structure; no second copy is actually made. When individual elements are altered as in `a[[3, 4]] = 7`, some copying and resetting of pointers needs to occur so that `b[[3, 4]]` is not altered at the same time; destructive operations are not allowed in *Mathematica*. In a linear solver for large problems, one would, of course, be concerned about such things.

Computer problems

1. Implement a recursive algorithm for Gaussian elimination modeled after that described on page 133. There should be parameters `a` and `b` where `a` is the matrix of coefficients and `b` is the right-hand-side vector. *Important*: Normally in *Mathematica* one cannot assign a value to a parameter of a function within the definition of that function. Instead of overwriting `a` and `b`, it is recommended that you copy them into local variables and alter the copies as needed. The algorithm should return the value of $a^{-1}b$.

   There are many ways of doing this problem. You can do it without loops by using the *Mathematica* objects `Module`, `Length`, `Range`, `Outer[Times, ..., ...]`, ".", and `Prepend`.

   Execute your solver on the example

$$\begin{aligned} 3x + 5y - z &= 10, \\ 7x - 2y + 3z &= 12, \\ x + 5y - 4z &= -1. \end{aligned}$$

2. Do a *Mathematica* implementation `ge` of the algorithm for Gaussian elimination given on page 135. The procedure should have as arguments `a` and `b` and should return the solution vector `x` as its value. To test your routine, define `a` to be some arbitrary nonsingular 3×3 matrix and `b` to be some arbitrary three-element vector (you might use `Table[Random[ ], ...]`), and compare your answer with that obtained with `LinearSolve[a, b]`. *Important*: Normally in *Mathematica* one cannot assign a value to a parameter of a function within the definition of that function. Instead of overwriting `a` and `b`, it is recommended that you copy them into local variables and alter the copies as needed.

3. Set up a system of linear equations (that is, assemble `a` and `b`) for the problem described below. Use `Reals` for the values. Consider a 7×7 square grid of points arranged and labeled as follows:

```
      +   +   +   +   +
  +   1   2   3   4   5   +
  +   6   7   8   9  10   +
  +  11  12  13  14  15   +
  +  16  17  18  19  20   +
  +  21  22  23  24  25   +
      +   +   +   +   +
```

Assume that temperatures are given at unlabeled points denoted by +'s as follows: 100.0 along the top, 50.0 along the right side, and 0.0 elsewhere. The temperature at a point labeled with a number is unknown but is assumed to be the average of temperatures at the four nearest neighbors. In other words there are 25 unknown temperatures, and for each unknown temperature there is an equation that says that that temperature is the average of four other temperatures, some or all of which are also unknown. (Suggestion: Initialize the matrix to zero. For each label n put five entries into the nth row of the matrix and/or right-hand-side vector: one for the grid point itself and one for each of its four neighbors. To detect when n is a point adjacent to the left or right boundary, use Mod[n, 5].) After you assemble your 25×25 matrix and your 25-element right-hand-side vector, do the following: Print the first seven rows and columns of the matrix using MatrixForm[ ], and print the first seven right-hand-side entries.

4. Apply ge from Problem 2 to the equations in Problem 3 and get a Timing. Also get a Timing for LinearSolve. Print the 25 solution values as a 5×5 array using Partition[...,5] and MatrixForm.

4.4 Partial Pivoting (and Scaling)

4.4.1 Partial pivoting

With exact arithmetic mathematical pivoting would be enough. However, floating-point arithmetic introduces roundoff error and the situation is different. Let us consider what might go wrong. Intuition suggests that if a zero pivot is fatal, one that is approximately zero may be dangerous. Although the reasoning is questionable, the conclusion is correct. For example, suppose we are using four-digit rounded arithmetic. For the system

$$10000. \begin{bmatrix} 0.0002000 & 2.000 \\ 2.000 & 2.000 \end{bmatrix} \begin{bmatrix} x \\ y \end{bmatrix} = \begin{bmatrix} 2.000 \\ 4.000 \end{bmatrix}$$

we would use as a multiplier the number shown to the left of it. Elimination introduces a couple of *relatively* small roundoff errors resulting in

$$\begin{bmatrix} 0.0002000 & 2.000 \\ 0 & -20000. \end{bmatrix} \begin{bmatrix} \hat{x} \\ \hat{y} \end{bmatrix} = \begin{bmatrix} 2.000 \\ -20000. \end{bmatrix}.$$

Back substitution then gives

$$\hat{y} = (-20000.)/(-20000.) = 1.000,$$
$$\hat{x} = (2.000 - 2.000 \times \hat{y})/0.0002000 = 0.$$

This does not satisfy the original equations very well. The true solution is

$$y = 0.99989998\cdots,$$
$$x = 1.00010001\cdots,$$

so the true solution is not well approximated either. You may notice the cancellation in the formation of $\hat{x}$. This amplifies the small error in $\hat{y}$. (Note, however, that the subtraction itself is exact.) There is another more illuminating way of explaining the large error in $\hat{x}$. The computation involves two erroneous operations,

$$-20000.\;\hat{+}\;2.000 = -20000. \quad \text{and} \quad -20000.\;\hat{+}\;4.000 = -20000.,$$

which have errors of magnitudes 2 and 4. These are tiny relative to the results of the two addition operations, but they are large compared to the elements of the original matrix. In fact, the values 2 and 4 in the additions above might as well have been zero. In other words, rounding -20002 and -20004 is equivalent to

$$\text{changing} \quad \begin{bmatrix} 0.0002 & 2 \\ 2 & 2 \end{bmatrix} \begin{bmatrix} x \\ y \end{bmatrix} = \begin{bmatrix} 2 \\ 4 \end{bmatrix} \quad \text{to} \quad \begin{bmatrix} 0.0002 & 2 \\ 2 & 0 \end{bmatrix} \begin{bmatrix} \tilde{x} \\ \tilde{y} \end{bmatrix} = \begin{bmatrix} 2 \\ 0 \end{bmatrix}.$$

These large roundoff errors could occur only because of the generation of large intermediate results.

The important principle in controlling roundoff error is to

AVOID VERY LARGE INTERMEDIATE RESULTS.

More specifically, keep the coefficients of the reduced matrices from getting large *relative* to those of the original matrix. This can be accomplished by keeping the multipliers small using a device known as **partial pivoting**. For the problem we have been considering,

$$\begin{bmatrix} 0.0002000 & 2.000 \\ 2.000 & 2.000 \end{bmatrix} \begin{bmatrix} x \\ y \end{bmatrix} = \begin{bmatrix} 2.000 \\ 4.000 \end{bmatrix},$$

this means interchanging the two rows so the pivot is the larger of the two numbers in the first column. This gives

$$0.0001000 \begin{bmatrix} 2.000 & 2.000 \\ 0.0002000 & 2.000 \end{bmatrix} \begin{bmatrix} x \\ y \end{bmatrix} = \begin{bmatrix} 4.000 \\ 2.000 \end{bmatrix}$$

with the multiplier shown to the left of the system. It has absolute value less than 1. Elimination results in

$$\begin{bmatrix} 2.000 & 2.000 \\ 0 & 2.000 \end{bmatrix} \begin{bmatrix} \hat{x} \\ \hat{y} \end{bmatrix} = \begin{bmatrix} 4.000 \\ 2.000 \end{bmatrix}$$

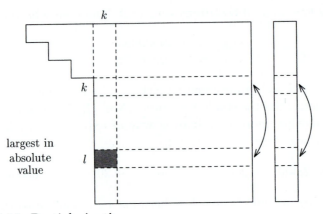

Figure 4.13: Partial pivoting

where the roundoff errors are tiny. Back substitution yields the following solution, which we compare to the exact solution:

$$\hat{y} = 1.000, \qquad\qquad\qquad \hat{x} \;=\; 1.000,$$
$$y = 0.99989998\cdots, \qquad\qquad x \;=\; 1.00010001\cdots.$$

The computed result is very good. Given below, and illustrated in Figure 4.13, is the partial pivoting algorithm for general linear systems of equations:

> **for** $k := 1$ **to** $n - 1$ **do**
>   find $l \in [k : n]$ that maximizes $|A[l,\, k]|$;
>   **for** $j := k$ **to** n **do** $A[k,\, j] \leftrightarrow A[l,\, j]$ **end for**;
> $B[k] \leftrightarrow B[l]$;
>   subtract multiples of kth row from remaining rows
> **end for**

Thus, partial pivoting keeps the multipliers less than or equal to 1 in absolute value, so that no rapid coefficient growth occurs as multiples of one row are subtracted from others. As a consequence the elements of reduced matrices are not large compared to the elements of A, which in turn implies that rounding errors are tiny compared to the elements of A.

The following example is not only another illustration of the instability of Gaussian elimination without pivoting, it is also a demonstration of how to separate systematically the effects of different roundoff errors in a calculation and thus identify the offending errors in an unstable calculation.

Example 4.3 In this example[4] we express the problem in a more direct way that avoids having to give names to the solution values. This is desirable because almost every step of the computation involves roundoff error, which changes the solution. More precisely, instead of expressing the elimination process as

$$A\boldsymbol{x} = \boldsymbol{b} \longrightarrow A'\boldsymbol{x}' = \boldsymbol{b}' \longrightarrow A''\boldsymbol{x}'' = \boldsymbol{b}'' \longrightarrow \cdots$$

where $\boldsymbol{x} \approx \boldsymbol{x}' \approx \boldsymbol{x}''$, we write

$$A^{-1}\boldsymbol{b} \approx (A')^{-1}\boldsymbol{b}' \approx (A'')^{-1}\boldsymbol{b}'' \approx \cdots.$$

The problem is to compute

$$\begin{bmatrix} 6.000 & 2.000 & 2.000 \\ 2.000 & 2.000/3.000 & 1.000/3.000 \\ 1.000 & 2.000 & -1.000 \end{bmatrix}^{-1} \begin{bmatrix} -2.000 \\ 1.000 \\ 0. \end{bmatrix}, \text{ whose exact value is } \begin{bmatrix} 2.6 \\ -3.8 \\ -5. \end{bmatrix}.$$

With four-digit decimal floating-point arithmetic, Gaussian elimination without pivoting gives $[1.335 \quad 0. \quad -5.003]^{\mathrm{T}}$, which is a poor result. To locate the sources of the error, we can compute, after each rounded operation, what the final result would be if the remainder of the calculation were to be performed without error. If we do so, we find that the accuracy is still good after elimination in the first column, for we get

$$\begin{bmatrix} 6.000 & 2.000 & 2.000 \\ 0 & 0.0001000 & -0.3333 \\ 0 & 1.667 & -1.333 \end{bmatrix}^{-1} \begin{bmatrix} -2.000 \\ 1.667 \\ 0.3334 \end{bmatrix}, \text{ whose exact value is } \begin{bmatrix} 2.6009\cdots \\ -3.8003\cdots \\ 5.0026\cdots \end{bmatrix}.$$

After computing the multiplier we have

$$\begin{bmatrix} 6.000 & 2.000 & 2.000 \\ 0 & 0.0001000 & -0.3333 \\ 0 & 0 & -1.333 - 16670.(-0.3333) \end{bmatrix}^{-1} \begin{bmatrix} -2.000 \\ 1.667 \\ 0.3334 - 16670.(1.667) \end{bmatrix},$$

whose exact value is as above. Multiplication by the multiplier gives

$$\begin{bmatrix} 6.000 & 2.000 & 2.000 \\ 0 & 0.0001000 & -0.3333 \\ 0 & 0 & -1.333 + 5556. \end{bmatrix}^{-1} \begin{bmatrix} -2.000 \\ 1.667 \\ 0.3334 - 27790 \end{bmatrix}$$

whose exact value is

$$\begin{bmatrix} 2.9341\cdots \\ -4.7995\cdots \\ -5.0029\cdots \end{bmatrix}.$$

---

[4]From K.E. Atkinson (1985).

The solution of the problem is dramatically altered because of the roundoff errors of 0.111 and 1.11 generated by the two multiplications. These errors are as large as the original data. Thus, we see again that large numbers imply large errors. Subsequent roundoff errors associated with these large numbers also significantly alter the solution.

4.4.2 Error estimates

How accurate is Gaussian elimination with partial pivoting? It is difficult to make useful a priori statements about the effect of roundoff error. Theoretical and empirical evidence suggests that

$$\beta^{-n}\text{cond}(A)$$

is a ballpark estimate for the relative error and that the relative residual is somewhat smaller. In fact, it is a noteworthy feature of partial pivoting that it does better in making the residuals small than it does in making the errors small.

Example 4.4 If we determine a polynomial that interpolates some function at 1, 1.01, 1.02 by solving for coefficients of powers of the independent variable, we get the matrix

$$\begin{bmatrix} 1 & 1 & 1 \\ 1 & 1.01 & 1.0201 \\ 1 & 1.02 & 1.0404 \end{bmatrix},$$

whose condition number is 120000. A matrix obtained in this way is known as a *Vandermonde matrix*. If a solution is computed using 53-bit floating-point arithmetic, we might expect a relative error $\|\hat{x} - x\|/\|x\|$ of order

$$10^{-16} \cdot \text{cond}(A) \approx 10^{-11}.$$

With floating-point numbers the goals of minimizing the norm of the errors and the norm of the residuals are slightly incompatible. For example, consider the system

$$\begin{bmatrix} -1 & 9 \\ -2 & 9 \end{bmatrix} \begin{bmatrix} x \\ y \end{bmatrix} = \begin{bmatrix} 10 \\ 8 \end{bmatrix},$$

which has solution $x = 2, y = 1.333\cdots$. Assuming four-digit decimal floating-point numbers, the nearest pair of machine numbers is $x = 2.000, y = 1.333$. *But* it is the pair $x = 1.998, y = 1.333$ that minimizes the norm of the residuals. This is explained in Figure 4.14 where the two equations are shown as straight lines intersecting at the solution of the system, pairs of machine numbers are shown as crosses, and the set of all pairs (x, y) yielding a residual norm of at most 0.001 is shown as the shaded parallelogram. Residual norms of other magnitudes would correspond to parallelograms that are likewise centered on the solution but scaled up

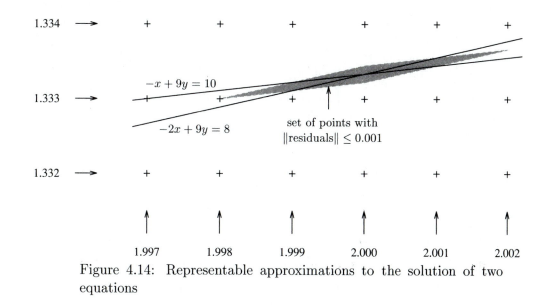

Figure 4.14:   Representable approximations to the solution of two equations

or down. We see that $x = 1.998, y = 1.333$ is the only pair of machine numbers that has a residual norm as small as 0.001. One can imagine even more extreme situations in which the shaded parallelogram is extremely elongated, but these cannot be as clearly drawn.

⋆ 4.4.3 Scaling

Unfortunately there is a complication associated with the application of partial pivoting. Consider yet again the example

$$\begin{bmatrix} 0.0002000 & 2.000 \\ 2.000 & 2.000 \end{bmatrix} \begin{bmatrix} x \\ y \end{bmatrix} = \begin{bmatrix} 2.000 \\ 4.000 \end{bmatrix}.$$

Multiplying the first equation of this system by a factor 10^5 gives

$$\begin{bmatrix} 20.00 & 20000.00 \\ 2.000 & 2.000 \end{bmatrix} \begin{bmatrix} x \\ y \end{bmatrix} = \begin{bmatrix} 20000.00 \\ 4.000 \end{bmatrix}.$$

If it is the error in the solution $\begin{bmatrix} x & y \end{bmatrix}^{\mathrm{T}}$ only that is of consequence, this scaling does not change the problem in any fundamental way. If the residual matters (as it does in polynomial interpolation), scaling *does* fundamentally alter the problem—the scaling should be done to give each residual the appropriate weighting. For the remainder of this subsection we *assume that the goal of the computation is small errors* rather than small residuals.

Scaling might affect the solution by the additional roundoffs that result from multiplication by the scale factors. One can and should avoid this by *using only powers of β as scale factors.* Then for Gaussian elimination *without pivoting,* scaling makes absolutely no difference; the floating-point computation is completely unaffected except for differences in the exponents of some of the intermediate results (and the possibility of underflow or overflow).

With partial pivoting the situation is much different, because this strategy compares magnitudes of numbers, and these depend on how the equations *happen* to be scaled. For our example, elimination proceeds without interchanging rows and we get

$$\begin{bmatrix} 20.00 & 200000. \\ 0 & -20000. \end{bmatrix} \begin{bmatrix} \dot{x} \\ \dot{y} \end{bmatrix} = \begin{bmatrix} 200000. \\ -20000. \end{bmatrix}.$$

Back substitution yields

$$\hat{x} = 0., \ \hat{y} = 1.000 \qquad \text{instead of} \qquad x = 1.00010001\cdots, \ y = .99989998\cdots,$$

for which

$$\text{errors} \approx \begin{bmatrix} -1 \\ 0.0001 \end{bmatrix}, \qquad \text{residuals} = \begin{bmatrix} 0 \\ 2 \end{bmatrix}.$$

The error is awful, but the residual is small relative to the norm of the right-hand side. Suppose, however, we interchange rows to get

$$\begin{bmatrix} 2.000 & 2.000 \\ 20.00 & 200000. \end{bmatrix} \begin{bmatrix} x \\ y \end{bmatrix} = \begin{bmatrix} 4.000 \\ 200000. \end{bmatrix}$$

and eliminate to get

$$\begin{bmatrix} 2.000 & 2.000 \\ 0 & 200000. \end{bmatrix} \begin{bmatrix} \check{x} \\ \check{y} \end{bmatrix} = \begin{bmatrix} 2.000 \\ 200000. \end{bmatrix}.$$

Back substituting gives

$$\check{x} = 1.000, \ \check{y} = 1.000, \qquad \text{errors} \approx \begin{bmatrix} -0.0001 \\ 0.0001 \end{bmatrix}, \qquad \text{residuals} = \begin{bmatrix} -20 \\ 0 \end{bmatrix}.$$

Note that the error norm is 10000 times smaller than before but the residual norm is 10 times larger. This illustrates that smaller residuals are not equivalent to smaller errors. It is also consistent with the statement that partial pivoting tends to yield the smallest residuals but not necessarily the smallest errors.

For partial pivoting, scaling, even by powers of β, indirectly affects the accuracy by affecting the choice of pivots. In fact, we can get partial pivoting to yield any ordering of the equations (except those orderings that have vanishing pivots) by an appropriate scaling of the equations.

How then should one scale? The best *practical* scaling is to divide each equation by the sum of the absolute values of the coefficients in that equation (or the nearest power of β), but this can be much worse than the best possible scaling. For this reason LAPACK leaves scaling up to the user, and the prevailing advice is to "accept the original matrix as given and not carry out any scaling."[5]

Review questions

1. Fully explain the purpose of partial pivoting.

2. It is a noteworthy feature of partial pivoting that it does better in making which smaller: the error or the residual?

Exercises

1. Would Gaussian elimination without pivoting be adequate for well-conditioned systems of equations? Explain.

2. Use Gaussian elimination with partial pivoting to solve $A\boldsymbol{x} = \boldsymbol{b}$ where

$$A = \begin{bmatrix} 2 & 1 & -1 \\ 4 & 0 & -1 \\ -8 & 2 & 2 \end{bmatrix}, \qquad \boldsymbol{b} = \begin{bmatrix} 6 \\ 6 \\ -8 \end{bmatrix}.$$

   Do not use other algorithms such as Gauss-Jordan.

3. Supply all the details for the algorithm on page 144. Do *not* do any operations with entire arrays or with "sections" of arrays.

4. Write an algorithm for Gauss-Jordan with partial pivoting to solve $A\boldsymbol{x} = \boldsymbol{b}$.

5. What are the equations for the four lines that bound the shaded parallelogram in Figure 4.14?

Mathematica notes

The *Mathematica* package `LinearAlgebra`GaussianElimination`` allows you to do Gaussian elimination with partial pivoting. The package defines two functions: `LUFactor[ ]` and `LUSolve[ ]` that together allow you to solve linear systems. The next section explains the advantages of this splitting, but for now we will just use them together.

Read in the package.   *In[1]:=* `<< LinearAlgebra`GaussianElimination``

---

[5]Forsythe, Malcolm, and Moler (1977), p. 38

Define a function to solve the matrix equation a . x == b.	`In[2]:= linsol[a_, b_] := LUSolve[LUFactor[a], b]`

Define a matrix a.

```
In[3]:= a = Table[1./N[i+j-1], {i,5}, {j,5}]
Out[3]= {{1., 0.5, 0.333333, 0.25, 0.2},
   {0.5, 0.333333, 0.25, 0.2, 0.166667},
   {0.333333, 0.25, 0.2, 0.166667, 0.142857},
   {0.25, 0.2, 0.166667, 0.142857, 0.125},
   {0.2, 0.166667, 0.142857, 0.125, 0.111111}}
```

Define a right-hand side b.

```
In[4]:= b = {1., 1., 1., 1., 1.}
Out[4]= {1., 1., 1., 1., 1.}
```

Find the solution to a . x == b.

```
In[5]:= x = linsol[a, b]
Out[5]= {5., -120., 630., -1120., 630.}
```

Evaluate the residuals.

```
In[6]:= a . x - b
```
$$Out[6]= \{-2.26485 \times 10^{-14}, -1.22125 \times 10^{-14}, 3.77476 \times 10^{-15},$$
$$1.33227 \times 10^{-15}, -1.22125 \times 10^{-15}\}$$

This package is particularly useful in conjunction with an alternative arithmetic such as that of `NumericalMath`ComputerArithmetic`` or interval arithmetic.

Read in the package.

```
In[7]:= << NumericalMath`ComputerArithmetic`
```

Set the arithmetic to be 4 digits in base 10.

```
In[8]:= SetArithmetic[4]
Out[8]= {4, 10, RoundingRule -> RoundToEven,
   ExponentRange -> {-50, 50}, MixedMode -> False,
   IdealDivide -> False}
```

Define a matrix of computer numbers.

```
In[9]:= a = Table[ComputerNumber[1/(i+j-1)],
           {i, 3}, {j, 3}]
Out[9]= {{1., 0.5, 0.3333}, {0.5, 0.3333, 0.25},
   {0.3333, 0.25, 0.2}}
```

Define a right-hand side.

```
In[10]:= b = Table[ComputerNumber[i],
           {i, 3, 5}]
Out[10]= {3., 4., 5.}
```

Solve the matrix equation `a . x == b`.

```
In[11]:= x = linsol[a, b]
Out[11]= {34.34, -247.7, 277.4}
```

Evaluate the residuals *within* the reigning arithmetic. This is *not* a good way to evaluate the residuals.

```
In[12]:= a . x - b
Out[12]= {0, -0.04, 0.01}
```

Set the arithmetic to use doubled precision.

```
In[13]:= SetArithmetic[8]
Out[13]= {8, 10, RoundingRule -> RoundToEven,
         ExponentRange -> {-50, 50}, MixedMode -> False,
         IdealDivide -> False}
```

Evaluate the residuals in the higher-precision arithmetic. Notice that the result is quite different.

```
In[14]:= r = a . x - b
Out[14]= {-0.05258, -0.03841, 0.000522}
```

Define the norm of a vector of `ComputerNumbers`.

```
In[15]:= norm[v_?VectorQ] :=
         ComputerNumber[Max[Abs[Normal /@ v]]]
```

Evaluate the relative residual.

```
In[16]:= norm[r]/norm[b]
Out[16]= 0.010516
```

This is the "correct" solution using eight-digit arithmetic.

```
In[17]:= cx = linsol[a, b]
Out[17]= {33.405481, -242.07603, 271.92481}
```

The errors in the solution.

```
In[18]:= err = x - cx
Out[18]= {0.934519, -5.62397, 5.47519}
```

The relative error in the solution.

```
In[19]:= norm[err]/norm[cx]
Out[19]= 0.020682078
```

You should be careful about changing the precision of the arithmetic when using `NumericalMath`ComputerArithmetic``. Note that setting the parameters in the arithmetic affects the result of the arithmetic, not the operands themselves. If you increase the precision, any of the old `ComputerNumbers` will still be representable numbers; but if you change the base or decrease the precision, an old `ComputerNumber` may no longer be representable in the new arithmetic. Any arithmetic done with an obsolete `ComputerNumber` will work, but it will use its old value; it will not be first coerced to the nearest `ComputerNumber` in the current arithmetic. This may or may not be what you want it to do. If you want coercion to occur, you need to be explicit and use `ComputerNumber[Normal[`*oldvalue*`]]`. This will coerce any `ComputerNumber` to the nearest `ComputerNumber` in the current arithmetic.

Computer problems

1. Do Computer Problem 1 of Section 4.3 for Gaussian elimination with partial pivoting modeled after the algorithm described on page 133. Additional useful *Mathematica* objects: `If`, `Abs`, `Max`, `Position[ ..., ...][[1, 1]]`, and `Join`.

2. Use `ComputerArithmetic` with six digits in base 10 and `GaussianElimination` to solve the matrix equation $Ax = b$ with A given by `Table[1/(i+j-1), {i, 4}, {j, 4}]` rounded to six digits and b given by `{1, 1, 1, 1}`. Is the relative error (defined in Section 4.2.2) comparable to the estimate given in this section? Is the relative residual smaller or larger?

3. Redo Computer Problem 2 with A given by `Table[1/(i+j-1), {i, 5}, {j, 5}]` and b given by `{1, 1, 1, 1, 1}`.

4. Define a function that takes a single integer argument k and uses `ComputerArithmetic` with k digits in base 10 and `GaussianElimination` to solve the system of equations $Ax = b$ with A given by `Table[1/(i+j-1), {i, 4}, {j, 4}]` rounded to k digits and b given by `{1, 1, 1, 1}`. The final result of the function should be the number of accurate digits in the solution as measured by $-\log_{10}(\|\hat{x} - x\|/\|x\|)$. Does the number of accurate digits in the solution vary with k in the way suggested in this section?

5. Redo Computer Problem 4 for the relative residual (defined in Section 4.2.2) rather than the relative error.

4.5 Linear-Equation Solvers

The actual implementation of Gaussian elimination in top-quality software such as LAPACK and its predecessor LINPACK is somewhat complicated. In particular, these packages split Gaussian elimination into two subroutines. It is the purpose of this section to explain this.

4.5.1 Basic idea

In certain situations, such as iterative improvement, nonlinear systems, and differential equations, we need to solve a sequence of linear systems that all have the same coefficient matrix but various right-hand sides that are not known until the preceding system is solved:

$$
\begin{aligned}
Ax^{(1)} &= b^{(1)}, \\
Ax^{(2)} &= b^{(2)} \quad \text{where } b^{(2)} \text{ depends on } x^{(1)}, \\
&\;\;\vdots \\
Ax^{(m)} &= b^{(m)} \quad \text{where } b^{(m)} \text{ depends on } x^{(m-1)}.
\end{aligned}
$$

In this situation we cannot solve all the systems at the same time, for example, by augmenting the first right-hand side with the others. What we could do to economize is to

compute A^{-1}, $\boxed{n^3 \text{ multiplications,}}$

$\boldsymbol{x}^k = A^{-1}\boldsymbol{b}^{(k)}, \qquad k = 1,\ 2,\ \ldots,\ m,$ $\boxed{n^2 \text{ multiplications each.}}$

However, there is a better way, and that is to split Gaussian elimination into two parts:

1. the part of Gaussian elimination involving only A:

Factor A $\boxed{\frac{1}{3}n^3 \text{ multiplications}}$

2. the rest of Gaussian elimination:

Solve $A\boldsymbol{x}^{(k)} = \boldsymbol{b}^{(k)}, k = 1,\ 2,\ \ldots,\ m$ $\boxed{n^2 \text{ multiplications each}}$

To be more precise, the first part is forward elimination on A (the right-hand side is irrelevant at this stage), and the second part is forward elimination on $\boldsymbol{b}$ and back substitution. The operations to be performed in Gaussian elimination (row interchanges and subtraction of multiples of pivot row from remaining rows) can be determined from the matrix A alone. To solve $A\boldsymbol{x}^{(1)} = \boldsymbol{b}^{(1)}, A\boldsymbol{x}^{(2)} = \boldsymbol{b}^{(2)}, \ldots, A\boldsymbol{x}^{(m)} = \boldsymbol{b}^{(m)}$ requires one call to *Factor* and m calls to *Solve*, one for each of $\boldsymbol{b}^{(1)}, \boldsymbol{b}^{(2)}, \ldots, \boldsymbol{b}^{(m)}$.

The structure of the two routines is diagramed below:

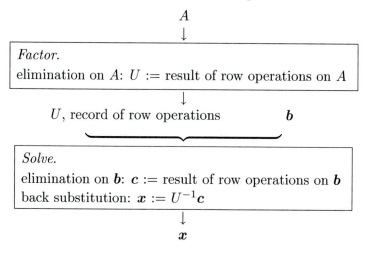

In order that the same row operations can be performed on b that are performed on A, the *Factor* routine creates a record of these operations, which is passed to the *Solve* routine.

4.5.2 Storage scheme

We first do an example for *Factor*. There are two arrays,

$$
A: \quad \begin{bmatrix} 2 & 6 & -2 \\ 1 & 3 & -4 \\ 3 & 6 & 9 \end{bmatrix} \qquad \text{and} \qquad IPIV: \quad \begin{bmatrix} \ \\ \ \\ \ \end{bmatrix},
$$

the first containing the original matrix and the second providing space to record row interchanges. After the first row interchange these arrays contain

$$
\begin{bmatrix} 3 & 6 & 9 \\ 1 & 3 & -4 \\ 2 & 6 & -2 \end{bmatrix}, \qquad \begin{bmatrix} 3 \\ \ \\ \ \end{bmatrix}.
$$

Note that in $IPIV[1]$ is stored the index of the row that was interchanged with the first row in the first step of elimination. Then we perform the first elimination and have

$$
\begin{bmatrix} 3 & 6 & 9 \\ \overline{1/3} & 1 & -7 \\ 2/3 & 2 & -8 \end{bmatrix}, \qquad \begin{bmatrix} 3 \\ \ \\ \ \end{bmatrix}.
$$

Note how the multipliers have overwritten the eliminated elements. Thus the array A does double duty: It holds the nonzero elements of the reduced coefficient matrix and the multipliers. This completes the first elimination step. After the second row interchange, the arrays contain

$$
\begin{bmatrix} 3 & 6 & 9 \\ \overline{1/3} & 2 & -8 \\ 2/3 & 1 & -7 \end{bmatrix}, \qquad \begin{bmatrix} 3 \\ 3 \\ \ \end{bmatrix}.
$$

Thus $IPIV[2]$ contains the index of the row that was interchanged with the second row in the second step of elimination. Note that *the multipliers are not interchanged.* Thinking in terms of recursion, the multipliers in the first $k-1$ columns are not part of the kth problem; interchanging them would only make a mess of the data. The second elimination gives

$$
\begin{bmatrix} 3 & 6 & 9 \\ \overline{1/3} & 2 & -8 \\ 2/3 & \overline{1/2} & -3 \end{bmatrix}, \qquad \begin{bmatrix} 3 \\ 3 \\ \ \end{bmatrix}
$$

where once again a multiplier overwrites an eliminated element. This completes the forward elimination on the coefficient matrix. The diagonal and upper triangular parts of the array

A contain the reduced matrix U, and the lower triangular elements contain the multipliers. The array $IPIV$ contains a record of row interchanges; the last location of $IPIV$ is unused. We shall see that we have all the information necessary to duplicate for the right-hand side what was done to the coefficient matrix.

We continue the same example now for *Solve*. Let array B contain right-hand side

$$\begin{bmatrix} 4 \\ -7 \\ 39 \end{bmatrix}.$$

Interchanging row 1 with row $IPIV[1] = 3$ gives

$$\begin{bmatrix} 39 \\ -7 \\ 4 \end{bmatrix}.$$

Subtracting multiples $A[2,1] = 1/3$ and $A[3,1] = 2/3$ of row 1 from rows 2 and 3 gives

$$\begin{bmatrix} 39 \\ -20 \\ -22 \end{bmatrix}.$$

Interchanging row 2 with row $IPIV[2] = 3$ gives

$$\begin{bmatrix} 39 \\ -22 \\ -20 \end{bmatrix}.$$

Subtracting multiple $A[3,2] = 1/2$ of row 2 from row 3 gives

$$\begin{bmatrix} 39 \\ -22 \\ -9 \end{bmatrix}.$$

Thus B contains a right-hand side that has undergone the same operations as the reduced matrix in the upper triangular part of A, and we can write

$$\begin{bmatrix} 3 & 6 & 9 \\ 0 & 2 & -8 \\ 0 & 0 & -3 \end{bmatrix} \begin{bmatrix} x_1 \\ x_2 \\ x_3 \end{bmatrix} = \begin{bmatrix} 39 \\ -22 \\ -9 \end{bmatrix}.$$

This we solve by back substitution:

$$\begin{aligned}
x_3 &= (-9)/(-3) = 3, \\
x_2 &= (-22 - (-8) \cdot 3)/2 = 1, \\
x_1 &= (39 - 6 \cdot 1 - 9 \cdot 3)/3 = 2.
\end{aligned}$$

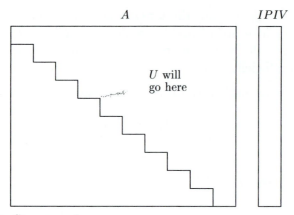

Figure 4.15: Storage scheme

Back substitution is *the* (efficient) way to compute $x = U^{-1}c$.

In general A is an $n \times n$ array of floating-point numbers and *IPIV* is an array of n integers, which are depicted in Figure 4.15. The way in which the algorithm uses this storage is shown in the following outline of *Factor*:

> **for** $k := 1$ **to** $n - 1$ **do**
>   determine pivot index l;
>   interchange rows k and l, columns k through n;
> $IPIV[k] := l$;
>   determine multipliers μ;
>   store multipliers where eliminated elements would go;
>   subtract multiples of row k from remaining rows
> **end for**

This is all illustrated in Figure 4.16. The multipliers for eliminating the kth variable are stored in $A[i, k]$, $i = k + 1, k + 2, \ldots, n$, and the index of the row that contains the kth pivot is stored in $IPIV[k]$. The output of *Factor* is shown in Figure 4.17 for a system of eight equations.

⋆ 4.5.3   Iterative improvement

Iterative improvement is a process that can be tacked onto the end of Gaussian elimination to clean up error that was made due to roundoff. It can yield solutions with machine-precision accuracy for a small additional cost.

Suppose we have *Factor*ed the coefficient matrix and have computed an approximation

$$x^{(1)} = Solve(A, IPIV, b).$$

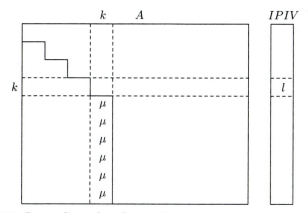

Figure 4.16: Recording the elimination process

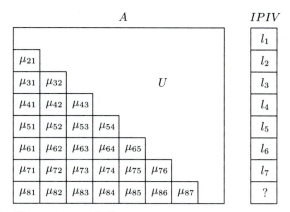

Figure 4.17: The output of *Factor*

The idea is to use the relationship

$$\text{residuals} = \boldsymbol{b} - A\hat{\boldsymbol{x}} = A(\boldsymbol{x} - \hat{\boldsymbol{x}}) = A(-\text{errors}).$$

Compared to what has already been done, it is computationally inexpensive to calculate the residual

$$\boldsymbol{r}^{(1)} = \boldsymbol{b} - A\boldsymbol{x}^{(1)}$$

and to use the available decomposition to solve $\boldsymbol{r}^{(1)} = A(-\text{errors})$ for the errors:

$$-\text{errors} \approx Solve(A, IPIV, \boldsymbol{r}^{(1)}) \stackrel{\text{def}}{=} \boldsymbol{c}^{(1)}.$$

We then add this approximation of the negative errors as a *correction*:

$$\boldsymbol{x}^{(2)} = \boldsymbol{x}^{(1)} + \boldsymbol{c}^{(1)}.$$

You might wonder, however, why the errors in solving for the correction $c^{(1)}$ should be any smaller than the errors in solving for $x^{(1)}$. Recall that the relative error is of order $u\,\mathrm{cond}(A)$, and thus it is similar for both $x^{(1)}$ and $c^{(1)}$. However, the *absolute* error in $c^{(1)}$ will be much smaller than that in $x^{(1)}$, normally. The limiting factor is usually the accuracy of the calculated residuals.

Example. From Section 4.4.3 we have the system

$$\begin{bmatrix} 20.00 & 200000. \\ 2.000 & 2.000 \end{bmatrix} \begin{bmatrix} x \\ y \end{bmatrix} = \begin{bmatrix} 200000. \\ 4.000 \end{bmatrix},$$

whose *Factor*ization is

$$A = \begin{bmatrix} 20.00 & 200000. \\ \boxed{0.1000} & -20000. \end{bmatrix}, \quad IPIV = \begin{bmatrix} 1 \end{bmatrix}$$

and whose computed solution is

$$x^{(1)} = \begin{bmatrix} 0. \\ 1.000 \end{bmatrix}.$$

All calculations are in four-digit decimal arithmetic. The computed residual is

$$r^{(1)} = \begin{bmatrix} 0. \\ 2.000 \end{bmatrix},$$

the correction is

$$c^{(1)} = \begin{bmatrix} 1.000 \\ -0.0001000 \end{bmatrix},$$

and the improved solution is

$$x^{(2)} = \begin{bmatrix} 1.000 \\ 0.9999 \end{bmatrix}.$$

You could not ask for a more accurate answer.

This process can be repeated. Given $x^{(k)}$, we compute

$$\begin{aligned} r^{(k)} &= b - Ax^{(k)}, \\ c^{(k)} &= Solve(A, IPIV, r^{(k)}), \\ x^{(k+1)} &= x^{(k)} + c^{(k)}. \end{aligned}$$

Normally this process is only of limited value unless the calculation of the residuals $r^{(k)}$ is done in higher precision than the rest of the calculation.

Exercises

1. Consider the system $A\boldsymbol{x} = \boldsymbol{b}$ where

$$A = \begin{bmatrix} 1 & 0 & 3 & 0 \\ 0 & 1 & 3 & -1 \\ 3 & -3 & 0 & 6 \\ 0 & 2 & 4 & -6 \end{bmatrix}, \qquad \boldsymbol{b} = \begin{bmatrix} -2 \\ -7 \\ 18 \\ -14 \end{bmatrix}.$$

  (a) Show step by step how *Factor* decomposes the matrix of coefficients and determines *IPIV*. More specifically, display the values of A and *IPIV* after each iteration of the outer loop on k.

  (b) Show step by step how *Solve* solves for the unknowns. More specifically, display the values of B after each iteration of the outer loop and at the completion of the procedure.

2. Do the preceding exercise for

$$A = \begin{bmatrix} 0 & 1 & 0 & 0 \\ 1 & 0 & 0 & 0 \\ 1 & 1 & 1 & 1 \\ 0 & 1 & 2 & 3 \end{bmatrix}, \qquad \boldsymbol{b} = \begin{bmatrix} 0 \\ 1 \\ -\frac{1}{2} \\ -\frac{1}{2} \end{bmatrix}.$$

3. Do Exercise 1 for the system

$$\begin{array}{rcl} 2x_1 + x_2 + x_4 &=& 1, \\ 3x_1 + 0.5x_2 + x_3 + x_4 &=& 2, \\ 4x_1 + 2x_2 + 2x_3 + x_4 &=& -1, \\ x_2 + x_3 + 2x_4 &=& 0. \end{array}$$

4. Solve $A\boldsymbol{x} = \boldsymbol{b}$ where $\boldsymbol{b} = [4 \quad 8 \quad -9 \quad 20]^{\mathrm{T}}$ and the factorization of A *returned* by *Factor* is given by

$$\text{array } A = \begin{bmatrix} 3 & -3 & 0 & 6 \\ 0 & 2 & 4 & 6 \\ \frac{1}{3} & \frac{1}{2} & 1 & -5 \\ 0 & \frac{1}{2} & 1 & 1 \end{bmatrix} \qquad \text{and} \qquad \text{array } IPIV = \begin{bmatrix} 3 \\ 4 \\ 3 \end{bmatrix}.$$

  Show your work.

5. (a) Supply all the details for the algorithm *Factor* on page 156. Do *not* do any operations with entire arrays or with "sections" of arrays.

(b) Supply all the details for the algorithm *Solve*.

(c) Obtain a precise count of the number of floating-point subtractions, multiplications, and divisions in *Factor* as a function of n. Present the operation count, clearly showing all steps.

(d) Repeat part (c) for all of *Solve*.

(e) As a check compare the sums of the counts in (c) and (d) for each of subtraction, multiplication, and division with the sums of the counts for forward elimination and back substitution in Section 4.3.

6. Write routines *Factor*(A) and *Solve*(A, b, x) that use Gauss-Jordan *without* pivoting to solve $Ax = b$. The routine *Solve* should make no changes to A. *Factor* should overwrite A with appropriate multipliers and "divisors."

7. Write routines *Factor*(A, *IPIV*) and *Solve*(A, *IPIV*, b, x) that use Gauss-Jordan with partial pivoting to solve $Ax = b$. The routine *Solve* should make no changes to A (or *IPIV*). *Factor* should overwrite A with appropriate multipliers and "divisors."

8. Why do we say, "You could not ask for a more accurate answer" in the example of iterative refinement?

Mathematica notes

Because the package `LinearAlgebra`GaussianElimination`` splits apart Gaussian elimination, it is quite easy to write a solver that does iterative improvement. The one difficulty is that the residual needs to be calculated in higher precision so that the new right-hand side is sufficiently accurate to effect improvement. When used in conjunction with `NumericalMath`ComputerArithmetic``, you can set the arithmetic to use higher precision before you calculate the residual and set it back to lower precision to calculate the improvement.

Computer problems

1. Define a function `linsol1[mat_, rhs_, digs_]` that takes a matrix and right-hand side, both of ordinary *Mathematica* numbers, converts them to `ComputerNumber`s of digs decimal digits, and calculates the solution vector of `ComputerNumber`s using iterative improvement. Use `LUFactor[ ]` just once and `LUSolve[ ]` several times to get convergence. Evaluate the residual using 2 digs precision and the improvement using digs precision. You will have to use `SetArithmetic[ ]` to change the precision. After you have lowered the precision, you should coerce the elements of the residual vector to be `ComputerNumber`s in the low-precision arithmetic before calculating the improvement. Use `ComputerNumber[Normal[#]]& /@` to do this. Print each iterate as the algorithm proceeds. Test it with `Table[1/(i+j-1), {i, 4}, {j, 4}]` and `{1, 1, 1, 1}`.

2. Define a function `linsol2[mat_, rhs_]` that takes a matrix and right-hand side of machine numbers and calculates the solution vector using iterative improvement. Use `LUFactor[ ]` just once and `LUSolve[ ]` several times to get convergence. Use the function `dble[ ]` on page 57 to coerce machine numbers to arbitrary-precision numbers with doubled precision for calculating the residual. Use `N[ ]` to convert the residual back to a list of machine numbers before calculating the improvement. Print each iterate as the algorithm proceeds. Test it with `Table[1./N[i+j-1], {i, 12}, {j, 12}]` and `Table[1., {12}]`.

4.6   Large Sparse Systems

The cost of solving large systems is very great unless there is a special property that can be exploited—for example, *sparsity*. A system is sparse if its coefficient matrix is mostly zeros, so much so that we do not store the entire matrix. Such matrices arise from

- networks, frame structures, and

- discretized differential equations: continuum mechanics, heat transfer, electromagnetism.

There are two types of methods for solving large sparse systems.

A *direct method* is one that is "exact" after a finite number of arithmetic operations in the absence of roundoff error. Such a method is usually a variant of Gaussian elimination with a special ordering of equations and variables. Efficiency is achieved by taking zeros into account. This can lead to fairly complicated data structures.

An *iterative method* defines a sequence of better and better approximations that converge to the solution only after an infinite number of iterations, even in exact arithmetic. (There is a relationship to iterative refinement, but we do not explore that here.) As an extremely simple example consider two unknown temperatures

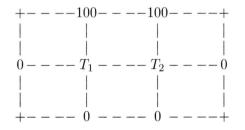

each of which is supposed to be the average of its four nearest neighbors. For example, we might be looking at the cross section of a bar whose upper face is kept at 100°F and whose three other faces are kept at 0°F. With an iterative method one begins with a guess; in the absence of any information one might use zero as an initial approximation. Then we improve T_1 by setting it equal to the average of its four neighbors. Then we improve T_2 in the same way using the improved value for T_1. We repeat this again and again, always using the best values available. The values obtained are shown in the following table:

k	$T_1^{(k)}$	$T_2^{(k)}$
0	0	0
1	25	31.25
2	32.812	33.203
3	33.301	33.325
4	33.331	33.333
5	33.333	33.333

The equations we are solving are

$$
\begin{aligned}
T_1 &= \tfrac{1}{4}(T_2 + 100 + 0 + 0), \\
T_2 &= \tfrac{1}{4}(0 + 100 + T_1 + 0),
\end{aligned}
$$

and the iteration we are using is

$$
\begin{aligned}
T_1^{(k)} &= \tfrac{1}{4}(T_2^{(k-1)} + 100 + 0 + 0), \\
T_2^{(k)} &= \frac{1}{4}(0 + 100 + T_1^{(k)} + 0),
\end{aligned}
$$

which is known as **Gauss-Seidel**.

The equations for the unknown temperatures are very crude approximations. A better approximation can be obtained by solving for a larger set of temperatures on a more refined set of grid points imposed on the cross section of the bar. Suppose that the bar cross section is defined by $0 \leq x \leq 3$ and $0 \leq y \leq 2$. Let us choose the spacing between grid points in the x and y directions to be $h = 1/N$ where N is an integer. The grid points are $(x, y) = (ih, jh)$, $i = 0, 1, \ldots, 3N$, $j = 0, 1, \ldots, 2N$. It is natural to use a doubly subscripted variable like u_{ij} to denote the unknown temperatures on a two-dimensional set of grid points. We are given the values of u_{ij} along the boundary:

$$
\begin{aligned}
\text{left}: && u_{0j} &= 0, && j = 1, 2, \ldots, 2N - 1, \\
\text{right}: && u_{3N,j} &= 0, && j = 1, 2, \ldots, 2N - 1, \\
\text{bottom}: && u_{i0} &= 0, && i = 1, 2, \ldots, 3N - 1, \\
\text{top}: && u_{i,2N} &= 100, && i = 1, 2, \ldots, 3N - 1.
\end{aligned}
$$

For interior points,

$$
u_{ij} = \tfrac{1}{4}(u_{i-1,j} + u_{i+1,j} + u_{i,j-1} + u_{i,j+1}), \quad i = 1, 2, \ldots, 3N - 1, \quad j = 1, 2, \ldots, 2N - 1;
$$

that is, each value is an average of its left, right, top, and bottom neighbor. This is still an approximation to the mathematical equations that govern temperature distribution, but the accuracy gets better as the grid spacing h gets smaller. In Gauss-Seidel we cycle through the unknowns, using the equation above to update the value of each unknown—we "relax" variable u_{ij} so that the (i, j)th equation is satisfied. Note the natural correspondence between equations and unknowns.

In an actual computer program we would store the unknowns in a two-dimensional array, although mathematically we think of them as constituting a column vector, *not a matrix.* Below is some code for doing one iteration, also known as a *sweep*, of Gauss-Seidel. It is assumed that the known values along the boundaries and guesses for the unknown values in the interior are loaded into the $(3N + 1) \times (2N + 1)$ array before beginning the iterations.

```
Do[
   Do[
      u[[i, j]] = 0.25 (u[[i-1, j]] + u[[i+1, j]]
                        + u[[i, j-1]] + u[[i,j+1]])
   , {i, 2, 3 N}]
, {j, 2, 2 N}]
```

The iteration is terminated when the residuals (the changes in `u[[i, j]]`) are less than some tolerance; *however*, the residuals should first be appropriately scaled, which in this case happens to mean multiplying them by $4h^{-2} = 4N^2$. Ideally, it is the error in the solution that we would like to control, but this is difficult to estimate.

Relaxation methods were popular in the 1930s for hand calculation; and it was observed that the corrections $u_{ij}^{\text{new}} - u_{ij}^{\text{old}}$ calculated by Gauss-Seidel were too conservative, that faster convergence was possible if one successively overcorrected or "overrelaxed" each unknown value. More specifically, each unknown is updated by adding to it some factor ω times the Gauss-Seidel correction computed using the current values of the other unknowns. This method is know as **successive overrelaxation**. Here is how it might be programmed:

```
Do[
   Do[
      correction = 0.25 (u[[i-1, j]] + u[[i+1, j]] + u[[i, j-1]]
                         + u[[i,j+1]]) -  u[[i, j]];
      u[[i, j]] = u[[i, j]] + omega * correction
   , {i, 2, 3 N}]
, {j, 2, 2 N}]
```

Note that $\omega = 1$ reduces this to Gauss-Seidel. The question remains: What is a good choice for the *relaxation parameter* ω? The answer is complicated. Here we will simply say that ω should always be between 1 and 2, that a value 1.9 is typical, and that the optimal value of ω increases as the number of equations gets larger. What is important is that even a trial-and-error choice for ω is likely to be much better than using Gauss-Seidel.

There are other, more complicated iterative methods, and with them it is possible to solve problems with as many as 1 million unknowns.

Computer problem

1. Use Gauss-Seidel iteration to solve Computer Problem 3 of Section 4.3.

4.7 LU Factorization

Here we consider Gaussian elimination without pivoting. Many practical problems can be identified for which pivoting is unnecessary (and even disadvantageous), for example, forces in a frame structure, currents in a resistance network, and temperature distribution. Matrices arising from problems like these share in common the property of being *symmetric positive definite*. A matrix A is said to be **symmetric** if $A^{\mathrm{T}} = A$, and it is said to be **positive definite** if $x^{\mathrm{T}} A x > 0$ for all $x \neq 0$. The definition of positive definite is not useful as a test. For a symmetric matrix a practical test is to perform Gaussian elimination without pivoting and observe the signs of the pivots. It can be shown that the matrix is positive definite if and only if all the pivots are positive.

Suppose that the result of *Factor*ing a matrix A is an array of values

$$\begin{bmatrix} u_{11} & u_{12} & \cdots & u_{1n} \\ l_{21} & u_{22} & \cdots & u_{2n} \\ \vdots & \ddots & \ddots & \vdots \\ l_{n1} & \cdots & l_{n,n-1} & u_{nn} \end{bmatrix}.$$

Then if we define

$$L = \begin{bmatrix} 1 & & & 0 \\ l_{21} & 1 & & \\ \vdots & \ddots & \ddots & \\ l_{n1} & \cdots & l_{n,n-1} & 1 \end{bmatrix}, \quad U = \begin{bmatrix} u_{11} & u_{12} & \cdots & u_{1n} \\ & u_{22} & \cdots & u_{2n} \\ & & \ddots & \vdots \\ 0 & & & u_{nn} \end{bmatrix},$$

it turns out that $LU = A$; indeed, it is a factorization of the original matrix A. The principal value of this fact is that it suggests new ways of implementing Gaussian elimination for solving $Ax = b$. Also, it indicates how to use the information generated by Gaussian elimination to solve both $A^{\mathrm{T}} y = c$ and $Ax = b$ without doing two factorizations. Finally, it explains terminology that people use for Gaussian elimination, such as the use of the name *"Factor"* for the part of Gaussian elimination that works on the coefficient matrix.

We will show that $LU = A$. The *main idea* of our demonstration is that a row operation can be expressed as premultiplication by some matrix, the matrix being obtained by performing the row operation on the identity matrix.

Example 4.5

Row operations	Matrix
subtract $2 \times \{1\}$ from $\{2\}$ subtract $3 \times \{1\}$ from $\{3\}$	$\begin{bmatrix} 1 & 0 & 0 \\ -2 & 1 & 0 \\ -3 & 0 & 1 \end{bmatrix}$

Below we see that premultiplication by the given matrix is equivalent to performing the given row operations:

$$\begin{bmatrix} 1 & 0 & 0 \\ -2 & 1 & 0 \\ -3 & 0 & 1 \end{bmatrix} \begin{bmatrix} a_{11} & a_{12} & a_{13} \\ a_{21} & a_{22} & a_{23} \\ a_{31} & a_{32} & a_{33} \end{bmatrix} = \begin{bmatrix} a_{11} & a_{12} & a_{13} \\ a_{21} - 2a_{11} & a_{22} - 2a_{12} & a_{23} - 2a_{13} \\ a_{31} - 3a_{11} & a_{32} - 3a_{12} & a_{33} - 3a_{13} \end{bmatrix}.$$

We demonstrate the existence of a factorization by executing the steps of forward elimination for

$$A = \begin{bmatrix} 6 & -2 & 2 & 4 \\ 12 & -8 & 6 & 10 \\ 3 & -13 & 9 & 3 \\ -6 & 4 & 1 & -18 \end{bmatrix}.$$

The first set of row operations and its embodiment in matrix form are

$$
\begin{array}{l}
\text{subtract } 2 \times \{1\} \text{ from } \{2\} \\
\text{subtract } \frac{1}{2} \times \{1\} \text{ from } \{3\} \\
\text{subtract } -1 \times \{1\} \text{ from } \{4\}
\end{array}
\qquad
M_1 = \begin{bmatrix} 1 & 0 & 0 & 0 \\ -2 & 1 & 0 & 0 \\ -\frac{1}{2} & 0 & 1 & 0 \\ 1 & 0 & 0 & 1 \end{bmatrix}.
$$

The result of the row operations is

$$M_1 A = \begin{bmatrix} 6 & -2 & 2 & 4 \\ 0 & -4 & 2 & 2 \\ 0 & -12 & 8 & 1 \\ 0 & 2 & 3 & -14 \end{bmatrix}.$$

We are not suggesting that we store the entire matrix M_1 in the computer, but rather we want to show that there is a simple algebraic way to express row operations. The second set of row operations and its matrix are

$$\text{subtract } 3 \times \{2\} \text{ from } \{3\} \qquad M_2 = \begin{bmatrix} 1 & 0 & 0 & 0 \\ 0 & 1 & 0 & 0 \\ 0 & -3 & 1 & 0 \\ 0 & \frac{1}{2} & 0 & 1 \end{bmatrix},$$
$$\text{subtract } -\tfrac{1}{2} \times \{2\} \text{ from } \{4\}$$

and the result of these row operations is

$$M_2 M_1 A = \begin{bmatrix} 6 & -2 & 2 & 4 \\ 0 & -4 & 2 & 2 \\ 0 & 0 & 2 & -5 \\ 0 & 0 & 4 & -13 \end{bmatrix}.$$

The third set of row operations and its matrix are

$$\text{subtract } 2 \times \{3\} \text{ from } \{4\} \qquad M_3 = \begin{bmatrix} 1 & 0 & 0 & 0 \\ 0 & 1 & 0 & 0 \\ 0 & 0 & 1 & 0 \\ 0 & 0 & -2 & 1 \end{bmatrix},$$

and the result of this is

$$M_3 M_2 M_1 A = \begin{bmatrix} 6 & -2 & 2 & 4 \\ 0 & -4 & 2 & 2 \\ 0 & 0 & 2 & -5 \\ 0 & 0 & 0 & -3 \end{bmatrix} \overset{\text{def}}{=} U.$$

Thus elimination reduces A to upper triangular form by multiplying by simple matrices.

For general n we obtain

$$U \overset{\text{def}}{=} M_{n-1} \cdots M_2 M_1 A.$$

Each matrix

$$M_k = \begin{bmatrix} 1 & & & & & & & & \\ & 1 & & & & & & & \\ & & \ddots & & & & & & \\ & & & 1 & & & & & \\ \hline & & & & 1 & & & & \\ & & & & -\mu_{k+1,k} & 1 & & & \\ & & & & -\mu_{k+2,k} & & 1 & & \\ & & & & \vdots & & & \ddots & \\ & & & & -\mu_{n,k} & & & & 1 \end{bmatrix}$$

where the kth row and column have been outlined and zero elements have been left blank. Thus, we have described elimination in terms of matrix products. A factorization of A is obtained by solving the equation above:

$$
\begin{aligned}
A &= (M_{n-1} \cdots M_2 M_1)^{-1} U \\
&= M_1^{-1} M_2^{-1} \cdots M_{n-1}^{-1} U.
\end{aligned}
$$

The inverse M_k^{-1} is simply M_k with its off-diagonal elements negated, for note that

$$
\begin{bmatrix}
1 & 0 & 0 & 0 \\
-\alpha & 1 & 0 & 0 \\
-\beta & 0 & 1 & 0 \\
-\gamma & 0 & 0 & 1
\end{bmatrix}
\begin{bmatrix}
1 & 0 & 0 & 0 \\
\alpha & 1 & 0 & 0 \\
\beta & 0 & 1 & 0 \\
\gamma & 0 & 0 & 1
\end{bmatrix}
= I.
$$

In the case of our 4×4 example,

$$
A = M_1^{-1} M_2^{-1} M_3^{-1} U
$$

where

$$
M_1^{-1} =
\begin{bmatrix}
1 & 0 & 0 & 0 \\
2 & 1 & 0 & 0 \\
\frac{1}{2} & 0 & 1 & 0 \\
-1 & 0 & 0 & 1
\end{bmatrix}, \quad
M_2^{-1} =
\begin{bmatrix}
1 & 0 & 0 & 0 \\
0 & 1 & 0 & 0 \\
0 & 3 & 1 & 0 \\
0 & -\frac{1}{2} & 0 & 1
\end{bmatrix}, \quad
M_3^{-1} =
\begin{bmatrix}
1 & 0 & 0 & 0 \\
0 & 1 & 0 & 0 \\
0 & 0 & 1 & 0 \\
0 & 0 & 2 & 1
\end{bmatrix},
$$

$$
U =
\begin{bmatrix}
6 & -2 & 2 & 4 \\
0 & -4 & 2 & 2 \\
0 & 0 & 2 & -5 \\
0 & 0 & 0 & -3
\end{bmatrix}.
$$

The nonzero off-diagonal elements of the first three matrices are the multipliers. The product of the first three matrices is

$$
M_1^{-1} M_2^{-1} M_3^{-1} =
\begin{bmatrix}
1 & 0 & 0 & 0 \\
2 & 1 & 0 & 0 \\
\frac{1}{2} & 3 & 1 & 0 \\
-1 & -\frac{1}{2} & 2 & 1
\end{bmatrix}
\overset{\text{def}}{=} L,
$$

which is a *unit* lower triangular matrix. Note that something very special has happened—the nonzero off-diagonal part of the product is simply the superposition of the off-diagonal parts of the factors, and hence the lower triangular elements of L are simply the multipliers. (This does *not* happen for the product $M_3 M_2 M_1$.) This completes the demonstration that $A = LU$.

It can be shown that with partial pivoting Gaussian elimination implicitly

1. computes a factorization

$$A = F_1 F_2 \cdots F_{2n-2} U$$

and

2. "divides" b by the factors of A:

$$
\begin{aligned}
A^{-1}b &= U^{-1} F_{2n-2}^{-1} \cdots F_2^{-1} F_1^{-1} b \\
&= U \text{ into}(F_{2n-2} \text{ into } (\cdots (F_2 \text{ into } (F_1 \text{ into } b)) \cdots)).
\end{aligned}
$$

Exercises

1. In Gaussian elimination with pivoting, a second kind of row operation is performed, namely, the interchange of two rows.

   (a) Interchanging the kth and lth rows is equivalent to premultiplication by what matrix?

   (b) What is the inverse of the matrix from part (a)?

   (c) What is the factorization $F_1 F_2 F_3 F_4 U$ that is determined by the example at the beginning of Section 4.5.2?

2. In Gauss-Jordan without pivoting, two kinds of row operations are performed.

   (a) One type of row operation is to divide the kth row by some nonzero value d. This is equivalent to premultiplication by what matrix?

   (b) The other type of row operation is to subtract a multiple m_i of the kth row from the ith row for each row $i \neq k$. This is equivalent to premultiplication by what matrix?

3. Let LU be an LU factorization of a 3×3 matrix A. Show that the elements of L and U can be explicitly determined one at a time. I.e., express $LU = A$ as a system of 9 equations in 9 unknowns and show how to solve for the unknowns.

Computer problem

1. `LUFactor[ ]` defined in `LinearAlgebra`GaussianElimination`` can be used to factor symbolic matrices. Since the entries are symbolic, no pivoting is done. Use `LUFactor[ ]` to find the lower and upper triangular matrix factors of

$$\texttt{Table[a[i,j], \{i, 4\}, \{j, 4\}]}$$

   Show that the product of these two matrices is the original matrix.

5. Interpolation

When you think of interpolation, you may think of determining intermediate values from tables:

x	0	0.1	0.2	0.3	0.4
$f(x)$	3.21	3.52	3.72	3.80	3.76

$f(0.25) = ?$

For a value like $f(0.5)$ that is off the end of the table, people use the word **extrapolation**. The generic term, which includes both possibilities, is **interpolation**. Applications of interpolation take many forms:

- One is to fill in the gaps of tables of data that are the result of physical experiment and observation. For example, United States census data are compiled only every 10 years, and population estimates are needed for other years, particularly future years.

- Functions that are known a priori but are time-consuming to evaluate can often be computed more quickly by interpolation from a table, especially now that so much computer memory is available. For example, molecular dynamics programs that do the direct calculation of all distances between atomic pairs spend as much as half the time taking square roots, and consequently there has been some use of tabulated square roots in this application.

- Interpolation is used to speed up operations to be performed on functions not known a priori but given by the user encoded in some programming language, for example, plotting or numerical integration. In the case of plotting it is usually less efficient to evaluate the function for every point on the display device than to evaluate the function at only a few points and fill in the rest by interpolation. Also, it is more convenient to construct the curve from device-independent graphics primitives, like line segments, rather than a sequence of points that depend on the resolution of the display device and the scale factor. As another example consider the problem of solving an equation $f(x) = 0$. One numerical method that is usually very efficient is the *secant method,* introduced in Chapter 3. It works by evaluating $f(x)$ at two different points and then constructing a polynomial of degree 1 (or less) that matches the function at those two points; see Figure 5.1. In constructing the polynomial we have in principle interpolated and extrapolated the two data points to all values of x. So we say that this polynomial *interpolates* $f(x)$ at those two points, and we shall use the word "interpolate" primarily

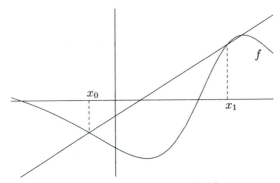

Figure 5.1: Linear interpolant—secant method

in this sense—to mean the construction of a simple function that matches another function at selected points. The constructed function is called an **interpolant**; in this case it is a **linear interpolant**. Finding the root of it is straightforward. If the root of the interpolant is close enough to being a root of $f(x)$, we are done; otherwise, the process is repeated using the root of the interpolant as one point together with the newer of the previous two points. Another method, known as **Muller's method**, samples the function $f(x)$ at three different points and constructs a **quadratic interpolant**, a polynomial of degree at most 2 that matches $f(x)$ at the three points. See Figure 5.2. One of the two roots of the quadratic is selected as a new point to replace the oldest of the three points used to construct the quadratic. Much more could be said about Muller's method, but here we want to highlight the role of polynomial interpolation in the derivation of numerical methods. In Section 5.7 we discuss a related method based on inverse quadratic interpolation.

- Interpolation is used by CAD systems to define curves from lists of coordinate positions specified interactively by a user with some computer graphics input device.

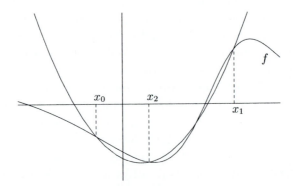

Figure 5.2: Quadratic interpolant—Muller's method

- Interpolation is the basis for most numerical methods for solving differential and integral equations, whose unknowns are functions. By interpolation the unknown functions are approximated in terms of their (unknown) values at specified points. These interpolants are substituted into a discretized form of the equations, which are then solved for the unknown values.

In addition, there is another well-known approximation technique, the *truncated Taylor series*, which is a generalized form of interpolation. With this included, it might be fair to say that interpolation is the most important topic in this book, especially because in its various forms it is the basis for the major part of numerical analysis.

There are various types of simple functions used for interpolation: polynomials, piecewise polynomials, sums of sines and cosines, sums of exponentials, and rational functions (ratios of polynomials). Except for Section 5.5, on piecewise polynomials, we confine our attention to polynomial interpolation.

You might wonder why polynomials are used so much in preference to other sets of functions. One reason is that there are mathematical theorems that assert the ability of polynomials to give good approximations to the kinds of functions likely to be encountered in practice. Another is that polynomials are easy to manipulate algebraically and efficient for computation. Also, the theory is quite simple. Finally, a set of polynomials of some given degree has no intrinsic length scale or origin for the independent variable: if $p(x)$ is a polynomial in x of degree $\leq n$, then $p(at + b)$ is, as a function of t, also a polynomial of degree $\leq n$. Other sets of functions have an intrinsic length scale and/or origin that may not be suitable for the problem under consideration.

The really important fact about polynomial interpolation is the existence of a unique interpolant, the topic of the second section.

This chapter contains the following sections:

5.1 Taylor Series

For creating approximations there is no tool better known than **Taylor series** expansions.

Theorem 5.1 *Let* $f(\circ)$ *be a function having* $n+1$ *continuous derivatives on some interval containing* a *and* x. *Then*

$$f(x) = \sum_{k=0}^{n}(x-a)^k \frac{f^{(k)}(a)}{k!} + (x-a)^{n+1}\frac{f^{(n+1)}(\xi)}{(n+1)!}$$

for some $\xi = \xi(x)$ *between* a *and* x.

What this says is that

$$f(x) = \text{truncated Taylor series} + \text{remainder term}$$

where the truncated series is a polynomial of degree $\leq n$ called the **Taylor polynomial** about $x = a$, which we shall denote by $p_n(x)$. Why should this polynomial be a reasonable approximation to $f(x)$? In what sense does this polynomial interpolate $f(x)$? To answer these questions, take the jth derivative of $p_n(x)$,

$$p_n^{(j)}(x) = \sum_{k=j}^{n}(x-a)^{k-j}\frac{f^{(k)}(a)}{(k-j)!},$$

and evaluate it at $x = a$:

$$p_n^{(j)}(a) = f^{(j)}(a).$$

This holds for $j = 0, 1, \ldots, n$. What we see is that $p_n(x)$ matches $f(x)$ and its first n derivatives at $x = a$, which suggests that $p_n(x)$ is a good approximation to $f(x)$ for $x \approx a$.

Example 5.1 The Taylor series for $\exp(x)$ about $x = 0$ is

$$1 + x + \frac{x^2}{2} + \frac{x^3}{6} + \cdots,$$

so the first three Taylor polynomials are 1, $1 + x$, and $1 + x + x^2/2$.

A polynomial $c_0 + c_1(x-a) + c_2(x-a)^2 + c_3(x-a)^3$, such as might be obtained from a Taylor series, can be evaluated efficiently using **Horner's rule**:

$$c_0 + (x-a)\,(c_1 + (x-a)\,(c_2 + (x-a)c_3)).$$

In numerical analysis we like to write $x = a + h$ where we think of h as a small fixed number, but, of course, it could be a variable. Similarly, we can write $\xi = a + \theta h$, where $0 < \theta < 1$. With these changes the Taylor expansion becomes

$$f(a+h) = \sum_{k=0}^{n} h^k\frac{f^{(k)}(a)}{k!} + h^{n+1}\frac{f^{(n+1)}(a+\theta h)}{(n+1)!}.$$

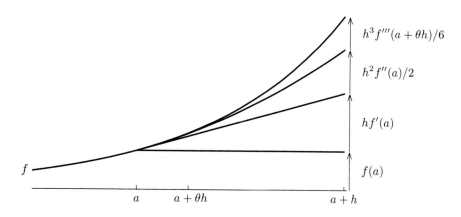

Figure 5.3: $f(x) = e^x$ together with its first three Taylor polynomials.

This equation is illustrated by Figure 5.3 for $f(x) = e^x$, $a = 0$, $h = 1.5$. In addition to the graph of $f(x)$ there are plotted the polynomials of degrees 0, 1, and 2 obtained by taking successively more terms of the Taylor expansion.

Example 5.2 To illustrate the use of Taylor polynomials, we derive a method for computing square roots. Setting $f(x) = x^{1/2}$, we have $f'(x) = \frac{1}{2}x^{-1/2}$, $f''(x) = -\frac{1}{4}x^{-3/2}$, and $f'''(x) = \frac{3}{8}x^{-5/2}$. This function has no derivatives at $x = 0$, so we choose another point $x = 1$ for the expansion. Substituting for $f(\circ)$ in

$$f(1+h) = f(1) + hf'(1) + \frac{h^2}{2}f''(1) + \frac{h^3}{6}f'''(1 + \theta h),$$

we get

$$\sqrt{1+h} = 1 + \frac{h}{2} - \frac{h^2}{8} + \frac{h^3}{16}(1 + \theta h)^{-5/2}.$$

To use this for computation, we would drop the remainder term. *However*, we should try to estimate the magnitude of the error. For illustration, let us suppose $|h| \leq 0.1$. Then we must have $-0.1 < \theta h < 0.1$, and taking worst-case values, we get

$$|\text{remainder}| < \frac{(0.1)^3}{16}(1 - 0.1)^{-5/2} < 0.000082.$$

The restriction on h may seem to limit the usefulness of the approximation, but this is not necessarily so. We can use it for any positive number if we can find a rough approximation to its square root, for example,

$$\sqrt{5} = 2.2\sqrt{\frac{5}{4.84}} = 2.2\left(1 + \frac{0.16}{4.84}\right)^{1/2} \approx 2.2\left[1 + \frac{1}{2}\left(\frac{0.16}{4.84}\right) - \frac{1}{8}\left(\frac{0.16}{4.84}\right)^2\right] = \frac{14881}{6655}.$$

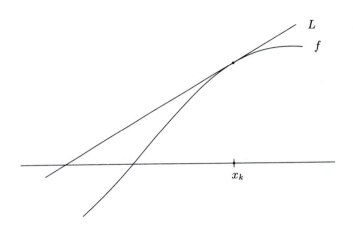

Figure 5.4: Local linearization

This method of finding square roots is more complicated than that of Section 1.3, and, as you might suspect, it is also less efficient.

As another application of the Taylor formula we give an alternative derivation of the Newton-Raphson method for solving $f(x) = 0$. Based on the use of the first two terms of the Taylor series,

$$f(x) \approx f(x_k) + f'(x_k)(x - x_k) \stackrel{\text{def}}{=} L(x),$$

which is a good approximation when $x \approx x_k$. The function $L(x)$ is a **local linearization** of $f(x)$. This is illustrated in Figure 5.4. The difference $L(x) - f(x)$ is truncation error. For Newton-Raphson the new approximation x_{k+1} is the root of $L(x)$. In other words,

$$f(x_k) + f'(x_k)(x_{k+1} - x_k) = 0,$$

which we solve to get the Newton-Raphson formula.

Another application of Taylor polynomials is to avoid cancellation difficulties, especially in situations where rearrangement is not possible. For example, the right-hand side of

$$x - \sin x = \frac{x^3}{3!} - \frac{x^5}{5!} + \frac{x^7}{7!} - \cdots$$

can be truncated and used for small x.

We can use a Taylor series expansion to analyze the convergence rate for functional iteration

$$x_{k+1} = g(x_k).$$

Letting $r = g(r)$ be the fixed point, we express the approximation as $x_k = r + e_k$, substitute this into the equation for the approximation, and expand as a Taylor series:

$$
\begin{aligned}
r + e_{k+1} &= g(r + e_k) \\
&= g(r) + g'(r)e_k + \tfrac{1}{2}g''(r)e_k^2 + \cdots,
\end{aligned}
$$

or

$$
e_{k+1} = g'(r)e_k + \tfrac{1}{2}g''(r)e_k^2 + \cdots.
$$

If $g'(r) \neq 0$ and $e_k \to 0$ as $k \to \infty$, then

$$
\lim_{k \to \infty} \frac{|e_{k+1}|}{|e_k|} = |g'(r)| > 0
$$

and the convergence is linear. Hence, $|g'(r)|$ is the asymptotic error constant (recall Section 3.3) and $|g'(r)| < 1$ is sufficient for local convergence of the iteration. Similarly, if $g'(r) = 0$ but $g''(r) \neq 0$, the convergence is quadratic. It is an exercise (Exercise 4) to show that convergence of Newton-Raphson is normally quadratic.

Before continuing, we examine more closely one aspect of Example 5.2, namely, the calculation of worst-case bounds. Note the word "bounds." For practical purposes it is not necessary to determine the exact worst-case value; it is all right to overestimate the magnitude of the error. (If you overestimate it by too much, you may sacrifice efficiency but not correctness.) This calculation can be done mechanically, i.e., by using rules, if you use interval operations. We start with $\theta \in [0,1]$ and $h \in [-0.1, 0.1]$. Then the remainder

$$
\begin{aligned}
\frac{h^3}{16}(1 + \theta h)^{-5/2} &\in \frac{[-0.1, 0.1]^3}{16}(1 + [0,\ 1][-0.1,\ 0.1])^{-5/2} \\
&= \frac{[-0.001, 0.001]}{16}([0.9, 1.1])^{-5/2} \\
&= \frac{[-0.001, 0.001]}{16}[1.1^{-5/2}, 0.9^{-5/2}] \\
&\subseteq [-0.000082, 0.000082].
\end{aligned}
$$

5.1.1 Big-oh notation

In working with an infinite power series there is difficulty in writing down the series because it has an infinite number of terms. In a case such as

$$
\frac{1}{1-h} = 1 + h + h^2 + \cdots,
$$

the difficulty is not great because the coefficients of the omitted terms are fairly obvious, but series can be much more complicated—so complicated, in fact, that we are content to know only the first few terms. The remaining terms involve higher powers of h, which can be neglected if h is small enough. In order to ensure that only correct coefficients are retained we need some way of keeping track of those whose coefficients are unknown. For this the big-oh notation is available. If we write

$$\frac{1}{1-h} = 1 + h + O(h^2), \tag{5.1}$$

we mean that there are terms involving h^2 and higher powers of h whose coefficients we have not bothered to keep track of. The "O" stands for "order" and we call "$O(h^2)$" a "term of order h^2." If we want to keep track of one additional term, we would write $1/(1-h) = 1 + h + h^2 + O(h^3)$. For one less term, we write $1/(1-h) = 1 + O(h)$.

Another example is

$$\exp(1 + h) = 1 + h + O(h^2).$$

This equation, however, may appear to contradict Equation (5.1) because $1/(1-h) \neq \exp(1 + h)$. There is no contradiction if we adopt the understanding that *the equal sign does not mean equality when used with the big-oh notation*—a loss of information is permitted when moving from the left-hand side to the right-hand side. A better notation, which you can use without confusing anyone, is to write

$$\frac{1}{1-h} \subseteq 1 + h + O(h^2),$$

and

$$\exp(1 + h) \subseteq 1 + h + O(h^2).$$

The idea here is that the big-oh represents the set of power series expansions whose lowest power term is given as the argument of the big-oh. It is easier, though, to be less formal and think of $O(h^2)$ simply as an unknown expansion consisting of powers of h with exponents ≥ 2.

With this interpretation of big-oh, we can work out the rules for operations. Simple examples are

- $2hO(h^2) = O(h^3)$,
- $O(h^2)O(h^2) = O(h^4)$,
- $O(h^3) + O(h^4) = O(h^3)$,
- $O(h^2) + h^2 = O(h^2)$.

These can be combined to do more complicated simplifications, such as

$$
\begin{aligned}
\exp(h + O(h^2)) &= 1 + (h + O(h^2)) + \tfrac{1}{2}(h + O(h^2))^2 + \tfrac{1}{6}(h + O(h^2))^3 + \cdots \\
&= 1 + (h + O(h^2)) + \tfrac{1}{2}(h^2 + O(h^3)) + \tfrac{1}{6}(h^3 + O(h^4)) + \cdots \\
&= 1 + h + O(h^2).
\end{aligned}
$$

We mentioned already the unorthodox and possibly confusing use of the equality sign with big-oh notation. There is another potential source of confusion, and that is that the expansion is not always performed about zero as it is for the variable h in this book. In particular, for the variable n, and others that typically represent integer values, it is usually an expansion about $n = \infty$ that is being considered. Thus $O(n^2)$ represents a series of terms involving n^2 and *lower* powers of n. There is little or nothing in the notation to decide what is meant. You must consider the context. The idea behind all uses of big-oh is that the terms represented by it are *negligible* compared to those terms given explicitly: for typical uses of h this occurs as $h \to 0$, and for n it occurs as $n \to \infty$.

⋆ 5.1.2 More about big-oh notation

The discussion of big-oh in the preceding subsection is a reasonable working definition that enables us to do manipulations easily. However, it is unduly restrictive and lacks the precision demanded by mathematicians, and computer scientists. Here we rectify the situation.

We say that a function of one variable $f(h)$ satisfies $f(h) = O(1)$ if there exist positive numbers C, D such that $|f(h)| \le C$ whenever $|h| \le D$, for example,

$$|\cos h| \le 1,$$

$$\left|\frac{\sin h}{h}\right| \le 1,$$

$$|h| \le 1 \qquad \text{if } |h| \le 1,$$

$$\left|\frac{1}{1-h}\right| \le 2 \qquad \text{if } |h| \le \tfrac{1}{2},$$

$$\text{or} \quad \left|\frac{1}{1-h}\right| \le \tfrac{3}{2} \qquad \text{if } |h| \le \tfrac{1}{3}.$$

On the other hand, $1/h \ne O(1)$.

We extend the definition of big-oh by defining $f(h) = O(g(h))$ to mean $f(h)/g(h) = O(1)$, which is equivalent to the existence of positive numbers C, D such that

$$|f(h)| \le C\,|g(h)| \quad \text{whenever } |h| \le D.$$

For example,

$$\frac{\sin h}{\sqrt{h}} = O(\sqrt{h}), \qquad h = O(h \ln h).$$

We would like to use big-oh not only as the right-hand side of an equal sign but as parts of expressions as we did in the preceding subsection. The way to do this is to define

$$O(g(h)) = \{\eta(h)\,|\,\eta(h) = O(g(h))\}.$$

For example,

$$O(1) = \left\{ \cos h, \ \frac{\sin h}{h}, \ h, \ \frac{1}{1-h}, \ \dots \right\}.$$

Operations with $O(\circ)$ are defined analogously to operations on sets of numbers. Thus, $O(1) + O(1) = O(1)$ and $O(h) \subseteq O(1)$. As noted in the preceding subsection, it is customary to write the latter as $O(h) = O(1)$ even though this notation is potentially misleading because $O(1) \neq O(h)$.

For purposes of manipulating big-oh quantities it may be easier, as an example, to think of $O(h^2)$ not as a set but as some specific but unknown quantity $\eta(h)$ such that $\eta(h)/h^2$ is bounded as $h \to 0$.

Review question

1. Let $p_n(x)$ be the Taylor polynomial of degree $\leq n$ for $f(x)$ about $x = a$. In what sense does $p_n(x)$ interpolate $f(x)$?

Exercises

1. Consider the approximation

$$\ln(1 + x) \approx x - \frac{x^2}{2} + \frac{x^3}{3}, \quad |x| \leq \tfrac{1}{10}.$$

   (a) Show that the magnitude of the error is bounded above by $1/(4 \cdot 9^4)$.

   (b) How can we use the above approximation and simple arithmetic to approximate $\ln 1.2$ without violating the restriction $|x| \leq \tfrac{1}{10}$ (and without adding more terms)? Hint: Exploit a property of the logarithm.

2. The expression $x - \sin x$ can be approximated for $|x| \leq 10^{-1}$ by $x^3/6$ with a relative error of magnitude less than 10^{-3}.

   (a) Derive the approximation $x^3/6$, and give the error term.

   (b) Show that the absolute error is less than or equal to 10^{-7} in magnitude.

   (c) Give an expression for the relative error, and show that it is less than or equal to 10^{-3} in magnitude. Hint: Use Taylor series to obtain a lower bound on $|x - \sin x|$.

3. Determine a low-degree polynomial approximation to $e^x - 1$, $|x| < 0.1$, having a *relative* error less than 10^{-5} in magnitude. Hint: Use Taylor series to obtain a lower bound on $|e^x - 1|$.

4. Newton-Raphson for $f(x) = 0$ has the form of functional iteration $x_{k+1} = g(x_k)$ with $g(x) = x - f(x)/f'(x)$.

(a) Show that convergence to a simple root r of $f(x)$ is quadratic provided that $f''(r) \neq 0$, and determine the asymptotic error constant.

(b) If we assume that $f(x)$ has a double root $x = r$ so that $f(r) = f'(r) = 0$ but $f''(r) \neq 0$, the method of analysis used for part (a) does not apply without some modification. Instead we can work from first principles by starting with

$$r + e_{k+1} = r + e_k - \frac{f(r + e_k)}{f'(r + e_k)}.$$

Determine the convergence rate and asymptotic error constant as follows: Separately expand numerator and denominator of the quotient in powers of e_k using the big-oh notation to represent higher order terms; then divide these two expansions and obtain an expansion for e_{k+1}.

(c) Use the method of analysis of part (b) to analyze convergence for a root of multiplicity m.

5. The chord method generates approximations to the root of r of a continuously differentiable function $f(x)$ by means of the following iteration:

$$x_{k+1} = x_k - \frac{f(x_k)}{f'(x_0)}.$$

Assuming that this converges, show that the order of convergence is (generally) 1. Determine the asymptotic error constant C.

6. Let $x \approx c^{1/3}$. By expressing x as $c^{1/3} + e$, determine the error in $c/x^2 \approx c^{1/3}$ as a Taylor expansion in powers of e up to $O(e^2)$.

7. Simplify (as much as possible): $O(h) - O(h)$, $\exp h + O(h^{3/2})$, $O(h)O(h^2)$, $\cos h + O(h)$. (Polynomials are simpler than elementary functions.)

8. Show that $O(h) - O(h) = 0$ is false.

Mathematica notes

Finding a Taylor polynomial with *Mathematica* is quite easy. `Series[ ]` will give you the Taylor series, and `Normal[ ]` will convert the series to a Taylor polynomial.

The second argument to `Series[ ]` specifies the variable, the center of expansion, and the order of approximation.

```
In[1]:= Series[Sqrt[1+h], {h, 0, 4}]
```

$$Out[1]= 1 + \frac{h}{2} - \frac{h^2}{8} + \frac{h^3}{16} - \frac{5 h^4}{128} + O[h]^5$$

There are several ways to generate a Taylor series in *Mathematica*. The most direct way is to use the function `Series[ ]`, the `OutputForm` of which is just the ordinary notation for

a series including a big-oh term. Combining a series with another expression will also result
in a series. Because of the big-oh term a series cannot be evaluated at a particular number.
On the other hand, it is often desirable to evaluate a *truncated* series at a particular value.
To convert a series to a "normal" expression, use the function `Normal[ ]`.

Start with a Taylor series expansion of
`Cos[h]` about $h = 0$.

$In[1]:=$ `s = Series[Cos[h], {h, 0, 5}]`

$$Out[1]= 1 - \frac{h^2}{2} + \frac{h^4}{24} + O[h]^6$$

`FullForm[ ]` shows what a series consists
of.

$In[2]:=$ `FullForm[s]`

$Out[2]//FullForm=$

`SeriesData[h, 0, List[1, 0, Rational[-1, 2], 0,`
   `Rational[1, 24]], 0, 6, 1]`

An operation on a series results in a series.

$In[3]:=$ `ls = Log[s]`

$$Out[3]= \frac{-h^2}{2} - \frac{h^4}{12} + O[h]^6$$

`Normal[ ]` is used to truncate a series
expansion.

$In[4]:=$ `diff = Normal[ls] - Log[Cos[h]]`

$$Out[4]= \frac{-h^2}{2} - \frac{h^4}{12} - Log[Cos[h]]$$

The error is $O[h]\wedge 6$.

$In[5]:=$ `Plot[diff, {h, -0.2, 0.2}, PlotRange -> All]`

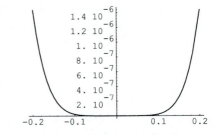

The function `CoefficientList[ ]` can be used to get a list of the coefficients of a polynomial.

Start with a polynomial.

$In[1]:=$ `p = Expand[(1 + 2x + 3y)\wedge3]`

$$Out[1]= 1 + 6\ x + 12\ x^2 + 8\ x^3 + 9\ y + 36\ x\ y + 36\ x^2\ y +$$
$$27\ y^2 + 54\ x\ y^2 + 27\ y^3$$

The coefficients of the powers of x in ascending order.

In[2]:= **CoefficientList[p, x]**

Out[2]= {1 + 9 y + 27 y^2 + 27 y^3, 6 + 36 y + 54 y^2,

12 + 36 y, 8}

The coefficients of the powers of y in ascending order.

In[3]:= **CoefficientList[p, y]**

Out[3]= {1 + 6 x + 12 x^2 + 8 x^3, 9 + 36 x + 36 x^2,

27 + 54 x, 27}

Given a list of coefficients, we can create a polynomial in an equally easy way.

The polynomial whose **CoefficientList** is {a, b, c, d}. Note the use of parentheses. Dot has a higher precedence than **Power**.

In[4]:= **{a, b, c, d} . (x^Range[0, 3])**

Out[4]= a + b x + c x^2 + d x^3

Computer problems

1. Use a Taylor polynomial to correctly evaluate

$$1. - (1. - 0.1^{40})^{40}$$

to at least 10 digits of accuracy without resorting to high-precision arithmetic. Check your answer using 60-digit arithmetic. Why does machine precision give a wrong answer when the expression is evaluated as written?

2. Use a Taylor polynomial to correctly evaluate $1. - \exp(x - \sin x)$ to at least 10 digits of accuracy at $x = 0.0001$ without resorting to high-precision arithmetic. Check your answer using 60-digit arithmetic.

3. Evaluate the following:

```
O[h] + O[h]
h + O[h]
h + O[h] ^ 2
Sin[x] - x + O[x]^3
```

4. Use **Series** to expand **Log[1 - x]** in powers of x up to x^10.

5. Evaluate

```
s = Sin[h] + O[h]^4
(s - (h - h^3/6))/h^4
(Sin[h] - (h - h^3/6))/h^4 + O[h]^4
```

6. Plot $\sin x$ and its Taylor polynomials about $x = 0$ for $0 \le x \le 2\pi$. Use the Taylor polynomials of degree 1, 3, 5, and 7.

7. Horner's rule is an efficient way to evaluate a polynomial. As an example, the polynomial $1+\frac{1}{2}x+\frac{1}{3}x^2+\frac{1}{4}x^3$ would be evaluated as $1+x(\frac{1}{2}+x(\frac{1}{3}+x\cdot\frac{1}{4}))$, with a saving of two or three multiplications. Use `CoefficientList[ ]` to define a function `horner[poly_, var_]` that takes a polynomial `poly` in a variable `var` and returns the polynomial in the nested form associated with Horner's rule. As another example, `horner[a x^3 - 3 x^2 + b c, x]` should give `b c + x^2 (-3 + a x)` (i.e., the result of slightly simplifying `((a x - 3) x + 0) x + b c )`.

5.2 Existence and Uniqueness

The interpolation problem is specified by a set of $n+1$ points (x_k, y_k), $k = 0, 1, \ldots, n$, pairs of **abscissas** (or **nodes**) and **ordinates** as shown in Figure 5.5. Numbering the points from zero on will prove to be convenient because the powers of x in a polynomial are also numbered from zero. For the theory to hold, it does not matter in what order we number the abscissas; in practice they are usually numbered from left to right. However, *the abscissas must be distinct*, which is mathematics jargon meaning that they are all different. This is because the graph of a polynomial can never go through two points, one of which is above the other. There are infinitely many polynomials that interpolate a given set of data; we seek a simple one—one of lowest degree. Precisely stated, the problem is to find a polynomial $p(x)$ of lowest degree such that

$$p(x_k) = y_k, \quad k = 0, 1, \ldots, n.$$

This constitutes $n + 1$ conditions on the polynomial. An arbitrary polynomial of degree m,

$$p(x) = a_0 + a_1 \, x + \cdots + a_m \, x^m,$$

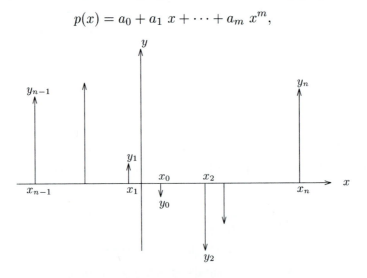

Figure 5.5: Graph of interpolation data

contains $m + 1$ different coefficients. Hence, it is natural to choose $m = n$, yielding the equations

$$
\begin{aligned}
a_0 + x_0\, a_1 + \cdots + x_0^n\, a_n &= y_0 \\
a_0 + x_1\, a_1 + \cdots + x_1^n\, a_n &= y_1 \\
\vdots \qquad \vdots \qquad\qquad \vdots \qquad &\;\; \vdots \\
a_0 + x_n\, a_1 + \cdots + x_n^n\, a_n &= y_n
\end{aligned}
$$

to be solved for $a_0, a_1, \ldots, a_n$.

Example 5.3 For the data

k	x_k	y_k
0	2	2
1	3	3
2	1	2
3	-1	1

we try the cubic polynomial $a + bx + cx^2 + dx^3$ and get the system of equations

$$
\begin{aligned}
a + 2b + 4c + 8d &= 2, \\
a + 3b + 9c + 27d &= 3, \\
a + b + c + d &= 2, \\
a - b + c - d &= 1,
\end{aligned}
$$

which can be solved using the methods of Chapter 4.

   This method of forming the interpolating polynomial is an example of the **method of undetermined coefficients**. For polynomial interpolation it always yields a system of *linear* equations, in which there are no powers of unknowns and no products of unknowns. We know from linear algebra that there are only three possibilities: no solution, exactly one solution, or infinitely many solutions. Moreover, there is exactly one solution if and only if the coefficients of the unknowns form a *nonsingular* matrix. So, the first question should be, "Is there always a unique solution to the polynomial interpolation problem?" The answer, given by the theorem that follows, is very satisfying.

Theorem 5.2 *There exists a unique polynomial of degree $\leq n$ that interpolates data at $n + 1$ distinct abscissas.*

Proof. The coefficients of the polynomial are determined by

$$
\begin{bmatrix}
1 & x_0 & \cdots & x_0^n \\
1 & x_1 & \cdots & x_1^n \\
\vdots & \vdots & & \vdots \\
1 & x_n & \cdots & x_n^n
\end{bmatrix}
\begin{bmatrix}
a_0 \\
a_1 \\
\vdots \\
a_n
\end{bmatrix}
=
\begin{bmatrix}
y_0 \\
y_1 \\
\vdots \\
y_n
\end{bmatrix}.
$$

We need to show that this matrix is nonsingular. Suppose it is singular. Then

$$
\begin{bmatrix}
1 & \cdots & x_0^n \\
\vdots & & \vdots \\
1 & \cdots & x_n^n
\end{bmatrix}
\begin{bmatrix}
\bar{a}_0 \\
\vdots \\
\bar{a}_n
\end{bmatrix}
=
\begin{bmatrix}
0 \\
\vdots \\
0
\end{bmatrix}
$$

has infinitely many solutions because $[0 \ 0 \ \cdots \ 0]^{\mathrm{T}}$ is a solution. Let $[\bar{a}_0 \ \bar{a}_1 \ \cdots \ \bar{a}_n]^{\mathrm{T}}$ be a solution other than $[0 \ 0 \ \cdots \ 0]^{\mathrm{T}}$. Then the polynomial $p(x) \overset{\text{def}}{=} \bar{a}_0 + \bar{a}_1 \, x + \cdots + \bar{a}_n \, x^n$ is of degree k where k is the greatest j such that $\bar{a}_j \neq 0$. We have $0 \leq k \leq n$. With $p(x)$ defined in this way the matrix equation above is equivalent to stating that $p(x)$ vanishes[1] at $n+1$ distinct points $x_0, x_1, \ldots, x_n$. However, this is not possible because a polynomial of degree k has at most k distinct roots and $k < n+1$. Hence, the matrix is nonsingular.

This theorem is not just a formality; Exercise 7 shows that it does not extend to interpolation of a function of two variables.

Review question

1. Theorem 5.2 requires the abscissas to be distinct. At what point does the proof break down if the abscissas are *not* distinct?

Exercises

1. Let $f(1) = -3$, $f(2) = 1$, $f(3) = 2$.

   (a) Find the interpolating polynomial of lowest degree.

   (b) Use this to find a good approximation to the root of $f(x)$. (Assume that $f(x)$ has exactly one root.)

2. Construct the lowest degree polynomial $p(x)$ interpolating a given function $f(x)$ such that

$$
\begin{aligned}
p(0) &= f(0) = 1, & p'(0) &= f'(0) = 1, \\
p(1) &= f(1) = 0, & p'(1) &= f'(1) = 0.
\end{aligned}
$$

---

[1] Recall from Chapter 3 that "vanish" means "become equal to zero."

3. Determine the polynomial $p(x)$ of lowest degree that interpolates $f(x) = x/(1+x^2)$ at $x = -1, 0, 1$ and whose derivative interpolates $f'(x)$ at $x = 0$. Show your work.

4. Why would Theorem 4.1 not be true if "of degree $\leq n$" were replaced by "of degree n"?

5. Let $p(x)$ be the unique polynomial of degree at most 100 that satisfies $p(j) = (-1)^j$, $j = 0, 1, \ldots, 100$. How do we know that the degree of $p(x)$ is exactly 100?

6. Which is a more accurate approximation of $x^7 + 1$: the Taylor polynomial of degree ≤ 7 about $x = 1$ or the polynomial of lowest degree that interpolates at $x = 0, 1, \ldots, 7$?

7. A linear polynomial in two variables has the form $p(x, y) = a + bx + cy$.

   (a) Show that there does not exist a linear polynomial that interpolates the data $f(1, 1) = 1$, $f(2, 2) = 3$, and $f(3, 3) = 2$.

   (b) Show that there is more than one linear polynomial that interpolates the data $f(1, 1) = 1$, $f(2, 2) = 3$, and $f(3, 3) = 5$.

Computer problems

1. Define a function `muc[ ]` that takes a list of abscissas, a list of ordinates, and a variable and returns the interpolating polynomial calculated by the method of undetermined coefficients. Do not forget to deal with the case where the abscissas are not distinct by giving an error message. Useful *Mathematica* functions: `LinearSolve[ ]` and `Message[ ]`.

5.3 Lagrange Form

The Lagrange form is a direct and relatively simple way of constructing the interpolating polynomial. It demonstrates the existence, but not the uniqueness, of the interpolating polynomial. It is used in the solution of differential equations by the *finite-element method*, which we mention again in Section 5.5.

We construct the Lagrange form for $n = 3$. The general case will then be discussed. The interpolation problem for $n = 3$ is to find $p(x)$ such that

$$p(x_0) = y_0, \ p(x_1) = y_1, \ p(x_2) = y_2, \ p(x_3) = y_3.$$

The key idea is to do four special simple cases that do not depend on the ordinates y_k:

0. Find $l_0(x)$ such that

$$l_0(x_0) = 1, \ l_0(x_1) = 0, \ l_0(x_2) = 0, \ l_0(x_3) = 0.$$

1. Find $l_1(x)$ such that

$$l_1(x_0) = 0, \ l_1(x_1) = 1, \ l_1(x_2) = 0, \ l_1(x_3) = 0.$$

2. Find $l_2(x)$ such that

$$l_2(x_0) = 0, \ l_2(x_1) = 0, \ l_2(x_2) = 1, \ l_2(x_3) = 0.$$

3. Find $l_3(x)$ such that

$$l_3(x_0) = 0, \ l_3(x_1) = 0, \ l_3(x_2) = 0, \ l_3(x_3) = 1.$$

These special interpolants we call **fundamental polynomials**. Their defining equations can be put more succinctly as

$$l_k(x_j) = \left\{ \begin{array}{ll} 1, & j = k, \\ 0, & j \neq k. \end{array} \right.$$

Because the fundamental polynomials are of degree at most 3, we know that their graphs are qualitatively like those of Figure 5.6. The key observation to be made is that for $l_0(x)$, and each of the others, we know all three roots. Therefore, we can write

$$l_0(x) = C(x - x_1)(x - x_2)(x - x_3)$$

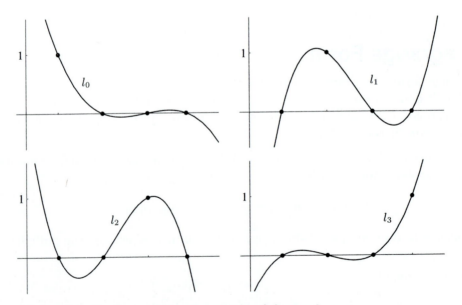

Figure 5.6: Fundamental polynomials of degree 3

where C is some constant. In doing this we have used three of the four conditions that define $l_0(x)$. The remaining condition is $l_0(x_0) = 1$, which implies

$$C(x_0 - x_1)(x_0 - x_2)(x_0 - x_3) = 1.$$

This gives us a value for C to substitute into our expression for $l_0(x)$. Likewise, we get expressions for the other three fundamental polynomials. What we end up with are the following:

$$l_0(x) = \frac{(x - x_1)(x - x_2)(x - x_3)}{(x_0 - x_1)(x_0 - x_2)(x_0 - x_3)},$$

$$l_1(x) = \frac{(x - x_0)}{(x_1 - x_0)} \frac{(x - x_2)(x - x_3)}{(x_1 - x_2)(x_1 - x_3)},$$

$$l_2(x) = \frac{(x - x_0)(x - x_1)}{(x_2 - x_0)(x_2 - x_1)} \frac{(x - x_3)}{(x_2 - x_3)},$$

$$l_3(x) = \frac{(x - x_0)(x - x_1)(x - x_2)}{(x_3 - x_0)(x_3 - x_1)(x_3 - x_2)}.$$

Note that these are well defined only if the x_j are distinct.

The fundamental polynomials are combined using the ordinates as weights to give the **Lagrange form** of the interpolating polynomial:

$$p(x) = y_0\, l_0(x) + y_1\, l_1(x) + y_2\, l_2(x) + y_3\, l_3(x).$$

To confirm that this interpolates, check any of the interpolating conditions; for example, observe that

$$\begin{aligned}
p(x_2) &= y_0\, l_0(x_2) + y_1\, l_1(x_2) + y_2\, l_2(x_2) + y_3\, l_3(x_2) \\
&= y_0 \cdot 0 + y_1 \cdot 0 + y_2 \cdot 1 + y_3 \cdot 0 \\
&= y_2.
\end{aligned}$$

It is also clear that this polynomial is of degree ≤ 3.

Example 5.4 Find the polynomial $p(x)$ of lowest degree that satisfies

$$p(x) = \sin \pi x \quad \text{at} \quad x = 0,\ \tfrac{1}{6},\ \tfrac{1}{2}.$$

The Lagrange construction gives

$$\begin{aligned}
p(x) &= \sin \pi 0\, l_0(x) + \sin \frac{\pi}{6}\, l_1(x) + \sin \frac{\pi}{2}\, l_2(x) \\
&= 0 \cdot \frac{(x - \frac{1}{6})(x - \frac{1}{2})}{(0 - \frac{1}{6})(0 - \frac{1}{2})} + \frac{1}{2} \cdot \frac{(x - 0)(x - \frac{1}{2})}{(\frac{1}{6} - 0)(\frac{1}{6} - \frac{1}{2})} + 1 \cdot \frac{(x - 0)(x - \frac{1}{6})}{(\frac{1}{2} - 0)(\frac{1}{2} - \frac{1}{6})},
\end{aligned}$$

which is shown graphically in Figure 5.7. Simplifying, we get

$$p(x) \;=\; \frac{1}{2}\cdot\frac{x(x-\frac{1}{2})}{-\frac{1}{18}} + 1\cdot\frac{x(x-\frac{1}{6})}{\frac{1}{6}}$$

$$\;=\; -9x(x-\tfrac{1}{2}) + 6x(x-\tfrac{1}{6}) = x(\tfrac{7}{2}-3x).$$

The error is plotted in Figure 5.8.

How does this differ from the polynomial obtained by the method of undetermined coefficients? The two must be identical because the interpolating polynomial is unique.

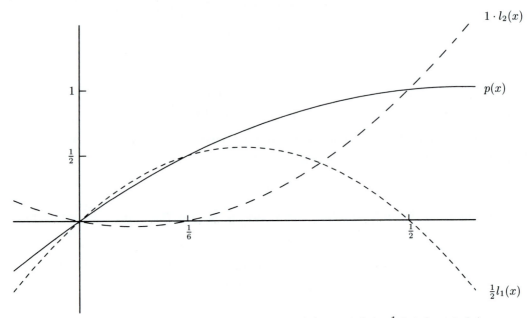

Figure 5.7: Construction of Lagrange form $p(x) = 0\cdot l_0(x) + \frac{1}{2}\cdot l_1(x) + 1\cdot l_2(x)$

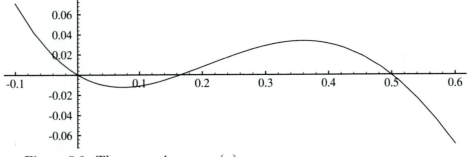

Figure 5.8: The error $\sin \pi x - p(x)$

In general, with $n + 1$ interpolating conditions $p(x_0) = y_0$, $p(x_1) = y_1$, $\ldots$, $p(x_n) = y_n$, the kth fundamental polynomial is

$$
\begin{aligned}
l_k(x) &= \frac{(x - x_0) \cdots (x - x_{k-1})(x - x_{k+1}) \cdots (x - x_n)}{(x_k - x_0) \cdots (x_k - x_{k-1})(x_k - x_{k+1}) \cdots (x_k - x_n)} \\
&= \prod_{\substack{j = 0 \\ j \neq k}}^{n} \frac{x - x_j}{x_k - x_j}.
\end{aligned}
$$

These are constructed to satisfy

$$
l_k(x_i) = \begin{cases} 1, & i = k, \\ 0, & i \neq k. \end{cases}
$$

The desired interpolant is

$$
p(x) = l_0(x)\, y_0 + l_1(x)\, y_1 + \cdots + l_n(x)\, y_n.
$$

If we evaluate $p(x)$ at some fixed x, what we see is a weighted sum of y_i's with coefficients that depend only on the values x_k. To verify that this is the interpolating polynomial, we note that

$$
\begin{aligned}
p(x_i) &= l_0(x_i)\, y_0 + \cdots + l_{i-1}(x_i)\, y_{i-1} + l_i(x_i)\, y_i + l_{i+1}(x_i)\, y_{i+1} + \cdots + l_n(x_i)\, y_n \\
&= 0 \cdot y_0 + \cdots + 0 \cdot y_{i-1} + 1 \cdot y_i + 0 \cdot y_{i+1} + \cdots + 0 \cdot y_n.
\end{aligned}
$$

Example 5.5 Suppose we want to derive a formula for approximating $f(\frac{3}{2})$ in terms of $f(0)$, $f(1)$, $f(2)$, and $f(3)$ where $f(x)$ is otherwise unknown. There is no one correct way to approximate in a situation like this. A generally good choice is polynomial interpolation, so let us do that. With $x_0 = 0$, $x_1 = 1$, $x_2 = 2$, and $x_3 = 3$ we have

$$
l_0\left(\tfrac{3}{2}\right) = \frac{(\tfrac{3}{2} - 1)(\tfrac{3}{2} - 2)(\tfrac{3}{2} - 3)}{(0 - 1)(0 - 2)(0 - 3)} = -\frac{1}{16}.
$$

Likewise, $l_1(\frac{3}{2}) = \frac{9}{16}$, $l_2(\frac{3}{2}) = \frac{9}{16}$, and $l_3(\frac{3}{2}) = -\frac{1}{16}$. The formula is

$$
f\left(\tfrac{3}{2}\right) \approx -\tfrac{1}{16} f(0) + \tfrac{9}{16} f(1) + \tfrac{9}{16} f(2) - \tfrac{1}{16} f(3).
$$

Supplementary note

Linear interpolation was known to the Old Babylonians nearly 4000 years ago.

Exercises

1. Obtain the Lagrange form of the interpolating polynomial for the data

   (a) $\dfrac{\begin{array}{c|ccc} x & 0 & 1 & 2 \\ \hline f(x) & 0 & -1 & 4 \end{array}}{}$

   (b) $\dfrac{\begin{array}{c|cccc} x & 1 & 3 & 6 & 10 \\ \hline f(x) & 1 & 2 & 3 & 4 \end{array}}{}$

   (Do not simplify.)

2. Let $p(x)$ be the lowest degree interpolating polynomial for $1/x$ at 1, $\frac{3}{2}$, 2. Give the Lagrange form for $p(x)$. (Do not simplify.)

3. Derive the secant method using the idea that we choose x_{k+1} to be a root of a linear interpolant $L(x)$ of $f(x)$.

4. Suppose that $p(x)$ interpolates a function at $x = 2, 3, 5, 7$. What is another polynomial that also interpolates the function at those points?

5. Obtain the (lowest degree) polynomial interpolating the function $f(x) = x^3 + x^2 + x + 1$ at the points $x = 0, 1$, and 2. Do this by subtracting from $f(x)$ (the appropriate multiple of) a cubic that vanishes at $x = 0, 1, 2$.

6. Suppose we have abscissas $x_0 \le x_1 \le x_2 \le \cdots \le x_9 \le x_{10}$ that are all different except that $x_3 = x_4$. An attempt to form the Lagrange interpolating polynomial for these abscissas breaks down. Explain precisely how and where it breaks down.

7. The most obvious way of forming the $n+1$ products $(x - x_0) \cdots (x - x_{j-1})(x - x_{j+1}) \cdots (x - x_n)$, $0 \le j \le n$, requires proportional to n^2 arithmetic operations. How can these products be formed so that the number of operations is proportional to n?

8. The Lagrange form of the interpolating polynomial is a weighted sum of $n + 1$ fundamental polynomials each of degree n. Under what condition in terms of $x_0, x_1, \ldots, x_n$, $y_0, y_1, \ldots, y_n$ will the sum not also be of degree n?

9. Let $q(x)$ be a polynomial of degree m, and let $p(x)$ be the polynomial of degree $\le n$ that interpolates $q(x)$ at $n+1$ distinct points $x_0, x_1, \ldots, x_n$. Precisely when is it true that $p(x) \equiv q(x)$?

★10. Show that the fundamental polynomials satisfy $\displaystyle\sum_{i=0}^{n} l_i(x) = 1$.

★11. If $P(x)$ denotes the polynomial of degree n such that $P(k) = k/(k+1)$ for $k = 0, 1, \ldots, n$, determine $P(n+1)$. (This problem is from the Fourth U.S.A. Mathematical Olympiad for high-school students.) If you cannot do this mathematically, use the computer to obtain a plausible conjecture.

Mathematica notes

The Lagrange interpolation formula is quite easy to program in *Mathematica*. The basic idea is to be able to turn a list such as {a, b, c, d, e} into a product of differences with a specified element dropped.

Start with a list of data.	`In[1]:= data = {a, b, c, d, e}`
	`Out[1]= {a, b, c, d, e}`
Delete the fourth element in the list of data.	`In[2]:= Drop[data, {4}]`
	`Out[2]= {a, b, c, e}`
Form the list of differences with x. Recall that the arithmetic operations are listable.	`In[3]:= x - %`
	`Out[3]= {-a + x, -b + x, -c + x, -e + x}`
Change the head List to Times.	`In[4]:= Times @@ %`
	`Out[4]= (-a + x) (-b + x) (-c + x) (-e + x)`

These operations can all be done in one short statement.

Drop the second element, form a list of differences with x, and finally change the head List to Times.	`In[5]:= Times @@ (x - Drop[data, {2}])`
	`Out[5]= (-a + x) (-c + x) (-d + x) (-e + x)`

Computer problem

1. Translate the Lagrange interpolation formula into *Mathematica* by defining a function with three arguments, the first being a list of abscissas, the second being an equally long list of ordinates, and the third being the name of the independent variable. Do not ask for any simplification. As a test try it on {0, 1/6, 1/2}, {0, 1/2, 1}, t. Then Expand the result.

5.4   Error Term

The error in interpolating a function $f(x)$ by a polynomial $p(x)$ is the difference $p(x) - f(x)$. This is a function of x that, in practice, is unknown. Nonetheless, we know that it vanishes at the interpolation nodes and probably changes sign at each node. With deeper analysis there is more that we can say about the error that is useful—information that can guide us in the application of interpolation and the design of algorithms.

5.4.1   Runge's phenomenon

You may wonder whether it is best to use as many data points as is practical. Equivalently, should the degree of an interpolating polynomial be as high as is practical? It all depends.

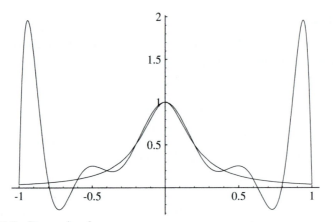

Figure 5.9: Runge's phenomenon

Example 5.6 Consider interpolating $f(x) = 1/(1 + 25x^2)$ for $-1 \leq x \leq 1$. This is a nice, smooth function and is a good candidate for approximation by a polynomial. Let $p_n(x)$ interpolate $f(x)$ at $n+1$ equally spaced points from -1 to 1. In Figure 5.9 we have plotted $f(x)$ and $p_{10}(x)$. What happens as we let let $n \to \infty$? The value of $p_n(x)$ converges to $f(x)$ but *only* for those x in the middle of the interval, in particular, only if $|x| < 0.7266768604776682 \cdots$. The sequence of values $p_n(x)$ diverges as $n \to \infty$ if $|x|$ is greater than this quantity. We see good approximation in the middle but not at the ends of the interval.

Example 5.6 demonstrates that high-degree polynomial interpolation *with equidistant nodes* can be unsatisfactory *at the ends of the interval*. However, with a smaller interval fairly high degree polynomial interpolation with equally spaced nodes can be satisfactory at the ends. For example, calculations in astronomy often use numerical methods based on 12th degree polynomial interpolation to solve Newton's equations of motion.

5.4.2 Chebyshev nodes

In applications where there is freedom in the choice of nodes, the best *general* choice is a set of **Chebyshev nodes**. Suppose for the sake of simplicity that we want a polynomial approximation whose worst-case error on the interval $-1 \leq x \leq 1$ is as small as possible. This is achieved, approximately, by using the Chebyshev nodes for $[-1, 1]$:

$$x_k \stackrel{\text{def}}{=} - \cos \left(\frac{k + \frac{1}{2}}{n + 1} \pi \right), \qquad k = 0,\ 1,\ \ldots,\ n.$$

A geometric prescription for these nodes is given by Figure 5.10 for the case $n + 1 = 10$. With only mild assumptions on the function $f(x)$, a statement can be made about the polynomial

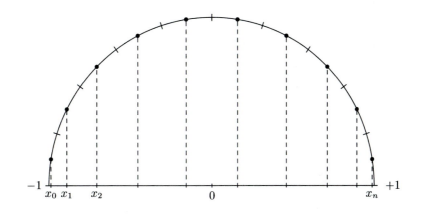

Figure 5.10: Chebyshev nodes

$p_n(x)$ that interpolates $f(x)$ at the Chebyshev nodes x_k, $k = 0, 1, \ldots, n$. What can be said is that if $f(x)$ has a continuous first derivative for $-1 \le x \le 1$, then

$$\lim_{n \to \infty} p_n(x) = f(x) \quad \text{for } -1 \le x \le 1.$$

(If $f(x)$ does not have a continuous first derivative, convergence may or may not occur.) A result like this does not guarantee that such a process can obtain the desired accuracy with reasonable computational effort, but it does increase our confidence in the process.

5.4.3 Error term stated

Having mentioned some interesting facts about the limit $n \to \infty$, we consider now the situation for a fixed n.

Theorem 5.3 *Let $p_n(\circ)$ be the unique polynomial of degree $\le n$ interpolating $f(\circ)$ at $n + 1$ distinct points $x_0, x_1, \ldots, x_n$. If $f(\circ)$ has a continuous $(n + 1)$th derivative on some interval containing $x_0, x_1, \ldots, x_n$, and x, then*

$$f(x) = p_n(x) + (x - x_0)(x - x_1) \cdots (x - x_n) \frac{f^{(n+1)}(\xi)}{(n + 1)!}$$

for some $\xi = \xi(x)$ between the least and greatest of $x_0, x_1, \ldots, x_n$, and x.

This theorem expresses a function as the sum of its interpolating polynomial and a *remainder* term. Especially worth noting, and yet expected, is that the remainder equals zero when x is an interpolation node.

You may notice that the remainder term is quite like something we have already encountered. It resembles the remainder term of the Taylor polynomial. If we let

$$x_1 \to x_0, \quad x_2 \to x_0, \quad \ldots, \quad x_n \to x_0,$$

it happens that the

$$\text{remainder term} \to (x - x_0)^{n+1} \frac{f^{(n+1)}(\xi)}{(n+1)!}$$

for some ξ between x_0 and x. It will be shown (in Section 5.6.5) that $p_n(x)$ has as its limit the Taylor polynomial. In the simplest case of $n = 0$ the interpolating polynomial is the same as the Taylor polynomial, and for both we have

$$f(x) = f(x_0) + f'(\xi)(x - x_0),$$

which is the *mean-value theorem*.

Let us examine the expression for the magnitude of the error:

$$|\text{error}| = |p_n(x) - f(x)| = \frac{|f^{(n+1)}(\xi)|}{(n+1)!} \prod_{k=0}^{n} |x - x_k|.$$

The point ξ appearing in this expression is unknown and, in practice, unknowable. It depends in a complicated way on f and each of the points $x_0, x_1, \ldots, x_n$ *and* x. It is often nearly as good to work with an upper bound on the error. Let $[a, b]$ be an interval containing all of the points, take

$$M_{n+1} \overset{\text{def}}{=} \max_{a \le \xi \le b} |f^{(n+1)}(\xi)|,$$

and put it into the expression above. This gives

$$|\text{error}| \le \frac{M_{n+1}}{(n+1)!} \prod_{k=0}^{n} |x - x_k|.$$

Only the second half of this bound depends on x. We see from this dependence that the nodes x_k should be chosen as close as possible to x, which is entirely to be expected. In Figure 5.11 we have plotted the particular case $\prod_{k=0}^{5} |x - x_k|$. Observe that the error bound is largest for extrapolation and is smallest for interpolation in the middle.

Exercises

1. Suppose we are given the data

x	0	1	2
$f(x)$	1	4	15

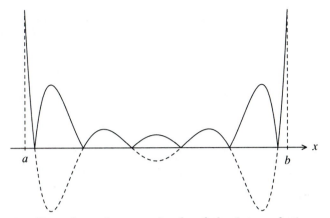

Figure 5.11: Bound on the magnitude of the interpolation error

(a) Form the Lagrange polynomial of degree ≤ 2 interpolating the given data. (Do not simplify.)

(b) Give a bound on the interpolation error at the point $x = \frac{1}{2}$ assuming that the magnitude of the third derivative of $f(x)$ is less than or equal to 6.

2. Use Lagrange interpolation to approximate $\sqrt{13}$ from the values of $\sqrt{x}$ for $x = 4, 9, 16, 25$. Show that the error term for this interpolation lies between $81/125000$ and $405/1024$. Determine the actual error.

3. Consider the use of quadratic interpolation to estimate $\ln(1.55)$ from the values of $\ln x$ at $x = 1.5, 1.6, 1.7$. Find an upper bound on the interpolation error without actually evaluating $\ln x$. Try to get the bound $1/27000 = 0.000037037037\cdots$.

4. Let $p(x)$ be the lowest degree interpolating polynomial for $1/x$ at $1, \frac{3}{2}, 2$. Give a reasonably good upper bound for the magnitude of the error $|p(x) - 1/x|$ for $1 \leq x \leq 2$.

Mathematica notes

The function `InterpolatingPolynomial[ ]` in *Mathematica* gives the Newton form of the interpolating polynomial to a set of data. The construction of the Newton form is explained in Section 5.6.

The interpolating polynomial in the variable x that passes through the points {1, a}, {2, b}, and {3, c}.

```
In[1]:= InterpolatingPolynomial[{a, b, c}, x]

Out[1]= a + (-a + b + (a - 2 b + c) (-2 + x)) (-1 + x)
                         ───────────────
                               2
```

Evaluating the polynomial at $x = 1, 2, 3$ gives a, b, c, respectively.

```
In[2]:= Expand[% /. x -> {1, 2, 3}]

Out[2]= {a, b, c}
```

The interpolating polynomial of
{{x0,y0},{x1,y1},{x2,y2}}.

```
In[3]:= InterpolatingPolynomial[
           {{x0,y0},{x1,y1},{x2,y2}}, x]
```

$$Out[3]= y0 + (x - x0) \left(\frac{-y0 + y1}{-x0 + x1} + \frac{(x - x1) \left(-\left(\frac{-y0 + y1}{-x0 + x1}\right) + \frac{-y1 + y2}{-x1 + x2}\right)}{-x0 + x2}\right)$$

The interpolating polynomial that
interpolates {{x0,y0}, {x1,y1}} *and* has
first and second derivatives yp0 and ypp0
at x == x0.

```
In[4]:= InterpolatingPolynomial[
           {{x0,{y0,yp0,ypp0}},{x1,y1}}, x]
```

$$Out[4]= y0 + (x - x0) \left(yp0 + (x - x0) \left(\frac{ypp0}{2} + \frac{(x - x0) \left(\frac{-ypp0}{2} + \frac{-yp0 + \frac{-y0 + y1}{-x0 + x1}}{-x0 + x1}\right)}{-x0 + x1}\right)\right)$$

The derivative at x == x0 is indeed yp0.

```
In[5]:= Expand[D[%, x] /. x -> x0]
Out[5]= yp0
```

Computer problems

1. In this problem we examine Runge's phenomenon with the function
   `f[x_] := 1./(1.+25.x^2)`.

   (a) Let `p[x_]` be the interpolating polynomial using 11 equally spaced nodes ranging
       from `-1.` to `1.`. Define `p[x_]` using `=` rather than `:=` so that the interpolating
       polynomial is constructed only once rather than each time `p[ ]` is evaluated. Plot
       `f[x]` and `p[x]` on the same set of axes. Use `PlotRange -> All`.

   (b) Repeat part (a) using the 11 Chebyshev nodes for the interval $[-1., 1.]$.

   (c) Plot the errors of the two interpolants.

2. Consider the function `f[x_] := 1./(1.+25.x^2)` *and its derivative* on the interval
   $[-1., 1.]$.

   (a) Using 11 equally spaced nodes, find the interpolant that interpolates both function
       values and first derivative values at the nodes. Plot the error in the interpolant.
       Does the inclusion of first derivative values defeat Runge's phenomenon?

   (b) Repeat part (a) using the 11 Chebyshev nodes for the interval $[-1., 1.]$.

(c) Consider the derivatives of the two interpolating polynomials. Plot the errors in these derivatives as approximations to the derivative of **f**. Note: Form polynomials and their derivatives using `Set` and `Expand`; otherwise, plotting takes too much time.

3. Let $p_n(x)$ interpolate $\sin x$ at $x = 0, h, \ldots, nh$ where $h > 0$. An error analysis suggests that for each $x \geq 0$, $p_n(x) \to \sin x$ as $n \to \infty$ if and only if $h \leq 1$. For each of $h = 0.9, 1.1$ and $n = 5, 10, 20, 40$ create $p_n(x)$ using `InterpolatingPolynomial[ ]` and plot $p_n(x) - \sin x$ on the interval $[0., 3.]$ using `PlotRange -> All`. Do the results support the conjecture that $p_n(x) \to \sin x$ as $n \to \infty$ if and only if $h \leq 1$?

5.5   Piecewise Polynomial Interpolation

An important idea is that of **piecewise polynomial interpolation**. As is shown in Example 5.6 the polynomial of highest possible degree is not always the most accurate choice, and it is computationally time-consuming. For these reasons it is much more common in practice to construct an interpolant by piecing together lower degree polynomials. There are two illustrations of this in this section: table construction and plotting.

Piecewise polynomial approximation is the basis of the **finite-element method** used heavily in civil and mechanical engineering to model solid structures as well as in other applications like fluid dynamics. A piecewise polynomial $s(x)$ is a function defined on some interval $[a, b]$ such that there is a partitioning of the interval $a = x_0 < x_1 < \cdots < x_m = b$ into subintervals on each of which $s(x)$ is equal to a (possibly) different polynomial. If the values of $s(x)$ at the partition points match those of the polynomials on each side, so that $s(x)$ is continuous, then $s(x)$ is said to be a C^0 piecewise polynomial. If first derivatives match, then $s(x)$ is a C^1 piecewise polynomial, etc. A C^2 piecewise cubic is known as a *spline*.

5.5.1   Table construction

It can be faster to interpolate the value of a function from a table than to compute it from scratch, and with plentiful computer memory it is practical to do this for frequently used functions. As an example suppose we wish to compute e^x, $0 \leq x \leq 1$, using *piecewise linear interpolation* from values of e^x tabulated for $x = 0, h, 2h, \ldots, 1 - h, 1$ where $h = 1/N$. Within each interval $x_{n-1} \leq x \leq x_n$ we interpolate from the two endpoints. (They are the nearest two tabulated values.) To determine n from x, we can compute the ceiling $\lceil x/h \rceil$. Graphically the piecewise linear interpolant is just the result of using straight line segments to connect points on the graph of e^x that have equally spaced x coordinates. This suggests that we can make the piecewise linear interpolant as close as we like to e^x by choosing the spacing h small enough. In order to minimize the number of tabulated values that must be stored, our choice of h should be just small enough to achieve the desired accuracy. Also, let us choose for h a nice round number. Suppose then that we wish to have the

$$|\text{error}| \leq 10^{-6}.$$

In the next paragraph we show that the

$$|\text{error}| \leq \frac{eh^2}{8}, \tag{5.2}$$

which is an upper bound on the magnitude of the error in terms of h alone. The desired accuracy is obtained if

$$\frac{eh^2}{8} \leq 10^{-6}.$$

This is satisfied by $h = 10^{-3}$, but not by $h = 2 \times 10^{-3}$.

The error for linear interpolation at x from x_{n-1} and x_n is

$$|\text{error}| \leq \frac{|f''(\xi)|}{2!}\,|(x - x_{n-1})(x - x_n)|$$

where $x_{n-1} < \xi < x_n$. We note that $f''(\xi) = e^\xi$ and $0 < \xi < 1$, so $|f''(\xi)| \leq e$. The graph of $|(x - x_{n-1})(x - x_n)|$ for $x_{n-1} \leq x \leq x_n$ is an inverted parabola that is symmetric about the midpoint $(x_{n-1} + x_n)/2$, so it achieves its maximum at the midpoint:

$$|(x - x_{n-1})(x - x_n)| \leq \left|\left(\frac{h}{2}\right)\left(-\frac{h}{2}\right)\right|.$$

Combining these bounds yields (5.2).

Now suppose we want to tabulate e^x, $0 \leq x \leq 1$, at equidistant nodes so that "centered" cubic interpolation is good for six-decimal-place accuracy. By "centered" we mean that the nearest two nodes to the left and the nearest two nodes to the right are used. As before, the big question is: What should we choose for the spacing $h = 1/N$ between consecutive nodes? The dependence of interpolated values on tabulated values is illustrated in Figure 5.12, for some arbitrary function $f(x)$. Note the necessity of tabulating two outside values. Each subinterval between successive nodes uses a different cubic polynomial, and together they form a piecewise cubic interpolant, illustrated in Figure 5.13. The goal is to choose a value for h such that $|\text{error}| \leq 10^{-6}$. In the next paragraph we show that

$$\max |\text{error}| \leq \frac{e^{1+h}}{4!}\left(\frac{9}{16}\right)h^4, \tag{5.3}$$

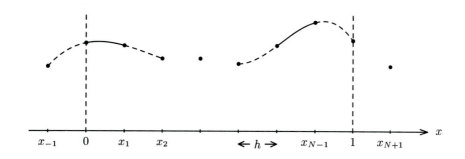

Figure 5.12: Dependence of interpolated values on tabulated values

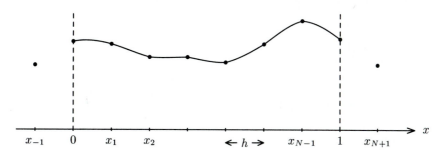

Figure 5.13: Piecewise cubic interpolant

so we want

$$\frac{e^{1+h}}{4!}\left(\frac{9}{16}\right)h^4 \le 10^{-6}. \tag{5.4}$$

The value $h = \frac{1}{10}$ does not satisfy this, but $h = \frac{1}{20}$ does. Comparing this to linear interpolation, we note that only 23 table entries are needed for cubic interpolation as opposed to 1001 for linear interpolation. The reason is that as h gets smaller, the h^4 in the piecewise cubic error bound decreases more rapidly toward zero than does the h^2 in the piecewise linear error bound.

Here we obtain error bound (5.3). Let x be an arbitrary point of $[0, 1]$, and choose n such that $x_{n-1} \le x \le x_n$. Then

$$|\text{error}| \;\le\; \frac{|f^{\text{iv}}(\xi)|}{4!}|x - x_{n-2}||x - x_{n-1}||x - x_n||x - x_{n+1}|$$

and

$$|f^{\text{iv}}(\xi)| \le \max_{-h \le \xi \le 1+h} e^{\xi} \;=\; e^{1+h}.$$

The part of the error bound that explicitly involves x is shown in Figure 5.14. Because of the uniform spacing of the nodes the graph is symmetric about the midpoint $x = \frac{1}{2}(x_{n-1} + x_n)$.

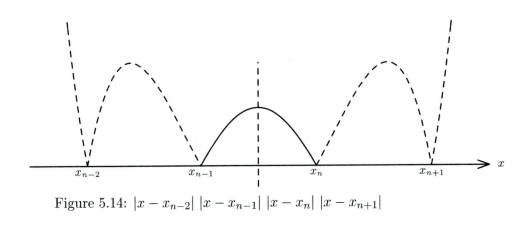

Figure 5.14: $|x - x_{n-2}|\, |x - x_{n-1}|\, |x - x_n|\, |x - x_{n+1}|$

(Proving this is Exercise 9 at the end of this section.) Hence, because x is restricted to the middle subinterval, the graph is maximized at the midpoint:

$$\text{maximum} \ = \ \left|\tfrac{3}{2}h\right|\ \left|\tfrac{1}{2}h\right|\ \left|-\tfrac{1}{2}h\right|\ \left|-\tfrac{3}{2}h\right| \ = \ \tfrac{9}{16}h^4.$$

Combining these bounds yields (5.3).

It is possible that the error bound of Equation (5.3) is misleading and that the actual worst-case error is much smaller. This happens not to be true in this case; in fact, the ratio of the error bound to the actual worst-case error approaches 1 as $h \to 0$:

$$\max |\text{error}| = \frac{e}{4!}\left(\frac{9}{16}\right)h^4 + O(h^5). \tag{5.5}$$

We see that the behavior as a function of h is dominated by some power of h, in this case h^4. This is typical of truncation error. The greater the power of h, the greater the reduction in error if h is made smaller. The exponent of h we call the **order of accuracy** of the method, and it is the primary measure of a method's ability to compute accurate values. For cubic interpolation the order is 4. Note that the order of *accuracy* here is not the same thing as the order of *convergence* for an iteration. Determining the order of accuracy of a method by error analysis is often a complicated and delicate process. Experiment is much more likely to yield the correct answer! To do an experiment, we need some way to compute actual errors, so we use problems for which this is not too difficult. The procedure then is as follows: First, compute actual errors for a finite sequence of h values that go to zero. Then, try to fit the behavior of the error to some power of h. To obtain a clear-cut result, use a log-log plot. To see why, we take logarithms in Equation (5.5):

$$(-\log_{10}(\max|\text{error}|)) = 4\,(-\log_{10} h) + \text{constant} + O(h). \tag{5.6}$$

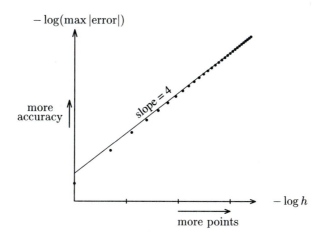

Figure 5.15: Decimal places of accuracy vs. log(number of points)

Minus signs have been inserted so that the left-hand side is decimal places of accuracy. The term $-\log_{10} h = \log_{10}(1/h)$ is a logarithmic measure of the number of points. If the $O(h)$ term is neglected, the relationship (5.6) between the two expressions in braces is linear with slope 4. Shown in Figure 5.15 is a rendition of the expected relationship. The plotted values of the accuracy should tend toward a straight line of slope 4 as $-\log_{10} h$ increases (if roundoff error is negligible).

5.5.2 Plotting

The question of how to plot a function of one variable is not only important and interesting in its own right, but it also illustrates a practical limitation of numerical methods. It is our first opportunity to explain the statement made concerning the "incorrectness" of numerical software.

The task is to plot $f(x)$, $a \le x \le b$, given the ability to evaluate $f(x)$ at any point but the desire to do so as little as possible. We can assume that the software and hardware of the plotting device can efficiently and accurately plot a polynomial function. (In practice these may be formed using instructions that draw points or line segments.) The main ideas are adequately illustrated if we consider approximating $f(x)$ by a piecewise linear function as pictured in Figure 5.16.

We shall pursue a simple strategy: For the given interval or some subinterval of it, evaluate $f(x)$ at the left endpoint, the midpoint, and the right endpoint. Use these three values to construct both a quadratic interpolant $q(x)$ and a piecewise linear interpolant $s(x)$ as shown in Figure 5.17 by the solid and dashed curves, respectively. Then:

1. Accept $s(x)$, $a \leq x \leq c$, if it is "close enough" to $q(x)$; otherwise, apply the algorithm to $[a, c]$.

2. Accept $s(x)$, $c \leq x \leq b$, if it is "close enough" to $q(x)$; otherwise, apply the algorithm to $[c, b]$.

By "close enough" we shall mean that the distance between the two curves is less than the expected resolution of the device. It might be sensible to give the user the option of requesting less accuracy.

The next question is one of computing the distance between the two curves. Let $[a, b]$ denote the interval *or subinterval* under consideration, and let c denote its center. Let us look at the left half of the interval. For $a \leq x \leq c$ we can form $s(x)$ as the linear polynomial that interpolates $f(x)$ at $x = a, c$ and $q(x)$ as the quadratic that interpolates at $x = a, c, b$. The distance between the graphs of the two functions is the length of the line segment PQ shown in Figure 5.18 where P is that point on the quadratic whose distance from the line segment

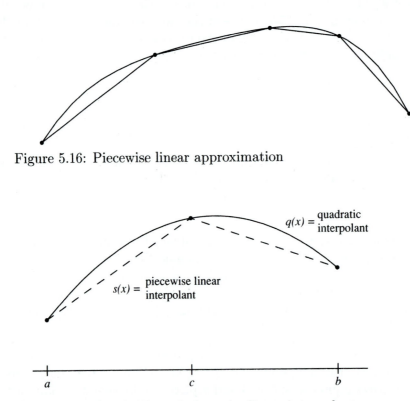

Figure 5.16: Piecewise linear approximation

Figure 5.17: Quadratic and piecewise linear interpolants

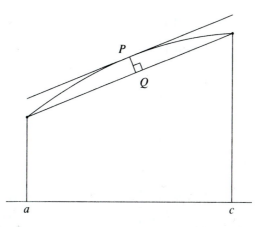

Figure 5.18: Maximum distance from quadratic to line segment

is maximum and Q is the point on the line segment nearest P. An elementary but tedious calculation (that is left as an exercise) shows

$$\text{max distance} = \frac{c-a}{8}\left(\frac{|f(b)-2f(c)+f(a)|}{\sqrt{(c-a)^2+(f(c)-f(a))^2}}\right). \tag{5.7}$$

Example 5.7 Suppose we are to plot $1/x, 1 \le x \le 2$, with tolerance $= 0.005$. For this function on the interval $[1,2]$ we construct the table

x	1	$\frac{3}{2}$	2
$f(x)$	1	$\frac{2}{3}$	$\frac{1}{2}$

The error estimate for $[1, \frac{3}{2}]$ is

$$\frac{\frac{3}{2}-1}{8}\left(\frac{|\frac{1}{2}-2\cdot\frac{2}{3}+1|}{\sqrt{(\frac{3}{2}-1)^2+(\frac{2}{3}-1)^2}}\right) = \frac{1}{16\sqrt{13}} = 0.017\cdots.$$

Because this is greater than 0.005, we should bisect $[1, \frac{3}{2}]$. Below is a tabulation of all the steps of the calculation:

Interval	Error estimate		Decision
$[1, 2]$	for $[1, \frac{3}{2}]$	$0.017\cdots$	bisect
	for $[\frac{3}{2}, 2]$	$0.019\cdots$	bisect
$[1, \frac{3}{2}]$	for $[1, \frac{5}{4}]$	$0.006\cdots$	bisect
	for $[\frac{5}{4}, \frac{3}{2}]$	$0.007\cdots$	bisect
$[\frac{3}{2}, 2]$	for $[\frac{3}{2}, \frac{7}{4}]$	$0.002\cdots$	OK
	for $[\frac{7}{4}, 2]$	$0.002\cdots$	OK
$[1, \frac{5}{4}]$	for $[1, \frac{9}{8}]$	$0.002\cdots$	OK
	for $[\frac{9}{8}, \frac{5}{4}]$	$0.002\cdots$	OK
$[\frac{5}{4}, \frac{3}{2}]$	for $[\frac{5}{4}, \frac{11}{8}]$	$0.001\cdots$	OK
	for $[\frac{11}{8}, \frac{3}{2}]$	$0.001\cdots$	OK

This strategy for partitioning the interval does not always work. For example, as shown in Figure 5.19, it would plot $\cos 4\pi x$, $0 \leq x \leq 1$, as a straight line. This might reasonably be regarded as bad luck. A more typical failure is shown in Figure 5.20 where the sampling points are too far apart to detect the blip in the function $\exp(-300(x - \frac{1}{3})^2)$.

The problem with the algorithm is that it begins with only three points, which is too few to resolve the ups and downs of more complicated functions. The algorithm will work if it begins with enough points. But there is no way of knowing how many is enough if all we can do is sample *values* of $f(x)$. The problem of deciding how many is enough must somehow be left to the user.

What we have said must also apply to the *Mathematica* command `Plot[f[x], {x, a, b}]` because it simply evaluates `f[x]` for numerical values of `x`. Without even knowing what strat-

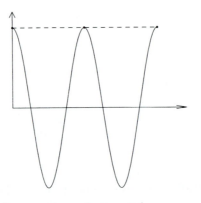

Figure 5.19: Sampling $\cos 4\pi x$, $0 \leq x \leq 1$

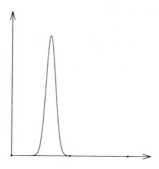

Figure 5.20: Sampling $\exp(-300(x - \frac{1}{3})^2)$

Figure 5.21: $f(x) = (x - c_1)(x - c_2) \cdots (x - c_N)$ and `Plot` of $f(x)$

egy it uses to choose sampling points,[2] we can deceive `Plot`. First call `Plot` with a function that is identically zero but has a monitoring device that records all arguments that it is given:

```
c = { }
zero[x_] := (AppendTo[c, x] ; 0.)
Plot[zero[x], {x, -2., 2.}]
```

Now `c` is a list of sampling points for `zero[ ]`. Next define a polynomial, pictured on the left in Figure 5.21, whose roots are the sampling points

```
f[x_] := Product[x-c[[k]], {k, 1, Length[c]}]
```

The result of `Plot[f[x], {x, -2., 2.}]` is shown on the right in Figure 5.21 and is a consequence of the inability to distinguish between `f[ ]` and `zero[ ]`.

---

[2]Other than that the strategy is deterministic.

Hence, we see that there is a limitation of purely numerical methods, which rely solely on sampling. To consider this issue more carefully, we need a clear statement of what an ideal computation should yield—of the best possible result obtainable *with the given data*. What are the given data? They are a massive *but finite* tabulation of values of $f(x)$ for all machine numbers x from a to b, encoded as a black-box procedure. For simplicity let us suppose that the best possible result is a piecewise linear interpolant of the entire table.[3] Practical necessity dictates that the computed result must be based on only a small sampling of the table, and thus arises the possibility of unannounced, unacceptable results. Such is a property of much numerical software, that the software sometimes fails to work *without warning*. This is discussed further in the concluding chapter.

If the deceptiveness of numerical software disturbs you, that is understandable. It is possible *for small problems* to build honest software by using elementary symbolic techniques to compute error bounds, just as you can calculate them by hand; but such software will not be written unless there is a demand from users.

Exercises

1. Suppose we have an array $y[0 : 9900]$, each of whose elements $y[n]$ contains the value $f(1 + 0.01n)$. Write an algorithm that, given a value x between 1 and 100, returns the result of linear interpolation from the two nearest tabulated values of $f(x)$. You may assume the availability of a floor or ceiling function.

2. Obtain good lower and upper bounds on the error in piecewise linear interpolation at $x = 1.13$ from a table for

$$\ln x, \quad x = 1, 1.1, 1.2, \ldots, 1.9, 2.$$

   Your answer should be a purely numeric expression, but it need not be evaluated. Do not use a value of the (natural) logarithm ln.

3. How accurately can $\ln x$ be determined by piecewise linear interpolation from a table for x in $[1, 2]$ if the difference between successive nodes is uniformly $h = 0.01$? Show your work.

4. Suppose that $\exp(x)$ is tabulated for $x = \ldots, -0.1, 0, 0.1, 0.2, \ldots$ and that at any given point $\bar{x}$ we approximate $\exp(\bar{x})$ by cubic interpolation of the nearest four tabulated values. Show that the *relative* interpolation error is bounded in absolute value by $\exp(0.2)/60000$.

5. Suppose we want the value y obtained by piecewise linear interpolation from a table of values for $\ln x$, $x = 2, 2 + h, 2 + 2h, \ldots, 3 - h, 3$ to satisfy

$$|y - \ln x| \leq 0.0001.$$

   How small must h be?

---

[3]If we are given a *formula* for the function, then the best possible result is defined by the formula.

6. (a) Suppose you have to create an equally spaced table of values of $\sin x$, $0 \le x \le 6.5$, in order to do linear interpolation later. Determine the largest spacing that can be used if the interpolation error must not exceed 0.0001.

   (b) What is the corresponding answer if quadratic interpolation is used? Assume we use the *nearest* three points and we extend the table to one outside point on each side.

7. Suppose you have to do a tabulation of $\sqrt{x}$, $1 \le x \le 100$, for $N + 1$ equally spaced values of x for interpolation from the $n+1$ nearest nodes by a polynomial of degree $\le n$ with error $\le 10^{-6}$.

   (a) How many values $N + 1$ are needed if $n = 0$?

   (b) How many values $N + 1$ are needed if $n = 1$?

   (c) How many values $N + 3$ are needed if $n = 2$, assuming the table is extended by one point at each end?

   (d) How can we use the table for $100 \le x \le 10000$?

8. A "readable" table gives the values of a function of x at points $x_n = nh$ where the spacing h is the product of a divisor of 10 and an integral power of 10. Examples:

Good table		Poor table		Poor table	
x	$f(x)$	x	$f(x)$	x	$f(x)$
1.0		1.1		2.0	
1.2		1.3		2.4	
1.4		1.5		2.8	
1.6		1.7		3.2	
1.8		1.9		3.6	
2.0		2.1		4.0	

   A "readable" table of values of $\cosh x$ for $0 \le x \le 2$ is required so that linear interpolation will yield six-decimal-place accuracy ($|\text{absolute error}| \le 10^{-6}$) for any value of x on this interval. Get a good bound on the error in terms of h, and then determine the maximum spacing h that satisfies the conditions.

9. Prove that $|x - x_{n-2}|\, |x - x_{n-1}|\, |x - x_n|\, |x - x_{n+1}|$ as a function of x is symmetric about the point $x = \frac{1}{2}(x_{n-1} + x_n)$ where x_{n-2}, x_{n-1}, x_n, and x_{n+1} are consecutive uniformly spaced points. The challenge here is to restate the problem mathematically.

10. Let $0 \le x \le 1$.

    (a) Explain why

$$\left| \prod_{k=1-m}^{m} (x - k) \right| \le ((\tfrac{1}{2})(\tfrac{3}{2}) \cdots (m - \tfrac{1}{2}))^2.$$

(b) Show that

$$\left| \prod_{k=-m}^{m} (x-k) \right| \leq (m+1)((\tfrac{1}{2})(\tfrac{3}{2}) \cdots (m-\tfrac{1}{2}))^2.$$

⋆11. Derive formula (5.7) for the maximum distance. This can be done with a computer algebra system. If you use *Mathematica*, you will find the following constructs useful: `D[`*expr*`, x]`, `Solve[`*lhs* `== ` *rhs*`, x]` (followed by `x /. %[[1, 1]]`), `Simplify[`*expr*`]`.

Mathematica notes

In Section 5.5.1 we showed how to find the order of accuracy by examining a log-log plot of the error. *Mathematica* has a package for drawing many kinds of specialized plots, including log-log plots, but the axes get labeled in the units of the original values rather than in units of their logarithms. An alternative is simply to take the `Log[ ]` of the data.

Start with some data representing error as a function of h. (These data contain a component of h^5 and h^6 as well as some rounding error.)

```
In[1]:= data = {{0.5, 25.44}, {0.25, 0.5509},
        {0.125, 0.0134}, {0.0625, 0.0003592},
        {0.03125, 0.00001029},
        {0.015625, 0.0000003071},
        {0.0078125, 0.00000000937}};
```

Convert the data to log-log data.

```
In[2]:= logdata = Log[data]
Out[2]= {{-0.693147, 3.23632}, {-1.38629, -0.596202},
        {-2.07944, -4.3125}, {-2.77259, -7.93163},
        {-3.46574, -11.4843}, {-4.15888, -14.9961},
        {-4.85203, -18.4858}}
```

We can see that the points nearly lie in a straight line and that the slope is about 5. (The scales on the axes are not the same.)

```
In[3]:= ListPlot[logdata]
```

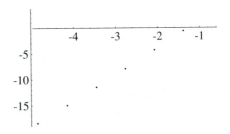

If we are only interested in the slope, we can calculate it without making a plot. The idea is to find it directly from the log-log data. However, it is unlikely that all of the log-log data will lie in a straight line; we need a straight line that best fits the data. In *Mathematica* we can use the function `Fit[ ]`.

The coefficient of the linear term is what
we want. Note that we do not get exactly 5
for the coefficient of `logh`. This is typical;
higher powers of `h` and rounding errors
have a significant effect.

```
In[4]:= Fit[logdata, {1, logh}, logh]
Out[4]= 6.65252 + 5.21111 logh
```

Computer problems

1. In the example on page 204 of `Plot[ ]` giving a completely erroneous result, we defined
   `f[x_] := Product[x-c[[k]], {k, 1, Length[c]}]`. Try repeating the example with
   `f[x_] = Expand[Product[x-c[[k]], {k, 1, Length[c]}]]`. Why does *Mathematica*
   give the correct plot when `f[ ]` is defined in this expanded way?

2. In this problem you are to implement piecewise cubic interpolation of the exponential
   function as described on page 198; that is, you are to define a function `exp[x_]` defined
   for `x` in the interval $[0., 1.]$ that gives the piecewise cubic interpolant of `Exp[x]` from the
   nearest four points on a mesh with spacing $h = 0.05$. Your function should refuse to
   evaluate for arguments outside the specified interval. The basic idea is first to construct a
   table of interpolating polynomials to use as needed. Use `InterpolatingPolynomial[ ]`
   to do this. The function `exp[x_]` should use the appropriate interpolating polynomial
   from the table. It is far too expensive to construct an interpolating polynomial each
   time it is needed. We will consider further refinements to the solution of this problem
   in the next section.

3. Implement the adaptive plotting strategy suggested in this section. You should use the
   Mathematica function `ListPlot[ ]` with the option `PlotJoined -> True` to draw the
   plot. Use recursion to implement the bisection. Note: Depending on your implementation, you may need to `Sort` the list of ordered pairs that you give `ListPlot[ ]`. They
   will be joined in the order in which they occur in the list, and if they are not in sorted
   order, the result will not even represent a function.

5.6   Newton Form

The Lagrange form of the interpolating polynomial is good for theoretical purposes (and for
special cases of interpolation in more than one variable). For most calculations the Newton
form is more convenient. Also, it has a bit less roundoff error and is more flexible. However,
the Newton form is more involved, making use of what are known as divided differences. Our
first encounter with divided differences will not show us how to compute them efficiently. It
is in the third subsection that this will be discussed.

5.6.1   The interpolating polynomial

The basic idea of the Newton form is to build a succession of interpolants of increasing
degree by utilizing one more data point with each successive interpolant. In Figure 5.22 is

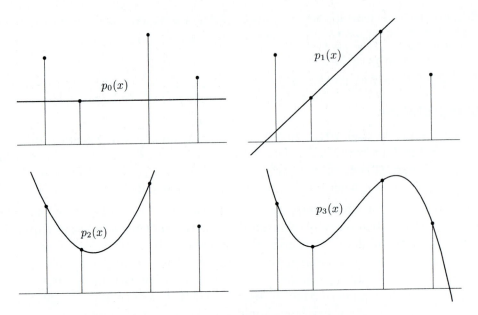

Figure 5.22: Building a succession of interpolants

shown a constant polynomial $p_0(x)$ interpolating one data point, a linear polynomial $p_1(x)$ interpolating two points, a quadratic polynomial $p_2(x)$ interpolating three points, and a cubic polynomial $p_3(x)$ interpolating four points. We explain the idea with an example.

Example 5.8

x_j	1	2	4
$f(x_j)$	1	$\frac{1}{2}$	$\frac{1}{4}$

We start with nothing as our approximation and add in a constant correction

$$p_0(x) = c_0,$$

which is determined by the first interpolating condition:

$$p_0(1) = 1 \quad \Rightarrow \quad c_0 = 1.$$

We add in a linear correction $(x - 1)c_1$, which, because it vanishes at $x = 1$, does not destroy what we have already done:

$$p_1(x) = 1 + (x - 1)c_1,$$

$$p_1(2) = \tfrac{1}{2} \quad \Rightarrow \quad 1 + (2 - 1)c_1 = \tfrac{1}{2} \quad \Rightarrow \quad c_1 = -\tfrac{1}{2}.$$

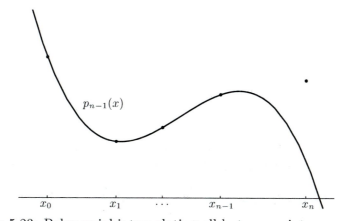

Figure 5.23: Polynomial interpolating all but one point

We add in a quadratic correction that does not change the values at $x = 1$ and $x = 2$:

$$p_2(x) = 1 + (x - 1)(-\tfrac{1}{2}) + (x - 1)(x - 2)c_2,$$

$$p_2(4) = \tfrac{1}{4} \quad \Rightarrow \quad 1 + (4 - 1)(-\tfrac{1}{2}) + (4 - 1)(4 - 2)c_2 = \tfrac{1}{4} \quad \Rightarrow \quad c_2 = \tfrac{1}{8}.$$

The idea is to make use of each polynomial in the sequence to help construct the next one. Suppose we have obtained one of the polynomials and we wish to construct the next one. Let the given polynomial $p_{n-1}(x)$ interpolate $f(x)$ at $x = x_0, x_1, \ldots, x_{n-1}$, as shown in Figure 5.23. We try constructing $p_n(x)$ as a correction to $p_{n-1}(x)$, in particular, a simple additive correction

$$p_n(x) = p_{n-1}(x) + \text{correction}.$$

The interpolation problem thus becomes that of constructing the correction $p_n(x) - p_{n-1}(x)$, which we hope is simpler. We use the interpolating properties of the two polynomials to get

$$\text{correction} = \begin{cases} 0, & x = x_0, x_1, \ldots, x_{n-1}, \\ f(x_n) - p_{n-1}(x_n), & x = x_n, \end{cases}$$

which is shown in Figure 5.24. We see that the correction has roots at the points $x = x_0, x_1, \ldots, x_{n-1}$. These must be all of its roots because the correction is a polynomial of degree $\leq n$. Hence, we can write the correction in the factored form

$$\text{correction} = (x - x_0)(x - x_1) \cdots (x - x_{n-1})c_n,$$

where the yet-to-be-determined coefficient c_n has been placed last in order to yield an ascending sequence of subscripts. From the value given for the correction at $x = x_n$ we get

$$c_n = \frac{f(x_n) - p_{n-1}(x_n)}{(x_n - x_0)(x_n - x_1) \cdots (x_n - x_{n-1})}.$$

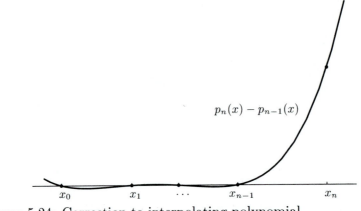

Figure 5.24: Correction to interpolating polynomial

This formula is *not for computing,* however—it is more sensitive to roundoff error than is necessary.

Four steps of this construction give

$$\underbrace{c_0}_{p_0(x)} + (x - x_0)c_1 + (x - x_0)(x - x_1)c_2 + (x - x_0)(x - x_1)(x - x_2)c_3 \,.$$

For computational purposes it is not necessary to expand out this polynomial. Instead, one should represent this polynomial by storing the nodes $x_0, x_1, \ldots, x_n$ and the Newton form coefficients $c_0, c_1, \ldots, c_n$. The polynomial can be efficiently evaluated by expressing it as

$$p_3(x) = c_0 + (x - x_0)(c_1 + (x - x_1)(c_2 + (x - x_2)c_3)).$$

We call this the **nested form** of the polynomial, and it avoids many extra multiplications. The special case $x_0 = x_1 = x_2$ is Horner's rule.

For reasons that become clear later, we call the c_j **divided differences.**

★ 5.6.2 Divided differences

From the preceding equations note that

$$
\begin{aligned}
p_0(x) &= c_0, \\
p_1(x) &= c_1 x + \text{lower degree term,}
\end{aligned}
$$

$$p_2(x) = c_2 x^2 + \text{lower degree terms,}$$
$$p_3(x) = c_3 x^3 + \text{lower degree terms.}$$

Thus c_k is the coefficient of x^k in the polynomial $p_k(x)$ that interpolates $f(x)$ at $x = x_0, x_1, \dots, x_k$, and it is sufficiently useful that it is accorded special notation.

Definition 5.4 *The kth divided difference*

$$f[x_0, x_1, \dots, x_k]$$

is the coefficient of x^k in the polynomial of degree $\leq k$ that interpolates $f(x)$ at $x = x_0$, x_1, ..., x_k.

If the degree is $< k$, the coefficient of x^k is 0.

Remark. The preceding definition may strike you as a rather indirect way of defining divided differences. To compensate for this, we give a closed-form formula. It is an exercise at the end of this section to verify (with the help of the Lagrange form) that

$$f[x_0, x_1, \dots, x_k] = \sum_{i=0}^{k} f(x_i) \prod_{\substack{j=0 \\ j \neq k}}^{k} \frac{1}{x_i - x_j}. \tag{5.8}$$

For example,

$$f[x_0] = f(x_0)$$
$$f[x_0, x_1] = \frac{f(x_0)}{x_0 - x_1} + \frac{f(x_1)}{x_1 - x_0}$$
$$f[x_0, x_1, x_2] = \frac{f(x_0)}{(x_0 - x_1)(x_0 - x_2)} + \frac{f(x_1)}{(x_1 - x_0)(x_1 - x_2)} + \frac{f(x_2)}{(x_2 - x_0)(x_2 - x_1)}.$$

Formula (5.8) is not worth remembering in detail. Also, this formula is *not for computing*. The main purpose of giving this formula is to make the idea of a divided difference more concrete.

What is worth remembering is the following restatement of the **Newton form** of the interpolating polynomial using divided-difference notation for the Newton coefficients:

$$\boxed{\begin{aligned} p_n(x) = f[x_0] + (x - x_0)f[x_0, x_1] + (x - x_0)(x - x_1)f[x_0, x_1, x_2] \\ + \cdots + (x - x_0)(x - x_1)\cdots(x - x_{n-1})f[x_0, x_1, \dots, x_n] \end{aligned}}$$

Remember, though, to use the nested form for computing.

An easy-to-prove consequence of our definition of divided differences is that their value does not depend on the ordering of the arguments:

Theorem 5.5 (Invariance Theorem) *The divided difference $f[x_0, x_1, \ldots, x_k]$ is invariant under all permutations of the arguments $x_0, x_1, \ldots, x_k$.*

Proof. The divided difference $f[x_0, x_1, \ldots, x_k]$ is the coefficient of x^k in the polynomial of degree $\leq k$ that interpolates $f(x)$ at $x = x_0, x_1, \ldots, x_k$. Because the interpolating polynomial is the same regardless of how $x_0, x_1, \ldots, x_k$ are ordered, the same must apply to the coefficient of x^k.

⋆ 5.6.3 Divided-difference recurrence

We now present a method for computing divided differences that is convenient, accurate, and efficient. The invariance theorem makes possible a short derivation of a recurrence relation for divided differences. In order to keep the ideas from getting lost in the notation, we derive the recurrence for a special case, that of a fourth divided difference $f[x_0, x_1, x_2, x_3, x_4]$. This is the coefficient of x^4 in the polynomial $p_4(x)$ that interpolates $f(x)$ at $x = x_0, x_1, x_2, x_3, x_4$. This polynomial has many Newton forms, depending on how these points are ordered. We shall give two such forms, using underbraces to mark how they differ. For the ordering x_1, x_2, x_3, x_0, x_4 the Newton form is

$$
\begin{aligned}
p_4(x) \;=\;& f(x_1) + (x - x_1)f[x_1, x_2] + (x - x_1)(x - x_2)f[x_1, x_2, x_3] \\
&+ (x - x_1)(x - x_2)(x - x_3)\underbrace{f[x_1, x_2, x_3, x_0]} \\
&+ (x - x_1)(x - x_2)(x - x_3)\underbrace{(x - x_0)f[x_1, x_2, x_3, x_0, x_4]},
\end{aligned}
$$

and for the ordering x_1, x_2, x_3, x_4, x_0 it is

$$
\begin{aligned}
p_4(x) \;=\;& f(x_1) + (x - x_1)f[x_1, x_2] + (x - x_1)(x - x_2)f[x_1, x_2, x_3] \\
&+ (x - x_1)(x - x_2)(x - x_3)\underbrace{f[x_1, x_2, x_3, x_4]} \\
&+ (x - x_1)(x - x_2)(x - x_3)\underbrace{(x - x_4)f[x_1, x_2, x_3, x_4, x_0]}.
\end{aligned}
$$

Equating these two forms of the same polynomial and canceling matching terms and factors gives

$$
f[x_1, x_2, x_3, x_0] + (x - x_0)f[x_1, x_2, x_3, x_0, x_4] = f[x_1, x_2, x_3, x_4] + (x - x_4)f[x_1, x_2, x_3, x_4, x_0].
$$

Using the invariance theorem, we get the recurrence

$$
f[x_0, x_1, x_2, x_3, x_4] = \frac{f[x_1, x_2, x_3, x_4] - f[x_0, x_1, x_2, x_3]}{x_4 - x_0}.
$$

It is an exercise at the end of this section to show that for general n we have

$$\boxed{\begin{aligned} f[x_0, x_1, \ldots, x_{n-1}, x_n] &= \frac{f[x_1, \ldots, x_{n-1}, x_n] - f[x_0, x_1, \ldots, x_{n-1}]}{x_n - x_0}, \\ f[x_0] &= f(x_0). \end{aligned}}$$

This you should use *for computing*. If you write it out for $n = 1$, you get

$$f[x_0, x_1] = \frac{f[x_1] - f[x_0]}{x_1 - x_0}.$$

For $n = 2$ you get

$$f[x_0, x_1, x_2] = \frac{f[x_1, x_2] - f[x_0, x_1]}{x_2 - x_0}.$$

Example 5.9 Suppose $f(x) = 1/x$ and we want to compute $f[1, 2, 4]$. Apply the recurrence to get

$$f[1, 2, 4] = \frac{f[2, 4] - f[1, 2]}{4 - 1}.$$

This requires that we apply the recurrence twice more to get

$$f[1, 2] = \frac{f[2] - f[1]}{2 - 1} = \frac{\frac{1}{2} - 1}{2 - 1} = -\frac{1}{2}$$

and

$$f[2, 4] = \frac{f[4] - f[2]}{4 - 2} = \frac{\frac{1}{4} - \frac{1}{2}}{4 - 2} = -\frac{1}{8}.$$

We now substitute these two values into the original expression to get

$$f[1, 2, 4] = \frac{-\frac{1}{8} - \left(-\frac{1}{2}\right)}{4 - 1} = \frac{1}{8}.$$

Example 5.10 There is no reason why the arguments of a divided difference cannot be variables. For $f(x) = x^3$ we get the following:

$$\begin{aligned} f[x, y] &= \frac{y^3 - x^3}{y - x} = x^2 + x\,y + y^2, \\ f[x, y, z] &= \frac{f[y, z] - f[x, y]}{z - x} = \frac{(y^2 + yz + z^2) - (x^2 + xy + y^2)}{z - x} = x + y + z, \\ f[x, y, z, w] &= \frac{f[y, z, w] - f[x, y, z]}{w - x} = \frac{(y + z + w) - (x + y + z)}{w - x} = 1, \\ f[x, y, z, w, v] &= 0. \end{aligned}$$

The expressions we get are special in many ways. In particular they nicely illustrate the invariance theorem, since it is clear that the ordering of the variables makes no difference.

Using the recurrence relation to go from higher divided differences to lower divided differences, as we did in Example 5.9, is cumbersome. To save writing, we should start with the lower differences and work up to the higher differences, in such a way that we compute only those divided differences that are needed. A systematic and easy-to-visualize method is to use a divided-difference table, which has the form

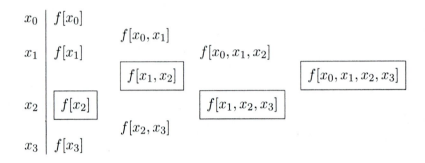

where the boxes should be ignored for the time being. The position of each entry in the table is related to the way in which it is computed. Consider a given entry, other than the original data in the first two columns—for example, $f[x_0, x_1, x_2]$. This entry is by definition a quotient. The numerator of this quotient is the difference of the entries to the immediate upper left, $f[x_0, x_1]$, and the immediate lower left, $f[x_1, x_2]$. The denominator is the difference of two node values that are found by taking the upper and lower diagonal paths from the given entry to the left edge of the table. For $f[x_0, x_1, x_2]$ this means x_0 and x_2.

To construct an interpolating polynomial, pick a path in the table that goes from left to right and consists of nearest-neighbor diagonal moves. The boxed entries of the table form such a path. Note that at the beginning of the path only the interpolation node x_2 is involved, but as we move to the right we pick up the points x_1, x_3, x_0 in that order. The entries selected by such a path can be used to construct a Newton-form interpolation polynomial. If we use the boxed entries, we get

$$p_3(x) = f[x_2] + (x - x_2)f[x_1, x_2] + (x - x_2)(x - x_1)f[x_1, x_2, x_3]$$
$$+ (x - x_2)(x - x_1)(x - x_3)f[x_0, x_1, x_2, x_3].$$

Different paths correspond to different orderings of the abscissas. However, not all orderings can be accommodated by any one table; for example, the ordering x_0, x_1, x_3, x_2 cannot be used with the above table because $f[x_0, x_1, x_3]$ is not in the table.

Example 5.11 Here is a divided-difference table:

$$
\begin{array}{c|l}
0 & 0. \\
  & \qquad\qquad 10.067 \\
2 & 20.134 \qquad\qquad\qquad 0.083667 \\
  & \qquad\qquad 10.318 \qquad\qquad\qquad 0.017333 \\
3 & 30.452 \qquad\qquad\qquad 0.17033 \\
  & \qquad\qquad 10.829 \\
5 & 52.110
\end{array}
$$

Note that after differencing two consecutive entries in a column we divided the result by the appropriate difference of node values. The Newton-form interpolating polynomial that uses the points in their tabulated order is

$$
\begin{aligned}
p_3(x) &= f[0] + (x-0)f[0,2] + (x-0)(x-2)f[0,2,3] \\
&\quad + (x-0)(x-2)(x-3)f[0,2,3,5] \\
&= 10.067x + 0.083667x(x-2) + 0.017333x(x-2)(x-3).
\end{aligned}
$$

Example 5.12 This is an unusual application of polynomial extrapolation. Define $f(k) = 1^2 + 2^2 + \cdots + k^2$. We will find the polynomial that interpolates this function at $k = 0, 1, \ldots, 8$. The divided-difference table is

$$
\begin{array}{c|ccccccc}
0 & 0 \\
  &   & 1 \\
1 & 1 &   & \frac{3}{2} \\
  &   & 4 &   & \frac{1}{3} \\
2 & 5 &   & \frac{5}{2} &   & 0 \\
  &   & 9 &   & \frac{1}{3} &   & 0 \\
3 & 14 &   & \frac{7}{2} &   & 0 &   & 0 \\
  &   & 16 &   & \frac{1}{3} &   & 0 &   & 0 \\
4 & 30 &   & \frac{9}{2} &   & 0 &   & 0 &   & 0 \\
  &   & 25 &   & \frac{1}{3} &   & 0 &   & 0 \\
5 & 55 &   & \frac{11}{2} &   & 0 &   & 0 \\
  &   & 36 &   & \frac{1}{3} &   & 0 \\
6 & 91 &   & \frac{13}{2} &   & 0 \\
  &   & 49 &   & \frac{1}{3} \\
7 & 140 &   & \frac{15}{2} \\
  &   & 64 \\
8 & 204
\end{array}
$$

The interpolating polynomial is

$$
\begin{aligned}
P(k) &= 0 + 1\cdot k + \tfrac{3}{2}k(k-1) + \tfrac{1}{3}k(k-1)(k-2) + 0 + 0 + 0 + 0 + 0 \\
&= \tfrac{1}{3}k(k + \tfrac{1}{2})(k+1).
\end{aligned}
$$

Evidently the polynomial $P(k)$ that interpolates $f(k)$ at $k = 0, 1, 2, 3$ also matches $f(k)$ at all other nonnegative integer values of k. One can verify by mathematical induction that $P(k) \equiv f(k)$.

★ 5.6.4 An important identity

By definition the remainder is $f(x) - p_n(x)$. We show here that the divided-difference notation enables us to write the remainder in another more suggestive, and yet compact, form. Applying the divided-difference recurrence *and* the symmetry property to $f[x_0, x_1, \ldots, x_{n-1}, x_n, x]$ yields

$$f[x_0, x_1, \ldots, x_{n-1}, x] = f[x_0, x_1, \ldots, x_{n-1}, x_n]$$
$$+ (x - x_n)f[x_0, x_1, \ldots, x_{n-1}, x_n, x]. \qquad (5.9)$$

This gives a way of expanding a divided difference with a variable x in it into a constant divided difference of the same order plus a remainder term involving a higher divided difference. Note how a new point x_n is introduced for the expansion. With $n = 0$ this gives

$$f[x] = f[x_0] + (x - x_0)f[x_0, x].$$

Applying the formula with $n = 1$ to the remainder term gives

$$f[x] = f[x_0] + (x - x_0)f[x_0, x_1] + (x - x_0)(x - x_1)f[x_0, x_1, x].$$

In this way we expand a function as polynomials of successively higher degree plus a remainder term. After $n + 1$ applications of Equation (5.9) we get the following important identity:

Proposition 5.6

$$f(x) = f[x_0] + (x - x_0)f[x_0, x_1] + \cdots$$
$$+ (x - x_0)\cdots(x - x_{n-1})f[x_0, x_1, \ldots, x_n]$$
$$+ (x - x_0)\cdots(x - x_{n-1})(x - x_n)f[x_0, x_1, \ldots, x_n, x]$$

which expresses $f(x)$ in terms of an interpolating polynomial (in Newton form) plus a remainder. The remainder is not a polynomial because of the x in the divided difference. It is some (probably complicated) function of x. This identity is not a deep mathematical result; it is merely a rewriting of $f(x)$ using the notation of divided differences.

Example 5.13 With $f(x) = 1/x$ and $x_0 = 1$, $x_1 = 2$, $x_2 = 4$ we have

$$
\begin{array}{c|l}
1 & 1 \\
 & \quad\quad -1/2 \\
2 & 1/2 \quad\quad\quad\quad\quad 1/8 \\
 & \quad\quad -1/8 \quad\quad\quad\quad\quad -1/(8x) \\
4 & 1/4 \quad\quad\quad\quad\quad 1/(8x) \\
 & \quad\quad -1/(4x) \\
x & 1/x
\end{array}
$$

From Proposition 5.6,

$$
\begin{aligned}
f(x) &= f[1] + (x-1)f[1,2] + (x-1)(x-2)f[1,2,4] \\
&\quad + (x-1)(x-2)(x-4)f[1,2,4,x],
\end{aligned}
$$

so

$$
\begin{aligned}
\frac{1}{x} &= 1 + (x-1)(-\tfrac{1}{2}) + (x-1)(x-2)\tfrac{1}{8} \\
&\quad + (x-1)(x-2)(x-4)\left(-\frac{1}{8x}\right).
\end{aligned}
$$

⋆ 5.6.5   Divided differences and derivatives

Divided differences look like approximations to derivatives. Here we determine the relationship. From Proposition 5.6,

$$
\text{remainder} = (x - x_0) \cdots (x - x_n) f[x_0, \ldots, x_n, x],
$$

and from Section 5.4.3,

$$
\text{remainder} = \frac{(x - x_0) \cdots (x - x_n)}{(n+1)!} f^{(n+1)}(\xi)
$$

for some ξ between the least and greatest of $x_0, \ldots, x_n, x$. Therefore (letting $n = k - 1$ and $x = x_k$),

$$
f[x_0, \ldots, x_{k-1}, x_k] = \frac{f^{(k)}(\xi)}{k!}.
$$

So we see that a kth divided difference is equal to the kth derivative at some point divided by $k!$ (do not forget the $k!$). All we can say for sure is that "some point" is between the least and greatest of the $k+1$ points that determine the divided difference. Without knowing more about $f(x)$, the best approximation[4] to ξ is

$$\xi \approx \frac{x_0 + x_1 + \cdots + x_k}{k+1}. \tag{5.10}$$

What else! Recall that a divided difference is a symmetric function of its arguments. Anyway, divided differences are useful as simple numerical approximations of derivatives.

Consider now what happens if we let $x_1 \to x_0$, $x_2 \to x_0$, ..., $x_n \to x_0$ in an interpolating polynomial $p_n(x)$. For cubic interpolation the Newton form is

$$
\begin{aligned}
p_3(x) \;=\;& f(x_0) + (x - x_0)f[x_0,\ x_1] + (x - x_0)(x - x_1)f[x_0,\ x_1,\ x_2] \\
& + (x - x_0)(x - x_1)(x - x_2)f[x_0,\ x_1\ ,x_2,\ x_3].
\end{aligned}
$$

Replacing divided differences by derivatives, we get

$$
\begin{aligned}
p_3(x) \;=\;& f(x_0) + (x - x_0)f'(\xi_1) + (x - x_0)(x - x_1)\frac{f''(\xi_2)}{2!} \\
& + (x - x_0)(x - x_1)(x - x_2)\frac{f'''(\xi_3)}{3!}
\end{aligned}
$$

where ξ_k is between the least and greatest of x_0, x_1, ..., x_k. In the limit ξ_k must go to x_0, yielding the Taylor polynomial

$$p_3(x) = f(x_0) + (x - x_0)f'(x_0) + (x - x_0)^2\,\frac{f''(x_0)}{2!} + (x - x_0)^3\,\frac{f'''(x_0)}{3!}.$$

This generalizes to arbitrary n. Hence, we see how the Taylor polynomial is a limiting case of polynomial interpolation.

Exercises

1. The problem of determining the coefficients c_0, c_1, ..., c_n for the Newton form can be expressed as a system of linear equations. What is this system in matrix notation for $n = 3$?

2. Let $(x[i], y[i])$, $i = 0$, 1, ..., N, be given data points. Consider the calculation of the coefficients $c[0]$, $c[1]$, ..., $c[N]$ of the Newton form.

   (a) Write an algorithm for the nested form of computing the value $p_k(x)$ of the first $k+1$ terms of the Newton interpolant assuming that $c[0]$, $c[1]$, ..., $c[k]$ are known.

---

[4]It can be shown that the kth derivative of $f(x)$ at ξ and at the nodal average differ by $O(h^2)$ where h is the average difference between successive points.

(b) Using part (a), write an algorithm for computing the coefficients $c[0]$, $c[1]$, $\ldots$, $c[N]$ based on the construction of Section 5.6.1.

3. Let P_L and P_N be the Lagrange and Newton polynomials of degree at most n that interpolate $f(x)$ at the points $x_0, x_1, \ldots, x_n$. Which is more accurate, assuming negligible roundoff error? Explain.

4. Verify the closed-form formula (5.8) using Definition 5.4 and the Lagrange form of the interpolating polynomial.

5. With $f(x) = 1/x$, what is (the simplified form of) $f[x_0, x_1, \ldots, x_n]$?

6. Verify for general n the recurrence relation for divided differences. This is primarily an exercise in getting the notation straight.

7. (a) Construct a divided-difference table from the following data:

x	1	3	6	10
$f(x)$	1	2	3	4

(b) Using part (a), construct the Newton form of the interpolating polynomial *in such a way* that as you add more terms you obtain first the interpolant for $x = 3$, then the one for $x = 3, 6$, then the one for $x = 3, 6, 1$, and finally the one for $x = 3, 6, 1, 10$.

8. Construct both the divided-difference form and the Lagrangian form of the cubic interpolating polynomial for the data

x	1	2	4	8
$f(x)$	0	1	2	3

9. Use the Newton form of interpolation to approximate $f(14)$ from the table

x	10	11	15
$f(x)$	70	69	68

Your answer should be a purely numeric expression, but it need not be evaluated.

10. Consider the table

x	2.0	2.2	2.4	2.6	2.8	3.0
$\log_{10} x$	0.30103	0.34242	0.38021	0.41497	0.44716	0.47712

Form a complete divided-difference table based on these values. Use interpolation by a fourth-degree interpolating polynomial in order to estimate $\log_{10} 2.1$.

11. Use Newton interpolation to determine a formula in closed form for $1^3 + 2^3 + \cdots + n^3$.

12. Use Newton interpolation to determine a formula in closed form for $1 \cdot 2 + 2 \cdot 3 + \cdots + n(n+1)$.

13. For the following table of data the x values are nodes and the y's are function values.

x	0.0	0.6	1.5	3.0	2.8	2.6	2.3	2.1	1.9	1.5
y	−0.8	−0.34	0.59	1.44	1.5	1.03	0.28	0.1	0.23	0.60

Suppose that the function value at $x = 1.2$ is approximated by Newton interpolation of all the data. Assume specifically that a divided-difference table is constructed using the data in the order given and that the nested form is used to evaluate the polynomial.

(a) What disaster occurs during this process?

(b) When does this occur? (Choose one.)

   I. In constructing the table
   II. In evaluating the nested form

(c') Answer this if your response to (b) is I. In which entry of the table does the problem occur?

(c'') Answer this if your response to (b) is II. After how many multiplications in the evaluation of the nested form does the problem occur?

14. Express $f[2,3,6]$ in terms of $f[2,3,4]$ and a higher difference.

15. Using mathematical induction, prove Proposition 5.6.

16. Obtain good lower and upper bounds on

$$\exp[x_0,\ x_1,\ x_2,\ x_3] \qquad \text{where } 0 \le x_0 < x_1 < x_2 < x_3 \le 1.$$

17. Estimate $f''(2)$ given

x	2.0	2.2	2.4
$f(x)$	0.30103	0.34242	0.38021

18. (calculator recommended) By means of quadratic interpolation with divided differences, estimate $f(2.2)$ from the values tabulated below. Obtain an error estimate by means of cubic interpolation. Form only that part of the divided-difference table that is needed for this problem. Make a good choice for the nodes. Maintain at least four significant *digits* of accuracy.

x	1.8	2.0	2.1	2.3	2.5	2.7	3.0
$f(x)$	0.5556	0.5000	0.4762	0.4348	0.4000	0.3704	0.3333

Mathematica notes

The notation we have used for divided differences may seem far removed from what is possible in a programming language, but with *Mathematica* it can be duplicated. Before discussing how divided-difference notation can be used, we need to discuss **patterns**.

We have used patterns before, to define rules; here we discuss some of their finer points. Suppose we have a function f [x], defined for certain values of x, and we wish to define divided differences for it. We can define first divided differences by

$$f[x\_, y\_] := (f[x] - f[y])/(x - y)$$

The expression to the left of the delayed assignment (:=) matches any expression having a head of f and two elements. The two elements can be arbitrary expressions and are formally represented by the names x and y. If this pattern occurs during the evaluation of a *Mathematica* expression, then it is transformed as specified by the expression to the right of the delayed assignment with the x and y replaced by the expressions they represent. In short, this is the usual definition for divided differences using *Mathematica* syntax.

But can we define divided differences of arbitrarily high order? In *Mathematica* this is quite easy. We add the rule

$$f[x\_, y\_\_, z\_] := (f[x, y] - f[y, z])/(x - z)$$

Here the __ matches a sequence of one *or more* elements of the expression, which in aggregate are represented by y. For example, in f[0, 1, 3, 9] the symbol y would represent the sequence 1, 3. Actually the two rules we have developed can be combined into one rule:

$$f[x\_, y\_\_\_, z\_] := (f[x, y] - f[y, z])/(x - z)$$

Here ___ matches a sequence of *zero* or more elements.

To see how this rule works in *Mathematica*, consider the following:

Define divided differences of f[ ].	*In[1]:=* f[x_, y___, z_] := (f[x, y] - f[y, z])/(x - z)
Turn on tracing for f.	*In[2]:=* On[f]

In[3]:= f[1, 2, 4, 7]

$$\text{f::trace: } f[1, 2, 4, 7] \longrightarrow \frac{f[1, 2, 4] - f[2, 4, 7]}{1 - 7}.$$

$$f::\text{trace: } f[1, 2, 4] \longrightarrow \frac{f[1, 2] - f[2, 4]}{1 - 4}.$$

$$f::\text{trace: } f[1, 2] \longrightarrow \frac{f[1] - f[2]}{1 - 2}.$$

$$f::\text{trace: } f[2, 4] \longrightarrow \frac{f[2] - f[4]}{2 - 4}.$$

$$f::\text{trace: } f[2, 4, 7] \longrightarrow \frac{f[2, 4] - f[4, 7]}{2 - 7}.$$

$$f::\text{trace: } f[2, 4] \longrightarrow \frac{f[2] - f[4]}{2 - 4}.$$

$$f::\text{trace: } f[4, 7] \longrightarrow \frac{f[4] - f[7]}{4 - 7}.$$

$$Out[3] = -\left(\frac{-(-f[1] + f[2] + \frac{f[2] - f[4]}{2})}{3} + \frac{\frac{-(f[2] - f[4])}{2} + \frac{f[4] - f[7]}{3}}{5} \right) / 6$$

Notice that f[2, 4] was evaluated twice. This double evaluation would not have happened if we had defined the rule for f[ ] to be

$$f[x\_, y\_\_\_, z\_] := f[x, y, z] = (f[x, y] - f[y, z])/(x - z)$$

since with this rule a *side effect* is to form another rule for each specific combination of arguments. In addition, since divided differences are symmetric in their arguments, a further improvement would be to give f[ ] the attribute Orderless. Even with these modifications, this is not an efficient way to implement divided differences. If performance is important, either separate lists or a list of lists should be used to store the divided-difference table.

Computer problems

1. Define a function dd[x_,y_] that gives the first entry of each column of the divided-difference table of a list y with respect to a list x. Test your function on x = Range[1,6], y = 1/x.

2. Define a function newt[z_,x_,d_,n_] that evaluates the interpolating polynomial of degree at most n-1 defined by the first n entries of x and d where d is obtained using dd[ ] of the previous problem. The evaluation should be at the point z. (It is possible

to define `newt[ ]` recursively using `Rest`.) Test your function on `x = Range[0,4]`, `d = dd[x,x^4], n = 5, z = 5`.

3. Implement the nested form of the Newton interpolation formula in *Mathematica* by defining a function with three arguments, the first being a list of abscissas, the second an equally long list of ordinates, and the third the name of the independent variable. Do not ask for any simplification. As a test, try it on `Range[4]`, `Range[4]^3`, `x`. Then `Expand` the result.

4. In this problem you are to implement piecewise cubic interpolation of the exponential function as shown in the example on page 198; that is, you are to define a function `exp[x_]` defined for x in the interval $[0., 1.]$ that gives the piecewise cubic interpolant of `Exp[x]` from the nearest four points on a mesh with spacing $h = 0.05$. Your function should refuse to evaluate for arguments outside the specified interval.

   (a) It is inefficient to form the divided-difference table for the nearest four points each time you need them. They should be evaluated once and used as appropriate. You should begin by constructing lists of the zeroth through third divided differences. Print the third divided differences as a check. (How big should they be?) Then define `exp[x_]`. Following is an example for the case of linear interpolation with $h = 0.25$.

```
xlist = 0.25 Range[0, 4];
ylist = Exp[xlist];
dylist = (Drop[ylist, 1] - Drop[ylist, -1])/0.25;
exp[x_] :=
    Module[{n = Floor[x/0.25 + 1]}, n = Min[n,4];
        ylist[[n]] + (x - xlist[[n]]) dylist[[n]]
    ] /; 0. <= x && x - 1. <= 0.
```

   Test with

```
Plot[exp[x] - Exp[x], {x, 0., 1.}, PlotRange->All]
```

   For piecewise cubics you will need two more lists, `ddylist` and `dddylist`, and the x list will need to include two points outside the interval.

   (b) The solution to part (a) does work, but it is vulnerable: the symbols `xlist`, `ylist`, etc. are floating around as global symbols, and they could accidentally be changed, destroying the function `exp[ ]`. In this part of the problem you are to alter your solution to part (a) such that it uses no global symbols (other than `exp` and built-in symbols). Following is a modification of our previous example that shows how to get the symbols inside a `Module` where they are relatively safe. (An alternative would be to actually type in all the numbers, but in the case of $h = 0.05$ there are many numbers and they need to be entered to `$MachinePrecision` precision (given by `InputForm`), not just the six digits that are displayed by default (`OutputForm`).

```
Clear[exp]   (* destroy the previous rule *)
xlist = 0.25 Range[0, 4];
ylist = Exp[xlist];
dylist = (Drop[ylist, 1] - Drop[ylist, -1])/0.25;
rule = Hold[exp /: exp[x_] :=
            Module[{n = Floor[x/0.25 + 1], xl, yl, dyl},
                 n = Min[n, 4];
                 xl = $xlist; yl = $ylist; dyl = $dylist;
                 yl[[n]] + (x - xl[[n]]) dyl[[n]]
              ] /; 0. <= x && x - 1. <= 0.];
rule = rule /. {$xlist -> xlist, $ylist -> ylist,
                $dylist -> dylist}
ReleaseHold[rule]
```

Notice how the data get spliced into the code for the function while it is being prevented from evaluation by `Hold`. The evaluation of the (Newton) interpolating polynomial should use the nested form. Use the following to test your function.

```
exp[$MinMachineNumber]
exp[0.]
exp[1.]
exp[1. - $MachineEpsilon]
exp[1. + $MachineEpsilon]
Log[exp[0.77]]
Plot[exp[x] - Exp[x], {x, 0., 1.}, PlotRange -> All]
```

Note: To get the desired effect from `ReleaseHold`, it must be on a line by itself. `ReleaseHold` removes a head of `Hold`, not `Hold` buried in the expression somewhere. You do not have to use `Hold` and `ReleaseHold`. You may use your editor to get the lists of data inside the `Module` defining the function, but then you must use numbers in their `InputForm` rather than their `OutputForm`.

5. Consider the polynomial that interpolates e^x at the nodes -1, $-\frac{1}{2}$, 0, $\frac{1}{2}$, and 1. The remainder term is

$$\frac{e^{\xi(x)}}{120}(x^2 - 1)(x^2 - \tfrac{1}{4})x.$$

Plot $\xi(x)$ on the interval $[-2, 2]$. Compare this with $\frac{1}{6}(x + \sum x_i) = x/6$ of Equation (5.10). (Note: The function $\xi(x)$ is not always uniquely determined, as it is here.)

6. We showed in this section that a Taylor polynomial is the limit of interpolating polynomials. We can also show this by brute force, but we had better use *Mathematica* as the brute. Even so, this can take several minutes.

   (a) Start with the `InterpolatingPolynomial` in x through the points `{x0,f[x0]}`, `{x1,f[x1]}`, `{x2,f[x2]}`, and `{x3,f[x3]}`.

(b) **Expand** the polynomial.

(c) Use **Together[ ]** to get the terms over a common denominator.

(d) Do **Limit[%, x1 -> x0, Analytic -> True]**. (Note: You need to use the option **Analytic -> True** or it will not use L'Hôpital's rule and it will not be able to evaluate the limit.)

(e) Take the **Limit** as **x2 -> x0**.

(f) Take the **Limit** as **x3 -> x0**.

(g) **Collect[%, {f[x0], f'[x0], f''[x0], f'''[x0]}]**.

(h) **Factor /@ %**.

7. The *Mathematica* functions **PolynomialQuotient[ ]** and **PolynomialRemainder[ ]** perform division of two polynomials in some designated variable and return, respectively, the quotient and remainder. Using these, write a routine to convert a polynomial in some designated variable to Newton form. The list of nodes should be given as the third argument and the nested Newton form returned as the value. *Do not* evaluate the polynomial at a sequence of points and reconstruct it by interpolation. Instead, rewrite the polynomial directly, using algebraic manipulation.

★5.7 Inverse Interpolation

This is a method for finding roots. We introduce it by means of an example. Suppose we wish to solve $f(r) = 0$ where $f(x) \stackrel{\text{def}}{=} x^2 - 2$ without computing a square root. If we evaluate $f(x)$ at three points,

x	$f(x)$
1	-1
2	2
3	7

we can, as shown in Figure 5.25, use quadratic interpolation to reconstruct $f(x)$, but this gets us nowhere. We shall describe another way to interpolate all three data points, which avoids having to extract the roots of a quadratic. We can write the equation of the curve as $x = f^{-1}(y)$ if we restrict x to a subinterval where $f(x)$ is either strictly increasing or strictly decreasing. For our example $x \geq 0$ suffices. We can, by interchanging the columns of the table, get a tabulation for $f^{-1}(y)$ at three increasing values of y. Figure 5.26 shows a plot of $f^{-1}(x)$ and the three tabulated values. These can be used to construct a quadratic interpolant for $f^{-1}(y)$, which can be evaluated at $y = 0$ to give an approximation to $f^{-1}(0) = r$. Using divided differences,

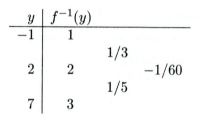

y	$f^{-1}(y)$		
-1	1		
		1/3	
2	2		$-1/60$
		1/5	
7	3		

we get for the interpolating quadratic

$$Q(y) = 1 + (y+1)(\tfrac{1}{3}) + (y+1)(y-2)(-\tfrac{1}{60}).$$

Hence, $r = f^{-1}(0) \approx Q(0) = \frac{41}{30} = 1.366\cdots$.

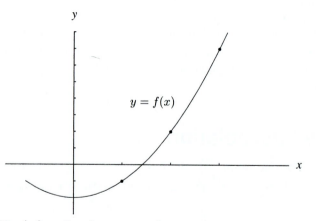

Figure 5.25: A function known at three points

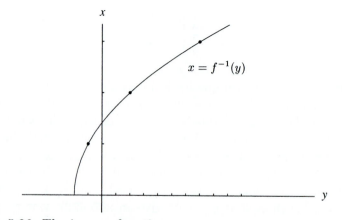

Figure 5.26: The inverse function

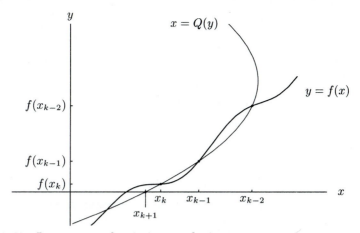

Figure 5.27: Inverse quadratic interpolation

More generally, to solve $f(r) = 0$ given

$$y_{k-2} = f(x_{k-2}), \quad y_{k-1} = f(x_{k-1}), \quad y_k = f(x_k),$$

we approximate $f^{-1}(y)$ by a quadratic $Q(y)$. We can do this by computing divided differences

y	$f^{-1}(y)$		
y_k	x_k		
		$x_{k,k-1}$	
y_{k-1}	x_{k-1}		$x_{k,k-1,k-2}$
		$x_{k-1,k-2}$	
y_{k-2}	x_{k-2}		

To minimize roundoff error effects, it is best to order the points according to how close we expect they are to the root. The quadratic interpolant is

$$Q(y) = x_k + (y - y_k)x_{k,k-1} + (y - y_k)(y - y_{k-1})x_{k,k-1,k-2},$$

which is illustrated in Figure 5.27, where the x and y axes have their usual orientation. We have $r = f^{-1}(0) \approx Q(0) \overset{\text{def}}{=} x_{k+1}$. This method is called **inverse quadratic interpolation**, and its order is $1.839286755\cdots$, the solution of $p^3 = p^2 + p + 1$.

Contrast this with Muller's method, which constructs a quadratic interpolant having either no root or two roots.

Example 5.14 Following is an example of inverse quadratic interpolation for $f(x) = x^2 - 4$:

$$x_0 = 6,$$
$$x_1 = 4,$$

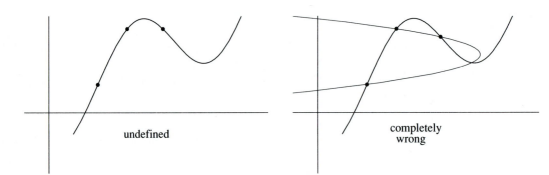

Figure 5.28: Pitfalls of inverse quadratic interpolation

$$x_2 = 1,$$
$$x_3 = 1.70285714285714285714285714285714285714285714285714285714285714285714285714285714285714285714285714285857,$$
$$x_4 = 2.06710757667554983116338385015273676316692581780897948116105360827362 9711,$$
$$x_5 = 2.00431950389365223103303782937232018140018676770185708848992214149688 8206,$$
$$x_6 = 1.99998823196618566168275040193529495847521547333783009221378580854833 4116,$$
$$x_7 = 1.99999999958475872316575857472059851424664680741185460039882254535698 1184,$$
$$x_8 = 2.00000000000000002634190567894510149811325493323830987866926365516008 927,$$
$$x_9 = 2.00000000000000000000000000000000001609027791542300702658314689013831 252920,$$
$$x_{10} = 1.99999999999999999999999999999999999999999999999999999999999999978000071 6377.$$

Inverse quadratic interpolation has a higher order of convergence than secant and thus, of all the methods we have studied, it is the most efficient, *when it works*. However, as shown in Figure 5.28, the inverse quadratic interpolant might be undefined or completely wrong in the sense that it goes through the data points in the wrong order. Use this method only if the three points are strictly increasing or strictly decreasing. Otherwise, apply linear interpolation to the two most recent iterates—the secant method. (Note: Because the inverse of a linear function is also a linear function, we could also think of the secant method as inverse linear interpolation.) For a practical rootfinder, supplement these two methods with bisection for reliability.

Exercises

1. Write down for the method of inverse quadratic interpolation the nested form of the formula for x_{k+1} in terms of x_k, $x_{k,k-1}$, $x_{k,k-1,k-2}$, y_k, and y_{k-1}.

2. Given that $f(2) = -6$, $f(3) = -1$, $f(4) = 6$, use inverse quadratic interpolation to estimate the root of $f(x)$.

Mathematica notes

Recall that the Taylor's series expansion of a function about a point $x = x_0$ is closely related to the limit of interpolating polynomials as the nodes converge to the center of expansion. Just as we can do inverse interpolation, we can find the inverse of a function represented by a series. In *Mathematica* this is very easy to do with the function InverseSeries[ ].

The series expansion of e^x about $x = 0$. This is valid for x near 0.

$In[1]:=$ **Series[Exp[x], {x, 0, 6}]**

$$Out[1] = 1 + x + \frac{x^2}{2} + \frac{x^3}{6} + \frac{x^4}{24} + \frac{x^5}{120} + \frac{x^6}{720} + O[x]^7$$

The series expansion for $x = \log y$ about $y = 1$.

$In[2]:=$ **InverseSeries[%, y]**

$$Out[2] = (-1 + y) - \frac{(-1 + y)^2}{2} + \frac{(-1 + y)^3}{3} - \frac{(-1 + y)^4}{4} +$$

$$\frac{(-1 + y)^5}{5} - \frac{(-1 + y)^6}{6} + O[-1 + y]^7$$

If y is near 1, h must be near 0. This is a more familiar form of the series expansion of the logarithm function.

$In[3]:=$ **% /. y -> 1+h**

$$Out[3] = h - \frac{h^2}{2} + \frac{h^3}{3} - \frac{h^4}{4} + \frac{h^5}{5} - \frac{h^6}{6} + O[h]^7$$

Since we know the inverse function for the exponential, we can find its series expansion directly.

$In[4]:=$ **Series[Log[1+h], {h, 0, 6}]**

$$Out[4] = h - \frac{h^2}{2} + \frac{h^3}{3} - \frac{h^4}{4} + \frac{h^5}{5} - \frac{h^6}{6} + O[h]^7$$

Computer problems

1. Find the exact (real) solution of $p^3 = p^2 + p + 1$ and Simplify[ ] the result.

2. In this problem we will derive several rootfinding methods that can be made to have arbitrarily high order. They are in general not practical because they require knowledge of several of the derivatives of the function. They do, however, have limited use, for example in inverting the function $f(x) = \int_0^x e^{-t^2}\, dt$, where you get as many of the derivatives as you desire at practically no extra cost.

   (a) Start with the first-order series expansion of f[x] about xn: Series[f[x], {x, xn, 1}]. This is an approximation to f[x] for x near xn.

(b) Use `InverseSeries[%, y]` to find a series expansion for `x` (the value of the inverse of the function `f`) in terms of `y` near `f[xn]`.

(c) Use `Normal[ ]` to turn the series into an algebraic expression, and then replace `y` by `0`. The result is Newton's method.

(d) Start with the second-order series expansion `Series[f[x], {x, xn, 2}]` and repeat parts (b) and (c). Experimentally find the convergence rate of this method.

(e) Start with the third-order series expansion and repeat parts (b) and (c). Experimentally find the convergence rate of this method.

6. Least-Squares Approximation

The following example is based on personal experience with installing a pipe organ. The pitch of a pipe in a pipe organ is determined by its length, with the 12 pipes in an "8-foot" octave ranging from about 8 feet at CC to about 4 feet at C, an octave higher. The diameters of the pipes also decrease as you go up the scale, with the rate of decrease depending on several factors. It so happened that a partial shipment of an 8-foot octave of pipes had arrived, and it was more convenient to cut and mount a bracket that was to hold the pipes than to wait for the entire shipment to arrive. The bracket needed accurate holes cut in it for the pipes. The holes had to be large enough to accommodate the pipes snugly. The actual data have been long forgotten, but five of the 12 pipes from the 8-foot octave had arrived. To complete the bracket, the diameters of the other seven pipes had to be closely estimated based on the diameters of the five known pipes. Suppose the data, in inches, for the five pipes were as follows: $CC^\sharp : 7\frac{13}{16}$, $DD^\sharp : 7\frac{3}{8}$, $EE : 7\frac{3}{16}$, $GG^\sharp : 6\frac{7}{16}$, and $AA : 6\frac{1}{4}$.

The diameters of pipes decrease geometrically as you proceed up the musical scale, but the rate of decrease is unknown. If we number the 12 pipes 1 through 12, we are looking for a formula for the diameter of the xth pipe of the form

$$d(x) = ab^x.$$

This formula is called the *model*. The constants a and b are known as the *parameters* of the model. The problem is to determine the values of a and b. Once these values are known, the diameters of the other seven pipes can be calculated.

Notice that we have two unknowns, and if we insert the data into the model we get five equations:

$$
\begin{aligned}
d(2) &= 7.8125 &&= ab^2, \\
d(4) &= 7.375 &&= ab^4, \\
d(5) &= 7.1875 &&= ab^5, \\
d(9) &= 6.4375 &&= ab^9, \\
d(10) &= 6.25 &&= ab^{10}.
\end{aligned}
\tag{6.1}
$$

A system of five equations in two unknowns poses difficulties. We could pick any two of the pipes and use their diameters to find the values of a and b that satisfy that subset of the data, but *which* two pipes should be used? For example, if we use GG$^\sharp$ and AA, we get $a = 8.39948$ and $b = 0.970874$. These values suggest that CC$^\sharp$ should have a diameter of about 7.91731, which is about 0.105 too large. The problem is that the data contain errors. There are errors both in the manufacturing of the pipes and in the measuring of the pipes. If there were no errors, *any* pair of pipes would suffice to solve for a and b exactly. This sort of difficulty can be expected to arise whenever you have an *overdetermined* system of equations, i.e., when there are more equations than there are unknowns. By forcing two of the equations to be exactly satisfied we may cause the others to exhibit large errors. We would like to choose values that allow all of the equations to be approximately satisfied instead of forcing two of them to be exactly satisfied.

We need a clear understanding of just what the problem is before we can go about trying to solve it. As we saw above, there is no solution to the problem given by Equations (6.1) because the system is overdetermined. We can look at the residuals, though, and try to make them small. That is, we can try to choose a and b so as to make each of

$$
\begin{aligned}
r(2) &= 7.8125 - ab^2, \\
r(4) &= 7.375 - ab^4, \\
r(5) &= 7.1875 - ab^5, \\
r(9) &= 6.4375 - ab^9, \\
r(10) &= 6.25 - ab^{10}
\end{aligned}
\tag{6.2}
$$

small. In particular, we want to find a and b such that the residual vector $\boldsymbol{r} = [r(2)\ r(4)\ r(5)\ r(9)\ r(10)]^{\mathrm{T}}$ is as small as possible. A question arises, however, as to what we mean by "small." Three possibilities are

maximum-norm:	$\max\ \{|r(2)|, |r(4)|, |r(5)|, |r(9)|, |r(10)|\},$
1-norm:	$\frac{1}{5}(|r(2)| + |r(4)| + |r(5)| + |r(9)| + |r(10)|),$
2-norm:	$\sqrt{\frac{1}{5}(r(2)^2 + r(4)^2 + r(5)^2 + r(9)^2 + r(10)^2)},$

and there are still others. The values of a and b that minimize each of these norms are approximately $a = 8.2483$ and $b = 0.972691$, $a = 8.25908$ and $b = 0.972589$, and $a = 8.25217$ and $b = 0.972664$, respectively. The minimum residual vectors for each of the three norms are

maximum-norm:	$[-0.008545\quad 0.008545\quad -0.005589\quad -0.008545\quad 0.003389]^{\mathrm{T}},$
1-norm:	$[\ \ 0.000000\quad 0.015071\quad \ \ 0.000000\quad -0.006256\quad 0.004956]^{\mathrm{T}},$
2-norm:	$[-0.005326\quad 0.011171\quad -0.003238\quad -0.007171\quad 0.004548]^{\mathrm{T}}.$

These residuals are the errors in predicting the diameters of the pipes from the model. This problem is difficult to solve with any of these norms, but the 2-norm is the least difficult.

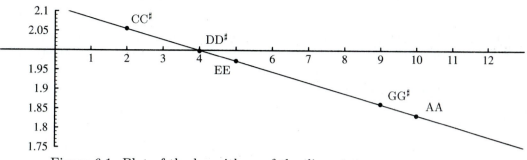

Figure 6.1: Plot of the logarithms of the diameters

The above problem with the model $d(x) = ab^x$ is an example of the *nonlinear least-squares approximation problem*. Nonlinear least-squares approximation is a difficult problem, and we will not attempt to solve it. Sometimes we can reformulate the problem as a *linear least-squares problem*. Consider the logarithms of the diameters: 2.05573, 1.9981, 1.97234, 1.86214, and 1.83258. This corresponds to rewriting the model in the form

$$\ln d(x) = \ln a + x \ln b.$$

Now the model is a linear in the unknowns, i.e., the unknowns $\ln a$ and $\ln b$ enter into the model in a linear way. (In this example, x also enters into the model in a linear way, but x is not an unknown.) If we plot the logarithms of the diameters against x, we should be able to draw a straight line nearly through the points. See Figure 6.1.

When we linearize the problem and try to minimize the 2-norm of the residual vector, we get a still different result: $a = 8.25188$ and $b = 0.97267$. The minimum residual vector for this solution is

$$[-0.000705 \quad 0.001503 \quad -0.000456 \quad -0.001095 \quad 0.000753]^{\mathrm{T}}.$$

These residuals are the errors in predicting the logarithms of the diameters of the pipes. The errors in the diameters are

$$[-0.005508 \quad 0.011090 \quad -0.003274 \quad -0.007045 \quad 0.004710]^{\mathrm{T}}.$$

We have different solutions because we have different ideas of what it means to have "good" values for a and b.

Linearizing the problem is seldom possible, and even when it is, the reformulation changes the problem. As we saw above, the solution to the reformulated problem is different from the solutions to the original problem. For some problems, it makes little difference which solution is used. In the problem above, any of the solutions would have suggested that the diameters of the missing pipes were very nearly what would be predicted. In other problems the choice of norm can make an important difference. Choosing a model and choosing a norm for the residual vector are important decisions. They are part of the specification of a data-fitting problem, but they are not a part of numerical analysis. In this chapter we will consider the solution of linear least-squares approximation problems, i.e., problems in which the parameters of the model enter into it in a linear way and where the 2-norm of the residual vector is to be minimized. We will also mention what some of the other norms might be appropriate for and under what conditions the 2-norm of the residual is justified.

This chapter contains the following sections:

6.1 The Linear Least-Squares Problem

In the introduction we looked at fitting the model

$$f(x) = c_1 + c_2 x$$

(with different notation) to some data. It is common to allow higher powers of x in the model. Thus the problem becomes that of fitting a polynomial to a set of data points $\{(x_i, y_i)\}_{i=1}^{m}$.

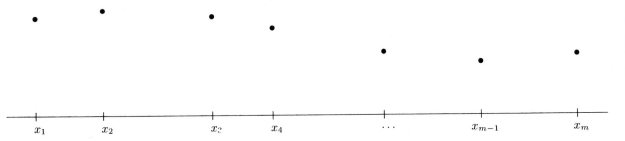

In particular, after choosing the degree of the polynomial, the problem is to find the values of each of the coefficients $c_1, c_2, \ldots, c_n$ such that the polynomial

$$f(x) = c_1 + c_2 x + c_3 x^2 + \cdots + c_n x^{n-1}$$

best fits the data. Once we have found values for c_j, $1 \le j \le n$, those particular values will identify our solution, which we will denote as $\hat{f}(x)$, as opposed to the general model $f(x)$.

With interpolation, we chose the degree $n - 1$ of the polynomial high enough to pass through all the points, namely $n = m$. Here we consider the case $n < m$. In general, we can no longer get an exact match, so there will be discrepancies between the actual data and the values given by the model. In fact, it is unlikely that *any* of the data points will exactly agree with the polynomial.

A further generalization is to allow terms in the model that are not just powers of x. The general model for linear least-squares approximation is a linear combination of **basis functions** $\{f_1(x), f_2(x), \ldots, f_n(x)\}$:

$$f(x) = c_1 f_1(x) + c_2 f_2(x) + \cdots + c_n f_n(x).$$

This linear combination is called the **model**. Since we do nothing with the basis functions except evaluate them at the points x_i, $1 \le i \le m$, this further generalization does not affect the difficulty of obtaining the solution. For concreteness, you can think of the basis functions $f_1(x), f_2(x), \ldots, f_n(x)$ as being the powers of x: $1, x, \ldots, x^{n-1}$.

Following are two applications for such approximations:

- Data compression. The coefficients of a simple model take less storage than do all the data points. For example, to set up a database for average daily temperatures for cities around the world, it would be more efficient to store a few coefficients rather than 366 temperature values.

- Smoothing. Many times, data are given that are known to contain error. If the error is random, it is possible to reduce it by statistical smoothing techniques, one of which is least-squares fitting. In fact, in applications such as geodesy (see Exercise 3 of Section 6.2), redundant measurements are taken in order to enable the effects of errors to be reduced in this way.

The best approximation $\hat{f}(x)$ to given data by a linear combination of basis functions is the one for which the residuals $y_i - \hat{f}(x_i)$ are smallest. However, the residuals are a sequence of values, and it is not obvious what "smallest" should mean. The answer to this depends on the application and should be part of the *statement of the problem*. (The role of numerical analysis is limited to computing *precisely defined* quantities and does not include deciding what the problem should be.) Three possibilities for measuring the size of the residuals are

$$\max_{1 \le i \le m} |y_i - f(x_i)|, \qquad \frac{1}{m} \sum_{i=1}^{m} |y_i - f(x_i)|, \qquad \sqrt{\frac{1}{m} \sum_{i=1}^{m} |y_i - f(x_i)|^2}.$$

After choosing a measure for the size of the residual, the problem is to find the $f(x)$ that minimizes it. We .denote that particular $f(x)$ by $\hat{f}(x)$. The special case $n = 1, f_1(x) \equiv 1$ is approximation by some constant c: Minimizing the first of these gives for c the average of the least and greatest of the y_i, minimizing the second gives the median, and minimizing the third gives the mean (or average). Which, then, do we choose? If data compression is our purpose, then the first seems appropriate. If smoothing is our goal, then the nature of the

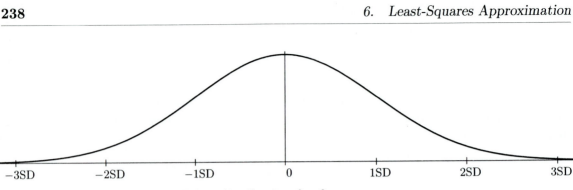

Figure 6.2: Probability distribution for δ_i.

errors must be known or guessed. Assume that the given data y_i are equal to $g(x_i) + \delta_i$ where $g(x_i)$ is $f(x_i)$ for particular values of the coefficients c_j and δ_i are independent random errors with expected values equal to zero. The "ideal solution" $g(x)$ is unknown and unknowable; the best that we can hope for is that the solution we find, $\hat{f}(x)$, will be close to $g(x)$. If the errors δ_i lie in some interval $[-\Delta, \Delta]$ with all values equally probable, then the second of the measures above is appropriate for determining the most likely $\hat{f}(x)$. In situations where the errors δ_i arise from an accumulation of many independent random errors, the δ_i tend to be *normally* distributed. If the δ_i are independent and normally distributed with mean 0 and equal standard deviations, then the third measure above is appropriate for determining the most likely $\hat{f}(x)$. This measure, called the root-mean-square (RMS), is the square root of the average of the squares of the individual residuals.

Often, though, the standard deviations of the errors are known to vary. For example, if we know that a particular data point has very little error, we will want it to very nearly satisfy the model. Likewise, if we know that a data point is contaminated with a large error, we will want to give it very little weight. If we know values $s_i > 0$ such that for each i, s_i is proportional to the standard deviation of δ_i, we should scale each of the residuals $y_i - f(x_i)$ by $1/s_i$ and use

$$\sqrt{\frac{1}{m} \sum_{i=1}^{m} \left(\frac{y_i - f(x_i)}{s_i} \right)^2} \tag{6.3}$$

as a measure of the size of the residual. This measure is called the *weighted RMS*. Note that if we multiply each of the s_i by a constant, we will change the value of the weighted RMS at the minimum but the $f(x)$ that gives the minimum will be the same.

It is rare that all of these assumptions are satisfied. In many cases the general model is flawed and the "ideal solution" $g(x)$ does not even exist or the errors are biased or not normally distributed. In such cases the use of the weighted RMS of the residuals is not rigorously justified but we use it anyway if no other method can be justified either, because it turns out that the weighted RMS norm is in general far easier to use than any other norm for solving approximation problems. If we know nothing about the relative sizes of the standard deviations of the errors, we need to assume something about them, most likely that they are equal, and use $s_i = 1$ for each i. The process of finding the solution is not affected by the validity of the problem.

The choice of which functions to use as a basis depends on two things. The first thing to consider is what an appropriate model for the problem might be. The model may be chosen for theoretical reasons or for convenience. For periodic data it is natural to use a periodic model such as a linear combination of sines and cosines. We say that a function $g(x)$ defined for all real x is *periodic* with *period* P if $g(x+P) \equiv g(x)$. Assuming a period of P, for example, we might choose as a model

$$f(x) = a_0 + a_1 \cos\left(\frac{2\pi}{P}x\right) + b_1 \sin\left(\frac{2\pi}{P}x\right) + a_2 \cos\left(2\frac{2\pi}{P}x\right) + b_2 \sin\left(2\frac{2\pi}{P}x\right).$$

The choice of a model is not a part of numerical analysis, and we will not discuss it further.

The other thing to consider in choosing a basis is how best to represent the model. A polynomial can be represented in several ways as a linear combination of basis functions. For example,

$$\begin{aligned} p(x) &= -2x + 2x^2 + 4x^3 \\ &= 0(1) + (-2)(x^1) + 2(x^2) + 4(x^3) \\ &= 1(1) + 1(x) + 1(2x^2 - 1) + 1(4x^3 - 3x). \end{aligned}$$

The difference between using $\{1, x, x^2, x^3\}$ and $\{1, x, 2x^2 - 1, 4x^3 - 3x\}$ as a basis is one of roundoff error. Mathematically the problems are equivalent, but one or the other may exhibit much better roundoff behavior. We will discuss this problem later.

Note that we are using the term *model* in a different sense from the way we defined it in Chapter 1. The use in this chapter is more restricted and is standard terminology for the study of least-squares approximation. *Model* in the sense of the rest of this book is more abstract and consists of both the *model* as used in the chapter and the criterion for best approximation.

Supplementary note

Information on the statistical assumptions underlying least-squares approximation can be found in

> Stephen M. Pizer, *Numerical Computing and Mathematical Analysis*, Science Research Associates, Chicago, 1975.

Mathematica notes

Linear least-squares approximation in *Mathematica* can be done with the function Fit[ ]. Fit[ ] takes three arguments: the data, the model (in the form of a list of basis functions), and the variable used in the representation of the basis functions.

Read in the normal distribution package.   *In[1]:= << Statistics`NormalDistribution`*

Define a random error to be used to   *In[2]:= err := Random[NormalDistribution[0, 1]];*
generate data. This approximates errors
from the standard normal distribution.
Each evaluation of **err** will result in a
different value.

Some data with some random noise.   *In[3]:= data = Table[{x,1+2x+x^2+err},*
                                                          {x, -1, 1, 1/100}];

The data in graphical form.   *In[4]:= pd = ListPlot[data]*

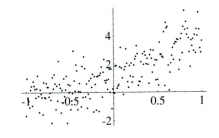

The least-squares approximation to the   *In[5]:= m = Fit[data, {1, x, x^2}, x]*
data.
                                               Out[5]= 1.02614 + 2.18259 x + 0.988171 x^2

A plot of the least-squares approximation.   *In[6]:= Plot[m, {x, -1, 1}]*

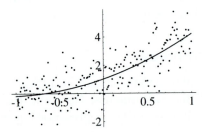

Show them together.   *In[7]:= Show[{%, pd}]*

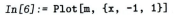

Computer problems

1. Use `Fit[ ]` to find a quadratic approximation to e^x on the interval $[-1., 1.]$. Use 21 data points on the interval with equal spacing between them. On separate graphs, plot the solution and plot its error as an approximation to e^x.

2. Use `Fit[ ]` to interpolate $\sin x$ at 0, $\pi/4$, $\pi/2$, $3\pi/4$, and π with a quartic polynomial.

3. Approximate e^x by a linear combination of 1, $\cos x$, $\sin x$, $\cos 2x$, and $\sin 2x$ on the interval $[1., 2.]$. Use 21 data points on the interval with equal spacing between them.

4. Use `FindMinimum[ ]` to find the values of the coefficients c_1, c_2, and c_3 in the model $c_1 + c_2 x + c_3 x^2$ that minimize the RMS residual for the data $\{(1, 1), (2, 1), (3, 2), (4, 3)\}$. Compare the result with that from `Fit[ ]`.

5. Use `FindMinimum[ ]` to find the least-squares solution to Equations (6.2).

6.2 The Normal Equations

Let us consider first the case where all of the residuals are equally important, i.e., where $s_i = 1$ for each i. We will see later how the problem changes when this is not the case. The problem of fitting a polynomial of degree $n - 1$ can be written as

$$
\begin{aligned}
c_1 &+ c_2 x_1 &+ \cdots &+ c_n x_1^{n-1} &\approx y_1, \\
c_1 &+ c_2 x_2 &+ \cdots &+ c_n x_2^{n-1} &\approx y_2, \\
&\vdots & &\vdots &\vdots \\
&\vdots & &\vdots &\vdots \\
c_1 &+ c_2 x_m &+ \cdots &+ c_n x_m^{n-1} &\approx y_m,
\end{aligned}
$$

which is known as an *overdetermined* system of linear equations because $m > n$. (Recall that the x_i and y_i are given; the c_j are the unknowns.) This can be expressed in matrix notation as

$$
Ac \approx y
$$

where A is a "tall" nonsquare matrix, the unknown c is a "short" vector, and y is a "tall" vector:

$$
A = \begin{bmatrix}
1 & x_1 & \cdots & x_1^{n-1} \\
1 & x_2 & \cdots & x_2^{n-1} \\
\vdots & \vdots & & \vdots \\
\vdots & \vdots & & \vdots \\
1 & x_m & \cdots & x_m^{n-1}
\end{bmatrix}, \quad
c = \begin{bmatrix}
c_1 \\
c_2 \\
\vdots \\
c_n
\end{bmatrix}, \quad
y = \begin{bmatrix}
y_1 \\
y_2 \\
\vdots \\
\vdots \\
y_m
\end{bmatrix}.
$$

The vectors c and y are artificial constructs in m- and n-dimensional space, and it is probably not fruitful to try to relate them to the two-dimensional plots of the data.

The residual vector is

$$r \stackrel{\text{def}}{=} y - Ac.$$

The problem is to minimize the RMS norm of this vector. If we could fit the model to the data exactly, there would be no discrepancies and it would make no difference which norm we chose to minimize; the residual would be 0 for any norm. Usually there will be discrepancies and minimizing one norm will result in a different solution from that given by a different norm. If we use the Euclidean norm,

$$\|u\|_2 \stackrel{\text{def}}{=} \sqrt{\sum_{i=1}^{m} u_i^2},$$

the least-squares problem becomes

$$\min_{c} \|y - Ac\|_2$$

where the constant factor $\sqrt{1/m}$ has been removed from the function to be minimized.

The solution to the least-squares problem is the solution c to the linear system

$$A^{\mathrm{T}}Ac = A^{\mathrm{T}}y.$$

The equations in this system of equations are known as the **normal equations**. It is as though we had multiplied both sides of the overdetermined system $Ac \approx y$ by A^{T} and changed approximate equality to equality. Note that $A^{\mathrm{T}}Ac = A^{\mathrm{T}}y$ is no longer overdetermined. The equation consists of a "small" square matrix $A^{\mathrm{T}}A$ times the "short" unknown vector c set equal to a "short" vector $A^{\mathrm{T}}y$—a system of n linear equations in n unknowns that can be solved by the usual techniques.

We need to discuss the possibility that $A^{\mathrm{T}}A$ may be singular because if it is we will not get a solution. It is easy to see that there will be a problem if we choose as our model $f(x) = c_1 x + c_2 x$: there cannot possibly be a unique solution because interchanging c_1 and c_2 results in an equivalent solution. It happens that we cannot solve for c_1 and c_2 because the matrix $A^{\mathrm{T}}A$ is singular.

The question of singularity is closely tied to the concept of linear dependence. If we have two vectors v and $2v$, we see that $2v$ can be gotten from v by multiplying by 2 or we can go the other way by multiplying by $\frac{1}{2}$. We call this property linear dependence, but the idea is more general. A set of k vectors $\{v_1, v_2, \ldots, v_k\}$ is said to be **linearly dependent** if one of the vectors can be written as a linear combination of the others. Otherwise the set of vectors is said to be **linearly independent**. For example, the set of vectors $\{[1\ 2\ 3]^{\mathrm{T}}, [2\ 0\ 1]^{\mathrm{T}}, [8\ 4\ 9]^{\mathrm{T}}\}$ is linearly dependent because $[8\ 4\ 9]^{\mathrm{T}} = 2[1\ 2\ 3]^{\mathrm{T}} + 3[2\ 0\ 1]^{\mathrm{T}}$.

It can be shown (Exercise 1) that the matrix $A^T A$ is nonsingular if and only if A has linearly independent columns. It can also be shown (Exercise 2) that if A is constructed from $1, x, \ldots, x^{n-1}$ evaluated at m distinct points where $m \geq n$, then A has linearly independent columns.

If we use $\{1, x, x^2, \ldots, x^{n-1}\}$ as the set of basis functions, a typical coefficient of the matrix $A^T A$ is

$$
\begin{aligned}
(A^T A)_{ij} &= e_i^T A^T A e_j \\
&= (A e_i)^T A e_j \\
&= \begin{bmatrix} x_1^{i-1} & x_2^{i-1} & \cdots & x_m^{i-1} \end{bmatrix} \begin{bmatrix} x_1^{j-1} \\ x_2^{j-1} \\ \vdots \\ x_m^{j-1} \end{bmatrix} \\
&= x_1^{i+j-2} + x_2^{i+j-2} + \cdots + x_m^{i+j-2};
\end{aligned}
$$

so there are only $2n - 1$ different coefficients to form. For a different basis there could be as many as $n(n+1)/2$ coefficients to calculate.

Example 6.1 Suppose we wish to fit the data

x_i	0	1	2	3	4
y_i	2	5	4	6	9

to a linear polynomial $c_1 + c_2 x$. This is conveniently expressed as the overdetermined system

$$
\begin{bmatrix} 1 & 0 \\ 1 & 1 \\ 1 & 2 \\ 1 & 3 \\ 1 & 4 \end{bmatrix} \begin{bmatrix} c_1 \\ c_2 \end{bmatrix} \approx \begin{bmatrix} 2 \\ 5 \\ 4 \\ 6 \\ 9 \end{bmatrix}.
$$

Let us assume that each right-hand-side value contains an independent, normally distributed error of the same standard deviation. To determine the best approximation we premultiply both sides of the overdetermined system by the transpose of the coefficient matrix to get the normal equations

$$
\begin{bmatrix} 5 & 10 \\ 10 & 30 \end{bmatrix} \begin{bmatrix} c_1 \\ c_2 \end{bmatrix} = \begin{bmatrix} 26 \\ 67 \end{bmatrix}.
$$

Solving this for c_1 and c_2 gives the best-fit linear polynomial

$$
p(x) = 2.2 + 1.5x.
$$

The residuals $y_i - p(x_i)$ are

$$-0.2, \quad 1.3, \quad -1.2, \quad -0.7, \quad 0.8.$$

For weighted least squares there is a small change that we must make. Rather than trying to solve the overdetermined system

$$Ac \approx y,$$

we want to give various weights to each of the equations in this system. In particular, the relative importance of each residual should be inversely proportional to the standard deviation of the assumed error giving rise to that residual. Thus, if S is the diagonal matrix with s_i as the ith diagonal element, the overdetermined system we want to solve is

$$S^{-1}Ac \approx S^{-1}y$$

and the residual we want to minimize is

$$r = S^{-1}y - S^{-1}Ac.$$

The Euclidean norm of this residual is minimized by the solution to

$$(S^{-1}A)^{\mathrm{T}}(S^{-1}A)c = (S^{-1}A)^{\mathrm{T}}(S^{-1}y). \tag{6.4}$$

Example 6.2 Continuing with the previous example, if the standard deviations are proportional to $s = \{0.1, 0.2, 0.2, 0.4, 0.5\}$, the overdetermined system is

$$\begin{bmatrix} 10 & 0 & 0 & 0 & 0 \\ 0 & 5 & 0 & 0 & 0 \\ 0 & 0 & 5 & 0 & 0 \\ 0 & 0 & 0 & 2.5 & 0 \\ 0 & 0 & 0 & 0 & 2 \end{bmatrix} \begin{bmatrix} 1 & 0 \\ 1 & 1 \\ 1 & 2 \\ 1 & 3 \\ 1 & 4 \end{bmatrix} \begin{bmatrix} c_1 \\ c_2 \end{bmatrix} \approx \begin{bmatrix} 10 & 0 & 0 & 0 & 0 \\ 0 & 5 & 0 & 0 & 0 \\ 0 & 0 & 5 & 0 & 0 \\ 0 & 0 & 0 & 2.5 & 0 \\ 0 & 0 & 0 & 0 & 2 \end{bmatrix} \begin{bmatrix} 2 \\ 5 \\ 4 \\ 6 \\ 9 \end{bmatrix}.$$

When we evaluate this, we get

$$\begin{bmatrix} 10 & 0 \\ 5 & 5 \\ 5 & 10 \\ 2.5 & 7.5 \\ 2 & 8 \end{bmatrix} \begin{bmatrix} c_1 \\ c_2 \end{bmatrix} \approx \begin{bmatrix} 20 \\ 25 \\ 20 \\ 15 \\ 18 \end{bmatrix};$$

so the best linear polynomial is

$$p(x) = \frac{9350}{4361} + \frac{6156}{4361}x \approx 2.144 + 1.4116x$$

and the residuals are approximately

$$-0.144004, \quad 1.44439, \quad -0.967209, \quad -0.378812, \quad 1.20958.$$

The general problem of linear least-squares fitting can be written as

$$
\begin{aligned}
c_1 f_1(x_1) &+& c_2 f_2(x_1) &+& \cdots &+& c_n f_n(x_1) &\approx y_1, \\
c_1 f_1(x_2) &+& c_2 f_2(x_2) &+& \cdots &+& c_n f_n(x_2) &\approx y_2, \\
&\vdots& &\vdots& & &\vdots& \quad\vdots \\
&\vdots& &\vdots& & &\vdots& \quad\vdots \\
c_1 f_1(x_m) &+& c_2 f_2(x_m) &+& \cdots &+& c_n f_n(x_m) &\approx y_m.
\end{aligned}
$$

The only difference between this and fitting a polynomial is that in writing the system as

$$A\boldsymbol{c} \approx \boldsymbol{y},$$

the matrix A becomes

$$
A = \begin{bmatrix}
f_1(x_1) & f_2(x_1) & \cdots & f_n(x_1) \\
f_1(x_2) & f_2(x_2) & \cdots & f_n(x_2) \\
\vdots & \vdots & & \vdots \\
\vdots & \vdots & & \vdots \\
f_1(x_m) & f_2(x_m) & \cdots & f_n(x_m)
\end{bmatrix}.
$$

In finite precision, using powers of x as basis functions is usually a poor choice. It leads to a matrix $A^{\mathrm{T}}A$ that can be very ill-conditioned. Powers of x give rise to columns of A that are nearly linearly dependent, meaning that the columns are vectors pointing in nearly the same "direction." We know that in three dimensions the inner product provides an easy test for a right angle between two vectors. More generally we say that vectors $\boldsymbol{u}$ and $\boldsymbol{v}$ are **orthogonal** if $\boldsymbol{u}^{\mathrm{T}}\boldsymbol{v} = 0$. Ideally the columns of A should be mutually orthogonal, in which case we say that the functions $f_1, f_2, \ldots, f_n$ form an **orthogonal system**. In this case $A^{\mathrm{T}}A = D$ where D is some diagonal matrix, because it is the result of taking inner products between columns of A:

$$(A^{\mathrm{T}}A)_{ij} = (A\boldsymbol{e}_i)^{\mathrm{T}}(A\boldsymbol{e}_j).$$

Hence, the optimal $\boldsymbol{c}$ is simply $D^{-1}A^{\mathrm{T}}\boldsymbol{y}$.

It turns out that with equally spaced periodic data the "trigonometric polynomials" are orthogonal, which makes them particularly well suited for least-squares approximation. More specifically, if $x_i = x_1 + (i-1)h$ and y_{m+i} is assumed to be the same as y_i, then the functions

$$
1, \cos\left(\frac{2\pi}{mh}x\right), \ \sin\left(\frac{2\pi}{mh}x\right), \ \cos\left(2\frac{2\pi}{mh}x\right), \ \sin\left(2\frac{2\pi}{mh}x\right), \ldots
$$

are orthogonal. For example, if n is odd, then the model

$$
f(x) = c_1 + c_2 \cos\left(\frac{2\pi}{mh}x\right) + c_3 \sin\left(\frac{2\pi}{mh}x\right) + \cdots + c_{n-1}\cos\left(\left(\frac{n-1}{2}\right)\frac{2\pi}{mh}x\right) + c_n \sin\left(\left(\frac{n-1}{2}\right)\frac{2\pi}{mh}x\right)
$$

with equal weights at the x_i will result in the normal equations being independent of each other. The jth normal equation will involve only the unknown c_j.

Exercises

1. Show that the matrix $A^{\mathrm{T}}A$ is nonsingular if and only if A has linearly independent columns.

2. Show that A has linearly independent columns if it is constructed from $1, x, \ldots, x^{n-1}$ evaluated at m distinct points where $m \geq n$.

3. Suppose that point A was measured to have an elevation of 1.0 km above sea level, that point B was measured to have an elevation of 1.4 km above sea level, and that point B was measured to have an elevation 0.5 km greater than that of point A. Assume that the measurement errors are independent random variables with identical normal distributions. What are the most likely elevations of the two points?

4. Show that in forming the matrix $A^{\mathrm{T}}A$ for the normal equations with a general set of basis functions, only $n(n-1)/2$ elements need to be calculated.

Mathematica notes

Only square nonsingular matrices have inverses. If the matrix A is invertible and we want to solve

$$A\boldsymbol{c} = \boldsymbol{y},$$

we express the solution as

$$\boldsymbol{c} = A^{-1}\boldsymbol{y}.$$

There is a generalization of the inverse to any rectangular matrix known as the pseudo-inverse. The pseudo-inverse of any invertible square matrix is just its inverse. If $A^{\mathrm{T}}A$ is nonsingular, then the pseudo-inverse is given by

$$A^{\dagger} = (A^{\mathrm{T}}A)^{-1}A^{\mathrm{T}}.$$

Hence, to minimize the 2-norm of the residual of the overdetermined system

$$A\boldsymbol{c} \approx \boldsymbol{y},$$

we can express the solution as

$$\boldsymbol{c} = A^{\dagger}\boldsymbol{y}.$$

The *Mathematica* function `PseudoInverse[ ]` computes the pseudo-inverse of a matrix; but just as one should almost never compute the inverse of a matrix, one should almost never compute the pseudo-inverse, either.

Computer problems

1. Verify that the best linear polynomial for data in Example 6.2 is $p(x) = 9350/4361 + (6156/4361)x$.

2. Let $A = $ `Table[i^j, {i, 6}, {j, 0, 3}]`, and $y = $ {-1188, 4524, -6076, 3299, 0, 0}. Solve $Ac \approx y$ for c. What is the 2-norm of the residual? Give several examples showing that small perturbations of c result in larger residuals than those for c. That is, offer evidence that c does indeed give the smallest 2-norm of the residual.

3. Set up the overdetermined systems of linear equations for Computer Problems 1–4 on page 241. Use `PseudoInverse[ ]` to solve the systems.

4. There are four properties of a pseudo-inverse, namely $ABA = A$, $BAB = B$, $(AB)^T = AB$, and $(BA)^T = BA$ where B is the pseudo-inverse of A. Let a be given by `Table[i^j, {i, 5}, {j, 3}]`, and let b be its pseudo-inverse. Verify that b satisfies the four properties of a pseudo-inverse.

5. In this problem we will verify numerically that the functions 1, $\cos(\frac{2\pi}{mh}x)$, $\sin(\frac{2\pi}{mh}x)$, $\cos(2\frac{2\pi}{mh}x)$, $\sin(2\frac{2\pi}{mh}x)$, ... evaluated at $x_j = j$ with $h = 1$ and $m = 4$ are orthogonal.

   (a) Let mesh = `Table[N[(2*Pi*j)/7], {j, 7}]`.

   (b) Let c0 = `Cos[0. mesh]`. Let c1 = `Cos[1. mesh]` and s1 = `Sin[1. mesh]`. Similarly define c2, s2, c3, and s3.

   (c) Let the matrix a be the transpose of {c0, c1, s1, c2, s2, c3, s3} (we want the columns of a to be these vectors) and evaluate `Transpose[a] . a`. Display the result using `MatrixForm[ ]`. `Chop[ ]` can be used to make the result more readable by converting all very small numbers to 0.

   (d) Repeat the above with eight mesh points rather than seven.

6. We mentioned in this section that it is better to use basis functions that are orthogonal. In this problem we examine the advantages of this. Consider the data

$$\texttt{Table[\{x, Sin[x]\}, \{x, 995., 1005.\}]}.$$

   (a) Approximate the data using the basis functions `Table[x^k,{k,0,10}]`. Calculate the residual and its 2-norm. Use `Fit[ ]` for this problem.

   (b) Approximate the data using the basis functions `Table[(x-1000.)^k,{k,0,10}]`. Calculate the residual and its 2-norm.

   (c) Verify that `ChebyshevT[4, (x-1000)/5]` is a polynomial in x of degree 4. We want to use these polynomials as basis functions but we want to prevent their evaluation with symbolic arguments. Let `cheby[k_,x_?NumberQ] := ChebyshevT[k,(x-1000.)/5.]` and use `Table[cheby[k,x],{k,0,10}]` as the basis functions to approximate the data. Calculate the residual and its 2-norm.

(d) It can be shown that each of the three sets of basis functions can represent any polynomial in x of degree at most 10. Moreover, the problem is really one of interpolation, and the residuals are entirely due to rounding since the system is not overdetermined. Which of the three solutions suffers the least from rounding?

7. We examine Runge's phenomenon again. We know that for the function $f(x) = 1/(1 + 25x^2)$, equally spaced data are not good for interpolation, especially as the number of data points becomes large. With least-squares approximation we should be able to do better, at least for low-degree approximations. It has been claimed that for m equally spaced data points, least-squares approximation of degree n should not be performed for $n > 2\sqrt{m}$. For $n = m - 1$ we have interpolation and Runge's phenomenon. Verify experimentally that the effects of Runge's phenomenon do not begin to appear until $n \approx 2\sqrt{m}$.

8. In this problem we will fit a model to the data representing average daily temperature highs in Champaign, Illinois for the years 1891 through 1990. (We will ignore the fact that the standard deviation for February 29 is about twice as large as the standard deviation for each of the other days of the year.) The data, given month by month, are

33 32 32 32 32 31 30 30 29 29 30 30 30 31 31 31 31 31 31 32 33 34 35 35 33 33 32 32 32 33 33
32 31 30 35 37 34 33 32 35 38 36 36 38 37 38 36 37 41 37 40 39 39 41 42 42 42 43 42 (43)
44 44 46 45 41 46 44 45 45 45 47 46 47 47 47 47 46 49 49 50 48 50 51 48 47 49 53 55 54 54 55
57 58 55 53 56 60 59 58 57 58 60 61 61 62 63 64 67 66 65 68 68 69 65 65 67 66 66 65 67 69
70 70 71 71 72 70 69 69 67 71 68 69 71 72 73 73 73 76 76 76 78 78 76 77 78 77 77 76 77 78 80
78 76 79 81 82 82 82 82 82 83 81 83 83 82 82 81 82 82 84 86 84 83 83 82 84 84 86 86 86 87 87
88 87 84 84 84 85 86 86 84 85 86 86 86 87 85 85 86 87 86 86 86 87 85 85 85 86 86 86 84 85 85
84 85 85 83 84 83 84 83 83 82 82 82 83 84 84 82 84 85 84 83 83 82 82 83 83 84 85 85 86 85 84
82 83 83 81 82 82 83 82 82 80 79 80 80 79 78 77 78 80 77 77 75 76 74 74 74 76 74 74 76 73
74 74 72 73 70 68 68 69 69 69 69 70 70 70 69 67 67 63 63 64 66 67 65 61 59 60 59 58 58 60 60
58 58 55 53 55 53 53 52 53 52 53 52 54 53 55 54 52 51 47 48 46 47 46 45 46 45 43 39 38 39
41 44 44 44 44 41 41 39 36 37 38 36 36 36 36 34 37 38 38 36 34 37 37 36 36 35 36 36 35 36 35

These data obviously contain noise due to finite sampling; for example, no one would seriously believe that March 5 can be expected to be 5 degrees colder than March 3. We will smooth these data to get more believable expected daily highs.

(a) Enter these data as a list of 366 numbers. (As an alternative, use the fake data given by

```
data = Table[Round[Random[Real, {58, 65}] +
            46.72 BesselJ[1, .02094 (Mod[k+73, 366]-183)]],
        {k, 366}];
```

For consistency, type SeedRandom[23] before generating data.)

(b) The expected daily high is a periodic function of t with period 366 if the *climate* remains constant. Form the normal equations for fitting the model

$$c_1 + c_2 \sin\left(\frac{2\pi}{366}t\right) + c_3 \cos\left(\frac{2\pi}{366}t\right) + c_4 \sin\left(2\frac{2\pi}{366}t\right) + c_5 \cos\left(2\frac{2\pi}{366}t\right)$$

to the data. Note: If you use `Pi` for π in this model, *Mathematica* will not evaluate, say, `Sin[2. Pi/366. 79.]` to a number. Every time it encounters the nonnumerical result it will try to evaluate it again and will waste a *lot* of time trying to evaluate each `Sin` and `Cos` each of the thousands of times they are encountered in the process of forming the normal equations. Use instead `pi = N[Pi]` or `a = N[2 Pi/366]`.

(c) Solve the normal equations one at a time by assuming that the very small off-diagonal elements of the coefficient matrix are zero.

(d) Show a `ListPlot` of `data` and a plot of your solution together on the same graph.

6.3   Two Derivations of the Normal Equations

There are two ways to derive the normal equations. The most straightforward way is to use partial derivatives to minimize the 2-norm of the residual with respect to the unknown coefficients. This derivation is presented in Section 6.3.1. As an alternative that avoids partial derivatives, we can follow a more circuitous route that relies on orthogonality and takes us to one of the central ideas of applied mathematics and numerical analysis. That derivation is presented in Section 6.3.2.

⋆ 6.3.1   Using partial derivatives

We start by showing how to minimize the 2-norm of the residual vector in the organ-pipe problem. Recall that the problem is to minimize the square root of the sum of the squares of the individual residuals. To simplify our task, we instead minimize the square of that quantity,

$$\|r\|_2^2 = (2.05573 - \ln a - 2\ln b)^2 + (1.9981 - \ln a - 4\ln b)^2 + (1.97234 - \ln a - 5\ln b)^2$$
$$+ (1.86214 - \ln a - 9\ln b)^2 + (1.83258 - \ln a - 10\ln b)^2$$

where the unknowns are $\ln a$ and $\ln b$. It is inconvenient to write this sum explicitly, so we use subscripted variables and summation notation:

$$\|r\|_2^2 = \sum_{i=1}^{5}(y_i - c_1 - c_2 x_i)^2$$

where x_i, y_i are the data and the unknowns c_1 and c_2 are $\ln a$ and $\ln b$, respectively. From calculus of several variables, we know that at the minimum of $\|r\|_2^2$, we have

$$0 = \frac{\partial}{\partial c_1}\|r\|_2^2 = \sum_{i=1}^{5} 2(y_i - c_1 - c_2 x_i)(-1),$$

$$0 = \frac{\partial}{\partial c_2}\|r\|_2^2 = \sum_{i=1}^{5} 2(y_i - c_1 - c_2 x_i)(-x_i).$$

Splitting these sums into three parts and dividing by -2, we get

$$0 = \sum_{i=1}^{5} y_i - \sum_{i=1}^{5} c_1 - \sum_{i=1}^{5} c_2 x_i,$$

$$0 = \sum_{i=1}^{5} y_i x_i - \sum_{i=1}^{5} c_1 x_i - \sum_{i=1}^{5} c_2 x_i^2.$$

Moving the unknown terms to the left-hand sides of the equations and factoring out the unknowns from the sums, we get the normal equations

$$c_1 \sum_{i=1}^{5} 1 + c_2 \sum_{i=1}^{5} x_i = \sum_{i=1}^{5} y_i,$$

$$c_1 \sum_{i=1}^{5} x_i + c_2 \sum_{i=1}^{5} x_i^2 = \sum_{i=1}^{5} y_i x_i.$$

Finally, we can write this in matrix notation as

$$\begin{bmatrix} 1 & 1 & 1 & 1 & 1 \\ x_1 & x_2 & x_3 & x_4 & x_5 \end{bmatrix} \begin{bmatrix} 1 & x_1 \\ 1 & x_2 \\ 1 & x_3 \\ 1 & x_4 \\ 1 & x_5 \end{bmatrix} \begin{bmatrix} c_1 \\ c_2 \end{bmatrix} = \begin{bmatrix} 1 & 1 & 1 & 1 & 1 \\ x_1 & x_2 & x_3 & x_4 & x_5 \end{bmatrix} \begin{bmatrix} y_1 \\ y_2 \\ y_3 \\ y_4 \\ y_5 \end{bmatrix}.$$

Note how the matrix products give rise to the sums in the summation form of the equations.

In general, we have more than two unknowns. The problem is to find the values of c_j for $1 \leq j \leq n$ that minimize

$$\|r\|_2^2 = \sum_{i=1}^{m} \left(y_i - \sum_{k=1}^{n} a_{ik} c_k \right)^2.$$

From calculus of several variables, we know that at the c that minimizes $\|r\|$, we have for each j, $1 \leq j \leq n$,

$$\frac{\partial}{\partial c_j}\|r\|_2^2 = 0.$$

Using the chain rule for derivatives, we get

$$
\begin{aligned}
0 = \frac{\partial}{\partial c_j}\|r\|_2^2 &= \sum_{i=1}^{m} 2 \left(y_i - \sum_{k=1}^{n} a_{ik}c_k \right) \frac{\partial}{\partial c_j} \left(y_i - \sum_{k=1}^{n} a_{ik}c_k \right) \\
&= 2\sum_{i=1}^{m} \left(y_i - \sum_{k=1}^{n} a_{ik}c_k \right) (-a_{ij})
\end{aligned}
$$

where the last simplification results the fact that y_i and a_{ik} are simply numbers and the fact that for each i, $\partial c_k/\partial c_j = 0$ for $k \neq j$, and $\partial c_j/\partial c_j = 1$.

By splitting the last sum into two parts we can continue the derivation as follows:

$$0 = \sum_{i=1}^{m} a_{ij}y_i - \sum_{i=1}^{m} \left(\sum_{k=1}^{n} a_{ik}c_k \right) a_{ij}.$$

By moving one sum to the left-hand side of the equation and reversing the order of summation we get

$$\sum_{k=1}^{n} \left(\sum_{i=1}^{m} a_{ij}a_{ik} \right) c_k = \sum_{i=1}^{m} a_{ij}y_i.$$

This equation must hold for each j where $1 \leq j \leq n$. By combining all of these equations and writing the result in matrix notation, we get the normal equations

$$A^{\mathrm{T}}Ac = A^{\mathrm{T}}y$$

of Section 6.2.

⋆ 6.3.2 Using linear algebra

Here we use geometric reasoning to discover the solution to the linear least-squares problem and algebra to validate it. Before we begin, we need some ideas from linear algebra.

A geometric concept that we need is that of a *subspace*. A nonempty subset S of a k-dimensional vector space is said to be a **linear subspace** if (i) the sum of any two vectors in S is also in S and (ii) any scalar multiple of any vector in S is also in S. For example, if our space is three-dimensional, then the entire space itself is a subspace, as is any plane or straight line. A common way in which subspaces arise is as the **span** of a set of vectors $\{v_1, v_2, \ldots, v_p\}$, which we define as the set of all linear combinations

$$\alpha_1 v_1 + \alpha_2 v_2 + \cdots + \alpha_p v_p.$$

Note that the span of a set of p linearly independent vectors is a p-dimensional subspace. Thus the span of a single nonzero vector is a line, and the span of two independent vectors is a plane.

The subspace that we are interested in is the set of all linear combinations of the columns of the matrix $A = [a_1 \ a_2 \ \ldots \ a_n]$:

$$Ac = c_1 a_1 + c_2 a_2 + \cdots + c_n a_n.$$

This subspace is called the *column space* of A. In particular, we want to find the one vector in the column space of A that is closest to y, i.e., find the values c_j, $1 \le j \le n$, that give

$$\min_{c_1, c_2, \ldots, c_n} \|y - (c_1 a_1 + c_2 a_2 + \cdots + c_n a_n)\|_2.$$

We begin by examining this problem for $n = 1$ and $m = 2$, where the problem is to minimize $\|y - c_1 a_1\|_2$. The subspace spanned by the one column of A is a straight line passing through the origin of the two-dimensional plane, and the problem is to find that vector on this straight line that is closest to y. The solution is to "project" a perpendicular from y to the straight line as shown in Figure 6.3. Such a choice makes the residual $r = y - c_1 a_1$ orthogonal to the straight line that is the column space of A:

$$r \perp \text{span of } a_1.$$

Clearly the perpendicular to the line determines the minimal distance.

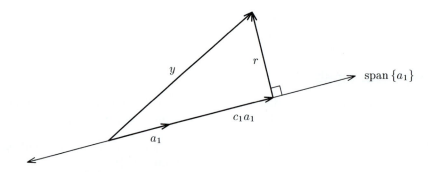

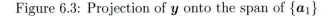
Figure 6.3: Projection of y onto the span of $\{a_1\}$

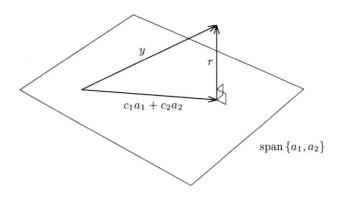

Figure 6.4: Projection of $\boldsymbol{y}$ onto the span of $\{\boldsymbol{a}_1, \boldsymbol{a}_2\}$

Consider now the case $n = 2$ and $m = 3$, where $\boldsymbol{y}$ is some vector in three-dimensional space and the two columns of A span a plane passing through the origin. (If the two columns are linearly dependent and not both zero, they span a straight line.) The vector in the column space of A nearest $\boldsymbol{y}$ is such that its difference from $\boldsymbol{y}$ is perpendicular to the plane, as shown in Figure 6.4. For $\boldsymbol{r}$ to be perpendicular to the space spanned by $\boldsymbol{a}_1$ and $\boldsymbol{a}_2$ is equivalent to

$$\boldsymbol{r} \perp \boldsymbol{a}_1, \boldsymbol{a}_2.$$

Generally, then, the idea is to make the residual

$$\boldsymbol{r} = \boldsymbol{y} - (c_1 \boldsymbol{a}_1 + c_2 \boldsymbol{a}_2 + \cdots + c_n \boldsymbol{a}_n)$$

orthogonal to the subspace spanned by $\boldsymbol{a}_1, \boldsymbol{a}_2, \ldots, \boldsymbol{a}_n$. (The derivation that we are undertaking involves a nonrigorous appeal to geometric intuition. The conclusion that we reach will be verified algebraically.) The condition we have just stated is "clearly" equivalent to

$$\boldsymbol{r} \perp \boldsymbol{a}_1, \boldsymbol{a}_2, \ldots, \boldsymbol{a}_n.$$

In other words,

$$
\begin{aligned}
\boldsymbol{a}_1^{\mathrm{T}} \boldsymbol{r} &= 0, \\
\boldsymbol{a}_2^{\mathrm{T}} \boldsymbol{r} &= 0, \\
&\vdots \\
\boldsymbol{a}_n^{\mathrm{T}} \boldsymbol{r} &= 0,
\end{aligned}
$$

or

$$
\begin{bmatrix}
\boldsymbol{a}_1^{\mathrm{T}} \\
\boldsymbol{a}_2^{\mathrm{T}} \\
\vdots \\
\boldsymbol{a}_n^{\mathrm{T}}
\end{bmatrix}
\boldsymbol{r} = \boldsymbol{0}.
$$

Continuing, we have, with matrix notation,

$$A^{\mathrm{T}}\boldsymbol{r} = \boldsymbol{0},$$

$$A^{\mathrm{T}}(\boldsymbol{y} - A\boldsymbol{c}) = \boldsymbol{0},$$
$$A^{\mathrm{T}}A\boldsymbol{c} = A^{\mathrm{T}}\boldsymbol{y}.$$

What we have just done is geometric reasoning; it is not a proof. We give here a proof that the reasoning was correct. Let $\boldsymbol{c}$ be the solution of the normal equations. To show that this minimizes the Euclidean norm of the residual, we look at what would happen if we used instead $\boldsymbol{c} + \boldsymbol{d}$. Then the norm of the residual would be

$$
\begin{aligned}
\|\boldsymbol{y} - A(\boldsymbol{c}+\boldsymbol{d})\|_2 &= \|\boldsymbol{r} - A\boldsymbol{d}\|_2 \\
&= \sqrt{(\boldsymbol{r} - A\boldsymbol{d})^{\mathrm{T}}(\boldsymbol{r} - A\boldsymbol{d})} \\
&= \sqrt{\boldsymbol{r}^{\mathrm{T}}\boldsymbol{r} - \boldsymbol{r}^{\mathrm{T}}A\boldsymbol{d} - \boldsymbol{d}^{\mathrm{T}}A^{\mathrm{T}}\boldsymbol{r} + \boldsymbol{d}^{\mathrm{T}}A^{\mathrm{T}}A\boldsymbol{d}}.
\end{aligned}
$$

Because of the normal equations, $\boldsymbol{r}^{\mathrm{T}}A$ and $A^{\mathrm{T}}\boldsymbol{r}$ are zero. Hence, the residual simplifies to

$$
\begin{aligned}
\|\boldsymbol{y} - A(\boldsymbol{c}+\boldsymbol{d})\|_2 &= \sqrt{\|\boldsymbol{r}\|_2^2 + \|A\boldsymbol{d}\|_2^2} \\
&\geq \|\boldsymbol{r}\|_2 \\
&= \|\boldsymbol{y} - A\boldsymbol{c}\|_2.
\end{aligned}
$$

In other words, the residual for $\boldsymbol{c} + \boldsymbol{d}$ for *any* $\boldsymbol{d}$ is at least as great as the residual for the solution $\boldsymbol{c}$ of the normal equations.

Exercise

1. Using partial derivatives, derive the normal equations for weighted linear least-squares approximation. That is, derive Equation (6.4) as the condition that minimizes Equation (6.3).

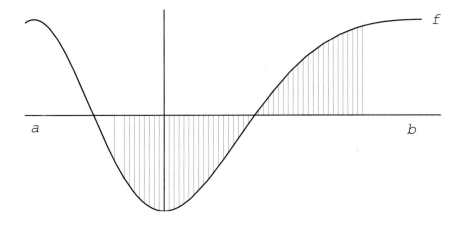

7.   Numerical Differentiation and Integration

Before learning integral calculus, the problem of finding areas seems very difficult; and learning how to find areas under curves with calculus can give an initial sense of excitement and power. This is later tarnished by the realization that most integrals are not amenable to analytical techniques. However, numerical techniques provide a nearly universal tool that although not exact can yield arbitrary accuracy. What is particularly gratifying is that with only modest computational effort and the right techniques one can approximate an integral to astonishing accuracy. Also very important is that numerical techniques for problems of differentiation and integration are the basis for numerical methods for differential and integral equations and are useful for solving nonlinear equations. Computing the definite integral for a function of one variable is sometimes called **quadrature**. The literal meaning of this word is "squaring," which is an ancient word for "computing area." For multiple integrals in two (or more) variables the term *cubature* is sometimes used.

This chapter contains the following sections:

7.1 Numerical Differentiation

Why differentiate numerically? Are not analytical techniques for differentiation universally applicable? Generally they are, but it is not always easy to automate analytical techniques despite the existence of computer algebra systems like *Mathematica*. Also, there are functions whose values are known only at a discrete set of points, for which only numerical methods are applicable. For example, a researcher interested in determining the forces exerted by an athlete might use cinematography to record position of the athlete's arm every 1/24 second. Then Newton's second law of motion is applied:

$$\text{force} = \text{mass} \cdot \frac{d^2}{dt^2}(\text{position}).$$

However, as we stated earlier, the main reason for studying this topic is its usefulness in the derivation of numerical methods, especially finite-difference techniques for differential equations, which are a central problem of scientific computation. Apart from its usefulness there is another reason for introducing numerical differentiation: It enables us to illustrate the important technique of *Richardson extrapolation* in the simplest possible setting.

If in the definition of the derivative we stop short of the limit, we obtain the **one-sided difference**

$$f'(a) \approx \frac{f(a+h) - f(a)}{h}$$

as an approximation. As illustrated by Figure 7.1, the slope $f'(a)$ of the tangent to the graph of a function $f(x)$ at a point $x = a$ is approximated by the slope of the secant that cuts the graph of $f(x)$ at two points, $x = a$ and $x = a + h$. It is fairly evident that this is a crude approximation unless h is very small. Nonetheless, it finds use in numerical methods for solving nonlinear equations where the derivative approximation is merely a means to some other end.

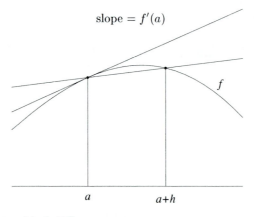

Figure 7.1: One-sided difference

The definition

$$(\text{truncation}) \text{ error} = \frac{f(a+h) - f(a)}{h} - f'(a)$$

does not provide a sense of the size of the error because of the cancellations that occur. To get a proper sense of the error, we can do a fairly elementary type of error analysis based on an expansion of the error in powers of the parameter h. We will see that this is useful in comparing the accuracy of algorithms and in constructing accurate algorithms via the method of undetermined coefficients. To express the error in powers of h, we do a Taylor expansion

$$f(a+h) = f(a) + hf'(a) + \frac{h^2}{2} f''(a) + \frac{h^3}{6} f'''(a) + \cdots$$

and do a substitution to get

$$\text{error} = \cdots = \frac{h}{2} f''(a) + \frac{h^2}{6} f'''(a) + \cdots.$$

Better still, by using a Taylor series with remainder,

$$f(a+h) = f(a) + hf'(a) + \frac{h^2}{2} f''(a + \theta h),$$

we get

$$\text{error} = \frac{h}{2} f''(a + \theta h)$$

where, as usual, θ is some number between 0 and 1. We see from this that the order of accuracy is 1.

It does not take much imagination (see Figure 7.2) to recognize that the **centered difference** approximation

$$f'(a) \approx \frac{f(a+h) - f(a-h)}{2h}$$

(obtained by taking the slope of the line cutting the graph of $f(x)$ at $x = a - h$ and $x = a + h$) is more accurate than a one-sided difference. To confirm this, we analyze the

$$\text{error} = \frac{f(a+h) - f(a-h)}{2h} - f'(a).$$

To pull h out into the open, we use

$$f(a+h) = f(a) + hf'(a) + \frac{h^2}{2} f''(a) + \frac{h^3}{6} f'''(a) + \cdots,$$

$$f(a-h) = f(a) - hf'(a) + \frac{h^2}{2} f''(a) - \frac{h^3}{6} f'''(a) + \cdots,$$

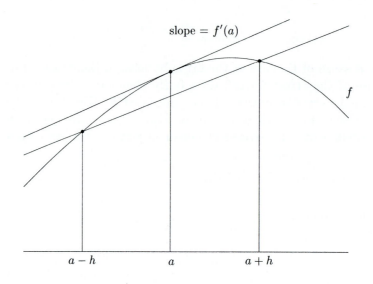

Figure 7.2: Centered difference

which combine to give

$$f(a+h) - f(a-h) = 2hf'(a) + \frac{h^3}{3}f'''(a) + \frac{h^5}{60}f^{v}(a) + \cdots.$$

Hence, the

$$\text{error} = \frac{h^2}{6}f'''(a) + \frac{h^4}{120}f^{v}(a) + \cdots.$$

Better still, with remainder terms we would get

$$\text{error} = \frac{h^2}{6}\left(\frac{f'''(\xi_-) + f'''(\xi_+)}{2}\right)$$

where ξ_- is between $a - h$ and a and ξ_+ is between a and $a + h$. This expression for the error is better because it is much more precise than, say, $O(h^2)$ or $(h^2/6)f'''(a) + O(h^3)$. Very large numbers can be hidden in the big-oh notation. The expression $(f'''(\xi_-) + f'''(\xi_+))/2$ can be simplified. Clearly its value is between $f'''(\xi_-)$ and $f'''(\xi_+)$. If $f'''(x)$ is continuous for $a - h \leq x \leq a + h$, then by the **intermediate-value theorem** $f'''(x)$ attains every value between $f'''(\xi_-)$ and $f'''(\xi_+)$ and, in particular, at some point $x = \xi$, say, $f'''(x)$ attains the average of the two values. See Figure 7.3. Therefore, the error $= (h^2/6)f'''(\xi)$, and the order of accuracy is 2, which confirms the superiority of a centered difference. The significance of second-order accuracy is best seen by taking (negative) logarithms

$$(-\log_2 |\text{error}|) = 2\left(\log_2(1/h)\right) - \log_2 |\tfrac{1}{6}f'''(\xi)|$$

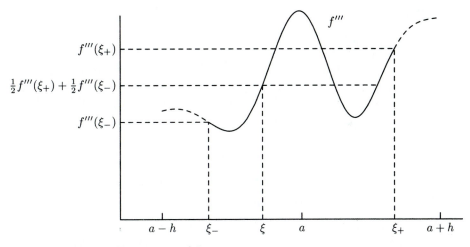

Figure 7.3: Existence of ξ

and plotting (binary places of) accuracy versus $\log_2(1/h)$ as shown in Figure 7.4. As $1/h \to +\infty$, we have $\xi \to a$ and the last term becomes constant.

To get more accurate formulas for derivative approximations, we need a systematic approach. The one-sided and centered-difference approximations are both based on linear interpolation. To generalize this, let $p(x)$ interpolate $f(x)$ at $x_0, x_1, \ldots, x_n$. An approximation to

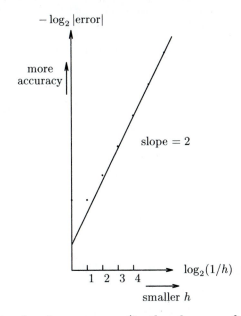

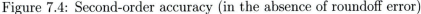

Figure 7.4: Second-order accuracy (in the absence of roundoff error)

the kth derivative is obtained thus:

$$f^{(k)}(a) \approx p^{(k)}(a)$$
$$= l_0^{(k)}(a)f(x_0) + l_1^{(k)}(a)f(x_1) + \cdots + l_n^{(k)}(a)f(x_n),$$

where we have used the Lagrange form to highlight the dependence on values of $f(x)$.

The order of accuracy of a numerical differentiation rule based on polynomial interpolation satisfies two rules:

RULE 1 Order $\geq$ number of points $-$ number of derivatives.

RULE 2 If $x_0, x_1, \ldots, x_n$ are symmetric about $x = a$, the order is even.

Example 7.1 Suppose we are to approximate $f''(a)$ given $f(a-h)$, $f(a)$, $f(a+h)$. Quadratic interpolation gives

$$f(x) \approx p(x) = \frac{(x-a)(x-a-h)}{(-h)(-2h)}f(a-h) + \frac{(x-a+h)(x-a-h)}{(h)(-h)}f(a)$$
$$+ \frac{(x-a+h)(x-a)}{(2h)(h)}f(a+h),$$

so

$$f''(a) \approx p''(a) = \frac{f(a+h) - 2f(a) + f(a-h)}{h^2}.$$

Rule 1 implies that the order is $\geq 3 - 2 = 1$, and rule 2 implies that the order is even. Hence the order is at least 2.

There is a very general device known as **Richardson extrapolation** that can combine the results from multiple applications of a simple low-accuracy formula in order to produce a high-accuracy result. It works for formulas whose accuracy is a function of some parameter h that can be freely chosen.

As an example we consider the formula

$$D(h) \stackrel{\text{def}}{=} \frac{f(a+h) - f(a-h)}{2h} \approx f'(a).$$

The idea of extrapolation is that if we know "basically" how the error of $D(h)$ behaves as a function of h, then we can extrapolate results obtained for several different values of h to the limit

$$\lim_{h \to 0} D(h) = f'(a).$$

With Taylor expansions we have shown that

$$D(h) = f'(a) + \frac{h^2}{6} f'''(a) + \frac{h^4}{120} f^{\mathrm{v}}(a) + \cdots. \tag{7.1}$$

For h twice as large we have

$$D(2h) = f'(a) + 4\frac{h^2}{6} f'''(a) + 16\frac{h^4}{120} f^{\mathrm{v}}(a) + \cdots. \tag{7.2}$$

We see that the first and dominant term of the error in $D(2h)$ is four times that of $D(h)$, so we can write

$$\begin{aligned} D(h) &= f'(a) + \text{ error,} \\ D(2h) &\approx f'(a) + 4 \cdot \text{ error.} \end{aligned}$$

Eliminating the error and solving gives

$$f'(a) \approx \tfrac{4}{3} D(h) - \tfrac{1}{3} D(2h).$$

More precisely, eliminating the *dominant* h^2 error term in (7.1) and (7.2) gives

$$4D(h) - D(2h) = 3f'(a) - \frac{h^4}{10} f^{\mathrm{v}}(a) + \cdots,$$

and dividing by 3 gives the new and more accurate formula

$$D_1(h) \stackrel{\text{def}}{=} \frac{4D(h) - D(2h)}{3} = f'(a) - \frac{h^4}{30} f^{\mathrm{v}}(a) + \cdots.$$

The order of accuracy is 4. Expressed in terms of values of $f(x)$ the formula is

$$D_1(h) = \frac{4}{3} \cdot \frac{f(a+h) - f(a-h)}{2h} - \frac{1}{3} \cdot \frac{f(a+2h) - f(a-2h)}{4h}.$$

Note that the idea of eliminating the dominant term of the error does not depend on knowing $f'''(a)$ or even the constant $\frac{1}{6}$. We need to know only that the dominant error term has the form constant$\cdot h^2$.

Example 7.2 With $f(x) = 1/x$, $a = 2$, and $h = 0.5$, we have

$$\begin{aligned} D(0.5) &= \frac{f(2.5) - f(1.5)}{1} = -0.266666 \cdots, \\ D(1) &= \frac{f(3) - f(1)}{2} = -0.333333 \cdots, \\ D_1(0.5) &= \tfrac{4}{3}(-0.266666) - \tfrac{1}{3}(-0.333333) = -0.244444. \end{aligned}$$

We have shown how to do one extrapolation. We could do another extrapolation by applying the idea to the new formula $D_1(h)$, the form of whose error expansion we have determined. If we extrapolated from the values $D_1(h)$ and $D_1(2h)$, this would involve the use of $D(h)$, $D(2h)$ *twice*, and $D(4h)$. Note how appropriate combinations of values of h economize on the amount of computation.

It is not necessary to use values of h that differ by a factor of 2. If in (7.1) we substitute Rh for h, where $R > 1$ is fixed, we get

$$D(Rh) = f'(a) + R^2 \frac{h^2}{6} f'''(a) + R^4 \frac{h^4}{120} f^{\mathrm{v}}(a) + \cdots .$$

Eliminating the dominant error term between this and (7.1) gives

$$R^2 D(h) - D(Rh) = (R^2 - 1) f'(a) - R^2 (R^2 - 1) \frac{h^4}{120} f^{\mathrm{v}}(a) + \cdots ,$$

and a division yields the improved formula

$$\frac{R^2 D(h) - D(Rh)}{R^2 - 1} = f'(a) - R^2 \frac{h^4}{120} f^{\mathrm{v}}(a) + \cdots$$

of order of accuracy 4. For example, $R = 3$ yields a formula that uses $f(a - 3h)$, $f(a - h)$, $f(a + h)$, $f(a + 3h)$ to approximate $f'(a)$.

As an example of a different type of error behavior, consider the *first-order* formula

$$D(h) \stackrel{\text{def}}{=} \frac{f(a) - f(a - h)}{h} \approx f'(a).$$

This has an expansion

$$D(h) = f'(a) - \frac{h}{2} f''(a) + \frac{h^2}{6} f'''(a) + \cdots ,$$

which for h twice as great is

$$D(2h) = f'(a) - 2 \frac{h}{2} f''(a) + 4 \frac{h^2}{6} f'''(a) + \cdots .$$

Combining the two expansions to eliminate the dominate h error term yields the approximation

$$2D(h) - D(2h) = f'(a) - 2 \frac{h^2}{6} f'''(a) + \cdots ,$$

whose order of accuracy is 2. Thus, we have determined a new formula,

$$D_1(h) \overset{\text{def}}{=} 2D(h) - D(2h)$$
$$= \frac{\frac{3}{2}f(a) - 2f(a-h) + \frac{1}{2}f(a-2h)}{h}.$$

Note that, as before, the derivation of these formulas requires only a knowledge of which powers of h are present.

Returning to the first example, there is another way to think about Richardson extrapolation. We use two values $D(H)$ and $D(2H)$ of $D(h)$ to construct the function of the form $\alpha + \beta h^2$ that interpolates $D(h)$ at $h = H$, $2H$. We then set $h = 0$ in the interpolant, thus extrapolating from positive values of h to the limiting value $\alpha \approx D(0) = f'(a)$. See Figure 7.5.

There is an important matter that we have not yet addressed. Because the truncation error gets smaller as $h \to 0$, it would seem logical to choose h as small as possible. In the case of some function $f(x)$ whose numerical values are available from some black-box procedure, h could be as small as 1 ulp, the spacing between successive machine numbers. Unfortunately, this will not be very accurate because there is another source of error that we have not yet mentioned. Before we do so, let us recall from Section 5.5.2 that, in principle, a black-box procedure is a tabulation (in which a table lookup might be rather costly) defined for an enormously long sequence of consecutive machine numbers. The entries of this or any other table will almost invariably contain data error, if only because of their finite precision. By statistical *smoothing* techniques it is often possible to recover to a great degree the true function underlying the data; for example, a least-squares approximation by a high-degree

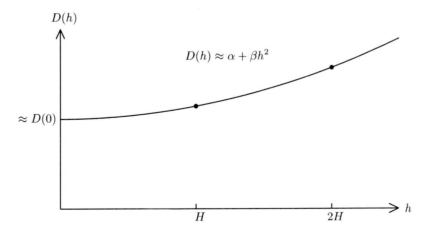

Figure 7.5: Richardson extrapolation

polynomial or trigonometric polynomial could be used for smoothing. Let $\bar{f}(x)$ denote our theoretically *best possible*[1] estimate of the true function. The difference $\delta(x) \overset{\text{def}}{=} f(x) - \bar{f}(x)$ we call *noise*. Thus, the *complete* computational problem is to smooth the data to determine $\bar{f}(x)$ and then evaluate $\bar{f}'(a)$. In practice it may be too costly to compute $\bar{f}(x)$, and smoothing may be neglected. The *complete* computational error in a centered-difference approximation that omits smoothing is

$$\frac{\delta(a+h) - \delta(a-h)}{2h} + \left(\frac{\bar{f}(a+h) - \bar{f}(a-h)}{2h} - \bar{f}'(a) \right).$$

The first term is the propagated noise, and the second is the usual truncation error. As $h \to 0$ the term due to noise gets larger and larger. Thus, if one neglects to do smoothing, one should not choose h too small. Noise also has an effect in interpolation and numerical integration but it is much less dramatic than in numerical differentiation.

Review questions

1. What mathematical tool is generally needed to obtain an expansion of the truncation error in powers of h?

2. Which derivative appears in the dominant term of an error expansion for a pth-order approximation to a first derivative? a second derivative? Does it change for a symmetric formula?

3. What is a one-sided difference approximation to a first derivative? a centered-difference approximation? a centered-difference approximation to a second derivative?

4. What is the order of accuracy of a one-sided difference approximation to a first derivative? a centered-difference approximation? a centered-difference approximation to a second derivative?

5. Do an expansion in powers of h for the error in one-sided difference approximation to a first derivative. A centered-difference approximation. A centered-difference approximation to a second derivative.

Exercises

1. Consider the formula

$$f''(a) \approx \frac{f(a+h) - 2f(a) + f(a-h)}{h^2}.$$

Determine the dominant term in an expansion of the error in powers of h.

---

[1] Deciding what this means is more in the domain of modeling than of computation.

2. For the approximation

$$f\left(a + \frac{h}{2}\right) \approx \frac{1}{2}(f(a) + f(a+h)) - \frac{h}{8}(f'(a+h) - f'(a)),$$

determine the dominant term in an expansion of the error in powers of h.

3. Given $f(0) = 0$, $f(1) = 1$, $f(2) = 5$, $f(3) = 13$, estimate $f''(0)$ by cubic polynomial interpolation.

4. Show that the simple centered-difference approximation to the first derivative can be obtained by interpolation at $a - h$, a, $a + h$. *Use this fact* to conclude that this approximation is exact for a function that is a quadratic polynomial.

5. Show how to estimate $f'(x_0), f'(x_1), \ldots, f'(x_N)$ from the values $f(x_0), f(x_1), \ldots, f(x_N)$ using quadratic interpolation in the best possible way for each point x_n. Assume that $x_n = a + n\,h, n = 0, 1, \ldots, N.$

6. (a) For

$$D(h) \stackrel{\text{def}}{=} \frac{f(a+h) - f(a)}{h},$$

   obtain the expansion

$$3D(h) - 2D(\tfrac{3}{2}h) = f'(a) - \frac{h^2}{4}f'''(a) + \cdots.$$

   (b) Given the data

x	1	1.2	1.3
$f(x)$	3.1	3.9	4.0

   calculate an approximation to $f'(1)$ using a formula of second-order accuracy. Use part (a).

7. Let

$$D(h) \stackrel{\text{def}}{=} \frac{f(a+h) - f(a-h)}{2h} \quad \text{and} \quad D_1(h) \stackrel{\text{def}}{=} \frac{4D(h) - D(2h)}{3}.$$

Give the details of a second extrapolation as suggested in this section. That is, derive a formula $D_2(h)$.

Mathematica notes

The *Mathematica* package `NumericalMath`NLimit`` defines, among other things, the function `ND[ ]` for doing numerical differentiation. `ND[ ]` has three options: `WorkingPrecision`, `Scale`, and `Terms`. `WorkingPrecision` is the precision of the arithmetic used to evaluate the derivative. `Scale` is the initial stepsize used in the decreasing sequence of steps. With `Scale -> h` the sequence is `h, h/2, h/4, ....` `Terms` is the total number of steps in the sequence to which Richardson extrapolation is applied. When higher-order derivatives are evaluated, additional terms are prepended to the sequence. Thus, with `Scale -> h` and `Terms -> 3`, the sequence for a second derivative is 2h, h, h/2, h/4.

Read in the package.

`In[1]:= << NumericalMath`NLimit``

A function whose derivative we seek. The `Print[ ]` in it is just so we can monitor where it gets evaluated.

`In[2]:= f[x_?NumberQ] := (Print[{x, Cos[x]}]; Cos[x])`

Find the derivative numerically at `x == 1` using five terms.

`In[3]:= ND[f[x], x, 1., Terms -> 5]`

```
{1., 0.540302}
{2., -0.416147}
{1.5, 0.0707372}
{1.25, 0.315322}
{1.125, 0.431177}
{1.0625, 0.48669}
```

`Out[3]= -0.841471`

The second derivative at the origin.

`In[4]:= ND[f[x], {x, 2}, 0., Scale -> 0.2]`

```
{0., 1.}
{0.4, 0.921061}
{0.2, 0.980067}
{0.1, 0.995004}
{0.05, 0.99875}
{0.025, 0.999688}
{0.0125, 0.999922}
{0.00625, 0.99998}
{0.003125, 0.999995}
```

`Out[4]= -1.`

Left derivatives are evaluated by making `Scale` negative.

`In[5]:= ND[f[x], {x, 2}, 0., Scale -> -0.2]`

```
{0., 1.}
{-0.4, 0.921061}
{-0.2, 0.980067}
{-0.1, 0.995004}
{-0.05, 0.99875}
{-0.025, 0.999688}
{-0.0125, 0.999922}
{-0.00625, 0.99998}
{-0.003125, 0.999995}
```

`Out[5]= -1.`

Computer problems

1. Use `ND[ ]` to find the derivatives of the following at the indicated points:

   (a) `Sin[x]` at $x = 1$.

   (b) `Log[x + 1/Pi]` at $x = 0$.

2. With the option `WorkingPrecision -> Infinity`, `ND[ ]` can be used to give symbolic results. Define a function `nd[expr_, n_]` to be `Expand[ND[expr, x, x0, Scale -> h, WorkingPrecision -> Infinity, Terms -> n-1]]` where `x`, `x0`, and `h` are global variables.

   (a) Consider `nd[f[x], n]` with $n = 2$, 3, 4, 5. What values of the function `f` are used in the formula using `n` values of `f`?

   (b) We can get an error expansion if we use `Normal[Series[f[x], {x, x0, 7}]]` in place of `f[x]` directly. What is the error in the formula using four values of `f`?

3. Redo Computer Problem 2 for second derivatives and third derivatives.

4. An alternative approach to numerical differentiation is simply to differentiate an interpolating polynomial.

   (a) Consider the interpolating polynomial in x for the points $(a, f(a))$, $(a-h, f(a-h))$, $(a-2h, f(a-2h))$, and $(a-3h, f(a-3h))$. Find the derivative of this polynomial with respect to x, replace x by a, and `Expand` the result. Do not display anything but the final result; the intermediate expressions get rather large and are uninteresting. (This is called a *backward differentiation formula*. Formulas of this sort are important for solving certain types of differential equations.)

   (b) Find the series expansion about $h = 0$ of the result of part (a). (Include enough terms in the series that you get more than the constant term.) The dominant term is $f'(a)$. What is the dominant term *in the error* if this expression is used as an approximation to $f'(a)$?

5. In this problem you will find several different centered-difference formulas and examine their respective errors as approximations to the derivative.

   (a) Consider the interpolating polynomial in x for the points $(a-h, f(a-h))$, $(a, f(a))$, and $(a + h, f(a + h))$. Find the derivative of this polynomial with respect to x, replace x by a, and `Expand` the result. Do not display anything but the final result; the intermediate expressions get rather large and are not important.

   (b) Find the series expansion about $h = 0$ of the result of part (a). (Include enough terms in the series that you get more than the constant term.) The dominant term is $f'(a)$. What is the dominant term *in the error* if this expression is used as an approximation to $f'(a)$?

   (c) Repeat parts (a) and (b) for the five-point formula using the points $(a - 2h, f(a - 2h))$, $(a - h, f(a - h))$, ... $(a + 2h, f(a + 2h))$ and the seven-point formula using the points $(a - 3h, f(a - 3h))$, $(a - 2h, f(a - 2h))$, ... $(a + 3h, f(a + 3h))$.

   (d) For each of the three difference formulas make a table of the approximations to $f'(3.)$ with $h = 0.1, 0.01, 0.001, \ldots, 10.^{-15}$ and $f(x) = \ln x$. Display the resulting lists showing all digits. (Use `SetPrecision[ ]` with `$MachinePrecision` digits.)

(e) Use `ListPlot[ ]` with `PlotJoined -> True` to plot the decimal places of accuracy for each of the lists. Use different plot styles (e.g., `PlotStyle -> Dashing[{0.01, 0.01}]`) to distinguish among them and combine them using `Show[ ]` with `AspectRatio -> Automatic`. Do the initial slopes agree with what you would expect from the form of the dominant term in the error? Why do the graphs all make sudden turns downward? (Answer with *Mathematica* comments.)

7.2 Simple Quadrature Rules

Assignment of a letter grade for a course involves *rounding* a value taken from a near-continuum to one of five possibilities. The rounding error ranges, say, from -0.5 grade point to $+0.5$ grade point with all possibilities assumed to be equally probable. (Of course, there is also a measurement error, but that is a different matter.) It is thus theoretically possible for the grade-point *average* (GPA) to be off by $+0.5$ or -0.5 due to accumulated rounding error. But how likely is this? Out of 6000 students who graduate, how many will have a GPA that is 0.1 grade point too low or worse because of roundoff error? Assuming 40 courses of equal weight, it can be shown that the probability of having a GPA accumulated rounding error in the range α to β is approximately

$$\sqrt{\frac{240}{\pi}} \int_\alpha^\beta \exp(-240x^2)\, dx.$$

This kind of integral cannot be exactly expressed in terms of elementary functions, but it occurs so often that there is a special function, called the error function, that can be used to obtain its value. Otherwise, we would have a problem of numerical integration, in particular, the numerical approximation of the value of a definite integral $\int_a^b f(x)\, dx$. We start the section with three well-known rules. It is worthwhile learning their coefficients and their order of accuracy. Then we discuss the process by which one can determine other rules and their orders of accuracy.

7.2.1 Composite quadrature rules

An integral is computed numerically by breaking it into small pieces. In particular, the area under the function curve is broken into narrow strips determined by some partition of the interval of integration $[a, b]$:

$$a = x_0 < x_1 < \cdots < x_N = b.$$

How to choose the partition is a difficult question. It affects the accuracy of the calculation. A method for automating the partitioning is given in Section 7.5, but it has its limitations. Once a partition has been determined, the idea is to write

$$\int_a^b f(x)\, dx = \int_{x_0}^{x_1} f(x)\, dx + \int_{x_1}^{x_2} f(x)\, dx + \cdots + \int_{x_{N-1}}^{x_N} f(x)\, dx$$

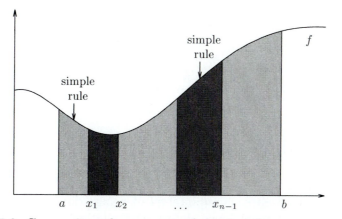

Figure 7.6: Composite rule as a sum of simple rules

and use some **simple rule** to approximate each of the integrals on the right. The repeated use of a simple rule in this way is often called a **composite rule**. See Figure 7.6.

7.2.2 Three simple rules

The **trapezoid rule**

$$\int_a^{a+h} f(x)\,dx \approx h\frac{f(a) + f(a + h)}{2} \stackrel{\text{def}}{=} T$$

approximates an integral by the area of the trapezoid defined by the values of the integrand at the endpoints $x = a$ and $x = a+h$. See Figure 7.7. The area is the width h of the trapezoid times its average height $\frac{1}{2}(f(a) + f(a + h))$. This formula is based on linear interpolation; it

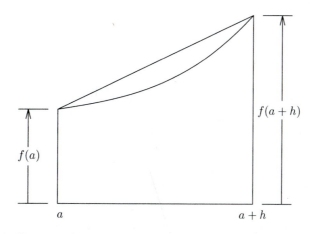

Figure 7.7: Trapezoid rule

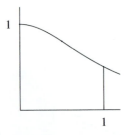

Figure 7.8: A quarter of π

is the exact integral for the linear polynomial that interpolates $f(x)$ at $x = a$ and $x = a + h$. If the trapezoid rule is used on each subinterval of a partition, the result is the *composite trapezoid rule*. This is based on piecewise linear interpolation at the points of the partition. Such an approximation gets better as the spacing between the points gets smaller.

Example 7.3 Consider the numerical approximation of

$$\int_0^1 \frac{dx}{1 + x^2} = \arctan 1 = \frac{\pi}{4} = 0.785398\cdots$$

shown in Figure 7.8. The use of the simple trapezoid rule with spacing 1 yields

$$T_1(1) = \tfrac{1}{2} \cdot 1 + \tfrac{1}{2} \cdot \tfrac{1}{2} = 0.75$$

and that of the 2-fold trapezoid rule with spacing $\frac{1}{2}$ yields

$$T_2(\tfrac{1}{2}) = \tfrac{1}{4} \cdot 1 + \tfrac{1}{2} \cdot \tfrac{4}{5} + \tfrac{1}{4} \cdot \tfrac{1}{2} = 0.775.$$

The **midpoint rule**

$$\int_a^{a+h} f(x)\, dx \approx h f\left(a + \frac{h}{2}\right) \overset{\text{def}}{=} M$$

approximates the integral by the area of a rectangle of height $f(a + h/2)$ and width h, as shown in Figure 7.9. It can be regarded as being the exact value of the integral of the constant polynomial that interpolates $f(x)$ at $x = a + h/2$. Of course, in practice, the midpoint rule would usually be applied repeatedly, as a composite rule.

It is natural to ask: Which of the two rules is more accurate? We will give a geometric argument showing that the midpoint rule is more accurate if $f''(x) > 0$ on the interval. A similar argument holds if $f''(x) < 0$. In a practical situation we would partition the intervals into subintervals small enough that one or the other of these two inequalities would hold for most subintervals. The argument proceeds by changing the way we picture each of

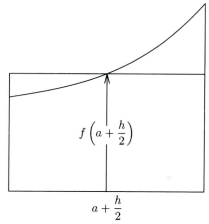

Figure 7.9: Midpoint rule

the two rules. The midpoint rule gives the area under any straight line that passes through $(a+h/2,\ f(a+h/2))$, in particular that line with slope $f'(a+h/2)$. This is shown in Figure 7.10 as the long slanted line that is tangent to the graph of $f(x)$ at the midpoint. (This line is the first-degree Taylor polynomial approximation of $f(x)$ about the midpoint.) Dark shading depicts the error in the midpoint rule. Note the piecewise linear function that lies just above the light shading. If both pieces have the same slope and if the jump is exactly at the midpoint, then the area under this curve is the same as that given by the trapezoid rule. Hence the area with light shading represents the error in the trapezoid rule. Because of the positive second derivative of $f(x)$, the trapezoid error is greater than the midpoint error. Less obvious is the ratio of the two errors. Taylor's formula $f(x) \approx f(a) + (x-a)f'(a) + \frac{1}{2}(x-a)^2 f''(a)$

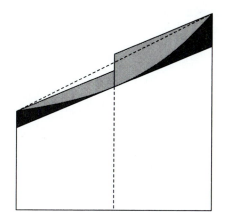

Figure 7.10: Trapezoid error (light shading) and midpoint error (dark shading)

suggests that $f(x)$ is approximately a parabola. From calculus we know that the area under a parabola is one-third the area of the rectangle that contains it. This would remain true if we were to apply a vertical shear to both the parabola and its containing box so as to transform this box into a parallelogram with two vertical sides. On this basis we suggest that the area in Figure 7.10 with dark shading is approximately half of that with light shading. In other words,

$$M \text{ error} \approx -\tfrac{1}{2} \cdot T \text{ error}.$$

Assuming the accuracy of the equation above, we can combine the trapezoid and midpoint rules so that their errors approximately cancel. If we write

$$T = \int_a^b f(x)\, dx + \text{error},$$

we have by observation

$$M \approx \int_a^b f(x)\, dx - \tfrac{1}{2} \cdot \text{error}.$$

To cancel the errors, we take one part trapezoid and two parts midpoint, obtaining

$$\tfrac{1}{3}T_f + \tfrac{2}{3}M_f \approx \int_a^b f(x)\, dx.$$

We rewrite the left-hand side in terms of values of $f(x)$, and we obtain the justly popular **Simpson rule**

$$S \overset{\text{def}}{=} h\left(\frac{1}{6}f(a) + \frac{2}{3}f\left(a + \frac{h}{2}\right) + \frac{1}{6}f(a + h)\right),$$

also known as *Simpson's one-third rule* to distinguish it from Simpson's three-eighths rule. The formula expresses an area as a width h times a weighted average of values of $f(x)$ from left, center, and right with a full *two-thirds* of the weight on the center value. Remember the weights

$$\frac{1}{6}, \quad \frac{2}{3}, \quad \frac{1}{6},$$

and you remember the Simpson rule.

7.2.3 Error term

An approximation is of no value without *some* estimate of its error. Often error estimates require advanced mathematics, but not in this case.

By definition the

$$\text{trapezoid error} = \frac{h}{2}(f(a) + f(a + h)) - \int_a^{a+h} f(x)\, dx.$$

Here h is a small parameter that is to be chosen with accuracy in mind, assuming the use of this approximation as part of a composite rule. We use a Taylor expansion about $x = a$ to get

$$f(a + h) = f(a) + hf'(a) + \frac{h^2}{2}f''(a) + \cdots.$$

A similar expansion is possible for the $f(x)$ occurring in the integral:

$$\int_a^{a+h} f(x)\,dx = \int_a^{a+h} \left(f(a) + (x - a)f'(a) + \frac{(x - a)^2}{2}f''(a) + \cdots \right) dx$$

$$= \left[(x - a)f(a) + \frac{(x - a)^2}{2}f'(a) + \frac{(x - a)^3}{6}f''(a) + \cdots \right]_a^{a+h}$$

$$= hf(a) + \frac{h^2}{2}f'(a) + \frac{h^3}{6}f''(a) + \cdots.$$

Therefore, after substitution the

$$\text{error} = \frac{h^3}{12}f''(a) + \frac{h^4}{24}f'''(a) + \frac{h^5}{80}f^{iv}(a) + \frac{h^6}{360}f^{v}(a) + \frac{h^7}{2016}f^{vi}(a) + \cdots.$$

In the trapezoid rule there exists a kind of symmetry about $x = a + h/2 \overset{\text{def}}{=} c$. We could regard the interval to be fixed at its center c with a variable width h. In terms of c and h the

$$\text{error}_T = \frac{h}{2}\left(f\left(c - \frac{h}{2}\right) + f\left(c + \frac{h}{2}\right) \right) - \int_{c-h/2}^{c+h/2} f(x)\,dx.$$

Expanding about $x = c$, we get

$$\text{error}_T = \frac{h^3}{12}f''(c) + \frac{h^5}{480}f^{iv}(c) + \frac{h^7}{53760}f^{vi}(c) + \cdots. \tag{7.3}$$

The advantage of this is that even powers of h are not present.

An expansion about the midpoint is just as natural for the midpoint rule. We get

$$\text{error}_M = hf(c) - \int_{c-h/2}^{c+h/2} f(x)\,dx$$

$$= -\frac{h^3}{24}f''(c) - \frac{h^5}{1920}f^{iv}(c) - \frac{h^7}{322560}f^{vi}(c) + \cdots. \tag{7.4}$$

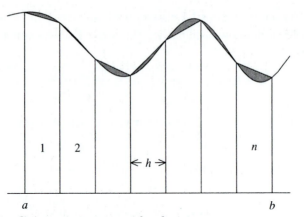

Figure 7.11: Composite trapezoid rule error

Because the Simpson rule is a weighted average of the trapezoid and midpoint rules, so is its error:

$$S \;=\; \tfrac{1}{3}T \;+\; \tfrac{2}{3}M,$$

$$\int_a^b f(x)\,dx \;=\; \tfrac{1}{3}\int_a^b f(x)\,dx \;+\; \tfrac{2}{3}\int_a^b f(x)\,dx,$$

$$\Rightarrow \qquad \text{error}_S \;=\; \tfrac{1}{3}\cdot \text{error}_T \;+\; \tfrac{2}{3}\cdot \text{error}_M.$$

Consequently, from (7.3) and (7.4),

$$\text{error}_S = \frac{h^5}{2880}f^{\text{iv}}(c) + \frac{h^7}{241920}f^{\text{vi}}(c) + \cdots . \tag{7.5}$$

The order of accuracy is the first and foremost measure of a method's power to approximate. For quadrature, some care is needed in determining the order. If we look at a simple rule, then as $h \to 0$ so does $\int_a^{a+h} f(x)\,dx$. Hence, an approximation of zero would in the limit give the correct result! The correct approach is to consider a situation in which the true value that we are approximating is independent of the parameter h. For quadrature we should instead consider the error in

$$\int_a^b f(x)\,dx \approx \text{composite rule with uniform spacing } h = \frac{b-a}{N}.$$

Let us consider, as an example, the error in the composite trapezoid rule, pictured in Figure 7.11. The error in the composite rule is a sum of the errors from each interval. The error in the kth subinterval is $(h^3/12)f''(c_k) + O(h^5)$ where c_k is the midpoint of the kth subinterval. Because $hf''(c_k)$ is the midpoint-rule approximation to the integral of $f''(x)$ on the interval

$[x_{k-1}, x_k]$, we can write

$$\text{error from } k\text{th subinterval} = \frac{h^3}{12} f''(c_k) + O(h^5)$$

$$= \frac{h^2}{12} \left(\int_{x_{k-1}}^{x_k} f''(x)\, dx + O(h^3) \right) + O(h^5)$$

$$= \frac{h^2}{12} \int_{x_{k-1}}^{x_k} f''(x)\, dx + O(h^5).$$

Summing up the errors and using the fact that $N = (b-a)/h$, we have that

$$\underbrace{O(h^5) + O(h^5) + \cdots + O(h^5)}_{N \text{ times}} = O(h^4)$$

and consequently that

$$\text{error} = \frac{h^2}{12} \int_a^b f''(x)\, dx + O(h^4).$$

This means that the trapezoid rule is second-order accurate provided that the coefficient of h^2 is nonzero, which will be true if $\int_a^b f''(x)\, dx = f'(b) - f'(a)$ is nonzero. Similarly it can be shown that

$$\text{composite midpoint rule error} = -\frac{h^2}{24} \int_a^b f''(x)\, dx + O(h^4),$$

$$\text{composite Simpson rule error} = \frac{h^4}{2880} \int_a^b f^{\text{iv}}(x)\, dx + O(h^6).$$

7.2.4 Systematic derivation

The following is a schematic representation of the rules we have studied in detail:

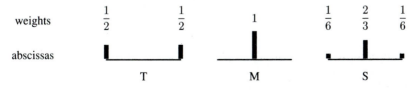

The trapezoid and Simpson rules are the first two of the **closed Newton-Cotes** formulas. These have equally spaced abscissas that include the endpoints. The midpoint rule is the first of the **open Newton-Cotes** formulas. These have equally spaced abscissas that exclude the endpoints. Formulas can usually be characterized by the location of their abscissas. If these are given, one can systematically determine the weights so as to maximize the order. We will illustrate three, closely related, derivation techniques using as an example the rule

$$\int_a^{a+h} f(x)\,dx \approx h(w_1 f(a-h) + w_2 f(a) + w_3 f(a+h)).$$

This is not a Newton-Cotes formula. (It occurs in the "integration" of differential equations.) The three derivation techniques are polynomial integration, undetermined coefficients in the analysis of the error term, and a simplified way of using undetermined coefficients.

polynomial interpolation

The idea is that we approximate the integrand by the polynomial that interpolates it at the chosen nodes:

$$
\begin{aligned}
\int_a^{a+h} f(x)\,dx &\approx \int_a^{a+h} (l_0(x)f(a-h) + l_1(x)f(a) + l_2(x)f(a+h))\,dx \\
&= \int_a^{a+h} l_0(x)\,dx \cdot f(a-h) + \int_a^{a+h} l_1(x)\,dx \cdot f(a) + \int_a^{a+h} l_2(x)\,dx \cdot f(a+h) \\
&= \cdots = \frac{-h}{12} \cdot f(a-h) + \frac{2h}{3} \cdot f(a) + \frac{5h}{12} \cdot f(a+h).
\end{aligned}
$$

Hence, the weights are merely the exact integrals of the Lagrange fundamental polynomials.

undetermined coefficients—error expansion

We begin by forming an expression for the (truncation) error with the weights left undetermined and doing an expansion of the error in powers of h:

$$
\begin{aligned}
\text{error} &= h(w_1 f(a-h) + w_2 f(a) + w_3 f(a+h)) - \int_a^{a+h} f(x)\,dx \\
&= \cdots \\
&= h(w_1 + w_2 + w_3 - 1)f(a) + h^2\left(-w_1 + w_3 - \tfrac{1}{2}\right)f'(a) \\
&\quad + h^3\left(\frac{w_1}{2} + \frac{w_3}{2} - \frac{1}{6}\right)f''(a) + h^4\left(-\frac{w_1}{6} + \frac{w_3}{6} - \frac{1}{24}\right)f'''(a) + \cdots. \quad (7.6)
\end{aligned}
$$

Each of the above terms depends on the function $f(x)$ in a different way and is independent of the others. The idea is to make the error as small as possible by making as many as possible of these terms equal to zero. We start first with the largest terms, namely, those having the lowest powers of h, and require their coefficients to vanish. Since there are three unknown weights, we set up three equations

$$
\begin{aligned}
w_1 + w_2 + w_3 &= 1, \\
-w_1 + w_3 &= \tfrac{1}{2}, \\
\tfrac{1}{2}w_1 + \tfrac{1}{2}w_3 &= \tfrac{1}{6}.
\end{aligned}
\tag{7.7}
$$

(There are many more equations that could be set up to get higher order terms to vanish; but unless the lower order terms vanish first, it does little good to get the higher order terms to vanish.) These can be solved to get

$$
w_1 = -\tfrac{1}{12}, \qquad w_2 = \tfrac{2}{3}, \qquad w_3 = \tfrac{5}{12}.
$$

Then we have the error $= (h^4/24)f'''(a) + \cdots$.

undetermined coefficients—easy way

Let us examine the error given by (7.6) with undetermined weights w_1, w_2, w_3 for special choices of $f(x)$, namely $f(x) \equiv 1$, $f(x) = x - a$, $f(x) = (x-a)^2$, ... These are special because each $f^{(k)}(a)$ vanishes for all but one value of k, greatly simplifying the error expansion (7.7). In particular,

$$
\begin{aligned}
f(x) &\equiv 1 &\Rightarrow&\quad \text{error} = h(w_1 + w_2 + w_3 - 1), \\
f(x) &= x - a &\Rightarrow&\quad \text{error} = h^2(-w_1 + w_3 - \tfrac{1}{2}), \\
f(x) &= (x-a)^2 &\Rightarrow&\quad \text{error} = 2h^3\left(\frac{w_1}{2} + \frac{w_3}{2} - \frac{1}{6}\right).
\end{aligned}
$$

Note that the first equation of the set of three equations (7.7) is equivalent to requiring that the error vanish when $f(x) \equiv 1$. Also, the second equation is equivalent to requiring that the error $= 0$ for $f(x) = x - a$, and the third equation is equivalent to requiring the error $= 0$ for $f(x) = (x-a)^2$. Hence, we can obtain the equations for the weights by making

$$
\int_a^{a+h} f(x)\, dx \approx h(w_1 f(a-h) + w_2 f(a) + w_3 f(a+h))
$$

hold exactly for $f(x) = 1, x - a, (x-a)^2$.

From the four rules we have studied, you may have observed that the weights used to form the weighted average do not depend on a or h, but only on the location of the abscissas relative to the interval $[a, a+h]$. For simplicity we may choose $a = 0$ and $h = 1$ and restate the determining conditions as follows: Make

$$
\int_0^1 f(x)\, dx \approx w_1 f(-1) + w_2 f(0) + w_3 f(1)
$$

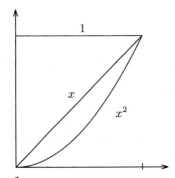

Figure 7.12: Powers of x

hold exactly for $f(x) = 1$, x, x^2. We would like it to work for higher powers of x also, but we have only three coefficients to choose. These functions are sketched in Figure 7.12. For $f(x) \equiv 1$ we have

$$\int_0^1 f(x)dx = 1, \quad f(-1) = 1, \quad f(0) = 1, \quad \text{and} \quad f(1) = 1,$$

and the formula above is exact only if

$$1 = w_1 \cdot 1 + w_2 \cdot 1 + w_3 \cdot 1.$$

For $f(x) = x$ we have

$$\int_0^1 f(x)dx = \tfrac{1}{2}, \quad f(-1) = -1, \quad f(0) = 0, \quad \text{and} \quad f(1) = 1,$$

and the formula is exact only if

$$\tfrac{1}{2} = w_1 \cdot (-1) + w_2 \cdot 0 + w_3 \cdot 1.$$

Similarly, requiring the formula to be exact for $f(x) = x^2$ yields the equation

$$\tfrac{1}{3} = w_1 \cdot 1 + w_2 \cdot 0 + w_3 \cdot 1.$$

These three equations for w_1, w_2, w_3 are equivalent to those obtained previously by error expansion.

It is natural to ask how the method of undetermined coefficients for quadrature rules relates to the method of undetermined coefficients for interpolating polynomials. In the case of quadrature rules we determine a *formula*[2] by making it exact when applied to particular

---

[2]Mathematicians use the term *functional*, which is a mapping from a function to a number.

functions. In the case of interpolation we determine a *function* by making it exact when evaluated at particular *numerical values*.

Choosing to make a quadrature formula exact for the particular functions $f(x) = 1, x, x^2$ may seem very special. However, it can be shown (Exercise 13) that, in fact, the formula is exact for any linear combination of these three functions. In other words, it is exact for all quadratic polynomials and those of lower degree.

As another example of the method of undetermined coefficients, we derive **Simpson's three-eighths rule**. This is the four-point closed Newton-Cotes formula, so we want to make

$$\int_{-1}^{1} f(x)\, dx \approx 2(w_1 f(-1) + w_2 f(-\tfrac{1}{3}) + w_3 f(\tfrac{1}{3}) + w_4 f(1))$$

hold exactly for $f(x) = 1,\ x,\ x^2,\ x^3$. The interval was chosen to be $[-1,\ 1]$ in the hope that this would simplify the algebra. The factor 2 on the right-hand side is the width of the interval. The number of unknowns can be reduced by symmetry arguments. In particular, there is the symmetry of abscissas with respect to the interval of integration. Also, this formula is determined so that it is exact for all cubic polynomials, and there is symmetry in the *set* of cubic polynomials. By this we do not mean that a particular cubic has symmetry. Rather we mean that the mirror image of a cubic is also a cubic. That is what we mean when we say that the set of cubics is symmetric. What this suggests is that the weights should not be biased to either the left or right but should be symmetric:

$$w_3 = w_2, \quad w_4 = w_1.$$

With this in mind we set up the equations arising from the conditions stated at the beginning:

$$
\begin{aligned}
1: \quad & 2(w_1 + w_2 + w_2 + w_1) && = 2, \\
x: \quad & 2\left(-w_1 - \frac{w_2}{3} + \frac{w_2}{3} + w_1\right) && = 0, \\
x^2: \quad & 2\left(w_1 + \frac{w_2}{9} + \frac{w_2}{9} + w_1\right) && = \tfrac{2}{3}.
\end{aligned}
$$

The equation for x is automatically satisfied, as is the equation for x^3. The solution is $w_1 = \tfrac{1}{8}$, $w_2 = \tfrac{3}{8}$, hence the name of the method.

7.2.5 Accuracy and exactness

For the kinds of methods we are considering, if the order of accuracy is p, then the

$$\text{composite formula} = \int_a^b f(x)\, dx \; + \; \text{constant} \cdot h^p \cdot \int_a^b f^{(p)}(x)\, dx + \cdots.$$

Therefore, assuming that further terms in the expansion involve yet higher derivatives of $f(x)$, such a formula must be exact for polynomials of degree $\leq p - 1$.

The formulas we have covered can be summarized as in the following table.

Formula	Number of abscissas	Order	Exact for polynomials of degree
midpoint	1	2	1
trapezoid	2		
$-\frac{1}{12}, \frac{2}{3}, \frac{5}{12}$	3	3	2
Simpson	3	4	3
Simpson $\frac{3}{8}$	4		

This table illustrates two general principles. One is that for formulas based on polynomial interpolation the order is greater than or equal to the number of abscissas. The other is that symmetric formulas are of even order, regardless of the number of abscissas.

One can derive Newton-Cotes formulas of higher order. It turns out that the high-order formulas have some negative weights, and this can result in greater than necessary error for nonsmooth integrands. Also, for high order there is a problem with amplification of integrand noise due to large positive and negative weights.

Both the midpoint and Simpson formulas are of one order higher than expected on the basis of the number of nodes. For an explanation look at Figure 7.13. It is clear that the integral of a linear polynomial is the same as that of the constant polynomial that interpolates it at the midpoint of the interval, which explains why the midpoint rule is exact for linear polynomials. The quadratic polynomial that interpolates a cubic at the points $x = -1$, 0, 1 differs from the cubic by some constant multiple of the polynomial $(x + 1)x(x - 1)$, whose integral for $-1 \leq x \leq 1$ vanishes. Hence, because of the special choice of nodes the quadratic has the same integral as the cubic. This idea of a special choice of nodes is pursued further in the next section.

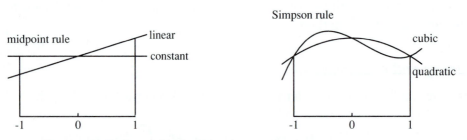

Figure 7.13: Formulas having extra accuracy

Review questions

1. Which derivative appears in the dominant term of an error expansion for a pth-order approximation to an integral?

2. What is (a) the trapezoid rule? (b) the midpoint rule? (c) the Simpson rule?

3. What is the order of accuracy of (a) the trapezoid rule? (b) the midpoint rule? (c) the Simpson rule?

4. Do an expansion in powers of h for the error in (a) the simple trapezoid rule, (b) the simple midpoint rule, (c) the simple Simpson rule.

5. What is the relationship between the dominant term in an expansion of a simple rule and that for the corresponding composite rule?

Exercises

1. What is the numerical value of the 2-fold Simpson rule[3] approximation for

$$\int_1^{2.6} \frac{dx}{x}?$$

Your answer should be wholly numeric but need not be simplified.

2. Consider the sum $H_n \stackrel{\text{def}}{=} \sum_{k=1}^{n} \frac{1}{k}$.

   (a) This is the composite-midpoint-rule approximation of some *simple* integral. What is that integral?

   (b) Use part (a) to approximate H_n. Simplify your answer.

3. Consider the quadrature rule

$$\int_a^{a+h} f(x)\, dx \approx h(-\tfrac{1}{12}f(a-h) + \tfrac{2}{3}f(a) + \tfrac{5}{12}f(a+h)).$$

   (a) What is the corresponding composite rule for the integral $\int_a^b f(x)\, dx$ with uniformly spaced nodes $a+jh$ for appropriate integer values j where $h = (b-a)/N$? Simplify your answer so that it is expressed as a linear combination of values of $f(x)$.

   (b) Rewrite your answer to (a) as the composite trapezoid rule T_N plus simple correction terms.

---

[3] The composite rule with the Simpson rule applied to each of two equal subintervals.

4. Show that the simple (one-third) Simpson rule is exact for $\int_{-a}^{a} f(x)\,dx$ if $f(x)$ is an odd function (this means that $f(-x) = -f(x)$).

5. Provide the missing details for showing that Equation (7.4) holds.

6. Provide the missing details for showing that Equation (7.5) holds.

7. Consider the approximation

$$\int_{a}^{a+h} f(x)dx \approx h(\tfrac{1}{4}f(a) + \tfrac{3}{4}f(a + \tfrac{2}{3}h)).$$

Expand the error in powers of h, obtaining the first nonzero term.

8. Consider the approximation

$$\int_{a}^{a+h} f(x)\,dx \approx h(\tfrac{3}{2}f(a) - \tfrac{1}{2}f(a - h)).$$

Expand the error in powers of h, obtaining the first nonzero term.

9. Provide the missing details for showing that Equation (7.6) holds.

10. What is the Simpson three-eighths rule for the interval $[c - h/2,\ c + h/2]$? Do an asymptotic expansion of the truncation error up to $O(h^7)$.

11. Derive a quadrature rule of the form

$$\int_{0}^{\infty} e^{-x} f(x)\,dx \approx w_0 f(0) + w_1 f(2),$$

approximating $f(x)$ by the lowest degree interpolating polynomial.

12.   (a) Derive a quadrature formula of the form

$$\int_{-h}^{h} f(x)\,dx \approx h(\alpha f(-\tfrac{2}{3}h) + \beta f(0) + \gamma\, f(\tfrac{2}{3}h))$$

that attains the maximum order of accuracy possible.

  (b) Expand the error in powers of h, obtaining the first nonzero term.

13. Consider a quadrature formula

$$\int_{-1}^{1} f(x)dx \approx \sum_{k=1}^{n} w_k f(x_k)$$

where the abscissas x_k and weights w_k have given numerical values. Show that if the formula is exact for $f(x) = 1, x, x^2$, it is also exact for any quadratic polynomial $q(x) = ax^2 + bx + c$.

14. By a change of variables express the integral $\int_a^b f(x)\,dx$ as $\int_{-1}^1 g(t)\,dt$. What is $g(t)$?

15. Suppose in an approximation to an integral by some composite rule we halve the spacing h of the partition.

  (a) How would this reduction in h be expected to affect the error if the rule is first-order accurate?

  (b) What if the rule were second-order accurate?

  (c) What if the rule were pth-order accurate?

  (d) If the error drops from 0.034518 to 0.013243, what is the apparent order of accuracy? Do not assume that the order is an integer or a nice rational number.

Computer problems

1. Mathematicians often write $\int_a^b f(x)\,dx$ as $\int_a^b f$. This is proper because a function $f = f(\circ)$ exists independently of whatever label we use for the independent variable, and it may be convenient to avoid naming the dummy variable. This style is also used in programming languages like Fortran. Define a *Mathematica* function `integrate[f_, a_, b_]` that uses the built-in routine `Integrate` to determine $\int_a^b f$ analytically where $f = f(\circ)$ is a function of one variable. Any additional variables that you use must be made local. Test it with `integrate[Sin, 0, Pi]`.

2. Define a function `trap[f_, a_, b_, n_]` that returns the approximation to $\int_a^b f(x)\,dx$ given by the composite trapezoid rule with n equally spaced subintervals. For $n = 1, 2, 4, 8, 16, 32, 64$ apply this to $\int_0^{2\pi} \exp(\sin x)\,dx$ using 96 digits of precision. Taking the $n = 64$ approximation as the correct value, calculate the errors for the other values of n, use `N[ ]` to reduce them to machine numbers, and print them. From these construct a table of $\log_2 n$ versus $-\log_2(|\text{error}|)$. Use a *Mathematica* comment to answer the following question: If the order of accuracy were p, what kind of behavior would you expect to see in the second row/column of the table? (This type of convergence is called *exponential convergence* and can be expected from the trapezoid rule if the integrand is periodic with infinitely many continuous derivatives and the interval of integration is an integer multiple of the period.)

3. In this exercise we use *Mathematica* to derive Simpson's rule. Begin by obtaining a symbolic polynomial interpolant in `x` for the points `{a, f[a]}`, `{b, f[b]}`, and `{c, f[c]}` using `InterpolatingPolynomial` or an interpolation routine you developed. Then substitute `(a+b)/2` for `c`, `Simplify`, `Integrate` from `a` to `b`, and `Simplify` again.

4. This problem is a particularly interesting use of *Mathematica*. We automate the method of undetermined coefficients.

(a) An approximation formula such as the midpoint rule for quadrature,

$$\int_0^1 f(x)\,dx \approx f(\tfrac{1}{2}),$$

might be represented in *Mathematica* by

`midpt[f_] := Module[{x},Integrate[f[x],{x, 0, 1}] ] == f[1/2]`

In a similar manner create the formula

$$\int_0^1 f(x)\,dx \approx af(0) + bf(1)$$

and name it `trap`. "Evaluate" `trap` for the function $f(x) \equiv 1$. (In *Mathematica* this can be done most conveniently by substituting the "pure function" `1&` for `f_`.) Do this again for the function $f(x) = x$ (which can be written as `#&` in *Mathematica*.) You have in this way created two equations that could be solved for the undetermined coefficients a and b. See what happens if you do this yet again for the function $f(x) = x^k$ (which can be written as `#^k&` in *Mathematica*).

(b) Write a function `muc[formula_, n_]` that when given a formula defined for general functions `f_` will return a `List` of equations for the first `n` powers of x beginning with x^0. (Note that we define $x^0 \equiv 1$.) Then create the formula

$$f'(0) \approx c_0 f(0) + c_1 f(-1) + c_2 f(-2),$$

call it `bdf`, and use `muc` to set up a system of three equations. (Programming tip: There is no need to use a list or indexed variables for the three coefficients.) Apply the *Mathematica* function `Solve` to this system. Then pick out the first (and only) solution using `[[1]]` and apply this rule to `bdf[f]` where `f` is a symbol having no value. (Use `/.` to do the substitution.)

5. (a) Define a function `simp[f_, a_, b_, n_]` that returns the approximation to $\int_a^b f(x)\,dx$ given by the composite Simpson rule with n equally spaced subintervals. Test your routine on $\int_0^1 x^3\,dx$ for $n = 3$ by printing the result. (What should you get? Answer to yourself.)

(b) For *each* of the integrals

    (i) $\int_0^1 \max\{0,\ x - \tfrac{1}{5}\}\,dx$,   (ii) $\int_0^1 x^{3/4}\,dx$,

    (iii) $\int_0^1 x^{5/3}\,dx$,   (iv) $\int_0^1 x^{7/2}\,dx$,

do the following: Obtain, but do not print, the n-fold Simpson rule approximations for $n = 1, 2, 4, 8, 16, 32, 64$. Somehow obtain the correct value and use it to calculate and print the digits of accuracy for all seven approximate values. Construct a list of corresponding values of $\log_{10} n$ and do a linear fit of digits of accuracy versus $\log_{10} n$ as indicated below:

```
data = Transpose[{logn,digits}];
Print[ line = Fit[data, {1, x}, x] ];
plot = Plot[line, {x, 0., 2.}, DisplayFunction -> Identity];
listplot = ListPlot[ data, DisplayFunction -> Identity,
                            PlotStyle -> PointSize[0.02]];
Show[plot, listplot, DisplayFunction -> $DisplayFunction]
```

For each problem use a *Mathematica* comment to answer the following question: What is the likely order of accuracy of the approximation (in the limit as $n \to \infty$, assuming no roundoff error)? (If you have any doubts, you can redo the fit, leaving out the data for small values of n and/or including data for larger values of n.)

7.3   Gaussian Quadrature Rules

It has been suggested that the nodes can be specially chosen to get a higher order of accuracy. In fact, with n weights and n abscissas at our disposal we can make the formula exact for $f(x) = 1, x, \ldots, x^{2n-1}$ and, indeed, any polynomial of degree $\leq 2n - 1$. To illustrate the idea, we derive the three-point Gauss formula

$$\int_{-1}^{1} f(x)\, dx \approx w_1 f(x_1) + w_2 f(x_2) + w_3 f(x_3),$$

where the parameters w_1, w_2, w_3 and x_1, x_2, x_3 are to be determined. We should set up equations for these parameters by requiring that the formula be exact for $f(x) = 1$, x, x^2, x^3, x^4, x^5 and hence for all quintic polynomials. This would result in a rather formidable set of *nonlinear* equations involving powers of the abscissas. Fortunately we can simplify the equations. We expect that the formula will have symmetry—there is no reason why the left side of the interval should be treated differently from the right. As before, this is true because the *set* of quintic polynomials is symmetric. Hence, we expect that the abscissas will be positioned symmetrically about the origin as shown in Figure 7.14. Algebraically this is expressed

$$x_2 = 0, \qquad x_1 = -x_3.$$

Symmetry for the weights means
$$w_1 = w_3.$$

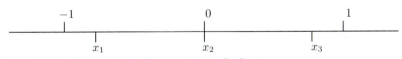

Figure 7.14: Symmetrically positioned abscissas

The ultimate justification for these simplifying assumptions is that they succeed. These three conditions reduce the number of unknown parameters to three:

$$\int_{-1}^{1} f(x)\, dx \approx w_3 f(-x_3) + w_2\ f(0) + w_3\ f(x_3).$$

If we check this formula for the first six powers of x, we discover that both the left- and right-hand sides of the approximate equality are zero for $f(x) = x,\ x^3,\ x^5$. In fact, the choice of symmetric parameters make the formula exact for all odd powers of x, all linear combinations of odd powers of x, and all functions, such as $\sin x$, having power series involving only odd powers of x. Thus, only three conditions remain to determine the three parameters w_2, w_3, and x_3:

$$
1:\quad \int_{-1}^{1} 1\, dx \quad =\quad w_3 \cdot 1 \quad\quad +\quad w_2 \cdot 1 \quad +\quad w_3 \cdot 1,
$$

$$
x^2:\quad \int_{-1}^{1} x^2\, dx \quad =\quad w_3(-x_3)^2 \quad +\quad w_2 \cdot 0^2 \quad +\quad w_3 x_3^2,
$$

$$
x^4:\quad \int_{-1}^{1} x^4\, dx \quad =\quad w_3(-x_3)^4 \quad +\quad w_2 \cdot 0^4 \quad +\quad w_3 x_3^4,
$$

which simplify to

$$
\begin{aligned}
w_3 \quad + \quad w_2 \quad + \quad w_3 \quad &= \quad 2, \\
w_3 x_3^2 \quad\quad\quad + \quad w_3 x_3^2 \quad &= \quad \tfrac{2}{3}, \\
w_3 x_3^4 \quad\quad\quad + \quad w_3 x_3^4 \quad &= \quad \tfrac{2}{5}.
\end{aligned}
$$

These further simplify to

$$
w_2 = 2 - 2w_3, \quad w_3 x_3^2 = \tfrac{1}{3}, \quad w_3 x_3^4 = \tfrac{1}{5},
$$

whose unknowns can be solved for in the order

$$
x_3^2 = \tfrac{3}{5}, \quad w_3 = \tfrac{5}{9}, \quad w_2 = \tfrac{8}{9}.
$$

With the coefficients thus determined, the three-point Gauss formula is

$$
\int_{-1}^{1} f(x)\, dx \approx \tfrac{5}{9} f\left(-\sqrt{\tfrac{3}{5}}\right) + \tfrac{8}{9} f(0) + \tfrac{5}{9} f\left(\sqrt{\tfrac{3}{5}}\right).
$$

The formula is exact for all polynomials of degree ≤ 5 and has order of accuracy 6.

Example 7.4 We can apply the three-point Gauss formula to $\int_{0}^{1}(1+x^2)^{-1} dx$ if we extend the formula to an arbitrary interval of integration. This is the subject of Exercise 5. Alternatively we can transform the integral and then apply the formula:

$$\int_0^1 \frac{dx}{1+x^2} = \int_0^2 \frac{(1/2)dx}{1+(x/2)^2} = \int_{-1}^1 \frac{2\,dx}{4+(x+1)^2}$$

$$\approx \frac{5}{9} \cdot \frac{2}{4+(-\sqrt{3/5}+1)^2} + \frac{8}{9} \cdot \frac{2}{4+(0+1)^2} + \frac{5}{9} \cdot \frac{2}{4+(\sqrt{3/5}+1)^2}$$

$$= \frac{2132}{2715} = 0.78539\cdots.$$

The error is merely $-0.00013\cdots$. In practice, $\pm\sqrt{3/5}$ would be replaced by floating-point approximations.

There are tables and computer programs that give the parameters of higher order Gauss formulas. Gauss formulas are also known as **Gauss-Legendre formulas**. The n-point formula has order of accuracy $2n$. These are the formulas of choice if one wants to use a quadrature formula with predetermined abscissas, such as happens in the solution of differential and integral equations. For other situations one can use composite rules with automatic partitioning, as discussed in the sections that follow.

Exercises

1. Determine numbers $x_1 < x_2 < x_3$ such that the quadrature rule

$$\int_{-1}^1 f(x)\,dx \approx \tfrac{2}{3}f(x_1) + \tfrac{2}{3}f(x_2) + \tfrac{2}{3}f(x_3)$$

   is exact for polynomials of degree as high as possible. Exploit symmetry.

2. Show how to determine x_2, w_1, and w_2 to maximize the order of accuracy of the formula

$$\int_{-1}^1 f(x)\,dx \approx w_1 f(-1) + w_2 f(x_2).$$

   (Warning: Note the lack of symmetry.)

3. Suppose we wish to determine constants x_3, w_3, w_4 so that the quadrature rule

$$\int_{-1}^1 f(x)\,dx \approx w_4\,f(-1) + w_3\,f(-x_3) + w_3\,f(x_3) + w_4\,f(1)$$

   has the highest possible order of accuracy. Determine three equations that could be solved to get x_3, w_3, w_4. (You need not solve the equations.)

4. Determine an expression of the form $Ch^{p+1}f^{(p)}(c)+O(h^{p+2})$ for the error of the quadrature rule

$$\frac{h}{2}f\left(c-\frac{h}{2\sqrt{3}}\right)+\frac{h}{2}f\left(c+\frac{h}{2\sqrt{3}}\right)\approx\int_{c-h/2}^{c+h/2}f(x)\,dx;$$

   i.e., determine p and C.

5. Apply the three-point Gauss rule *appropriately* to the problem of approximating

$$\int_{1}^{2}\ln(x)\,dx.$$

   (You need not evaluate the answer.)

6. Consider the approximation

$$\int_{-1}^{1}f(t)\,dt\approx f(-\sqrt{1/3})+f(\sqrt{1/3}).$$

   Generalize this formula to approximate

$$\int_{a}^{b}g(x)\,dx.$$

   The generalized formula should be expressed in terms of a,b, and g.

7. A function $f(x)$ is said to be *odd* if $f(-x)\equiv-f(x)$. Show that the three-point Gauss formula is exact for any odd (integrable) function.

8. Consider a numerical quadrature rule of the form

$$\int_{0}^{1}xf(x)dx\approx wf(a)$$

   where w and a are constants to be determined. Determine w and a so that the formula is exact when $f(x)$ is a polynomial of degree $\leq n$ where n is as great as possible.

Mathematica notes

The package `NumericalMath`GaussianQuadrature`` provides functions that calculate weights, abscissas, and error terms for Gauss-Legendre quadrature.

Read in the package.   *In[1]:=* << NumericalMath`GaussianQuadrature`

Find the abscissa-weight pairs for 7-point Gauss-Legendre quadrature on the interval [2, 3] using 20-digit numbers.

```
In[2]:= GaussianQuadratureWeights[7, 2, 3, 20]
Out[2]= {{2.02544604382862, 0.0647425},
         {2.1292344072003, 0.139853},
         {2.297077424311301, 0.190915}, {5/2, 0.20898},
         {2.702922575688699, 0.190915},
         {2.8707655927997, 0.139853},
         {2.97455395617138, 0.0647425}}
```

The error in the 7-point Gauss-Legendre quadrature rule for the function f on the interval a to b. The 14th derivative of f is understood to be evaluated at some unknown point.

```
In[3]:= GaussianQuadratureError[7, f, a, b]
                          -20          15  (14)
Out[3]= -6.49241 10    (-a + b)   f
```

Computer problems

1. Redo part (b) of Computer Problem 4 of Section 7.2 for

$$\int_0^1 xf(x)\,dx \approx w_1 f(x_1) + w_2 f(x_2).$$

In this case there will be two solutions, and you should pick the one for which $x_1 < x_2$.

2. Use 12-point Gauss-Legendre quadrature with 50-digit arithmetic to find an approximation to $\int_{-1}^1 e^x\,dx$. Show that the actual error agrees with that suggested by `GaussianQuadratureError[ ]`.

7.4 Numerical Error Estimates

Mention has been made of the possibility of choosing a partition for a composite rule automatically. To do this, we need some way of knowing whether or not a partition is too coarse. What we need is some estimate of the accuracy, and what we develop in this section is a technique that provides a "calculated guess" of the error.

The trapezoid rule will be used to illustrate the idea. We know that

$$T_N(h) = \int_a^b f(x)\,dx + \frac{h^2}{12}\int_a^b f''(x)dx + O(h^4).$$

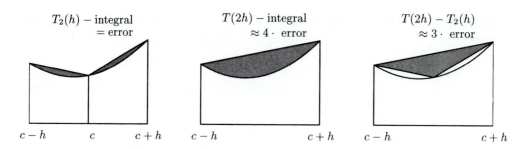

Figure 7.15: Error in trapezoid rules

where $T_N(h)$ denotes the N-fold trapezoid rule with spacing $h = (b-a)/N$. By forming $T_N(h)$ for different values of h we can deduce an estimate of the error. Let

$$T_2(h) = \int_{c-h}^{c+h} f(x)\, dx + \text{ error}$$

be the approximation we would like to use. Then

$$T(2h) \approx \int_{c-h}^{c+h} f(x)\, dx + 4 \cdot \text{ error.} \tag{7.8}$$

(Why do we not have exact equality?) This approximation is essentially free because the necessary values of $f(x)$ have already been computed to form $T_2(h)$. Subtracting gives us

$$T(2h) - T_2(h) \approx 3 \cdot \text{ error.}$$

Figure 7.15 gives a graphical interpretation of these three equations. Dividing by 3, we get

$$\text{error} \quad \approx \quad \frac{T(2h) - T_2(h)}{3} \quad \overset{\text{def}}{=} \quad \text{error estimate}$$

$$= \quad \cdots \quad = \quad \frac{h^2}{12}(2h)\frac{f(c+h) - 2f(c) + f(c-h)}{h^2}.$$

The final expression given for the error estimate is not a surprise. It is exactly the theoretical error term given initially for the composite trapezoid rule except that $f''(x)$ is replaced by a divided-difference estimate of the second derivative in terms of already computed values of $f(x)$.

Example 7.5 Recall from Example 7.3 (page 270) the approximations $T_2(\frac{1}{2}) = 0.775$ and $T_1(1) = 0.75$ to the integral

$$\int_0^1 \frac{dx}{1+x^2} = \frac{\pi}{4} = 0.785398\cdots.$$

Our estimate of the error in $T_2(\frac{1}{2})$ is

$$\frac{T_1(1) - T_2(\frac{1}{2})}{3} = -0.008333\cdots;$$

the actual error is $-0.010398\cdots$.

Remark. Given an estimate of the error (sign and magnitude), there is a temptation to subtract this from the approximate value to obtain an

$$\text{improved approximation} \overset{\text{def}}{=} T_2(h) - \text{error estimate}$$
$$= \frac{4 \cdot T_2(h) - T(2h)}{3}$$
$$= 2h\frac{f(c-h) + 4f(c) + f(c+h)}{6}.$$

This we recognize as Simpson's rule. However, we are left with no error estimate (for the improved approximation). We could use the magnitude of the old error estimate as an *estimated* error bound for the improved approximation, which is justified if this approximation really is an improvement.

Example 7.5 (continued) Subtracting out the error estimate gives

$$\text{improved } T_2(\tfrac{1}{2}) = 0.783333\cdots,$$

which has an error of only $-0.002065\cdots$. One cannot help but marvel at the high accuracy of Simpson's rule.

Let us see how to adapt the idea for estimating error to the Simpson rule. We know the

$$\text{composite Simpson rule} = \int_a^b f(x)\,dx + \frac{h^4}{2880}\int_a^b f^{iv}(x)dx + O(h^6).$$

For the simple and 2-fold Simpson rules sketched in Figure 7.16 we have

$$S_2(h) = \int_{c-h}^{c+h} f(x)\,dx + \text{ error},$$
$$S(2h) \approx \int_{c-h}^{c+h} f(x)\,dx + 16 \cdot \text{ error},$$
$$S(2h) - S_2(h) \approx 15 \cdot \text{ error},$$
$$\text{error estimate} \overset{\text{def}}{=} \frac{S(2h) - S_2(h)}{15} \approx \text{ error}.$$

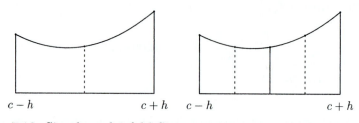

$$c - h \qquad\qquad\qquad c + h \qquad c - h \qquad\qquad\qquad c + h$$

Figure 7.16: Simple and 2-fold Simpson

Note that the error estimate for $S_2(h)$ is cheap, because the values needed for $S(2h)$ are available from the computation of $S_2(h)$.

Remark. As with the 2-fold trapezoid rule we can obtain an

$$\text{improved } S_2(h) \stackrel{\text{def}}{=} S_2(h) - \text{error estimate.}$$

The resulting formula is known as *Bode's rule*, and it has an order of accuracy equal to 6.

7.4.1 Error bounds

A more delicate analysis, which is beyond the scope of this book, yields remainder terms

$$T = \int_a^{a+h} f(x)\, dx + \frac{h^3}{12} f''(\xi_{\mathrm{T}}),$$

$$M = \int_a^{a+h} f(x)\, dx - \frac{h^3}{24} f''(\xi_{\mathrm{M}}),$$

$$S = \int_a^{a+h} f(x)\, dx + \frac{h^5}{2880} f^{\mathrm{iv}}(\xi_{\mathrm{S}}).$$

These error terms are more satisfactory than error expansions because there is a definite limit to their size, and this depends on only a relatively low order derivative of the integrand. The error terms for the trapezoid and midpoint rules imply that the true result must be between the values computed with these two rules, provided that $f''(x)$ does not change sign on the interval of integration. The error term for the Simpson rule is very small, at least for many functions likely to be encountered in practice.

The error in the composite trapezoid rule is

$$\begin{aligned}
\text{error} &= \frac{h^3}{12} f''(\xi_1) + \frac{h^3}{12} f''(\xi_2) + \cdots + \frac{h^3}{12} f''(\xi_N) \\
&= \frac{Nh^3}{12} \cdot \frac{f''(\xi_1) + f''(\xi_2) + \cdots + f''(\xi_N)}{N},
\end{aligned}$$

and we have an average of values for $f''(x)$. If the second derivative is continuous, then by the intermediate-value theorem, it will somewhere, say at $x = \xi$, be equal to this average value:

$$\text{error} = \frac{h^2}{12}(b - a)f''(\xi).$$

Similarly it can be shown that

$$\text{composite-midpoint-rule error} \quad = \quad -\frac{h^2}{24}(b - a)f''(\xi_{\text{M}}),$$

$$\text{composite-Simpson-rule error} \quad = \quad \frac{h^4}{2880}(b - a)f^{\text{iv}}(\xi_{\text{S}}).$$

Note that the remainder terms for the corresponding simple rules are obtained for the special case $N = 1$, by setting $b - a = h$.

The remainder term in a quadrature rule can be used to obtain a rigorous bound on the magnitude of the error. This can be done by the computer using symbolic differentiation and interval analysis—the unknown ξ is replaced by the interval known to contain ξ.

Supplementary note

An excellent reference on error analysis is Ralston and Rabinowitz (1978).

Review question

1. Let T_N denote the approximation to $\int_a^b f(x)\,dx$ obtained from the composite trapezoid rule with N subintervals. The error is $(b - a)(h^2/12)f''(\xi_N)$ where $h = (b - a)/N$ and ξ_N lies somewhere between a and b. Derive an error estimate for T_2 in terms of T_1 and T_2. On what assumption does the accuracy of this estimate depend?

Exercises

1. Is (7.8) exact if $f(x)$ is a quadratic polynomial? Explain.

2. Derive Bode's rule as suggested by the remark just before Section 7.4.1.

3. Consider the 3-fold midpoint rule

$$\int_a^{a+3h} f(x)\,dx \approx hf\left(a + \frac{h}{2}\right) + hf\left(a + \frac{3h}{2}\right) + hf\left(a + \frac{5h}{2}\right) \stackrel{\text{def}}{=} M_3(h).$$

From the three given values of $f(x)$ construct an estimate of the error in $M_3(h)$. Recall that the midpoint rule has order of accuracy 2. (Note: Your final answer must not involve other values or derivatives of $f(x)$.)

4. Let T_N denote the approximation to $\int_a^b f(x)\, dx$ obtained from the composite trapezoid rule with N subintervals of equal length.

   (a) Criticize the following analysis. Because

   $$T_1(2h) = \int_a^b f(x)\, dx + \frac{b-a}{12} h^2 f''(\xi)$$

   and

   $$T_2(h) = \int_a^b f(x)\, dx + \frac{b-a}{12} \left(\frac{h}{2}\right)^2 f''(\xi)$$

   we have

   $$\tfrac{4}{3}T_2 - \tfrac{1}{3}T_1 = \int_a^b f(x)\, dx.$$

   (b) Explain why the conclusion is impossible.

5. For the composite Simpson rule with N equally spaced subintervals we have

   $$\int_a^b f(x)\, dx = S_N - \frac{h^4}{2880}(b-a) f^{\text{iv}}(\xi)$$

   where $h = (b-a)/N$ and $a < \xi < b$. It can be shown that $\left| \dfrac{d^4}{dx^4}\left(\dfrac{1}{1+x^2}\right) \right| \le 24$, for $0 \le x \le 1$. Use this to show that the magnitude of the error for S_2 applied to $\displaystyle\int_0^1 \frac{dx}{1+x^2}$ is bounded by $\frac{1}{1920}$.

6. For the composite trapezoid rule with N equally spaced subintervals we have

   $$\int_a^b f(x)\, dx = T_N - \frac{h^2}{12}(b-a) f''(\xi), \quad a < \xi < b.$$

   Determine a reasonable value of N that will ensure an absolute error no greater than $\frac{7}{2400}$ for the composite trapezoid rule approximation of

   $$\int_0^{14} t \cos t \, dt.$$

7. Consider the use of the N-fold Simpson rule to approximate

   $$\ln 3 = \int_1^3 \frac{dx}{x}.$$

   How large must N be so that the magnitude of the error is no greater than 10^{-6}?

Mathematica **notes**

One of the many advantages of using *Mathematica* to study numerical analysis is that it allows us to obtain formulas that would otherwise be too tedious to derive. For example, we mentioned that correcting for the dominant error in Simpson's rule results in Boole's rule, but a lot of effort is required to get a formula. Here and in the problems that follow we show how this can be done in *Mathematica* quite easily.

Start with a 6-term Taylor expansion of f[x] about $x = 0$.

$In[1]:=$ **fs[x_] = Normal[Series[f[x], {x, 0, 5}]]**

$$Out[1]= f[0] + x\ f'[0] + \frac{x^2\ f''[0]}{2} + \frac{x^3\ f^{(3)}[0]}{6} +$$

$$\frac{x^4\ f^{(4)}[0]}{24} + \frac{x^5\ f^{(5)}[0]}{120}$$

The corresponding approximation to $\int_{-h}^{h} f(x)\,dx$.

$In[2]:=$ **int = Integrate[fs[x], {x, -h, h}]**

$$Out[2]= 2\ h\ f[0] + \frac{h^3\ f''[0]}{3} + \frac{h^5\ f^{(4)}[0]}{60}$$

The elementary trapezoid rule applied to the approximation **fs**.

$In[3]:=$ **t1 = Expand[h fs[-h] + h fs[h]]**

$$Out[3]= 2\ h\ f[0] + h^3\ f''[0] + \frac{h^5\ f^{(4)}[0]}{12}$$

The 2-fold trapezoid rule applied to **fs**.

$In[4]:=$ **t2 = Expand[h/2 fs[-h] + h fs[0] + h/2 fs[h]]**

$$Out[4]= 2\ h\ f[0] + \frac{h^3\ f''[0]}{2} + \frac{h^5\ f^{(4)}[0]}{24}$$

The corresponding approximation to the simple Simpson rule.

$In[5]:=$ **s1 = Expand[t2 - (t1-t2)/3]**

$$Out[5]= 2\ h\ f[0] + \frac{h^3\ f''[0]}{3} + \frac{h^5\ f^{(4)}[0]}{36}$$

The dominant error in Simpson's rule.

$In[6]:=$ **s1 - int**

$$Out[6]= \frac{h^5\ f^{(4)}[0]}{90}$$

Caution: If you do this without using big-oh, as we did above, you should mentally keep track of the first omitted term or use more than enough terms.

Computer problems

1. In this problem we derive some explicit formulas for Simpson's rule, Bode's rule, and further corrected rules for $\int_{-h}^{h} f(x)\,dx$. Do *not* use an approximate representation for the function. You are to find explicit formulas involving values of f at the nodes.

   (a) Define a routine t[n_] that gives the n-fold trapezoid rule in terms of the values of the function f[ ] at the nodes. For reasons of efficiency you should define it to Expand the result and remember that result for future reference. Use t[n_] := t[n] = Expand[...]. A useful *Mathematica* function is Sum[ ].

   (b) Define the improved rules:

   $$
   \begin{aligned}
   &\texttt{s[n\_] := s[n] = Expand[t[2n]-(t[n]-t[2n])/(2\textasciicircum 2-1)]} \\
   &\texttt{r[n\_] := r[n] = Expand[s[2n]-(s[n]-s[2n])/(2\textasciicircum 4-1)]} \\
   &\texttt{q[n\_] := q[n] = Expand[r[2n]-(r[n]-r[2n])/(2\textasciicircum 6-1)]} \\
   &\texttt{p[n\_] := p[n] = Expand[q[2n]-(q[n]-q[2n])/(2\textasciicircum 8-1)]}
   \end{aligned}
   $$

   (c) What is the 4-fold Simpson rule, s[4]?

   (d) What is the 2-fold Bode rule, r[2]?

   (e) What is p[1]?

2. In this problem we examine the errors in the rules defined in Computer Problem 1. If you have solved that problem, you will first need to Clear the symbols t, s, r, q, and p, or things will not work correctly.

   (a) Start by defining an approximate representation of f:

   $$\texttt{fs[x\_] = Normal[Series[f[x], \{x, 0, 10\}]]}$$

   (b) Define a function t[n_] that gives the approximate representation of the n-fold trapezoid rule. For reasons of efficiency you should define it to Expand the result and remember that result for future reference. Use t[n_] := t[n] = Expand[...]. A useful *Mathematica* function is Sum[ ].

   (c) Define s, r, q, and p as in Computer Problem 1.

   (d) Find the error in each of s[1], r[1], q[1], and p[1] as approximations to the integral of fs.

3. Recall from Section 7.2 that the probability of having a GPA that is at least 0.1 grade point too low owing to accumulated rounding error is approximately

$$\sqrt{\frac{240}{\pi}} \int_{-0.5}^{-0.1} \exp(-240x^2)\,dx.$$

You will use this as a benchmark to compare NIntegrate[ ] with your own iterative *but nonadaptive* composite Simpson integrator.

(a) The integrand above has an antiderivative that can be expressed in terms of the error function erf(x). Ask *Mathematica* for the derivative of `Erf[x]`. Define a function $g(x)$ such that $g'(x) = \sqrt{240/\pi}\exp(-240x^2)$. Validate your answer by asking *Mathematica* for the derivative of $g(x)$. Then use $g(x)$ (and the fundamental theorem of calculus) to compute the "true value" of the integral given above. Compute from this the number of students out of 6000 who will have a GPA that is 0.1 grade point too low or worse because of roundoff error.

(b) Define a *Mathematica* function

$$f[x\_] := (nfns = nfns + 1; Exp[-240. x x])$$

(The `nfns = nfns + 1` causes `nfns` to be incremented each time the function `f[ ]` is evaluated.) Using `NIntegrate[ ]` with `PrecisionGoal -> Infinity` and `AccuracyGoals` of $m = 4, 5, \ldots, 10$ decimal places of accuracy, determine in each case the actual decimal places of accuracy (do not forget the `Sqrt[240./N[Pi]]` in front of the integral) and the base 10 logarithm of the number of evaluations of `f[ ]`. Use `Table[ ]` to do this, and have it produce a table of ordered pairs, the first number in each pair being the logarithm of the number of evaluations and the second number the decimal places of accuracy. Did `NIntegrate[ ]` always achieve the requested `AccuracyGoal`?

(c) Write a numerical integration routine that has arguments f, a, b, and *decpl* and uses the composite Simpson rule, *with a uniform partition*, to approximate $\int_a^b f(x)\,dx$ with an estimated error of at most *decpl* decimal places of accuracy. Do this by generating a sequence of composite Simpson rule approximations: simple Simpson, 2-fold Simpson, 4-fold Simpson, ... and by using 1/15 of the difference between two successive approximations as an estimate of the error in the more refined of the two approximations (cf. page 291). You should reuse the `f` values from one approximation in the next; i.e., *never* evaluate `f` more than once at the same point. (Hint: A simple way to do this is to form a sum of f values at "even" points and another at "odd" points.)

(d) Redo part (b) using your iterative composite Simpson routine.

(e) `Show` the combined `ListPlots` of the data tabulated in parts (b) and (c) using two different plot styles to join the points for each of the data sets.

7.5   Global Adaptive Quadrature

The error estimates developed in the preceding section can be used to estimate the error in a $2N$-fold rule by adding together the estimates for N different 2-fold rules. If this sum is too great, one could uniformly subdivide the subintervals and try again. However, there is usually no reason (other than simplicity) why the partition must be uniform. Perhaps the greatest benefit would be gained from the subdivision of only those subintervals that contribute the most to the overall error estimate. In this section we develop this idea into an algorithm that *automatically* determines an *efficient* partition that is fine enough for the desired accuracy.

To demonstrate the potential benefits of a nonuniform partition that is *adapted* to the integrand, we examine a simple example. Consider

$$\int_0^1 \sqrt{x}\,dx \approx \text{composite trapezoid rule}$$

for some partition $0 < x_1 < x_2 < \cdots < x_{N-1} < 1$. In this particularly simple case it can be proved that an optimal choice of these points is given by the formula $x_j = (j/N)^2$, meaning that no other choice of the $N - 1$ points gives as small an error in the composite trapezoid rule. For comparison, a uniform partition is given by $x_j = j/N$. An illustration for $N = 4$ is given for both of these partitions in Figure 7.17. You can see that the optimal partition, with the points placed closer together where the integrand varies more rapidly, yields a piecewise linear interpolant that fits the integrand much better. An especially meaningful comparison of the two types of partitions is obtained by looking at the smallest value of N, which measures the computational cost, needed to attain some given level of accuracy. The difference in cost is dramatic:

digits of accuracy	1	2	3	4	5	6
uniform		2	6	27	122	563	2610
optimal		2	4	11	34	106	334

Number of subintervals of N needed

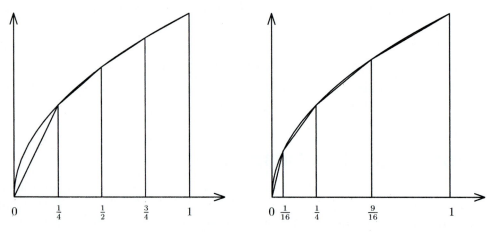

Figure 7.17: Uniform and optimal partitions

Figure 7.18: $\int_0^1 \exp^{-100x} \, dx$

The order of accuracy can be calculated by using for h the average spacing $(b-a)/N$. The result is an order of accuracy of 1.5 for uniform partitions and 2 for optimal partitions. The reduced order for the uniform partitions is somehow related to the infinite first derivative of $\sqrt{x}$ at $x = 0$. It is gratifying to know that it is possible, by adapting the partition to the integrand, to recover the normal second-order accuracy of the trapezoid rule. However, we have not shown that this is practical. Determining the optimal partition is probably much more difficult than calculating the integral in the first place! Nonetheless it may be possible to determine a *nearly optimal* partition that is nearly as good as an optimal one and much better than a uniform one. It was the purpose of this example to show the potential rewards of such an endeavor.

In order to gain an advantage from **adaptive quadrature** it is not necessary for the integrand to have a **singularity**, that is, an infinite derivative. More typical of problems needing nonuniform partitions is the integral $\int_0^1 \exp^{-100x} \, dx$, plotted in Figure 7.18, whose integrand has derivatives that vary greatly in magnitude as a function of x.

The idea, then, of adaptive quadrature is to adapt the partition to the integrand by concentrating samples where it varies most rapidly. How fine to make the partition could be determined on the basis of an *absolute error tolerance* ε:

$$\text{find } Q \text{ such that } \left| Q - \int_a^b f(x) \, dx \right| \leq \varepsilon$$

An *algorithm* to determine an appropriate partition has as ingredients

- some basic formula,
- some error estimator, and
- some initial partition.

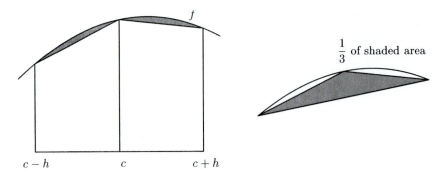

Figure 7.19: Formula T_2 and its error estimator

For a basic formula let us take the 2-fold trapezoid rule, pictured in Figure 7.19 for a generic interval $[c - h, c + h]$ with center c and half-width h. For an error estimator let us use the formula

$$\frac{h}{6}(f(c+h) - 2f(c) + f(c-h))$$

derived in the preceding section and sketched in Figure 7.19. For an initial partition P_1, let us take the entire interval, $P_1 : a < b$.

We illustrate the algorithm for refining the partition for the integral $\int_0^1 \sqrt{x}\,dx$. The initial interval $[0, 1]$ has center $c = \frac{1}{2}$ and half-width $h = \frac{1}{2}$. The error estimate is

$$\frac{\frac{1}{2}}{6}\left(1 - 2\sqrt{\tfrac{1}{2}} + 0\right) = -0.034518.$$

If this exceeds (in magnitude) the error tolerance, we subdivide and calculate errors for the subintervals as shown below:

P_1	|err est|
$[0, 1]$	0.034518

P_2	|err est|
$[0, \frac{1}{2}]$	0.012204$*$
$[\frac{1}{2}, 1]$	0.001039
$\sum$|err est| $=$	0.013243

The global error estimate shown above is the sum of the magnitudes of the local error estimates. Because these local error estimates are mere approximations, we take a conservative approach and prevent cancellation of the local error estimates by summing their magnitudes. If this sum exceeds the error tolerance, we continue the subdivision process by subdividing that subinterval whose error estimate is greatest (marked with an asterisk). In this case the parent interval $[0, \frac{1}{2}]$ is replaced, as shown below to the left, by its first child $[0, \frac{1}{4}]$; and its second child $[\frac{1}{4}, \frac{1}{2}]$ is appended to the list. There is no need to keep the intervals in their natural order. Yet another step of the refinement process is shown below to the right.

P_3	|err est|
$[0, \frac{1}{4}]$	0.004314*
$[\frac{1}{2}, 1]$	0.001039
$[\frac{1}{4}, \frac{1}{2}]$	0.000367
$\sum$|err est| $=$	0.005720

P_4	|err est|
$[0, \frac{1}{8}]$	0.001525*
$[\frac{1}{2}, 1]$	0.001039
$[\frac{1}{4}, \frac{1}{2}]$	0.000367
$[\frac{1}{8}, \frac{1}{4}]$	0.000130
$\sum$|err est| $=$	0.003061

Note that the error reduction in the total error that was achieved in going from P_2 to P_3 would not have been possible if we had chosen instead to subdivide $[\frac{1}{2}, 1]$. (Why?) The results of two more refinements are shown below.

P_5	|err est|
$[0, \frac{1}{16}]$	0.000539
$[\frac{1}{2}, 1]$	0.001039*
$[\frac{1}{4}, \frac{1}{2}]$	0.000367
$[\frac{1}{8}, \frac{1}{4}]$	0.000130
$[\frac{1}{16}, \frac{1}{8}]$	0.000046
$\sum$|err est| $=$	0.002121

P_6	|err est|
$[0, \frac{1}{16}]$	0.000539*
$[\frac{1}{2}, \frac{3}{4}]$	0.000167
$[\frac{1}{4}, \frac{1}{2}]$	0.000367
$[\frac{1}{8}, \frac{1}{4}]$	0.000130
$[\frac{1}{16}, \frac{1}{8}]$	0.000046
$[\frac{3}{4}, 1]$	0.000100
$\sum$|err est| $=$	0.001349

The development of the partition is shown graphically in Figure 7.20. The process would stop when $\sum$\|err est\| $\leq \varepsilon$. If you compare these partitions with the optimal ones given before, you see that they are quite similar.

Thus, in general, to get P_{n+1} we halve that subinterval of P_n that has the largest error estimate. With a basic formula of order p, the error in that subinterval is reduced by roughly $(\frac{1}{2})^p$.

The cost of searching for the error estimate of maximum magnitude could make this an unreasonably expensive process. For example, $N = 1000$ subintervals implies a total of ≈ 500000 comparisons if a linear search is used. A more efficient program would avoid most of these comparisons by maintaining (with pointers) a partial ordering of subintervals as a binary tree (such as is used in the heap sort). With such a device only about 10000 comparisons would be needed.

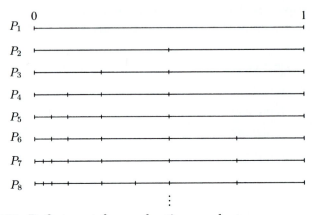

Figure 7.20: Refinement from adaptive quadrature

Our explanation of adaptive quadrature assumed the use of an absolute error tolerance. This is at variance with our emphasis on relative error. However, requesting a small pure relative error

$$\frac{|Q - \int_a^b f(x)\,dx|}{|\int_a^b f(x)\,dx|} \le \varepsilon$$

can be unreasonable, because, as depicted in Figure 7.21, the integral can be very small if there is severe cancellation due to sign changes in the integrand. On the other hand, the **modified relative error** accuracy criterion

$$\frac{|Q - \int_a^b f(x)\,dx|}{\int_a^b |f(x)|\,dx} \le \varepsilon, \tag{7.9}$$

with the absolute value inside the integral, is quite reasonable. Moreover, it is equivalent to requiring that Q be the exact integral of a function $\tilde{f}(x)$ that differs from $f(x)$ by at most ε in a relative sense:

$$Q = \int_a^b \tilde{f}(x)\,dx \quad \text{where} \quad |\tilde{f}(x) - f(x)| \le \varepsilon |f(x)|. \tag{7.10}$$

The proof of this fact is Exercise 3.

Figure 7.21: An integral that is nearly zero

What we have seen in this chapter is that numerical quadrature routines work by *sampling* $f(x)$. Reduced to simplest terms, an adaptive algorithm proceeds as follows:

Available information	Action
a, b	choose c_1; evaluate $f(c_1)$
$a, b, c_1, f(c_1)$	choose c_2; evaluate $f(c_2)$
$a, b, c_1, f(c_1), c_2, f(c_2)$	choose c_3; evaluate $f(c_3)$
$\vdots$	$\vdots$
$a, b, c_1, f(c_1), c_2, f(c_2), \ldots, c_N, f(c_N)$	approximate $\int_a^b f(x)dx$

The number of samples N will depend on the sample values, but it will be far less than the number of machine numbers in the range of integration. The structure of $f(x)$ is never examined by the algorithm. As a consequence, *uncertainty* is unavoidable in the accuracy[4] of the result. Therefore, it is desirable to give some control to the user by letting him or her specify an initial partition that is sufficiently fine to resolve the basic features of the integrand. The user may not have good information, but the algorithm begins with no information at all.

Results of guaranteed accuracy can be computed if the formula for $f(x)$ is differentiated several times and interval analysis is used.

Supplementary note

An alternative to global adaptive quadrature is *local* adaptive quadrature, which can be found in many numerical analysis textbooks. This is an approach that uses less storage but is not robust and requires more integrand evaluations for badly behaved integrands. *Global* adaptive quadrature can be found in Kahaner, Moler, and Nash (1989, p. 156).

Exercises

1. Show that the partition $0 < \frac{1}{4} < 1$ is optimal for the 2-fold trapezoid rule in evaluating $\int_0^1 \sqrt{x}\, dx$; e.g., show that a perturbation ε of the node $\frac{1}{4}$ increases the error in the trapezoid approximation.

2. Consider the example given in this section of partitions $P_1, P_2, \ldots, P_6$. What could we say for certain about $\sum |\text{err est}|$ for P_7 if we were given only the table of $|\text{err est}|$ for the subintervals of P_6? Of course, we could say that this sum is nonnegative, but what is the most that can be said for certain?

---

[4]For this purpose it is reasonable to define the best possible result as the composite trapezoid rule applied to a partition consisting of all machine numbers in the range of integration.

⋆3. Prove (7.10). Hint: Define

$$\tilde{f}(x) = f(x) + \delta|f(x)|$$

where δ is some constant yet to be determined.

Computer problem

1. (a) Implement the algorithm described in this section. There should be parameters `f_`, `a_`, `b_`, `eps_` where the first three have obvious meanings and `eps` is the absolute error tolerance. Return the approximation to the integral. Limit the number of subintervals to 100. If the estimated error has not converged to the tolerance by then, issue an error message and return the best estimate of the integral. Avoid computing the integrand more than once at each point. Following are some suggestions. There are six pieces of information you need to maintain about each subinterval: an error estimate, the length (or half-length) of the subinterval, the center, and the values of `f` at the endpoints and center of the subinterval. It would be nice to keep these six pieces of information together in a record (a list or data object with some other head) for each subinterval. If you do this, it will be awkward to find the record for the subinterval with the largest error estimate. An alternative is to have two separate lists: `err` being a list of estimated errors and `intinfo` being a list of records containing the other information about each subinterval. If you do this, you will need to be careful that the two lists are always updated together. To get the index of the subinterval with the largest error, use `Position[err, Max[err]]`. The basic structure of the algorithm should be

```
intgrt[f_, a_, b_, eps_] :=
    Module[{result, maxn=100, k, c, h, f0, f1, f2, err, toterr},
        (* Approximate the integral and the error for [a, b] *)
            . . .
        While[ toterr > eps  &&  Length[err]+1 <= maxn,
            (* Find the worst subinterval *)
                . . .
            (* Subtract off the approximation for that subinterval *)
                . . .
            (* Add on the approximation for the right half *)
                . . .
            (* Add on the approximation for the left half *)
                . . .
        ];
        If[ toterr > eps, Message[intgrt::conv, toterr]];
        result
    ]
```

(b) Apply your routine to $\int_{0.}^{1.} \sqrt{x}\, dx$ with an absolute error tolerance of $\frac{2.}{3.} \times 0.0001$ and with the function Timing wrapped around it. At the same time determine the number of function (that is, integrand) evaluations, by defining

$$\texttt{sqrt[x\_] := (nf = nf + 1; Sqrt[x])}$$

(or using the equivalent pure function) where nf is initialized to zero. For comparison, a uniform mesh would require 123 function evaluations and an optimal mesh only 35.

(c) Repeat part (b), but instead of simply counting the number of function evaluations accumulate the points in a list. Use

$$\texttt{sqrt[x\_] := (sq = Sqrt[x]; AppendTo[data, \{x, sq\}]; sq)}$$

where data has been initialized to the empty list { }. After evaluating $\int_{0.}^{1.} \sqrt{x}\, dx$, plot data using ListPlot[ ]. Where do most of the function evaluations occur?

(d) Apply your routine also to $\int_{0.}^{100.} e^{-x}\, dx$ with a tolerance of 0.0001 and look at the value of nf. Then apply the composite trapezoid rule from Computer Problem 2 of Section 7.2 to the same integral with the number of subintervals equal to nf - 1 . To get the true value apply N[Integrate[...]] to this problem. How many times smaller is the error of the adaptive integrator? (Answer this with a computation or with a *Mathematica* comment.)

8.   Ordinary Differential Equations

Differential equations are not the sort of thing we encounter in our daily life. Yet differential equations are an extremely important tool in most of science and engineering. They are also needed in the social sciences and other areas. The laws of nature are most often expressed as differential equations; for example, Maxwell's equations in electromagnetics,

$$
\begin{aligned}
\nabla \cdot \mathbf{D} &= \rho, \\
\nabla \times \mathbf{H} &= \mathbf{J} + \frac{\partial}{\partial t}\mathbf{D}, \\
\nabla \times \mathbf{E} &= -\frac{\partial}{\partial t}\mathbf{B}, \\
\nabla \cdot \mathbf{B} &= 0,
\end{aligned}
$$

sometimes sported on electrical engineering tee shirts, are partial differential equations. The goal of science is to understand nature, which often means finding differential equations. Engineering applies science, which often means solving differential equations. Much of what we have done up to now was in preparation for this topic.

Just as it is often difficult to evaluate an integral analytically, it is often difficult to solve an ordinary differential equation (ODE) analytically. In fact, it is almost never possible. And in most cases where an analytical solution is possible it is only because functions have been invented for this purpose—in particular, the elementary and special functions. Numerical analysis provides us with the tools to solve differential equations, both ordinary and partial, numerically.

This chapter contains the following sections:

8.1 A Single ODE

This section is a brief introduction to differential equations.

8.1.1 Examples and applications

We begin with two examples of **ordinary differential equations**.

Example 8.1

$$Y'(t) = -\tfrac{1}{50}(Y(t) - 20)$$

is an equation whose unknown is a *function* $Y(t)$ of one variable. The equation is expected to be satisfied identically for all t. What complicates the problem is that the equation contains not only the unknown function $Y(t)$ but also its derivative. Methods for solving such equations analytically consist of three steps:

1. Rearrange the equation (the tricky part).

2. Take an antiderivative, which introduces an arbitrary constant.

3. Rearrange the equation to give an explicit expression for $Y(t)$.

Later we discuss a method for obtaining the analytical solution to simple differential equations like this. Applying this method will yield the **general solution**

$$Y(t) = 20 + Ce^{-t/50}$$

where C is an arbitrary constant. The idea is that C can be given any numerical value and $Y(t)$ will solve the differential equation. To verify that this is a solution, we show that the left-hand side and the right-hand side are identically equal:

$$Y'(t) = -\frac{C}{50}e^{-t/50},$$

$$-\frac{1}{50}(Y(t) - 20) = -\frac{C}{50}e^{-t/50}.$$

Example 8.2 The general solution of

$$Y'(t) = 1 - Y(t)|Y(t)|$$

is rather complicated to state. One **particular solution** is

$$Y(t) = \begin{cases} \text{undefined,} & t \le -\pi/2, \\ \tan t, & -\pi/2 < t \le 0, \\ \tanh t, & t > 0. \end{cases}$$

It is plotted in Figure 8.1. It is not customary to bother stating for which values a function is undefined. We did it here to emphasize this possibility. Even the universe, according

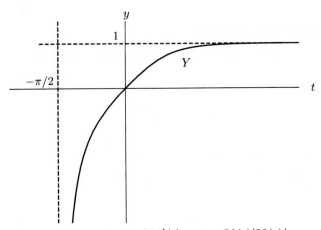

Figure 8.1: Particular solution of $Y'(t) = 1 - Y(t)|Y(t)|$

to current theories, was undefined at some point in the distant past. This example also underscores the fact that a function is not the same thing as a formula. The function $Y(t)$ is defined in two pieces, each by a different formula. Before verifying that $Y(t)$ satisfies the differential equation, we should establish that it is differentiable at $t = 0$, for this may not be obvious. First we note that it is continuous since both $\tan t$ and $\tanh t$ are 0 at $t = 0$. Differentiating, we have

$$Y'(t) = \begin{cases} \sec^2 t, & -\pi/2 < t < 0, \\ ?, & t = 0, \\ \operatorname{sech}^2 t, & t > 0. \end{cases}$$

We note that both $\sec^2 t$ and $\operatorname{sech}^2 t$ are equal to 1 at $t = 0$, and therefore $Y'(0)$ exists. Now we can verify that $Y(t)$ satisfies the ODE for $-\pi/2 < t \le 0$:

$$\begin{aligned} Y'(t) &= \sec^2 t, \\ 1 - Y(t)|Y(t)| &= 1 - (\tan t)|\tan t| = 1 - (\tan t)(-\tan t) = \sec^2 t, \end{aligned}$$

and for $t \ge 0$:

$$\begin{aligned} Y'(t) &= \operatorname{sech}^2 t, \\ 1 - Y(t)|Y(t)| &= 1 - (\tanh t)|\tanh t| = 1 - \tanh^2 t = \operatorname{sech}^2 t. \end{aligned}$$

It happens that each of the preceding examples arises from some physical situation in which the independent variable t represents time. There are other examples where position is the independent variable, which we might want to represent by x. Most often, ordinary differential equations model the behavior in time of some system that has distinct components, for example, celestial bodies, electric circuits, populations of different species, and concentrations of different chemicals. The "execution" of such models on the computer often goes by the name *continuous simulation,* for which special programming languages have been developed. The physical origins of Examples 8.1 and 8.2 are the subjects of the next two examples.

Example 8.3 Newton's law of cooling states that the temperature $T(t)$ of a body obeys

$$T'(t) = -k(T(t) - T_\infty)$$

where T_∞ is the (constant) temperature of its surroundings and k is some constant affecting the rate at which heat is lost, for example, $T_\infty = 20$ (in °C) and $k = 0.02$ (in minute^{-1}). A pictorial representation is given by Figure 8.2. Solving for $T(t)$ begins with the rearrangement

$$\frac{T'(t)}{T(t) - T_\infty} = -k.$$

Taking an antiderivative,

$$\ln |T(t) - T_\infty| = -kt + C_1,$$

introduces an arbitrary constant C_1. With the derivative of $T(t)$ no longer present we can solve algebraically:

$$\begin{aligned} |T(t) - T_\infty| &= \exp\left(C_1 - kt\right) \\ T(t) &= T_\infty \pm e^{C_1} e^{-kt} \\ T(t) &= T_\infty + C_2 e^{-kt} \end{aligned}$$

where $C_2 \stackrel{\text{def}}{=} \pm e^{C_1}$. We thus have a family of solutions, a few of which are depicted in Figure 8.3. We will show that through each point of the t-y plane there is exactly one solution. Normally we expect that a physical problem should have just one solution. This problem will have a unique solution if we supply an **initial condition** stating what the temperature is at some point in time, for example $T(0) = 95$. The most general initial condition is $T(t_0) = T_0$, and this will always determine a unique value for the arbitrary constant C_2 in the general

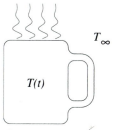

Figure 8.2: Something cooling

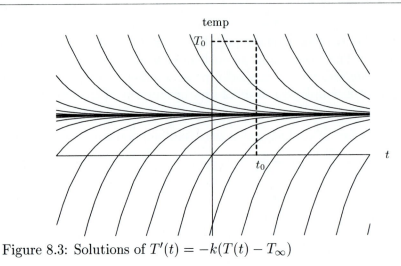

Figure 8.3: Solutions of $T'(t) = -k(T(t) - T_\infty)$

solution. (See Figure 8.3.) To obtain C_2, we substitute the general solution into the initial condition:

$$T_\infty + C_2 e^{-kt_0} = T_0.$$

We solve this to get $C_2 = (T_0 - T_\infty)e^{kt_0}$. Substituting back into the general solution, we have

$$T(t) = T_\infty + (T_0 - T_\infty)e^{-k(t-t_0)}$$

as the solution of the general **initial-value problem**.

Example 8.4 The downward velocity $V(t)$ of a falling body, pictorially represented in Figure 8.4, is subject to Newton's second law of motion, which equates the product of the mass m of the body and the downward acceleration $V'(t)$ to the sum of the forces acting downward on the body. If we consider the force of gravity and drag but neglect buoyancy, we get

$$mV'(t) = mg - \frac{\rho A C_0}{2}|V(t)|\,V(t)$$

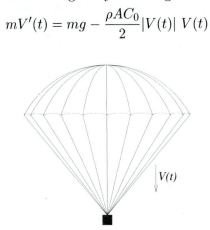

Figure 8.4: Something falling

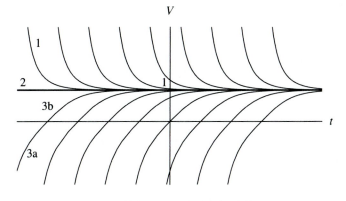

Figure 8.5: Solutions of $V'(t) = 1 - V(t)\,|V(t)|$

where ρ is the density of air, A is the area projected by the body onto a horizontal plane, and C_0 is the drag coefficient (which is a function of the shape of the body). We can choose physical units of length and time so that $g = 1, \rho A C_0/(2m) = 1$, and we get

$$V'(t) = 1 - |V(t)|\,V(t).$$

There are three kinds of solutions to this differential equation:

$$
\begin{aligned}
V(t) &= \coth(t - C_1), &\qquad t > C_1, &\qquad \{1\}\\
V(t) &\equiv 1, &\qquad &\qquad \{2\}
\end{aligned}
$$

$$
V(t) = \begin{cases}
\tan(t - C_3), & C_3 - \dfrac{\pi}{2} < t \le C_3, &\qquad \{3a\}\\[2mm]
\tanh(t - C_3), & t \ge C_3. &\qquad \{3b\}
\end{cases}
$$

These are illustrated in Figure 8.5. They represent, respectively, the cases where the initial downward velocity is greater than, equal to, and less than the free-fall velocity. If the initial motion is upward, then the formula for the solution changes when the body reaches its maximum height. Note that in cases 1 and 3 the solution does not exist before some point in time. This can be ascribed to the unrealistic assumption that the gravitational field is uniform. In reality, gravity will diminish with increasing altitude, as will the density ρ of the atmosphere.

Applications of numerical methods to ordinary differential equations have been important historically.[1]

When Newton's law of gravity was first proposed, it lacked decisive experimental confirmation. It already was possible using current methods to predict accurately the positions of planets and moons. In particular, it had been predicted that Halley's comet would return at

---

[1]S. G. Nash, ed., *A History of Scientific Computing*, ACM Press, New York, 1990; in particular, the article by C.W. Gear and R.D. Skeel on pages 88–105.

the end of 1748. As the due date approached in 1748, three scientists—Clairaut, Lalande, and Lepaute—did a calculation using the law of gravity to predict the return of Halley's comet. Lalande wrote, "During six months we calculated from morning to night, sometimes even at meals; ... it was necessary to calculate the distance of each of the two planets, Jupiter and Saturn, from the comet, separately for every successive degree, for 150 years."[2] Logarithm tables were probably all they had to work with. Their calculations predicted that the comet would return later than expected and reach its closest distance to the sun on April 13, 1749. This was off by only 31 days. Historians of science say that this was important evidence for the idea of a "clockwork universe," so it seems that the numerical solution of ODEs contributed to the Enlightenment of the 18th century.

Halley's comet returned again in 1835, and this was predicted with an error of only 5 days. The next return was in 1910, and the best prediction was off by only 2.7 days. A prize of 1000 German marks was awarded for this. The winning calculation took into account the effect of the seven planets from Venus out to Neptune.

On a similar scale were the computations performed by Norwegian mathematician Carl Störmer, who with his colleagues spent several years before 1907 calculating the orbits of electrons in the earth's magnetic field in order to explain the aurora borealis.

The discovery of Neptune was accomplished by calculations that attempted to account for unexplained discrepancies in the motion of Uranus. One of the discoverers was John Couch Adams, who in 1883 published the popular Adams methods for solving ODEs numerically. Later, irregularities were observed in the orbits of Uranus and Neptune, which led to the discovery of Pluto in 1930 and its moon Charon in 1978. However, subsequent calculations have shown that the masses of Pluto and Charon are 1000 times too small to account for the irregularities, so there is a search for a Planet X that is 3 to 5 times larger than the earth and 3 times further from the sun than Pluto.

Tabulations of future positions of the moon were historically important in navigation for determining longitude, and funding was available for computing these tables. One such set of calculations in 1929 by L.J. Comrie punched half a million cards.

A more down-to-earth application was exterior ballistics. An early expert in this area was an astronomy professor at the University of Chicago, F.R. Moulton. He obtained practical experience in 1918 by computing the trajectories of projectiles for the U.S. Army. These data were used to construct tables for aiming guns including anti-aircraft weapons.

The solution of ODEs was an important driving force behind the construction of computers. The first successful computer was a mechanical analog computer built by Vannevar Bush and others at MIT in 1930. Later, electrical models were built. However, the precision of analog computers was limited and was inadequate for applications such as astronomy.

---

[2]C. Sagan and A. Druyan, *Comet*, Random House, New York, 1985.

The numerical solution of differential equations was the motivation for Howard Aiken to plan the first automatic digital computing machine at Harvard. The result, in 1943, was a largely mechanical computer called the Mark I. The first working electronic digital computer, the ENIAC (Electronic Numerical Integrator And Computer), was designed with the intention of solving ordinary differential equations by imitating the techniques used on analog computers. It was completed in 1946. Just as the integrators in an analog computer operate in parallel, so did the arithmetic on each of the accumulators. About this time Bell Telephone Laboratories was building computers using electromagnetic relays, and, in particular, the Model III built in 1944 and the Model V built in 1947 were primarily for the purpose of solving systems of ODEs. Copies of these two computers went to the Ballistic Research Laboratory at the Aberdeen Proving Grounds, as did the ENIAC, which was funded for the purpose of doing ballistics calculations, and the ORDVAC, built at the University of Illinois.

Digital machines especially designed for the integration of ODEs continued to be built. They were called *digital differential analyzers* and were used in applications such as real-time control systems. Also, in recent times special-purpose machines have been constructed to solve many-body problems in molecular dynamics and astronomy. For example, the GRAPE project at the University of Tokyo is a parallel computer for studying astrophysics, plasmas, and systems of molecules. Recently, at MIT the Supercomputer Toolkit computed the orbits of the planets of the solar system 100 million years into the future and showed that all nine planets have chaotic orbits.

We have given one example of the analytical solution of a differential equation. We give here a similar example that uses Leibnitz's differentials, which may be more familiar to you. The equation $Y'(t) = Y(t)$ can be expressed

$$\frac{dy}{dt} = y$$

and solved by the following sequence of steps:

$$\frac{dy}{y} = dt,$$

$$\int \frac{dy}{y} = \int dt + C,$$

$$\ln|y| = t + C,$$

$$y = \pm e^{t+C} = C'e^t.$$

As another example we obtain the solution for Example 8.4. Using y as the dependent variable, we have

$$\frac{dy}{dt} = 1 - |y|y,$$

$$\frac{dy}{1 - |y|y} = dt,$$

$$\int \frac{dy}{1 - |y|y} = \int dt - C,$$

where the arbitrary constant has been given a negative sign for consistency with Example 8.4. This contains an absolute value, which is most easily handled by separately considering the cases $y \leq 0$ and $y \geq 0$. If necessary, the solution can be patched together later. For $y \leq 0$ we have

$$\begin{aligned} \arctan y &= t - C, \\ y &= \tan(t - C). \end{aligned}$$

For $y \geq 0$ we have

$$\frac{1}{2} \ln \left| \frac{1+y}{1-y} \right| = t - C.$$

To strip off the absolute values requires another case analysis. For $y < 1$ we have

$$y = \tanh(t - C),$$

and for $y > 1$ we have

$$y = \coth(t - C).$$

Also note that $y \equiv 1$ is a solution.

The analytical technique used in the preceding two examples for solving differential equations is called **separation of variables**. In its fullest generality this idea is applicable to any differential equation in which the right-hand side can be expressed as a product of a function of t only and a function of $Y(t)$ only. Often there is no dependence of the right-hand side function on t, in which case we say that the differential equation is **autonomous**. Such has been the case for the differential equations that we have solved analytically.

Example 8.5 Consider the initial-value problem

$$Y'(t) = -tY(t), \qquad Y(0) = 1.$$

We can divide by $Y(t)$ so that $Y(t)$ and $Y'(t)$ appear on the left-hand side only. Integrating this, we have

$$\int_0^t \frac{Y'(s)\,ds}{Y(s)} = \int_0^t -s\,ds,$$

and with the change of variables $y = Y(s)$ we get

$$\int_1^{Y(t)} \frac{dy}{y} = \int_0^t -s\,ds.$$

Thus, the problem has been reduced to that of integration:

$$[\ln y]_1^{Y(t)} = \left[\frac{-s^2}{2}\right]_0^t,$$

$$Y(t) = \exp\left(-\frac{t^2}{2}\right).$$

Analytical methods are often difficult or even impossible to apply; and unless they result in a relatively simple formula, they give little insight. For insight it is better to employ graphical methods. Consider

$$Y'(t) = \sin t \cdot Y(t).$$

This tells us that at any point (t, y) on a solution curve $y = Y(t)$ the slope $= \sin t \cdot y$. This formula could be used to tabulate slopes for various values of t and y as shown in Table 8.1. For example, $t = \pi/2$ and $y = 1$ gives a slope of 1, which is entered into the table. These data can be plotted by inserting little arrows of the appropriate slope at the appropriate point in the t-y plane. Then, as shown in Figure 8.6, solution curves can be drawn that are everywhere tangent to the little arrows. This is not very accurate, but much the same idea can be used to calculate highly accurate numerical solutions.

y	$-\pi$	$-\frac{5\pi}{6}$	$-\frac{\pi}{2}$	$-\frac{\pi}{6}$	0	$\frac{\pi}{6}$	$\frac{\pi}{2}$	$\frac{5\pi}{6}$	π
2	0	-1	-2	-1	0	1	2	1	0
1	0	$-\frac{1}{2}$	-1	$-\frac{1}{2}$	0	$\frac{1}{2}$	1	$\frac{1}{2}$	0
0	0	0	0	0	0	0	0	0	0
-1	0	$\frac{1}{2}$	1	$\frac{1}{2}$	0	$-\frac{1}{2}$	-1	$-\frac{1}{2}$	0
-2	0	1	2	1	0	-1	-2	-1	0

Table 8.1: Solution slopes

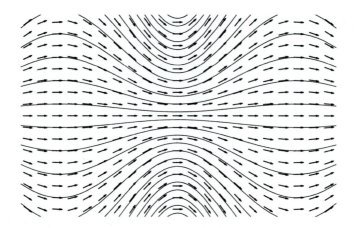

Figure 8.6: Curves tangent to solution slopes

8.1.2 The initial-value problem for a single ODE

Here we discuss the problem in its most general form. This is important if we want to write a program for solving an arbitrary differential equation. The differential equations we consider have the form

$$Y'(t) = f(t, Y(t))$$

where the **right-hand side** $f(t, y)$ is an expression, or more properly a function, of two variables. We regard the function $f(t, y)$ as specifying a slope at every point in the t-y plane, as depicted by the little arrows in Figure 8.7. The initial condition has the form

$$Y(a) = \eta$$

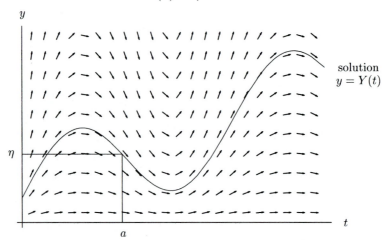

Figure 8.7: The general initial-value problem

where a and η are numbers. This specifies the point (a, η) in the t-y plane through which the solution $Y(t)$ must pass. Elsewhere $Y(t)$ is determined by the condition that it be everywhere tangent to the little arrows that fill the t-y plane.

Example 8.6 The choice

$$f(t,y) = -4(y + \cos t), \quad a = 0, \quad \eta = 1$$

corresponds to the ODE $Y'(t) = -4(Y(t) + \cos t)$ and the initial condition $Y(0) = 1$.

It is instructive to examine the special case $f(t,y) = f(t)$, where the right-hand side does not depend on the unknown. Integrating the differential equation in this case yields

$$\int_a^t Y'(s)\, ds = \int_a^t f(s)\, ds.$$

The initial condition implies that

$$Y(t) = \eta + \int_a^t f(s)\, ds.$$

The problem has been reduced to one of indefinite integration. All differential equations involve integration as part of their solution, and for this reason it is common for differential equations to use the word "integrating" to mean the same as "solving."

8.1.3 Stability

If we graph the set of solutions, we obtain a family of (normally) disjoint curves that go from left to right. An error in the initial condition will relocate us from one solution curve to another, so the propagation of such an error is governed by how the difference between the two solution curves changes as t increases. If the curves run "parallel" or converge (without ever actually meeting), the error will not grow. Such a problem is said to be **stable**. If the curves diverge, the error does grow, and the problem is said to be **unstable**. Both cases occur for the differential equation $Y'(t) = Y(t)(1 - Y(t))$, as shown in Figure 8.8. This differential equation has been used to describe population growth. Small populations are subject to exponential growth; large populations tend to a steady-state value.

Exercises

1. Suppose that an ODE has as its general solution $Y(t) = 3 + Ce^{-2t}$ where C is an arbitrary constant.

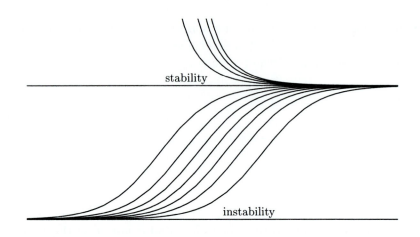

stability

instability

Figure 8.8: Stability and instability

    (a) Show that there exists a solution through any point (t_0, y_0) in the t-y plane.

    (b) Show that this is not true if instead $Y(t) = 3 + Ct$.

2. Obtain the general solution of $Y'(t) = Y(t)/t$ and also the particular solution for initial condition $Y(1) = \frac{1}{2}$.

3. Consider the differential equation

$$Y'(t) = Y(t)(1 - Y(t)).$$

    (a) Solve it for initial condition $Y(0) = \frac{1}{2}$.

    (b) Solve it for general initial conditions $Y(a) = \eta$. Indicate the interval on which the solution exists. (Be prepared to do a case analysis; and note that if the solution ceases to exist at a point, it does not exist beyond that point.)

4. Solve

$$Y'(t) = \frac{Y(t)^2}{t}, \quad t \geq 1,$$

given that $Y(1) = \eta$ where η is some number.

5. Although it is possible in unusual cases to have two solutions $Y_1(t)$ and $Y_2(t)$ to the ODE $Y'(t) = f(t, Y(t))$ coalesce, it is not possible for one solution to cross another solution at an angle. Explain.

6. Let $Y(t)$ solve an autonomous differential equation $Y'(t) = f(Y(t))$. Show that $\bar{Y}(t) \stackrel{\text{def}}{=} Y(t + c)$ where c is some constant is also a solution. Geometrically what is the relation between $\bar{Y}(t)$ and $Y(t)$?

Mathematica notes

The package `Graphics`PlotField`` defines `PlotVectorField[ ]`, which can be used to produce figures like Figures 8.6 and 8.7.

Read in the package.

In[1]:= `<< Graphics`PlotField``

A plot of arrows tangent to the solutions of $dy/dx = (\cos y)/(2 + \sin t)$.

In[2]:= `PlotVectorField[{1, Cos[y]/(2 + Sin[t])},`
        `{t, -6, 6}, {y, -6, 6},`
        `PlotPoints -> 20]`

The functions `DSolve[ ]` and `NDSolve[ ]` can be used to solve ordinary differential equations. Their syntax is similar, but for `NDSolve[ ]` you need to specify a domain for the solution. With either, you have the choice of solving for an expression that involves the independent variable or a function. For example, you might solve for `y[t]` or `y`. The distinction is purely one of form.

`DSolve[ ]` takes three arguments: a list containing the differential equation and initial condition, the unknown function, and the independent variable. As with `Solve[ ]`, the solution is given as a rule.

In[3]:= `DSolve[{y'[t] == t y[t], y[0] == 1}, y[t], t]`

Out[3]= `{{y[t] -> E`$^{t^2/2}$`}}`

If you solve for `y` rather than `y[t]`, you get a pure function for the solution.

In[4]:= `DSolve[{y'[t] == t y[t], y[0] == 1}, y, t]`

Out[4]= `{{y -> (E`$^{\#1^2/2}$` & )}}`

The solution given by `NDSolve[ ]` involves an `InterpolatingFunction`. An `InterpolatingFunction` can be evaluated at any place in its domain, and it carries with it a table of divided differences to do the interpolation. The divided differences themselves are not of direct use to users, so they are not displayed. The domain of the function is useful, and it is displayed.

With `NDSolve`, you have to specify the domain of the independent variable. The solution is given in the form of a rule involving an `InterpolatingFunction` defined on the specified domain. The "<>" indicates information not displayed.

```
In[5]:= NDSolve[{y'[t] == Sin[t] y[t], y[0] == 1}, y,
                {t, 0, 20}]

Out[5]= {{y -> InterpolatingFunction[{0., 20.}, <>]}}
```

You can evaluate the solution at any point in the domain. In particular you can `Plot` the solution. (The `Evaluate[y /. %[[1]]]` is for reasons of efficiency: `Plot[ ]` is `HoldAll`, and without the `Evaluate[ ]` the replacement would occur for each value of `t` rather than just once.)

```
In[6]:= Plot[Evaluate[y /. %[[1]]][t], {t, 0, 20},
            PlotPoints -> 75,
            Prolog -> Thickness[.001]]
```

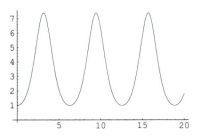

Computer problems

1. Use `PlotVectorField[ ]` to plot the tangent vectors to the solutions curves of

   (a) $Y'(t) = (\sin t)Y(t)$,

   (b) $Y'(t) = 1 + Y(t)^2$,

   (c) $Y'(t) = Y(t)(1 - Y(t))$.

2. Consider the ODE
$$Y'(t) = 1 - |Y(t)|^3.$$

   Use `NDSolve[ ]` to solve for `y[t]` on the interval $[0, 10]$ with the initial conditions

   (a) $Y(0) = -1$,

   (b) $Y(0) = -0.999$,

   (c) $Y(0) = -0.98$,

   (d) $Y(0) = -0.5$,

   (e) $Y(0) = 1.5$.

   Compare $y(10)$ of (a) and (b). Does this represent stability or instability? Compare $y(10)$ of (d) and (e). Does this represent stability or instability? What about (b) and (c)? Plot all five solutions together on the same set of axes.

8.2 Euler's Method

Numerical methods typically construct ODE solutions by obtaining their values on a finite set of **mesh points**

$$a = t_0 < t_1 < t_2 < \cdots < t_{n-1} < t_n < \cdots < t_N$$

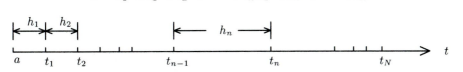

and filling in the gaps by interpolation. A mesh can be automatically chosen by an ODE integrator; the idea is similar in spirit to global adaptive quadrature but quite different in details. The difference between successive mesh points $h_n \overset{\text{def}}{=} t_n - t_{n-1}$ is called the **stepsize**. An ODE integrator generates the solution by marching forward in time t one step at a time: Given t_{n-1} and $y_{n-1} \approx Y(t_{n-1})$, it determines t_n and $y_n \approx Y(t_n)$. The entire process is started with the initial condition; it is continued by means of some discrete approximation to the differential equation. One step of such a process is graphed in Figure 8.9. Especially worth noting is that the numerical solution values y_{n-1} and y_n do not lie on the true solution. In fact, they do not even lie on the same solution. Rather, each step we take usually puts us on yet a different solution.

The simplest numerical method is Euler's method, but it gives a rather crude approximation. We introduce it for the example $V'(t) = 1 - V(t)^2$ where $V(t)$ represents an unknown velocity. The differential equation is a rule for determining $\frac{d}{dt}$ velocity (the acceleration) if we are given the velocity. Suppose we know the velocity at time t and want its value at time $t + \Delta t$. We can write

$$
\begin{aligned}
V(t + \Delta t) - V(t) &= \int_t^{t+\Delta t} V'(s)\,ds \\
&= \Delta t \cdot (\text{average } V' \text{ on } [t, t + \Delta t]) \\
&\approx \Delta t \cdot V'(t).
\end{aligned}
$$

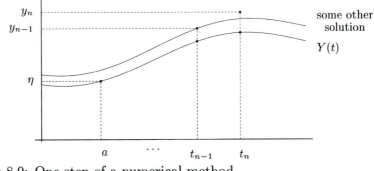

Figure 8.9: One step of a numerical method

That last step, in which the average acceleration is approximated by its initial value, is the basis of the Euler method. It is only an approximation because the acceleration is varying, as governed by the differential equation. We have computed, for the initial condition $V(0) = 0$, a few values using $\Delta t = 0.1$:

t	V	$V' = 1 - V^2$	$\Delta V \approx V' \cdot \Delta t$
0	0	1	0.1
0.1	0.1	0.99	0.099
0.2	0.199	0.96	0.096
0.3	0.295		

A derivation of Euler's method for the general ODE $Y(t) = f(t,\, Y(t))$ in the spirit of the preceding example is to imagine that $Y(t)$ denotes distance:

$$
\begin{aligned}
\text{distance} \ &= \ \text{time} \times \text{average velocity}, \\
Y(t_n) - Y(t_{n-1}) \ &= \ h_n \times \text{average } Y'(t) \\
&\approx \ h_n\, Y'(t_{n-1}) = h_n\, f(t_{n-1},\, Y(t_{n-1})).
\end{aligned}
$$

An alternative derivation of Euler's method is depicted in Figure 8.10. The idea is to use a linear approximation to the solution in the subinterval $[t_{n-1},\, t_n]$ such that its slope matches that of the ODE solution passing through the point $(t_{n-1},\, y_{n-1})$. This point is known, and the slope of the solution through it is given from the differential equation as $f(t_{n-1},\, y_{n-1})$. Equating this to the slope of the linear approximation gives

$$
\frac{y_n - y_{n-1}}{h_n} = f(t_{n-1}, y_{n-1}).
$$

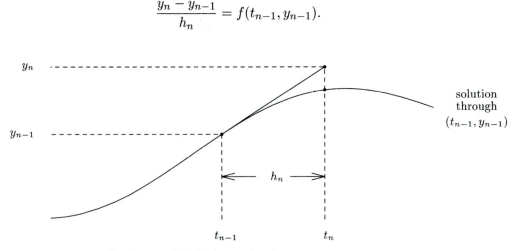

Figure 8.10: One step of Euler's method

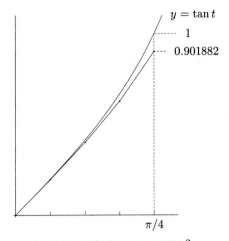

Figure 8.11: Euler's method for $Y'(t) = 1 + Y(t)^2$

This can be solved for the unknown value y_n to give the formula

$$y_n = y_{n-1} + h_n\, f(t_{n-1}, y_{n-1}).$$

Let us consider how to program such a method. We give a program for an example that will be considered again in Section 8.5. The differential equation is $Y'(t) = 1 + Y(t)^2$, the initial condition is $Y(0) = 0$, and we wish to calculate $Y(\pi/4)$. The program is written in *Mathematica*, but it resembles code written in other programming languages.

```
f[t_, y_] := 1. + y^2
eta = 0.
a = 0.; b = N[Pi]/4.
n = 4
Module[{h = (b-a)/n, t = a, y = eta}, (* local variables *)
    Print[t, y];
    Do[ y = y + h f[t, y];
        t = t + h;
        Print[t, y]
    ,{n}] (* n times *)
]
```

Note how new values of the solution overwrite old values. This would be important for reasons of storage economy if we were solving a very large system of differential equations. Also note that the code inside the `Module` is good for any differential equation; we need only redefine `f[t_,y_]`. Plots of the numerical solution and the true solution are given in Figure 8.11. Piecewise linear interpolation has been used to fill in the numerical solution.

It is said, "Newton in his *Principia* [of 1687] was the first to find approximate solutions of differential equations by numerical processes"[3] but that it was Leonhard Euler, in 1768, who "is basically responsible for the present-day methods."[4] Euler published a description of his method for the general problem

$$\frac{dy}{dx} = f(x, y).$$

In spite of its very low accuracy, the Euler method is used in some applications. For example, the first digital differential analyzer, MADDIDA, built in 1950, used the Euler method, but with a very small stepsize.

It is useful to know something about how errors arise in numerical solutions of differential equations. To explain the situation, we need to introduce the **local (discretization) error**. At time t_n we find ourselves at the point (t_n, y_n). It is (probably) not on the true solution but rather on some nearby solution $U(t)$. Mathematically this means that

$$U(t_n) = y_n \quad \text{and} \quad U'(t) = f(t, \, U(t)).$$

We call $U(t)$ the *local solution*. There is a (generally) different local solution for each solution point (t_n, y_n). If there is any danger of confusion, we can distinguish between them by using $U_n(t)$ for the local solution through the nth solution point. To advance the solution to t_{n+1}, the best we can do is follow the curve $y = U(t)$ exactly and compute $U(t_{n+1})$ exactly (unless we go back and use older information). The amount

$$d_{n+1} \stackrel{\text{def}}{=} y_{n+1} - U(t_{n+1})$$

is the local error. It is the error that should be attributed to the taking of the $(n+1)$th step. This is pictured in Figure 8.12. A useful expression can be obtained for the local error. Both y_{n+1} and $U(t_{n+1})$ can be expressed or expanded in terms of $U(t)$ at $t = t_n$. Employing the equations that define y_{n+1} and $U(t)$, we get

$$y_{n+1} = U(t_n) + h_{n+1} U'(t_n).$$

A Taylor formula with remainder gives

$$U(t_{n+1}) = U(t_n) + h_{n+1} U'(t_n) + \frac{h_{n+1}^2}{2} U''(\tau_{n+1}).$$

Substituting into the definition of local error, we get

$$d_{n+1} = -\frac{h_{n+1}^2}{2} U''(\tau_{n+1}).$$

---

[3]F. R. Moulton, *Differential Equations*, Macmillan, New York, 1930.

[4]H. H. Goldstine, *A History of Numerical Analysis from the 16th through the 19th Century*, Springer Verlag, New York, 1977.

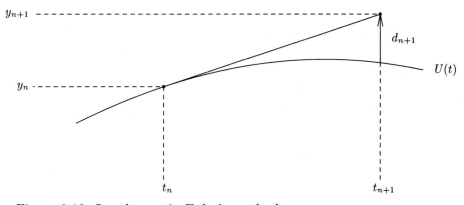

Figure 8.12: Local error in Euler's method

The error that we really care about, $e_n \stackrel{\text{def}}{=} y_n - Y(t_n)$, is often called the **global (discretization) error** to distinguish it from the local error. The relationship between the two is sketched in Figure 8.13. What we have is

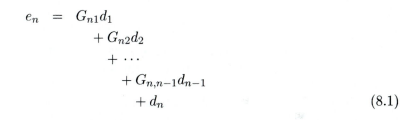

$$
\begin{aligned}
e_n \;=\; & G_{n1}d_1 \\
& + G_{n2}d_2 \\
& + \cdots \\
& + G_{n,n-1}d_{n-1} \\
& + d_n
\end{aligned}
\tag{8.1}
$$

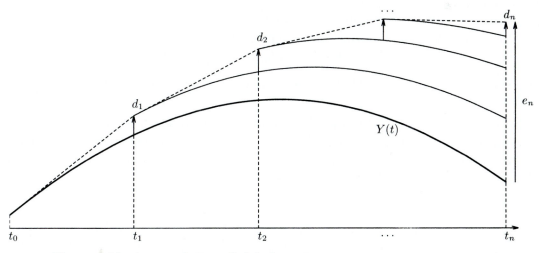

Figure 8.13: Accumulation of global error

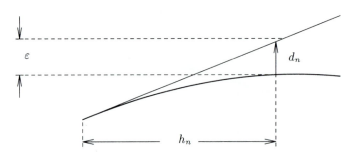

Figure 8.14: Stepsize selection

where each of the terms $G_{nj}d_j$ represents a difference between two neighboring solution curves at $t = t_n$. The *growth factor*

$$G_{nj} \overset{\text{def}}{=} \frac{\text{propagated } d_j}{d_j}$$

depends on the stability of the differential equation.

The general idea behind stepsize-selection mechanisms in ODE solvers is to choose h_n just small enough that

$$|d_n| \le \varepsilon \overset{\text{def}}{=} \text{local-error tolerance,}$$

where the **local-error tolerance** is some parameter, often specified by the user. It is clear from Figure 8.14 that reducing h_n reduces the local error, and, in fact, our local-error analysis shows a reduction like the square of h_n. To control the local error, one needs a local-error estimate. The details of how this is obtained are beyond the scope of this book. (See, however, Computer Problem 1 of Section 8.4.) The global error is shown by Equation (8.1) to depend on

- the sizes of the d_j, which are affected by ε,
- the growth factors G_{nj}, which are determined by the stability of the ODE,
- the number of steps n, which depends on the length of the interval and the ODE.

Only the first is under the control of the user; the last two depend on the *difficulty of the problem*.

Recall that the order of accuracy is that power of h to which the error is proportional. For ordinary differential equations the error of concern is the global error. Let us consider a uniform stepsize $h = (b - a)/N$ and look at the error $y_N - Y(b)$ at the end of the interval, as indicated in Figure 8.15. The global error is

$$e_n = \sum_{j=1}^{N} G_{nj}d_j = \sum_{j=1}^{N} O(h^2).$$

Hence, this error is proportional to $Nh^2 = (b - a)h$, making the order equal to 1.

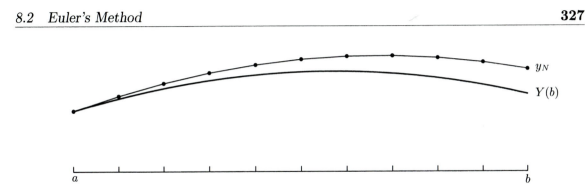

Figure 8.15: Global error at the end

The global error we are considering is pure truncation error, arising from the local truncation errors d_n added in at each step. Strictly speaking it should be called the *global truncation error*, because with the use of floating-point arithmetic there will be an additional error due to rounding. This will result in a *global rounding error*, which is the difference between the numerical solution computed with rounded arithmetic and the numerical solution computed with exact arithmetic. The overall global error is a sum of the global truncation error and the global rounding error.

The effects of roundoff can be significant for ODEs, especially in single precision. In both quadrature and ODEs the outer loop of the computation is essentially a long sum—the discrete analog of integration—and the many roundoff errors can add up to a significant error.

Example 8.7 Consider the application of Euler's method with uniform stepsize $h = 0.1$ to

$$Y'(t) = 0.234, \quad Y(0) = 1$$

for $0 \le t \le 1$ using four-decimal-digit rounded arithmetic. We get $y_0 = 1$ and

$$
\begin{aligned}
y_n &= y_{n-1} \,\hat{+}\, 0.1 \,\hat{\times}\, 0.234 = y_{n-1} \,\hat{+}\, 0.0234 \\
&= y_{n-1} + 0.023,
\end{aligned}
$$

because the digit 4 gets dropped when 0.0234 is added to a number of the form $1.d_2 d_3 d_4$. The computed value of y_{10} is thus 1.230 rather than 1.234. If we had used a stepsize $h = 0.01$, the computed value would be 1.200 at $t = 1$.

In the preceding example, smaller stepsizes lead to larger (global) roundoff errors. Let us look at the general situation. The equations for Euler's method are

$$y_1 = y_0 + h_1\, f(t_0,\, y_0), \quad \ldots, \quad y_N = y_{N-1} + h_N\, f(t_{N-1},\, y_{N-1}).$$

This is one big sum,

$$y_N = y_0 + \sum_{n=1}^{N} h_n\, f(t_{n-1}, y_{n-1}).$$

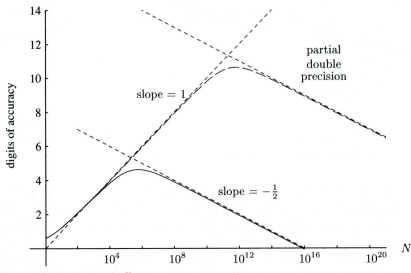

Figure 8.16: Roundoff error vs. truncation error

As suggested by Example 8.7, the major source of roundoff error is typically the floating-point addition. This gives a global roundoff error that is proportional to $\sqrt{N}$ for rounding (and proportional to N for chopping). With a uniform stepsize on an interval of length $b - a$ we have $h = (b-a)/N$, and hence the global truncation error, for Euler's method, is proportional to $1/N$. The combined effect of the two types of errors is shown in Figure 8.16. You notice from this graph that as N is increased there is a point at which the gain arising from the decreasing truncation error is overwhelmed by the increasing roundoff error.

One treatment for the roundoff error due to the long sum is partial double precision:

```
    ⋮
y = dble[eta]
    ⋮
y = y + dble[ h * f[t, N[y]] ]
    ⋮
```

Here N converts to machine precision, and dble converts to twice the machine precision (see page 57). Another remedy, which avoids higher precision, is magic adding (for references see page 67).

Review question

1. If the local truncation error $d_j = O(h)$, what can be said about the global error as $h \to 0$?

Exercises

1. Give a closed-form expression for y_N obtained by Euler's method with stepsize $1/N$ for $Y'(t) = Y(t)$, $Y(0) = 1$.

2. Show all the steps needed to obtain the equation $y_{n+1} = U(t_n) + h_{n+1}U'(t_n)$ in the analysis of the local error.

3. For the differential equation $Y'(t) = Y(t)$, a local error introduced into the numerical solution at mesh point t_n will have an effect on the numerical solution at some later mesh point t_N that is $\exp(t_N - t_n)$ times as great. Suppose we have a mesh $0 < 0.1 < 0.3 < 0.6 < 1.0$ with local errors $0.02, 0.01, 0.05, 0.04$ introduced at the end of each of the four steps in the order given. What is the global error at $t = 1.0$?

4. Express the propagated local error $G_{nj}d_j$ in Equation (8.1) in terms of local solutions $U_i(t)$.

Mathematica notes

The *Mathematica* function `NestList[ ]` produces a list of the successive iterates of some function, which must be specified as the first argument. Since that is exactly what Euler's method does, any differential equation of the form $Y'(t) = f(Y(t))$ can be solved very easily with Euler's method in *Mathematica* using `NestList[ ]`.

Choose a stepsize.

```
In[1]:= h = 0.1
Out[1]= 0.1
```

Use Euler's method to find an approximate solution to $Y'(t) = Y(t)/2$. The iterator function `(# + h #/2)&` represents the method $y_n = y_{n-1} + hy_{n-1}/2$. The second argument is the initial value, and the third argument is the number of steps to take.

```
In[2]:= NestList[(# + h #/2)&, 1., 20]
Out[2]= {1,, 1.05, 1.1025, 1.15763, 1.21551, 1.27628,
   1.3401, 1.4071, 1.47746, 1.55133, 1.62889, 1.71034,
   1.79586, 1.88565, 1.97993, 2.07893, 2.18287, 2.29202,
   2.40662, 2.52695, 2.6533}
```

Differential equations of the form $Y'(t) = f(t, Y(t))$ can handled in a similar way, but it is slightly more complicated. We will represent the numerical solution as a list of ordered pairs (t, y).

Choose a stepsize.

```
In[3]:= h = 0.1
Out[3]= 0.1
```

Define a function will take us from one point to the next point. This represents Euler's method for the ODE $Y'(t) = tY(t)$.

```
In[4]:= step[{t_, y_}] := {t + h, y + h t y}
```

Find an approximate solution to
$Y'(t) = tY(t)$.

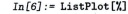
```
In[5]:= NestList[step, {0., 1.}, 20]
Out[5]= {{0., 1.}, {0.1, 1.}, {0.2, 1.01}, {0.3, 1.0302},
         {0.4, 1.06111}, {0.5, 1.10355}, {0.6, 1.15873},
         {0.7, 1.22825}, {0.8, 1.31423}, {0.9, 1.41937},
         {1., 1.54711}, {1.1, 1.70182}, {1.2, 1.88902},
         {1.3, 2.1157}, {1.4, 2.39075}, {1.5, 2.72545},
         {1.6, 3.13427}, {1.7, 3.63575}, {1.8, 4.25383},
         {1.9, 5.01952}, {2., 5.97323}}
```

Plot the numerical solution.

```
In[6]:= ListPlot[%]
```

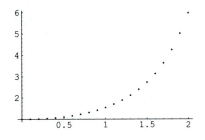

Computer problems

1. Redo the example of Figure 8.11 for the interval $[0, \pi/2]$ instead of $[0, \pi/4]$ using $N = 8$, then 16, and then 32. (The differential equation is $Y'(t) = 1 + Y(t)^2$; the initial condition is $Y(0) = 0$.) For each solution, use `ListPlot` with `PlotJoined -> True` to plot the numerical solution using piecewise linear interpolation to fill it in.

2. Define a function `euler[f_, y0_, {a_, b_, h_}]` that takes a function `f` of two arguments (corresponding to the function on the right-hand side of the ODE $Y'(t) = f(t, Y(t))$), an initial value `y0`, and the domain specification `{a, b, h}`. Your function `euler[ ]` should use Euler's method to find an approximate solution to the ODE on the interval $[a, b]$ using stepsize `h`. Test it on the ODE $Y'(t) = \sin(t)Y(t)$ on the interval $[0, 20]$ with initial condition $Y(0) = 1$. Use `ListPlot[ ]` with `PlotJoined -> True` to plot the approximate solution.

8.3 Systems of ODEs

We begin with two examples of systems of ODEs.

Example 8.8 We consider a simple model of a predator–prey relationship involving rabbits and foxes. Let $R(t)$ be the rabbit population at time t, and let $F(t)$ be the fox population.

The rate of change of the populations might be governed by the equations

$$R'(t) = 2R(t) - 0.01R(t)F(t),$$
$$F'(t) = -F(t) + 0.01R(t)F(t).$$

Noticeable in these equations is the negative effect that $F(t)$ has on $R'(t)$ and the positive effect of $R(t)$ on $F'(t)$. These differential equations cannot be solved separately because of the *coupling*; they have to be solved simultaneously. Also, to get a particular solution, initial conditions are required—one for each dependent variable, for example, $R(0) = 300$ and $F(0) = 150$.

Example 8.9 Consider the revolution of one body around another much larger body in outer space, as depicted in Figure 8.17. The position $(X(t),\ Y(t))$ of the smaller body obeys Newton's second law of motion, and under the assumption that the mass of the smaller body is negligible compared to the mass M of the larger body, the equations are

$$X''(t) = \frac{-GMX(t)}{[X(t)^2 + Y(t)^2]^{3/2}},$$
$$Y''(t) = \frac{-GMY(t)}{[X(t)^2 + Y(t)^2]^{3/2}},$$

where the force per unit mass has been determined from Newton's law of gravitational attraction with G as the universal gravitational constant. These constitute a pair of *second-order* ODEs. Undoing the two differentiations in each equation will introduce a total of four arbitrary constants. These can be nailed down by prescribing initial conditions for $X(t)$ and $Y(t)$

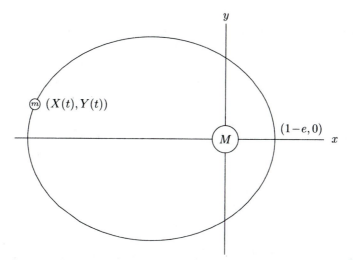

Figure 8.17: Revolution of one body around another

and their first derivatives. An example of initial conditions is given by

$$X(0) = 1 - e, \quad X'(0) = 0, \quad Y(0) = 0, \quad Y'(0) = \sqrt{GM\frac{1+e}{1-e}},$$

where e is some number such that $0 \leq e < 1$. The solution is known to be periodic with period $2\pi/\sqrt{GM}$.

Higher-order differential equations such as those of this example can be rewritten as a greater number of first-order equations by introducing additional dependent variables.

Example 8.9 (continued) If we introduce the velocity components $U(t) \stackrel{\text{def}}{=} X'(t)$ and $V(t) \stackrel{\text{def}}{=} Y'(t)$ as additional unknowns and use these definitions as additional equations, we get the initial-value problem

$$\begin{aligned} X'(t) &= U(t), & X(0) &= 1 - e, \\ Y'(t) &= V(t), & Y(0) &= 0, \\ U'(t) &= \frac{-GMX(t)}{[X(t)^2 + Y(t)^2]^{3/2}}, & U(0) &= 0, \\ V'(t) &= \frac{-GMY(t)}{[X(t)^2 + Y(t)^2]^{3/2}}, & V(0) &= \sqrt{GM(1+e)/(1-e)}, \end{aligned}$$

which has four first-order ODEs with four unknowns and four initial conditions.

The general initial-value problem for a system of two ODEs is

$$\begin{aligned} X'(t) &= f(t, X(t), Y(t)), & X(a) &= \xi, \\ Y'(t) &= g(t, X(t), Y(t)), & Y(a) &= \eta. \end{aligned}$$

A specific choice, for example, $f(t, x, y) = y$, $a = 0$, $\xi = 3.1$, $g(t, x, y) = (57.3 - 15000 \sin 100t)x$, $\eta = 0$, gives a problem that can actually be solved. A system of three ODEs has the form

$$\begin{aligned} X'(t) &= f(t, X(t), Y(t), Z(t)), & X(a) &= \xi, \\ Y'(t) &= g(t, X(t), Y(t), Z(t)), & Y(a) &= \eta, \\ Z'(t) &= h(t, X(t), Y(t), Z(t)), & Z(a) &= \zeta. \end{aligned}$$

It would certainly be a nuisance if we needed different programs for ODE systems of each different dimension. To handle any number of equations, we need to index the unknowns. We use superscripts for this purpose, because subscripts are already in use to denote values at particular mesh points. A general system of n ODEs can be written

$$\frac{d}{dt}Y^1(t) = f^1(t, Y^1(t), Y^2(t), \ldots, Y^n(t)), \quad Y^1(a) = \eta^1,$$

$$\frac{d}{dt}Y^2(t) = f^2(t, Y^1(t), Y^2(t), \ldots, Y^n(t)), \quad Y^2(a) = \eta^2,$$

$$\vdots$$

$$\frac{d}{dt}Y^n(t) = f^n(t, Y^1(t), Y^2(t), \ldots, Y^n(t)), \quad Y^n(a) = \eta^n.$$

The dependent variables can be collected together as a **state vector**

$$\boldsymbol{Y}(t) \stackrel{\text{def}}{=} \begin{bmatrix} Y^1(t) \\ Y^2(t) \\ \vdots \\ Y^n(t) \end{bmatrix}$$

that completely describes the physical system at time t. The state variables could be populations of different animal species or concentrations of different chemical species or branch currents and node potentials in an electric circuit. The initial condition tells us the state at time $t = a$:

$$\boxed{Y^i(a) = \eta^i, \quad i = 1, 2, \ldots, n.}$$

The ODE tells us how to go from the state at time t to the state at time $t + dt$ where dt is infinitesimal:

$$\frac{Y^i(t + dt) - Y^i(t)}{dt} = f^i(t, Y^1(t), Y^2(t), \ldots, Y^n(t))$$

$$\Downarrow$$

$$\boxed{\begin{aligned} Y^i(t + dt) = Y^i(t) + dt \cdot f^i(t, Y^1(t), Y^2(t), \ldots, Y^n(t)), \\ i = 1, 2, \ldots, n. \end{aligned}}$$

This is exactly true for only an infinitesimal time increment; for a finite time interval it is an approximation—in fact, it is Euler's method.

Using our customary notation, we look at Euler's method for the general system of two ODEs,

$$X'(t) = f(t, X(t), Y(t)),$$

$$Y'(t) = g(t, X(t), Y(t)).$$

Applying the method separately to each equation, we get

$$x_n = x_{n-1} + hf(t_{n-1}, x_{n-1}, y_{n-1}),$$

$$y_n = y_{n-1} + hg(t_{n-1}, x_{n-1}, y_{n-1}).$$

If for each successive value of n, we compute both x_n and y_n, the coupling presents no problem. The values of x_{n-1} and y_{n-1} will be available for computing x_n and y_n.

Following is a *Mathematica* function for computing by Euler's method the solution to the rabbit and foxes problem at equally spaced points from $t = 0$ to $t = 10$:

```
euler[n_] := (* n is the number of steps *)
   Module[{ h, soln, r, f, r1, f1}, (* local variables *)
      h = 10./N[n];
      soln = Table[{Null, Null, Null}, {n+1}];
           (* initialize to an array of n+1 triples *)
      r = 300.; f = 150.;
      soln[[1]] = {0., r, f};
      Do[ r1 = (2. - 0.01f) r; f1 = (0.01r - 1.) f;
         r = r + h r1; f = f + h f1;
         soln[[i+1]] = {i h, r, f}
      , {i, 1, n}];
      soln
   ]
```

The results of plotting the rabbit population for stepsize $h = 10/100$ and for stepsize $h = 10/200$ are shown in Figure 8.18. In the first run with $h = 0.1$ it appears that the rabbits died off. However, the second run with $h = 0.05$ shows that it was *truncation error* that killed them!

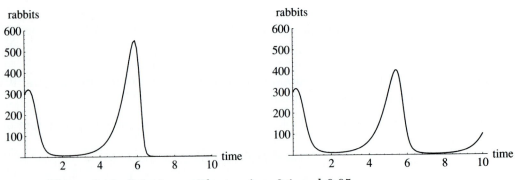

Figure 8.18: Solutions with stepsizes 0.1 and 0.05

Exercises

1. Consider the equations in Example 8.8 for rabbit and fox populations.

   (a) Is there a particular solution to this problem for which the rabbit and fox populations stay constant?

   (b) How many foxes must there be to bring about a decrease in the rabbit population?

   (c) What happens to the rabbit population if there are no foxes? Is this realistic for small R? for large R? Explain.

2. If $X(t)$ is the position and m the mass of a particle and if $V(x)$ is potential energy, then Newton's second law is

   $$m\ X''(t) = -V'(X(t)).$$

   (a) Prove that $\frac{1}{2}m(X'(t))^2 + V(X(t))$ is constant for all t.

   (b) What is the physical significance of what you proved in part (a)?

3. Show that if $X(t)$ and $Y(t)$ solve the differential equations of Example 8.9, then

   $$\frac{1}{2}\left(X'(t)^2 + Y'(t)^2\right) - \frac{GM}{[X(t)^2 + Y(t)^2]^{1/2}}$$

   is constant for all t. Monitoring this value is one way to check the accuracy of a numerical solution.

4. Write the following problem in standard form as a system of first-order ordinary differential equations with initial conditions:

   $$U'(t) = -U(t)V''(t), \quad U(1) = 1,$$

   $$V'''(t) + (U(t) - V(t))^2 = \frac{1}{t}, \quad V(1) = 0, \quad V'(1) = 1, \quad V''(1) = 0.$$

5. Determine t_n, r_n, f_n, r'_n, f'_n for $n = 0, 1$ for Euler's method applied to

   $$\begin{aligned} R' &= 2R - 0.1RF, & R(0) &= 300, \\ F' &= -F + 0.1RF, & F(0) &= 150 \end{aligned}$$

   with stepsize $h = 0.001$.

6. Apply one step of Euler's method with stepsize 0.1 to the initial-value problem

   $$Y'(t) = Y(t) - 2\ Z(t) + 4t, \qquad Y(0) = 1,$$

   $$Z'(t) = 3Y(t) - 4\ Z(t) + 5t, \qquad Z(0) = 2.$$

   Give a numerical answer.

Mathematica notes

The function `NDSolve[ ]` can be used to find solutions to systems of ordinary differential equations. As an example we consider the solution to the problem in Example 8.8.

Solve the problem.

```
In[1]:= sol = NDSolve[{r'[t] == 2r[t] - 0.01 r[t] f[t],
           f'[t] == -f[t] + 0.01 r[t] f[t],
           r[0] == 300, f[0] == 150},
          {r[t], f[t]}, {t, 0, 20}]

Out[1]= {{r[t] ->
         InterpolatingFunction[{0., 20.}, <>][t],
         f[t] -> InterpolatingFunction[{0., 20.}, <>][t]}}
```

Plot the rabbit population.

```
In[2]:= Plot[Evaluate[r[t] /. sol[[1]]], {t, 0, 20}]
```

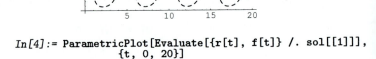

Plot both populations on the same set of axes.

```
In[3]:= Plot[Evaluate[{r[t], f[t]} /. sol[[1]]],
          {t, 0, 20}, PlotStyle ->
           {Dashing[{.02}], Dashing[{.007}]}]
```

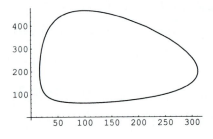

Plot the population orbit. This type of plot is sometimes called a phase-space plot.

```
In[4]:= ParametricPlot[Evaluate[{r[t], f[t]} /. sol[[1]]],
          {t, 0, 20}]
```

NDSolve[ ] returns the approximate solution to the ODE as an InterpolatingFunction, which you can use like any other function. However, it first finds the solution in the form of a list of values, just as you do when you use Euler's method or any other numerical ODE method. It then constructs the InterpolatingFunction from that list.

In some of the problems below you will need to manipulate solution lists. In particular you will need to extract columns from a matrix. One way to do that is to use an advanced feature of Part[ ]. In particular, a[[{1, 3, 4}, {3, 2}]] gives a 3 × 2 matrix consisting of the first, third, and fourth rows intersected with the third and second columns. Likewise, a[[Range[Length[a]], 3]] gives a *vector* consisting of the third column of the matrix a. (Range[Length[a]] evaluates to a specification of all the rows.)

Computer problems

1. Use NestList[ ] and Euler's method to solve the problem of the rabbits and foxes on the interval $0. \leq t \leq 20.$ with $h = 0.04, 0.02, 0.01$. Let the solution be represented by a list of triples (t_n, r_n, f_n), and define and use a function step[{t_, r_, f_}] that gives the next triple after {t, r, f}. Plot each solution separately in phase space.

2. This problem models (by classical mechanics) the interaction between two argon atoms. In particular, we determine their separation $R(t)$ in angstroms as a function of time t in picoseconds. At separations exceeding 3.816 Å there is a weak van der Waals attraction, and at closer distances there is a strong hard-core repulsion. Examining trajectories of the solutions in phase space—a parametric plot of $(R(t), R'(t))$—shows there are two types. Some trajectories are closed curves that represent an oscillating motion, characteristic of the solid or liquid phase. Others are open curves that go off to infinity, the gas phase. Each trajectory represents a different total energy of the system. The data for this problem come from a 1964 article by A. Rahman of Argonne National Labs (near Chicago), who was using machine language and Fortran on a CDC 3600 with floating-point arithmetic and an IBM 704 with fixed-point arithmetic in order to model up to 864 atoms. This was the first attempt to do molecular dynamics with a realistic force field. Today biomolecular modeling, and drug design in particular, is a major application of supercomputers. (Fortran is still the language used.)

   (a) Write a program for numerically solving the ODE $Y''(t) = f(Y(t))$, $0 \leq t \leq T$, given $Y(0)$, $Y'(0)$. Your program should have parameters f_, yinit_, ypinit_, tfinal_, h_, where f is a function rather than, say, an expression in y and the other parameters have obvious meanings. Your program should return a list of triples

   $$\{\{t_0, y_0, y_0'\}, \{t_1, y_1, y_1'\}, \ldots, \{t_N, y_N, y_N'\}\}$$

   where $t_{N-1} < t_{\text{final}} \leq t_N$. Important note: y' represents nothing more than the name of a subscripted variable (you might call it yp), not the derivative of y (which would not make much sense since y is not a function). Use a numerical method, attributed to Störmer and to Verlet, in which the $(n+1)$th step is

$$
\begin{aligned}
y'_{n+1/2} &= y'_n + \frac{h}{2}y''_n, \\
y_{n+1} &= y_n + hy'_{n+1/2}, \\
y''_{n+1} &= f(y_{n+1}), \\
y'_{n+1} &= y'_{n+1/2} + \frac{h}{2}y''_{n+1}.
\end{aligned}
$$

Note: Applying this method to $f(Y) = -Y$ to get $(Y(t), Y'(t))$ is a quick way to plot a good circle. (Use this fact to debug your program.) You will need to define a function that goes from $\{t_n, y_n, y'_n\}$ to $\{t_{n+1}, y_{n+1}, y'_{n+1}\}$. You could use NestList[ ] as the basic building block, but it is simpler just to use Table[ ] and assign values to variables within Table[ ].

(b) Apply your program to the problem

$$
R''(t) = 34.7 \left(\frac{3.4}{R(t)}\right)^7 \left[2\left(\frac{3.4}{R(t)}\right)^6 - 1\right], \quad 0 \le t \le 12.64,
$$

$$
R(0) = 6.46, \quad R'(0) = 0.
$$

Use a stepsize in the range 0.01 to 0.1. (Rahman used 0.01.) Do a ListPlot with $R(t)$ as the vertical axis and t as the horizontal axis. Label it "waveform."

(c) Do a ListPlot with $R'(t)$ as the vertical axis and $R(t)$ as the horizontal axis, thereby getting the trajectory in phase space. Label it "trajectory."

3. Use NDSolve[ ] to solve

$$
X''(t) = -X(t)(X(t)^2 + Y(t)^2)^{-3/2}, \quad X(0) = 0.1, \quad X'(0) = 0,
$$

$$
Y''(t) = -Y(t)(X(t)^2 + Y(t)^2)^{-3/2}, \quad Y(0) = 0, \quad Y'(0) = 4.4,
$$

$0 < t < 13$. Use ParametricPlot[ ] to plot the orbit $(X(t), Y(t))$ in the x-y plane. Repeat with $Y'(0) = 4.5$.

4. This problem illustrates the difference between waveform and phase-space plots and the meaning of instability.

(a) Duffing's equation
$$
Y''(t) + 0.05Y'(t) + Y(t)^3 = 7.5\cos t
$$

is given in a book by Thompson and Stewart as an example of chaotic behavior.[5] Use `NDSolve[ ]` to integrate this ODE up to $t = 6\pi$ for initial conditions

$$Y(0) = 3, \quad Y'(0) = 4$$

and use `Timing` to see how long it takes. You may have to increase the option `MaxSteps` to be more than 500.

(b) Plot $Y(t)$ versus t and label it "waveform."

(c) Use `ParametricPlot[ ]` to plot $Y'(t)$ versus $Y(t)$ and label it "trajectory." Note: Do the replacement with $/.$ before differentiating.

(d) Let $U(t)$ also satisfy Duffing's equation but with the slightly different initial conditions
$$U(0) = 3.01, \quad U'(0) = 4.01.$$

Use `NDSolve[ ]` to solve for $Y(t)$ and $U(t)$ simultaneously, as though they were a coupled system of ODEs. (Yes, this will require four initial conditions.) The advantage of combining the two problems is that their solutions will be calculated for the same set of mesh points $\{t_n\}$. (Also truncation errors will be similar for $Y(t)$ and $U(t)$, making comparison more reliable.) Use `Timing` to see how long it takes, and use the same integration interval as before.

(e) Plot the difference `u[t]` - `y[t]` and label it "effect of perturbation."

5. Consider a projectile being fired vertically from the surface of the earth. If $x(t)$ is its height and $v(t)$ is its upward velocity at time t, then (from Newton's second law of motion and his law of gravitation with rotation and atmospheric effects neglected) one can derive the ODE

$$X'(t) = V(t),$$
$$V'(t) = -g\frac{r^2}{(r + X(t))^2}.$$

Let $r = 6378.388\,\text{km}$ and $g = 0.00980621\,\text{km/sec}^2$. If the initial velocity is $\sqrt{2gr}$ or larger, the projectile will never fall back to earth. Use `NDSolve[ ]` to find the maximum height that a projectile starting with an initial velocity of 99% of $\sqrt{2gr}$ will reach. Note: `FindRoot[ ]` has a form that restricts the search to an interval.

---

[5]J.M.T. Thompson and H.B. Stewart, *Nonlinear Dynamics and Chaos: Geometrical Methods for Engineers and Scientists*, Wiley, New York, 1988.

8.4 Taylor-Series Methods

Analysis of the local error of the Euler method revealed that it used the first two terms of the Taylor expansion of the ODE solution $U(t)$ passing through the point $(t_n,\ y_n)$. The obvious improvement would be to add the third term. But can this be readily computed? The first term, $U(t_n) = y_n$, is available as a result of the previous step (or from the initial condition). The second term, $U'(t_n) = f(t_n,\ U(t_n))$, is available from the differential equation in terms of the first term, $U(t_n)$. If we can determine $U''(t_n)$, we can construct the approximation

$$U(t) \approx U(t_n) + (t - t_n)U'(t_n) + \frac{(t - t_n)^2}{2}U''(t_n),$$

which could be evaluated at $t = t_{n+1}$ to determine y_{n+1}. This is shown in Figure 8.19. The value of $U''(t_n)$ *can* be obtained, simply by differentiating the ODE and evaluating the resulting expression. This is best explained by means of an example.

Example 8.10 With $f(t, y) = t^2 + y^2$ we have

$$U'(t) = t^2 + U(t)^2,$$

so

$$U''(t) = 2t + 2U(t)U'(t).$$

Define $y'_n = U'(t_n)$ and $y''_n = U''(t_n)$. Note that the symbols y'_n and y''_n are merely names of numerical values; they cannot be derivatives of the numerical value y_n because a number

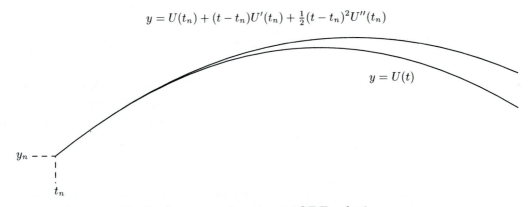

$$y = U(t_n) + (t - t_n)U'(t_n) + \tfrac{1}{2}(t - t_n)^2 U''(t_n)$$

$$y = U(t)$$

y_n

t_n

Figure 8.19: Taylor approximation to ODE solution

cannot be differentiated. With this understanding we have

$$
\begin{aligned}
y_n' &= t_n^2 + y_n^2, \\
y_n'' &= 2t_n + 2y_n y_n', \\
y_{n+1} &= y_n + h_{n+1} y_n' + \frac{h_{n+1}^2}{2} y_n''.
\end{aligned}
$$

For example, with $t_n = 2$, $y_n = 1$, and $h = 0.1$ we get $y_n' = 5$, $y_n'' = 14$, and $y_{n+1} = 1.57$. Be aware that y_{n+1} only approximates $U(t_{n+1})$.

The local error at the $(n+1)$th step is

$$
d_{n+1} = -\frac{h_{n+1}^3}{3!} U'''(t_n + \theta h_{n+1})
$$

for some unknown θ between 0 and 1. An error like this is committed at every step, and after a number of steps proportional to $1/h$ it accumulates to give a global error that is proportional to h^2. Hence, the order of accuracy is 2, and we call this the **second-order Taylor method**.

On the basis of the example you can see that more generally we can obtain

$$
\begin{aligned}
U'(t) &= f(t, U(t)), \\
U''(t) &= \frac{d}{dt} f(t, U(t)) \stackrel{\text{def}}{=} f_2(t, U(t), U'(t)), \\
&\;\;\vdots \\
U^{(p)}(t) &= \frac{d}{dt} f_{p-1}(t, U(t), \ldots, U^{(p-2)}(t)) \stackrel{\text{def}}{=} f_p(t, U(t), \ldots, U^{(p-1)}(t)).
\end{aligned}
$$

The symbols $f_j(\ldots)$ are names for the expressions we get when we differentiate; for Example 8.10 this is $f_2(t, y, z) = 2t + 2yz$. Once these expressions are generated we can use them at each step to generate values $y_n^{(j)} \stackrel{\text{def}}{=} U^{(j)}(t_n)$ of derivatives of the local solution:

$$
\begin{aligned}
y_n' &= f(t_n, y_n), \\
y_n'' &= f_2(t_n, y_n, y_n'), \\
&\;\;\vdots \\
y_n^{(p)} &= f_p(t_n, y_n, \ldots, y_n^{(p-1)}).
\end{aligned}
$$

The step can now be taken using

$$
y_{n+1} = y_n + h_{n+1} y_n' + \cdots + \frac{h_{n+1}^p}{p!} y_n^{(p)}.
$$

The local error is

$$d_{n+1} \stackrel{\text{def}}{=} y_{n+1} - U(t_{n+1}) = -\frac{h_{n+1}^{p+1}}{(p+1)!} U^{(p+1)}(t_n + \theta h_{n+1}).$$

Example 8.10 (continued) Here is a concrete realization of the *third*-order Taylor method:

```
...
y = eta; t = a; Print[t, y];
Do[ y1 = t^2 + y^2;
    y2 = 2. t + 2. y y1;
    y3 = 2. + 2.(y1^2 + y y2);
    y = y + h (y1 + h/2. (y2 + h/3. y3));
    t = t + h;
    Print[t, y]
  ,{n}]
...
```

Note the use of Horner's rule to evaluate the polynomial in h.

Extension of this method to a system of ODEs is possible. If first derivatives satisfy

$$
\begin{aligned}
R'(t) &= 2R(t) - 0.01R(t)F(t), \\
F'(t) &= -F(t) + 0.01R(t)F(t),
\end{aligned}
$$

then second derivatives are given by

$$
\begin{aligned}
R''(t) &= 2R'(t) - 0.01\left(R'(t)F(t) + R(t)F'(t)\right), \\
F''(t) &= -F'(t) + 0.01\left(R'(t)F(t) + R(t)F'(t)\right).
\end{aligned}
$$

Beginning with $r_n \approx R(t_n)$, $f_n \approx F(t_n)$, we can compute

$$
\begin{aligned}
r'_n &= 2r_n - 0.01 r_n f_n, \\
f'_n &= -f_n + 0.01 r_n f_n, \\
r''_n &= 2r'_n - 0.01\left(r'_n f_n + r_n f'_n\right), \\
f''_n &= -f'_n + 0.01\left(r'_n f_n + r_n f'_n\right), \\
r_{n+1} &= r_n + h\left(r'_n + \frac{h}{2} r''_n\right), \\
f_{n+1} &= f_n + h\left(f'_n + \frac{h}{2} f''_n\right).
\end{aligned}
$$

The Taylor method has a drawback: it is inconvenient and error-prone unless automatic differentiation is used, but software for doing this is not widely available (for Fortran and C programs at least). Hence, the method has not been popular.

The Taylor method is well suited for interval computation where some form of automatic differentiation is needed anyway in order to compute bounds on the truncation errors.

A general description of the step-by-step Taylor-series method was provided by Euler in his 1768 treatise. An application of the sixth-order Taylor-series method was published in 1878 by an American, G.W. Hill, who used it to generate numerical tables and graphs giving positions of the moon.

The Taylor-series method is also known as the *power-series* method. It is often taught as an analytical technique in which we express $Y(t) = \sum_{j=0}^{\infty} c_j (t - a)^j$, $a \le t \le b$, and substitute this into the initial condition and ODE in order to determine the coefficients c_j.

Exercises

1. For the differential equation $Y'(t) = tY(t)^2$ suppose we are given that $Y(2) = 1$. Determine the value of $Y'''(2)$.

2. Given $Y''(t) = tY'(t) + Y(t)^2$, $Y(1) = 1$, and $Y'(1) = 2$, determine $Y'''(1)$.

3. Obtain the equations for one step of the third-order Taylor-series method applied to $Y'(t) = tY(t)$.

4. Do the calculation of y_{n+1} in Example 8.10 using a fourth-order rather than a second-order Taylor method.

5. Write a complete algorithm that uses the second-order Taylor-series method with step-size 0.02 to compute the solution to

$$Y'(t) = tY(t) - Y(t)^2, \qquad Y(0) = 1$$

and prints the computed value of $Y(1)$.

6. In the text, equations are given for the numerical solution of the rabbits and foxes problem by the second-order Taylor method. Extend this example to the third-order Taylor method.

Mathematica notes

One of the big advantages of using a language such as *Mathematica* is that we can write programs that combine symbolic and numerical techniques. Here we examine how to find higher order derivatives symbolically and use Taylor-series methods for solving ODEs. We consider the differential equation

$$Y'(t) = \sin(t)Y(t)^2.$$

Start with the expression for $Y'(t)$. The notation makes it clear that y depends on t.

$In[1]:= \mathtt{f1 = Sin[t] \; y[t]\wedge 2}$

$Out[1]= \mathtt{Sin[t] \; y[t]}^{2}$

Find the successive higher order derivatives.

$In[2]:= \mathtt{f2 = D[f1,t]; \; f3 = D[f2,t]; \; f4 = D[f3,t]}$

$Out[2]= \mathtt{-(Cos[t] \; y[t]}^{2}\mathtt{) \; - \; 6 \; Sin[t] \; y[t] \; y'[t] \; +}$

  $\mathtt{6 \; Cos[t] \; y'[t]}^{2} \mathtt{+ \; 6 \; Cos[t] \; y[t] \; y''[t] \; +}$

  $\mathtt{6 \; Sin[t] \; y'[t] \; y''[t] \; + \; 2 \; Sin[t] \; y[t] \; y}^{(3)}\mathtt{[t]}$

Now replace the functional notation for y[ ] and its derivatives with atomic symbols. Recall that any numerical method for solving ODEs uses discrete variables, not continuous functions.

$In[3]:= \mathtt{\{f1, \; f2, \; f3, \; f4\} = \{f1, \; f2, \; f3, \; f4\} \; /.}$
    $\mathtt{\{y[t] \; -> \; y0, \; y'[t] \; -> \; y1,}$
    $\mathtt{y''[t] \; -> \; y2, \; y'''[t] \; -> \; y3\}}$

$Out[3]= \mathtt{\{y0}^{2}\mathtt{\; Sin[t], \; y0}^{2} \mathtt{\; Cos[t] \; + \; 2 \; y0 \; y1 \; Sin[t],}$

  $\mathtt{4 \; y0 \; y1 \; Cos[t] \; - \; y0}^{2} \mathtt{\; Sin[t] \; + \; 2 \; y1}^{2} \mathtt{\; Sin[t] \; +}$

  $\mathtt{2 \; y0 \; y2 \; Sin[t], \; -(y0}^{2} \mathtt{\; Cos[t]) \; + \; 6 \; y1}^{2} \mathtt{\; Cos[t] \; +}$

  $\mathtt{6 \; y0 \; y2 \; Cos[t] \; - \; 6 \; y0 \; y1 \; Sin[t] \; + \; 6 \; y1 \; y2 \; Sin[t] \; +}$

  $\mathtt{2 \; y0 \; y3 \; Sin[t]\}}$

Note that we must not change the rules for the f's again. We depend on the rules containing these symbols, whose values we will set and change repeatedly. This will have the effect of making the f's evaluate to different values.

The variables t and y get assigned numerical values as the ODE gets solved.

$In[4]:= \mathtt{\{t = 1.2, \; y = 0.3, \; h = 0.02\}}$

$Out[4]= \mathtt{\{1.2, \; 0.3, \; 0.02\}}$

The various derivatives for the Taylor series are merely the result of evaluating the f's. Note that the order of these evaluations is important because the later expressions for the f's involve the earlier values of the y's.

$In[5]:= \mathtt{\{y0 = y, \; y1 = f1, \; y2 = f2, \; y3 = f3, \; y4 = f4\}}$

$Out[5]= \mathtt{\{0.3, \; 0.0838835, \; 0.0795218, \; 0.0101784, \; -0.0631798\}}$

The new value of y using stepsize h and the values of the various derivatives at the old t and y.

$In[6]:= \mathtt{y = y0 + h(y1 + h/2.(y2 + h/3.(y3 + h/4. \; y4)))}$

$Out[6]= \mathtt{0.301694}$

Computer problem

1. Consider a projectile being fired vertically from the surface of the earth. If x is its height and $V(x)$ is its upward velocity, then (from Newton's second law of motion and law of

gravitation with rotation and atmospheric effects neglected) one can derive the ODE

$$V'(x) = -\frac{gr^2}{V(x)(r+x)^2}$$

where g is acceleration due to gravity (at the surface) and r is the earth's radius. The initial condition is $V(0) = v_i$. (If the initial velocity is less than the escape velocity $\sqrt{2gr}$, the projectile does not continue outward forever and $V(x)$ becomes undefined beyond some height x.) Use $r = 6378.388$ km and $g = 0.00980621$ km/sec^2. You are to solve this numerically using the fourth-order Taylor method.

(a) For each of the first four derivatives of $V(x)$ find expressions involving V, x, and derivatives of lower order than what the expression itself represents. Then replace the functional notation with atomic symbols.

(b) Define a function having a parameter v_i for the initial value $V(0)$ and a parameter x_f for the final value of x. The function should incorporate the derivation of the expressions for the derivatives from part (a) and compute a list of mesh points (values of x from 0 through x_f) and a list of corresponding approximations for $V(x)$. A list consisting of these two lists should be returned by the function. Each new mesh point $x + h$ is to be determined from the current mesh point x where h is chosen to satisfy

$$\left| \frac{h^4 v_n''''}{4!} \right| = ltol \overset{\text{def}}{=} 10.^{-4}.$$

Each value v_{n+1} is to be determined from the current value v_n by the fourth-order Taylor method. In no event should x go beyond x_f. Stop before this point if v_{n+1} becomes zero or negative[6] or the number of steps equals 100.

(c) Run the routine for $v_i = \sqrt{2.gr}$, $x_f = 10.^{12}$. Then after contemplating the results, enter the *Mathematica* comment `(* The foregoing computation is a striking illustration of the power of automatic stepsize control. *)`. Also run the routine for $v_i = 11.$, $x_f = 10.^{12}$. `ListPlot` the results after `Transpose`ing them.

8.5 Runge-Kutta Methods

The motivation for considering other methods is to avoid analytic derivatives and yet obtain the accuracy of the Taylor methods. Runge-Kutta (RK) methods satisfy these criteria.

---

[6]The analytical solution $V(x)$ does not become negative—it simply ceases to exist.

8.5.1 Runge's midpoint method

One of our derivations of Euler's method was based on the equality

$$U(t_n + h) = U(t_n) + h \left(\frac{1}{h} \int_{t_n}^{t_n+h} U'(t)dt \right).$$

The expression in large parentheses is the average of $U'(t)$ over the subinterval, and in Euler's method this is approximated by the value $U'(t_n)$. A better approximation would use the value $U'(t_n + h/2)$, but to get this from the differential equation $U'(t) = f(t, U(t))$ would require $U(t_n + h/2)$. The idea, due to Carl Runge in 1895, is to approximate $U(t_n + h/2)$ with an Euler step of stepsize $h/2$. It is true that we will be getting an error due to Euler's method, but it now has a less direct effect. The equations for Runge's midpoint method are

$$
\begin{aligned}
g_1 &= f(t_n, y_n), \\
y_{n+\frac{1}{2}} &= y_n + \frac{h}{2}g_1, \\
g_2 &= f\left(t_n + \frac{h}{2}, y_{n+\frac{1}{2}}\right), \\
y_{n+1} &= y_n + hg_2.
\end{aligned}
$$

The superior accuracy of this over Euler's method is well illustrated by Figure 8.20. In particular, you can see that $(t_n + h/2, y_{n+1/2})$ is much closer to $(t_n + h/2, U(t_n + h/2))$ than (t_n, y_n) is; so if $f(t, y)$ is smooth as a function of two variables, then g_2 will be much closer to $U'(t_n + h/2)$ than g_1 is. Note that each step will generate its own g_1 and g_2, but since we discuss only one step at a time it is not necessary to write this as $g_{1,n+1}$ and $g_{2,n+1}$.

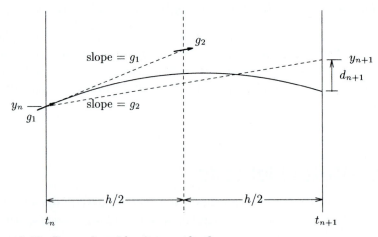

Figure 8.20: Runge's midpoint method

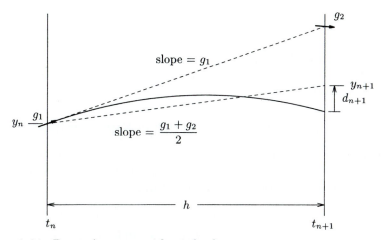

Figure 8.21: Runge's trapezoid method

8.5.2 Runge's trapezoid method

Another fairly accurate approximation to the average value of $U'(t)$ on the interval $[t_n,\ t_n+h]$ is to use the average at the two endpoints, $\frac{1}{2}U'(t_n)+\frac{1}{2}U'(t_n+h)$. We cannot evaluate $U'(t_n+h)$ from the differential equation until we have an *preliminary* approximation to $U(t_n+h)$, which we obtain from an Euler step of stepsize h. The method is illustrated in Figure 8.21, and the formula is

$$y_{n+1} = y_n + \frac{h}{2}g_1 + \frac{h}{2}g_2$$

where

$$
\begin{aligned}
g_1 &= f(t_n, y_n),\\
g_2 &= f(t_n + h, y_n + hg_1).
\end{aligned}
$$

This was also derived by Runge in 1895.

Example 8.11 Suppose $t_n = 2$, $y_n = 1$, $h = 0.1$, and the differential equation is $Y'(t) = t^2 + Y(t)^2$. Then

$$
\begin{aligned}
g_1 &= t_n^2 + y_n^2 = 5,\\
g_2 &= (t_n + h)^2 + (y_n + hg_1)^2 = 2.1^2 + 1.5^2 = 6.66,\\
y_{n+1} &= y_n + h\left(\frac{g_1 + g_2}{2}\right) = 1 + 0.1 \times 5.83 = 1.583.
\end{aligned}
$$

With `f[t_, y_] := t^2 + y^2` a program for one step is given by

```
(* given t, y *)
g1 = f[t, y]
g2 = f[t + h, y + h g1]
t = t + h
y = y + 0.5 h (g1 + g2)
```

8.5.3 General second-order two-stage Runge-Kutta methods

The two methods we have considered have a generalization based on the ideas of using a second-order two-point formula to approximate the average value of $U'(t)$ and using a preliminary Euler step to get to the second of the two points:

$$
\begin{aligned}
g_1 &= f(t_n, y_n), \\
g_2 &= f(t_n + \alpha h, y_n + \alpha h g_1), \\
y_{n+1} &= y_n + h\left(\left(1 - \frac{1}{2\alpha}\right)g_1 + \frac{1}{2\alpha}g_2\right).
\end{aligned}
$$

The choice $\alpha = \frac{1}{2}$ gives Runge's midpoint method and $\alpha = 1$ gives Runge's trapezoid method. The generalization to arbitrary α is due to Wilhelm Kutta in 1901. Normally it is the evaluation of $f(t, y)$ that dominates the computational cost, so we count each such evaluation within a step as a **stage**. Above we have a two-stage method: computing g_1 is the first stage, and computing g_2 is the second.

At the beginning of this section we mentioned the desire to duplicate the accuracy of Taylor methods without analytical differentiation. To bring out this idea, we can rearrange the above Runge-Kutta formula as

$$
y_{n+1} = y_n + hy'_n + \frac{h^2}{2}\left(\frac{f(t_n + \alpha h, y_n + \alpha h y'_n) - f(t_n, y_n)}{\alpha h}\right)
$$

where $y'_n = f(t_n, y_n)$. You see here the use of a numerical differentiation of a sort. It can be shown that in the limit as $\alpha \to 0$ we get the second-order Taylor method.

Also, it can be shown that the local error

$$
\begin{aligned}
d_{n+1} &= y_{n+1} - U_n(t_{n+1}) \\
&= \cdots \\
&= h^3 \text{ term} + \cdots,
\end{aligned}
$$

assuming $f(t, y)$ has continuous partial derivatives. Hence, because $N = (b - a)/h$, the global error

$$
e_N = \sum_{j=1}^{N} \text{propagated } d_j
$$

is proportional to h^2.

With a parameter α available, the natural question is how best to choose it. There is no clear best choice. It is an exercise at the end of this section to show that $\alpha = \frac{2}{3}$ makes the order 3 *in the special case* where f depends on t only. This would not be a bad choice for the more general case.

8.5.4   The classical fourth-order Runge-Kutta method

This method is popular and is sometimes referred to as *the* Runge-Kutta method. It is based on sampling the slope at four specially selected points, the location of each point depending on only the previously sampled slope. The recipe is

$$
\begin{aligned}
g_1 &= f(t_n, y_n), \\
g_2 &= f\left(t_n + \frac{h}{2}, y_n + \frac{h}{2}g_1\right), \\
g_3 &= f\left(t_n + \frac{h}{2}, y_n + \frac{h}{2}g_2\right), \\
g_4 &= f(t_n + h, y_n + hg_3), \\
y_{n+1} &= y_n + h(\tfrac{1}{6}g_1 + \tfrac{1}{3}g_2 + \tfrac{1}{3}g_3 + \tfrac{1}{6}g_4).
\end{aligned}
$$

This is pictured in Figure 8.22. If $f(t, y)$ depends on t alone, this is Simpson's rule. The method was proposed by Kutta in his 1901 article and hence might be called the *Kutta-Simpson method.*

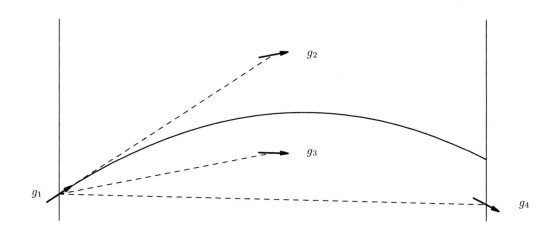

Figure 8.22: Classical fourth-order Runge-Kutta

Example 8.12 Suppose the differential equation is $Y'(t) = 1 + Y(t)^2$, the initial condition is $Y(0) = 0$, and we wish to calculate $Y(\pi/4)$. With stepsize $h = \pi/4 \approx 0.78540$, the Kutta-Simpson method generates the values

$$y_0 = 0, \qquad g_1 = 1,$$

$$y_0 + \frac{h}{2}g_1 = 0.39270, \quad g_2 = 1.1542,$$

$$y_0 + \frac{h}{2}g_2 = 0.45326, \quad g_3 = 1.2054,$$

$$y_0 + hg_3 = 0.94676, \quad g_4 = 1.8963,$$

$$y_1 = 0.99687.$$

The final value is in error by only -0.3%. By contrast, Euler's method with stepsize $h/4$ yields $y_4 = 0.90188$ with -9.8% relative error. The comparison is fair because each method uses four evaluations of $f(t, y)$. Be aware, though, that this does not mean that Kutta-Simpson is $9.8/0.3 \approx 33$ times better. If we used stepsizes only half as great, the Euler error would be cut in half but the Kutta-Simpson error would be *reduced by a factor of 16*.

8.5.5 A system of ODEs

The generalization of Runge-Kutta methods to a system of ODEs

$$
\begin{aligned}
Y'(t) &= f(t, Y(t), Z(t)), \\
Z'(t) &= g(t, Y(t), Z(t))
\end{aligned}
$$

is possible. For example, for Runge's midpoint method the formulas are

$$
\begin{aligned}
y'_n &= f(t_n, y_n, z_n), \\
z'_n &= g(t_n, y_n, z_n), \\
y'_{n+\frac{1}{2}} &= f\left(t_n + \frac{h}{2}, y_n + \frac{h}{2}y'_n, z_n + \frac{h}{2}z'_n\right), \\
z'_{n+\frac{1}{2}} &= g\left(t_n + \frac{h}{2}, y_n + \frac{h}{2}y'_n, z_n + \frac{h}{2}z'_n\right), \\
y_{n+1} &= y_n + h\, y'_{n+\frac{1}{2}}, \\
z_{n+1} &= z_n + h\, z'_{n+\frac{1}{2}}.
\end{aligned}
$$

Review questions

1. By visualizing their graphical interpretation, reproduce the equations for Runge's mid-point method.

2. Do the preceding problem for Runge's trapezoid method.

Exercises

1. Consider the Runge-Kutta method

$$
\begin{aligned}
g_1 &= f(t_n, y_n),\\
g_2 &= f(t_n + \tfrac{2}{3}h, y_n + \tfrac{2}{3}hg_1),\\
y_{n+1} &= y_n + \frac{h}{4}g_1 + \frac{3}{4}hg_2
\end{aligned}
$$

for the differential equation $Y'(t) = f(t, Y(t))$. Take one step of this method applied to

$$
Y'(t) = tY(t) - Y(t)^2, \quad Y(1) = 2
$$

with stepsize $h = 0.3$.

2. What method can be expressed as

$$
y_{n+1} = y_n + h_n\, f(t_n + \tfrac{1}{2}\,h_n,\ y_n + \tfrac{1}{2}\,h_n\, f(t_n, y_n)).
$$

3. In the spirit of Figures 8.20 and 8.21, sketch a picture of the general second-order two-stage Runge-Kutta method.

4. Below is given a graphical description of the $(n+1)$th step of a Runge-Kutta method:

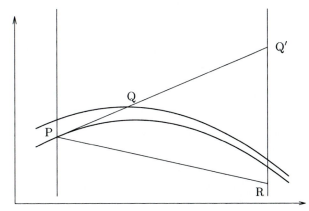

The two curves are solutions of $Y'(t) = f(t, Y(t))$. Point P has coordinates (t_n, y_n) and point R coordinates $(t_n + h, y_{n+1})$. Line segment $\overline{PQ}$ is tangent to the curve at P and is one-third the length of $\overline{PQ'}$. The slope of $\overline{PR}$ is $\frac{3}{2}g_2 - \frac{1}{2}g_1$ where g_2 is the slope at Q of the curve through Q and g_1 is the slope of $\overline{PQ}$. Write down the formulas that you would use to compute y_{n+1}.

5. Determine in *closed form* the numerical solution y_n for general h and n of $Y'(t) = Y(t)$, $Y(0) = 1$ obtained by Runge's midpoint method. Your answer should be of the form

$$y_n = \text{some expression involving } h \text{ and } n \text{ only.}$$

6. Consider the Runge-Kutta method of Exercise 1 applied to the differential equation $Y'(t) = f(t, Y(t))$. Now consider the special case where $f(t, y)$ depends on t alone, say $f(t, y) = \phi(t)$. In this case, what is the solution value y_2 in terms of $y_0, t_0, h,$ and ϕ *only*?

7. For Runge's trapezoid method applied to the initial-value problem $Y'(t) = 2Y(t)/t$ with $Y(1) = 1$, give a formula

$$y_{n+1} = \text{expression in terms of values } t, y_n, h \text{ only}$$

that is convenient for use on a calculator. Determine the value of the numerical solution at $t = 2$ for $h = \frac{1}{2}$ and for $h = \frac{1}{4}$, and determine the analytical solution $Y(t)$. By what factor is the error reduced in the numerical solution when h is reduced from $\frac{1}{2}$ to $\frac{1}{4}$?

8. Take two steps with Runge's midpoint method applied to the problem

$$Y'(t) = Y(t)^2, \quad Y(0) = 1$$

where $h = 0.2$. What is the analytic solution of

$$Y'(t) = Y(t)^2, \quad Y(a) = A?$$

Compute the global errors e_1, e_2, and the local errors d_1, d_2.

9. The arrangement
$$y_{n+1} = y_n + h(\tfrac{1}{6}g_1 + \tfrac{1}{3}g_2 + \tfrac{1}{3}g_3 + \tfrac{1}{6}g_4)$$
is a bit inefficient. How should one rearrange this expression to improve efficiency?

10. Show that the second-order two-stage RK method of Section 8.5.3 with $\alpha = \frac{2}{3}$ has a local error of order h^4 *in the special case* where f depends on t only.

11. Show that the general second-order two-stage RK method of Section 8.5.3 has a local error of order h^3 when $f(t, y) = a(t)y + b(t)$. Begin by showing that

$$f(t_n + \alpha h, \ y_n + \alpha h y_n') = f(t_n + \alpha h, \ U(t_n + \alpha h)) - a(t_n + \alpha h)\frac{(\alpha h)^2}{2}U''(\tau_{n+1})$$

where $U(t)$ is the local solution. Hint: What does the expression $f(t_n + \alpha h, \ U(t_n + \alpha h))$ represent?

Computer problems

1. Write a program for numerically solving the system of ODEs

$$Y'(t) = f(t, Y(t), Z(t)),$$
$$Z'(t) = g(t, Y(t), Z(t))$$

given $Y(0)$, $Z(0)$. Your program should have parameters f_, g_, yinit_, zinit_, tfinal_, h_, where f and g are functions rather than, say, expressions in y, z and the other parameters have obvious meanings. Your program should return a list of triples

$$\{\{t_0, y_0, z_0\}, \{t_1, y_1, z_1\}, \ldots, \{t_N, y_N, z_N\}\}$$

where $t_{N-1} < t_{final} \le t_N$. Use Runge's midpoint method, in which the $(n+1)$th step is

$$y'_n = f(t_n, y_n, z_n),$$

$$z'_n = g(t_n, y_n, z_n),$$

$$y'_{n+\frac{1}{2}} = f\left(t_n + \frac{h}{2}, y_n + \frac{h}{2}y'_n, z_n + \frac{h}{2}z'_n\right),$$

$$z'_{n+\frac{1}{2}} = g\left(t_n + \frac{h}{2}, y_n + \frac{h}{2}y'_n, z_n + \frac{h}{2}z'_n\right),$$

$$y_{n+1} = y_n + h\, y'_{n+\frac{1}{2}},$$

$$z_{n+1} = z_n + h\, z'_{n+\frac{1}{2}}.$$

2. In this problem you are to use your program from Computer Problem 1 to solve the rabbit and fox problem

$$R'(t) = 2R(t) - 0.01R(t)F(t),$$
$$F'(t) = -F(t) + 0.01R(t)F(t)$$

for $0 \le t \le 10$ and

$$R(0) = 300, \quad F(0) = 150.$$

(a) Use a stepsize in the range 0.01 to 0.1. Do a ListPlot with $R(t)$ as the vertical axis and t as the horizontal axis. You may find it useful to use solution[[Range[Length[solution]], {1, 2}]]. Label the axes "time" and "rabbits."

(b) Do a ListPlot with $F(t)$ as the vertical axis and $R(t)$ as the horizontal axis, thereby getting the trajectory in phase space. Label the plot "trajectory" and the axes "rabbits" and "foxes."

3. Write a program for numerically solving the system of ODEs

$$
\begin{aligned}
X'(t) &= f_1(X(t), Y(t), Z(t)), \\
Y'(t) &= f_2(X(t), Y(t), Z(t)), \\
Z'(t) &= f_3(X(t), Y(t), Z(t))
\end{aligned}
$$

given $X(0), Y(0), Z(0)$. Your program should have parameters f_, init_, tfinal_, h_, where f is a function that maps $\{x, y, x\}$ to $\{f_1(x, y, z), f_2(x, y, z), f_3(x, y, z)\}$; init_ is a list of the initial values of x, y, and z; and the other parameters have obvious meanings. Your program should return a list of triples

$$
\{\{x_0, y_0, z_0\}, \{x_1, y_1, z_1\}, \ldots, \{x_N, y_N, z_N\}\}
$$

where $t_{N-1} < t_{\text{final}} \le t_N$ (although the values of t are not to be included in the result). Use the classical fourth-order Runge-Kutta and take advantage of the Listable attribute of the arithmetic operations. Note that it is not necessary to keep track of the value of t. You should never refer to the individual variables x, y, or z (except in the definition of f[{x_, y_, z_}], which is separate from the program); the intermediate values g_1, g_2, g_3, and g_4 should be lists; and because the operations are Listable, you should not need to refer to parts of lists. (In fact, your program should work equally well with any size system of equations.)

4. Use your program from Computer Problem 3 to solve the Lorenz-attractor problem

$$
\begin{aligned}
X'(t) &= -3(X(t) - Y(t)), \\
Y'(t) &= -X(t)Z(t) + 26.5X(t) - Y(t), \\
Z'(t) &= X(t)Y(t) - Z(t)
\end{aligned}
$$

with initial conditions $\{X(0.), Y(0.), Z(0.)\} = \{0., 1., 0.\}$ on the interval $0. \le t \le 20.$ with stepsize $h = 0.04$. Use Show[Graphics3D[{Line[%]}], Axes -> Automatic] to plot the solution in three-dimensional space.

9.   Overview

Numerical analysis is the use of approximate numerical operations to obtain approximate solutions to quantitative problems having a mathematical specification. The process of solving an application problem can be broken into two phases

$$\begin{array}{ccccc} \text{physical} & \xrightarrow{\text{modeling}} & \text{mathematical} & \xrightarrow{\text{n.a.}} & \text{computer} \\ \text{reality} & & \text{model} & & \text{program} \end{array}$$

of which only the second is numerical analysis. The division between the two phases is not entirely clear-cut because deliberate simplifications are often made before the mathematical model is specified.

basic tools of approximation

Little would be possible without **rounding** the results of floating-point operations. The precision is a measure of the accuracy of this process. To solve an equation $f(x) = 0$, we can often rewrite it as $x = g(x)$ and use the **iteration**

$$x_{k+1} = g(x_k).$$

Newton-Raphson, for which $g(x) = x - f(x)/f'(x)$, is a systematic way of rewriting the equation. An iteration has order of convergence p if successive errors satisfy

$$|e_{k+1}| \sim C|e_k|^p$$

as $k \to \infty$. Linear convergence is an important special case in which the value of C is of special concern. To approximate a function defined for a continuum of values, we use another function characterized by some finite set of values, a process called **discretization**. This can be a *mesh function*, as illustrated in Figure 9.1, with intermediate values defined by polynomial or piecewise polynomial interpolation. Another example is a truncated Taylor series. If there is a mesh size parameter h, we say that the order of accuracy is p if the

$$|\text{discretization error}| \sim Ch^p$$

as $h \to 0$.

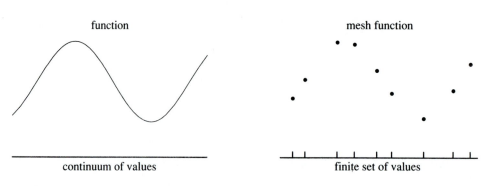

Figure 9.1: Discretization

roundoff vs. truncation error

Truncation error is due to truncating series, polynomial interpolation, quadrature rules, formulas for solving ODEs, terminating an iteration before convergence, etc. Quantitatively, truncation error is the difference between the answer computed by the numerical method using exact arithmetic and the true answer. Roundoff error is the difference between the answer computed by the numerical method with rounded arithmetic and the answer computed by the same method with exact arithmetic. Thus, the total computational error is

$$\text{error} \ = \ \text{truncation error} \ + \ \text{roundoff error.}$$

two kinds of problems

Technically a problem (in numerical analysis) is a mapping defined for a set of (input) data. For problems like the evaluation of

$$\sin(x),$$
$$A^{-1}\boldsymbol{b},$$
the roots of $a_n x^n + \cdots + a_1 x + a_0 = 0,$

the data are a finite set of numbers. Typically, roundoff error dominates. For other problems such as

$$\int_a^b f(x)\,dx,$$
find $Y(t)$, $a \le t \le b$ given $Y(a)$ and $Y'(t) = f(t, Y(t))$,
find the roots of $f(x) = 0,$

the (input) data include not only numbers but at least one function. Usually truncation error dominates. It is impractical to guarantee correct results if $f(x)$ can only be sampled.

ultimate products of activity in numerical analysis

A major goal of numerical analysis is the development of well-documented numerical software. Equally important are books describing numerical techniques, methods, and algorithms for applications. Also needed is a theory for creating numerical methods.

computational uncertainty

In most computations almost nothing is known for sure about the accuracy of the result. In some cases attempts are made to *estimate* the accuracy. In almost every case we cannot be certain about the accuracy of even the first digit! And this is a deliberate decision in the design of the numerical algorithm!! Why the uncertainty?

1. Failure to account for known errors
2. Unknown errors due to limited sampling

THE TWO
NUMERICAL
CRIMES

The first of these can be remedied with interval analysis; the second can be overcome by the use of symbolic computation.

Appendix A
Getting Started with *Mathematica*

An introduction to numerical methods should concentrate on the difficult task of getting good solutions to problems without becoming embroiled in too many of the technicalities associated with good performance, so important for large-scale computing. For this reason we prefer the use of a reasonably friendly and powerful interactive programming system like *Mathematica* to either Fortran or C. It has numerical, symbolic, and graphical capabilities, and it is easy to use as a calculator. (MATLAB is also good but is less powerful as a programming language and lacks symbolic capabilities. Maple has symbolic capabilities but lacks the powerful programming features.) *Mathematica* has a basic syntax that is simple and yet similar to that of mathematics. Also it provides concrete realizations of abstract mathematical concepts such as functions and functionals.

This appendix is designed to help you learn *Mathematica*. It is divided into three lessons that are numbered to correspond to the first three chapter numbers. Many sections of the main body of this book also contain notes about *Mathematica*. Those *Mathematica* notes are designed to help you work the specific computer problems in the respective sections, and (unless otherwise noted) you are not expected to need that material except for those problems. The discussion here is more general, and you are expected to know the material presented in lesson n to work the computer problems in chapters beginning with chapter n.

It is hoped that you will be able to learn what you need to know of *Mathematica* from this appendix and the *Mathematica* notes in the body of the book. This does not mean that it will teach you all there is to know about *Mathematica* by any means. *Mathematica* is a very large and complicated program, and this book is about numerical analysis. We assume that you have access to the *Mathematica* manual (Wolfram (1991)), but not necessarily on a continual basis. In addition it will be helpful to have access to the technical report *Guide to Standard Mathematica Packages*[1] for more extensive documentation of some of the functions that we will have cause to use that are defined in external packages. As will be pointed out, there is some help on-line, and *Mathematica* is interactive so you get immediate feedback as you learn how to use it. Additional help can be had from the growing list of books written to teach *Mathematica* and from other people who have had more experience.

---

[1]Published by Wolfram Research, Inc. and distributed with each copy of *Mathematica*.

We begin with the question of getting *Mathematica* started on your computer. This can vary considerably depending on the type of computer you have. *Mathematica* consists of two main parts: the "kernel," which does all the computational work, and the "front end," which is the interface you interact with directly. The kernel is functionally the same on all computers, but the front end can be either a "Notebook" interface or a text-based interface. As a general rule, to start *Mathematica* with a Notebook interface, you click the mouse on the *Mathematica* icon. To start *Mathematica* with a text-based interface, you type `math`. For further details you should seek local assistance. Likewise, entering commands and exiting from *Mathematica* are different with the different front ends. In either version you enter a command by typing it, but with the Notebook interface you press SHIFT-RETURN or ENTER on Macintosh and NeXT computers and SHIFT-ENTER or INSERT under Microsoft Windows, and with the text-based interface you press RETURN to get it to execute the command. To exit *Mathematica*, you choose the **Quit** menu item (Notebook interface) or type CONTROL-D or `Quit[ ]` (text-based interface).

This appendix contains the following material:

A.1 Lesson One
    A.1.1 What is *Mathematica*?
    A.1.2 *Mathematica* as a calculator
    A.1.3 Assigning values to symbols
    A.1.4 Some basic grammar and syntax
    A.1.5 Lists
    A.1.6 Defining your own functions
    A.1.7 Getting help
    A.1.8 Miscellanea
A.2 Lesson Two
    A.2.1 More on floating-point numbers
    A.2.2 Plotting functions and data
    A.2.3 Symbolic calculations
    A.2.4 Loops and conditionals
    A.2.5 Defining `Rules`
    A.2.6 Attributes of symbols
    A.1.7 The evaluation process
    A.2.8 Using external packages
    A.2.9 Miscellanea
A.3 Lesson Three
    A.3.1 Using pure functions
    A.3.2 More on patterns and rules
    A.3.3 How evaluation works
    A.3.4 The function `N[ ]`
    A.3.5 Delayed evaluation
    A.3.6 Miscellanea

A.1 Lesson One

A.1.1 What is *Mathematica*?

Before we get into the details of how to use *Mathematica* it will be helpful to have some idea of what it is, what it is good for, and what it is *not* good for. *Mathematica* has been advertised as "a system for doing mathematics by computer," and this is reasonably accurate, advertising hyperbole notwithstanding. For certain types of mathematics it is a very good tool. For other types of mathematics, such as Euclidean geometry, it is not very good at all. To be sure, many of the truths of Euclidean geometry can be studied quite effectively using *Mathematica*, but do not expect *Mathematica* to be able to produce axiomatic proofs; *Mathematica* will not do your thinking for you.

Mathematica does have its strengths and its weaknesses; and because those strengths and weaknesses are very different from what we humans have, *Mathematica* can be a very useful tool. Moreover, because of these differences, the way mathematics is studied is changing. Certain things that used to be very difficult or time-consuming can now be done much more easily and quickly by computer. In fact, some things that used to be completely impractical can now be done quite effectively. We cannot guarantee that *Mathematica* will be the last computer-algebra system that you will ever need to learn: who knows what the situation will be 20 or even 10 years from now? However, we can assure you that the time you spend learning *Mathematica* will be time well spent.

Mathematica is particularly good as a numerical, symbolic, and graphical calculator. Moreover, it handles everything in a unified way so you can get a symbolic result and graph it directly; you do not have to change to a different program or change the representation of the data. It is difficult to overstate the advantage gained by this unification. As an example of the usefulness of this we show how someone might approach the following problem:

Find b such that the graph of $y = b^x$ is tangent to the line $y = x$.

At this point do not concern yourself with the language of *Mathematica*. Our aim here is to demonstrate some of what *Mathematica* can do and how this might affect the way you approach a problem.

Plot x and 2^x on the same axes. We see that 2^x grows too rapidly.

```
In[1]:= Plot[{x, 2^x}, {x, 0, 4},
            AspectRatio -> Automatic]
```

Rather than enter a long command for each
guess, we define a command p[ ] that
draws a plot of the exponential function
with any given base b together with the line
$y = x$.

In[2]:= p[b_] := Plot[{x, b^x}, {x, 0, 5},
                      AspectRatio -> Automatic]

With base 1 the exponential function is
just the constant function $y = 1$.

In[3]:= p[1]

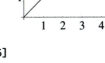

With base 1.5 the exponential function
again misses the line.

In[4]:= p[1.5]

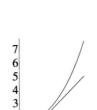

On the other hand, 1.4 is too small.

In[5]:= p[1.4]

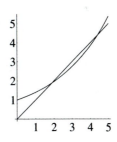

1.45 is very close. Note that this is not a
very accurate solution to the problem. It
does, however, make it clear just what the
problem is.

In[6]:= p[1.45]

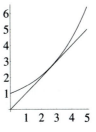

Define the function with which we are concerned.

$In[7]:= f[x_] := b^x$

Attempt to find the values of x and b that determine tangency.

$In[8]:= \text{Solve}[\{f[x] == x, f'[x] == 1\}, \{x, b\}]$

$Solve::dinv$:
  The expression b^x involves unknowns in more than one argument, so inverse functions can't be used.

$Out[8]= \text{Solve}[\{b^x == x, b^x \text{Log}[b] == 1\}, \{x, b\}]$

Mathematica was unable to find a solution symbolically.

Attempt to find the values of x and b numerically.

$In[9]:= \text{FindRoot}[\{f[x] == x, f'[x] == 1\},\\ \qquad \{x, 1\}, \{b, 2\}]$

We can at least guess that x is supposed to be e.

$Out[9]= \{x \to 2.71828, b \to 1.44467\}$

If it is true that x is e, then we can try using that to solve for b.

$In[10]:= \text{sol} = \text{Solve}[f[E] == E, b]$

We see that Solve[ ] can now handle it. Notice that we still are not guaranteed that there are no other solutions. (In fact, there *are* other, imaginary solutions).

$Solve::ifun$:
  Warning: Inverse functions are being used by Solve, so some solutions may not be found.

$Out[10]= \{\{b \to E^{1/E}\}\}$

We attempt to verify that both equations are satisfied.

$In[11]:= \text{check} = \{f[E] == E, f'[E] == 1\} \text{ /. sol}$

$Out[11]= \{\{(E^{1/E})^E == E, (E^{1/E})^E \text{Log}[E^{1/E}] == 1\}\}$

We need to simplify the result to decide.

$In[12]:= \text{PowerExpand}[\text{check}]$

This says that both equations were satisfied.

$Out[12]= \{\{\text{True}, \text{True}\}\}$

We see that they are tangent.

$In[13]:= p[E^{\wedge}(1/E)]$

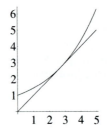

We can get a numerical approximation to the value of b to as many decimals as we want.

$In[14]:= N[E^{\wedge}(1/E), 45]$

$Out[14]= 1.44466786100976613365833910859643022305859 5453$

Notice that this problem, although not trivial, could have been solved by hand. Notice also that *Mathematica* was unable to solve it in the way we would have solved it by hand.[2] The way we solved this problem with *Mathematica* would be a rather impractical method without the aid of a computer. On the other hand, we can see much better what the problem is all about when we can produce graphs at the touch of a button. The way we do and learn mathematics has been forever changed.

So, *Mathematica* is a powerful calculator. It is also much more. It is a very high level programming language with roughly 1000 functions. For our purposes we will not need more than about 20 of them regularly and will probably use only about 50 to 100 at all. Some of these functions, such as `Plus`, are very low level while others are very powerful and allow considerable abstraction. The ability to concentrate on the mathematics and let the computer deal with the details is perhaps the most important reason for choosing *Mathematica* over a lower level language such as Fortran or C.

Of course, until you gain a certain familiarity with *Mathematica* you *will* need to concern yourself with getting it to do what you want. Since it is difficult to learn two things at once we suggest that you spend at least a few hours learning how to use *Mathematica before* you need to use it to solve problems in mathematics. Work through the examples in this appendix to start with. Actually type them into your computer and see the results. Learning *Mathematica*, or mathematics, is not a spectator sport. You certainly will not be able to learn all there is to know about *Mathematica*, but you will be able to learn enough that you will not have to refer to the manual for everything you enter.

A.1.2   *Mathematica* as a calculator

Mathematica can be used very much like a calculator for numerical calculations. There are some differences, however. These differences result from the fact that *Mathematica* uses several different types of numbers. The most obvious difference has to do with exact numbers: *Mathematica* can do exact calculations with integers and rational numbers, while most calculators are restricted to doing arithmetic with floating-point numbers and rounding the result to the nearest number that they can represent. Thus 1/3 on most calculators will result in something like 0.3333333333, while in *Mathematica* the result will be the rational number $\frac{1}{3}$. *Mathematica* can also work with floating-point numbers, but even here it is different from calculators. Calculators are restricted to a certain number of digits in their numbers (usually about 10 or 12), and the size of the largest number that they can represent is quite limited. *Mathematica* can work with very high precision numbers, and the largest number that it can represent is many orders of magnitude larger than that of any ordinary calculator.

---

[2]This situation is likely to change someday. Computer-algebra systems get more powerful all the time.

"*In[1]:=*" is written by *Mathematica* as an input prompt[3]; the "2 + 2 3" is the user's input. The entire next line is the system's response.

In[1]:= 2 + 2 3

Out[1]= 8

Raising something to a power is indicated by the "^" operator. Addition and subtraction use the obvious symbols. Multiplication can be indicated by either "*" or a space. Division uses "/".

In[2]:= 3^12

Out[2]= 531441

This large number is an integer. The input consists of two (exact) integers, and exact arithmetic is used with numbers that are not floating-point numbers.

In[3]:= 5^345

Out[3]= 13952482803738708279001264017399181633934448178989\
24146991120414096231245003342524017880886059780309603\
50408146208530556909840530131736756745657096447804250449\
61841032422915783794626949498926100654634836761847083159\
30430587008595466613769531259

Mathematica also does exact calculations with rational numbers.

In[4]:= 1/2 - 1/3 + 1/5 - 1/7

$$Out[4]= \frac{47}{210}$$

Mathematica represents the square root of −1 as I. All built-in functions and constants in *Mathematica* begin with an uppercase letter. This helps to avoid conflicts with user-defined functions and symbols.

In[5]:= Sqrt[-1]

Out[5]= I

Since the input is exact, no approximate calculations are allowed. In this case no exact simplification can be performed so nothing is changed. The "(* **perfect fifth** *)" is a comment entered by the user.

In[6]:= 2^(7/12) (**perfect fifth** *)*

$$Out[6]= 2^{7/12}$$

Most functions that do not have a standard mathematical abbreviation are spelled out in full in *Mathematica*. The function N[ ] is one of the few exceptions to this rule. The argument(s) of a function are enclosed in brackets ([ ]); parentheses are used only for algebraic grouping of terms.

The function N[ ] numerically evaluates an expression to give a result that is only approximately correct.

In[7]:= N[2^(7/12)]

Out[7]= 1.49831

---

[3]With the Notebook interface the input prompt does not appear until after the command is entered, but it gets inserted in front of what was entered.

Numbers entered with a decimal point are floating-point numbers. Approximate arithmetic is used with these numbers to give you a floating-point answer.

```
In[8]:= 2.^(4/12)  (* major third *)
Out[8]= 1.25992
```

Note that only six digits were displayed in the previous result. This is only to improve readability. *Do not assume that typing in* `1.25992` *will give you the same number!*

"`%`" refers to the previous result. "`==`" tests for equality (or approximate equality with floating-point numbers.)

```
In[9]:= % == 1.25992
Out[9]= False
```

Roughly speaking, the precision of a number is the number of significant digits used to represent it. Floating-point numbers can have nearly any precision, the main restriction being the amount of memory available. The global constant `$MachinePrecision` (between 16 and 19 on most computers) is in some sense a default precision. When you enter a floating-point number with fewer than `$MachinePrecision` digits, the precision is taken to be `$MachinePrecision`. `Precision[ ]` can be used to find the precision of a number. `SetPrecision[ ]` can be used to change the precision of a number. By setting the precision to be sufficiently high you can often expose small differences between numbers.

"`%%`" refers to the result two steps back. It is now clear that the two numbers are in fact different.

```
In[10]:= SetPrecision[{%%, 1.25992}, 20]
Out[10]= {1.2599210498948749862, 1.2599199999999992887}
```

If you enter a number with more than `$MachinePrecision` digits you get a number whose precision is roughly the number of digits.

```
In[11]:= Precision[12345.678998765432112345]
Out[11]= 22
```

We will discuss more features of floating-point numbers in Lesson Two, but you should be aware that floating-point arithmetic involves some subtleties. In *Mathematica* the precision of a result is, in many situations, chosen to reflect the perceived accuracy of that result.

Mathematica can also be used as a symbolic calculator. It knows about basic algebra and calculus and can be used to manipulate symbols. A symbol is a sequence of letters and digits that does not begin with a digit.

Mathematica automatically does very elementary simplifications.

```
In[12]:= x + 2x
Out[12]= 3 x
```

Like terms are automatically combined.

```
In[13]:= (2x^2 + 3x - 5) - 3(x^2 + 2x + 3)
                          2            2
Out[13]= -5 + 3 x + 2 x  - 3 (3 + 2 x + x )
```

We can use more than one variable.

```
In[14]:= Expand[(x+y)^3]
           3     2         2    3
Out[14]= x  + 3 x  y + 3 x y  + y
```

We can differentiate expressions.

```
In[15]:= D[Sin[x], x]
Out[15]= Cos[x]
```

A.1.3 Assigning values to symbols

Symbols can also be used in *Mathematica* to label the results of calculations. To assign a value to a symbol, you type *variable* = *value*.

This sets x equal to 3 and returns the result.	In[1]:= x = 9 - 2*3
	Out[1]= 3
If you evaluate x, you get 3.	In[2]:= x
	Out[2]= 3
When this is evaluated, x gets replaced by its value and the result is evaluated.	In[3]:= 2x + 3x
	Out[3]= 15
If you ask *Mathematica* about x, it shows the rule you made for x. The "Global`x" is just the complete name for x.	In[4]:= ?x
	Global`x
	x = 3

There are some differences between *Mathematica* and other programming languages. First of all, you can assign values that are not numbers.

Assign to y the value 2z + 3x. Note that z does not have a value but x does.	In[4]:= y = 2z + 3x
	Out[4]= 9 + 2 z
Ask what is known about y.	In[5]:= ?y
	Global`y
	y = 9 + 2*z
Assign a value to z.	In[5]:= z = 7
	Out[5]= 7
Assigning a value to z does not change the rule for y.	In[6]:= ?y
	Global`y
	y = 9 + 2*z
Evaluate y. Note that it now takes account of the value of z.	In[6]:= y
	Out[6]= 23
Change the value of z.	In[7]:= z = 11
	Out[7]= 11
Evaluate y again. Note that changing z caused the result of evaluating y to change.	In[8]:= y
	Out[8]= 31
Change the value of x.	In[9]:= x = 9
	Out[9]= 9

Changing the value of x did *not* change the value of y even though we originally defined y as y = 2z + 3x.	`In[10]:= y`
	
	`Out[10]= 31`

The reason changing z affects y but changing x does not is that the rule for y involves z but not x.	`In[11]:= ?y`
	
	`Global‘y`
	
	`y = 9 + 2*z`

The difference between the x and the z in the above example has to do with the fact that when we entered "y = 2z + 3x", the x had a value (3) but z did not. *When you enter an assignment with an "=", the rule that you get involves the values of all of the symbols at that time.* Symbols appearing in the rule that do not have values assigned to them get inserted directly into the rule as symbols. If they are later assigned values, those values will be used in subsequent evaluations.

It should be noted that *Mathematica* is quite different from more traditional programming languages with which you may be familiar. In many languages symbols refer to specific locations in memory. Not so with *Mathematica*. Symbols do not refer to locations in memory. You might think of a symbol as a label on a sheet of paper. Each symbol refers to a separate sheet of paper. When you create a symbol its sheet of paper is blank. If you associate a rule with a symbol, the sheet of paper corresponding to that symbol gets the rule written on it. If the rule contradicts an earlier rule, the earlier rule gets erased. There is no limit to the number of rules you can associate with the same symbol.

The simplest way to demonstrate how several rules can be associated with a single symbol is to use indexed variables. Mathematical variables are usually represented by symbols in *Mathematica*, but sometimes we want to talk about several related variables such as x_1, x_2, etc. In *Mathematica* this can be done with x[1], x[2], etc. Rules can be associated only with symbols, and the rules for the various x[n] are associated with x.

Make a rule that x[1] is to evaluate to 23. We are not restricted to using symbols for variables.	`In[1]:= x[1] = 23`
	
	`Out[1]= 23`

Note that the rule is associated with x.	`In[2]:= ?x`
	
	`Global‘x`
	
	`x[1] = 23`

Make a rule that x[2] is to evaluate to 12.	`In[2]:= x[2] = 29 - 17`
	
	`Out[2]= 12`

The rule x[2] = 12 is applicable, so the result is 12.	`In[3]:= x[2]`
	
	`Out[3]= 12`

There is no rule for x[7], so the result is just x[7] itself.	`In[4]:= x[7]`
	
	`Out[4]= x[7]`

The rules are used as they apply.

```
In[5]:= 3 x[1] - 2 x[2] + x[3]
Out[5]= 45 + x[3]
```

As in most programming languages, there is no problem with assigning a new value to a variable based on its current value. The right-hand side evaluates to 3 before the rule x[1] = 3 is formed.

```
In[6]:= x[1] = x[1] + 3
Out[6]= 26
```

We can clear all rules from the symbol x.

```
In[7]:= Clear[x]
```

There are no longer any rules associated with x.

```
In[8]:= ?x
Global`x
```

We have used the term "evaluate" to describe how rules are used. The process of evaluation is fundamental to how *Mathematica* works. There are identifiable steps in the evaluation process, but for now let us just say that to evaluate any expression, rules are applied repeatedly until none of the rules applies.

There are several different kinds of rules. The kind we saw above is formed with "=", or **Set**. When "=" is used, the expression to the right of the "=" is evaluated before the rule is formed. Another way to form a rule uses ":=", or **SetDelayed**. When ":=" is used, the expression to the right of the ":=" is *not* evaluated at all. The rule is simply formed with whatever is there. When we did x[2] = 29 - 17 above, it made little difference that we used "=" instead of ":=" since 29 − 17 will always evaluate to 12. But there are times when it makes a great deal of difference which kind of rule is used.

Start out with the rule that i is to evaluate to 1.

```
In[8]:= i = 1
Out[8]= 1
```

Make a rule for **next** that says whenever (*but not yet!*) **next** gets evaluated, evaluate the expression i = i+1.

```
In[9]:= next := (i = i+1)
```

This is the rule for **next**, just as we entered it.

```
In[10]:= ?next
Global`next
next := i = i + 1
```

Evaluating i results in 1.

```
In[10]:= i
Out[10]= 1
```

Evaluating **next** causes i to be incremented.

```
In[11]:= next
Out[11]= 2
```

Evaluate **next** three more times.

```
In[12]:= next; next; next
Out[12]= 5
```

The only rule for i is that it is to evaluate to 5.	*In[13]:=* **?i** Global`i i = 5
The rule for **next** has not changed since we entered it. Every evaluation of **next** gives a different result, but the rule itself is the same.	*In[13]:=* **?next** Global`next next := i = i + 1

Note that if instead of the rule **next := (i = i+1)**, we had made the rule **next = (i = i+1)**, two things would have been different. First of all the expression i = i+1 would have been evaluated and i would have been incremented. Second, the result of incrementing i would have been simply the number 2 with no reference to the symbol i. The rule for **next** would have been just **next = 2**.

Note that with ":=" it is easy to define "functions": you do not have to be concerned with whether any of the symbols have rules associated with them at the time you define your "function."

Define a "function" of **x**.	*In[13]:=* **y := 3x^2 + 4x - 7**
Assign a value to **x**.	*In[14]:=* **x = 2.3** *Out[14]=* 2.3
Evaluate **y** at **x**= 2.3.	*In[15]:=* **y** *Out[15]=* 18.07

There is a much better way to define functions, but this "quick and dirty" way is occasionally useful as a convenient way of forming a rule to evaluate an expression repeatedly. In fact, we can use this idea to write "programs" that do several operations.

This is basically how *Mathematica* works. There are other kinds of rules to learn about, and there are more details to how evaluation works, but the essential idea is that rules are used as they apply and evaluation continues until none of the rules is applicable. Such a process allows infinite recursion: What if a rule continues to be applicable? We will not discuss this problem now.

A.1.4 Some basic grammar and syntax

You may have noticed by now that some symbols we have used begin with a capital letter. Indeed, all symbols that are built into *Mathematica* begin with capital letters, e.g., **Plot**, **Sin**, **Precision**, **Pi**, **I**, etc. However, all functions that you as a user define *should* begin with a lowercase letter. This is not required; it is merely a convenient way to avoid conflicts. *Mathematica* has nearly 1000 built-in symbols and many more defined in external packages. If your own names begin with capital letters, you are likely to encounter name conflicts.

Another general rule about names is that they are usually complete words or combinations of words with each word capitalized. Thus we have names like **Plot**, **Precision**, **Show**, **ListPlot**, and **SetPrecision**. The main exception to this rule is that functions and constants that have a standard mathematical abbreviation take that abbreviation as their name. Thus we have `Sin`, `Tan`, `Exp`, and `Log`. This is not to say that there are no names consisting of a single letter. The symbols `C`, `D`, `E`, `I`, `N`, and `O` are defined, and we will have cause to use each of these in our study of numerical analysis.

Everything in *Mathematica* is an expression. An expression can either be an indivisible "atom" or be composed of other expressions. A nonatomic expression consists of a *head* followed by a (possibly empty) sequence of expressions, called *elements*, enclosed in brackets and separated by commas. Thus `Plus[1, x, Times[2.3, a]]` is a nonatomic expression. Its head is `Plus`, and its three elements are `1`, `x`, and `Times[2.3, a]`, each of which is itself an expression.

This is an atom.	`In[1]:= AtomQ[x]`
	`Out[1]= True`
This is not an atom.	`In[2]:= AtomQ[f[1-y, x, 3.7]]`
	`Out[2]= False`

An atom is an indivisible expression and can be a *number*, a *string*, or a *symbol*. There are four types of numbers: integers, rationals, reals, and complex numbers. A string is a sequence of characters enclosed in quotation marks, e.g., `"apple"`. A symbol is a sequence of letters and digits, beginning with a letter. Symbols are used as names for things. Some built-in symbols are `Plus`, `Pi`, and `Integrate`. `Plus` has rules associated with it that cause addition to occur. `Pi` has rules associated with it that allow it to be numerically evaluated to $3.1415926\cdots$. A symbol with no associated rules may be thought of as a mathematical variable.

We repeat: Everything in *Mathematica* is an expression. However, certain symbols such as `Plus` and `Set` have special forms for input and output that do not appear to have heads. It is much more convenient and readable to use `d = a + b + c` rather than `Set[d, Plus[a, b, c]]`. Lists also have a special form. A list in *Mathematica* is simply any expression with a head of `List`, but the special form for a list is the sequence of its elements enclosed in braces and separated by commas. Thus `List[a, 2, Plus]` is printed as `{a, 2, Plus}`.

The internal form of the expression `2 + 3x`.	`In[3]:= FullForm[2 + 3x]`
	`Out[3]//FullForm= Plus[2, Times[3, x]]`
Lists can be nested.	`In[4]:= FullForm[{{1, 2}, {x, y}}]`
	`Out[4]//FullForm= List[List[1, 2], List[x, y]]`

You can see the complete structure of any expression by asking for the `FullForm[ ]` of it.

The function `Head[ ]` can be applied to any expression. If the expression is a nonatomic expression, it will return the head of that expression. If `Head[ ]` is applied to a number, it will return `Integer`, `Rational`, `Real`, or `Complex`, depending on what type of number it is. If `Head[ ]` is applied to a string or a symbol, it will return `String` or `Symbol`, respectively.

The function `Part[ ]` can be used to extract particular elements from nonatomic expressions. Thus `Part[Plus[a, b, c], 2]` will return `b`. `Part[ ]` is most commonly used to extract elements of lists. It should be noted here that the head of an expression is regarded as part 0, and that **Part** can be used to extract the head of any expression. Finally, although there are no negative parts, the part specification can be negative. When you specify part $-n$, the element referred to is the nth element from the end. Thus the last part of an expression is part number -1.

The head of `Sin[x+y]` is `Sin`.	*In[5]:=* `Head[Sin[x+y]]`
	Out[5]= `Sin`
The head of a list is `List`.	*In[6]:=* `Part[{{1, 2}, {x, y}}, 0]`
	Out[6]= `List`
A simpler notation for extracting parts uses double brackets.	*In[7]:=* `{{1, 2}, {x, y}}[[1]]`
	Out[7]= `{1, 2}`
We can extract the first part of the last part using double brackets.	*In[8]:=* `{{1, 2}, {x, y}}[[-1, 1]]`
	Out[8]= `x`

Rational and complex numbers are atoms even though they look otherwise when you display them using **FullForm[ ]**. You cannot extract the numerator of a rational number or the imaginary part of a complex number using **Part[ ]**.

All computer languages have provisions for making comments, and *Mathematica* is no exception. A comment is made by typing a string of characters between the delimiters (* and *). When answering specific questions asked in the computer problems, your answer should consist of a *Mathematica* comment. Although excessive comments in a lengthy piece of *Mathematica* code are distracting, a few comments can be very helpful when it comes to trying to understand what a particular piece of code is supposed to do.

We close this subsection by recalling the five different types of paired delimiters that *Mathematica* uses.

( )	for mathematical grouping
{ }	for representing lists
[ ]	for forming expressions
[[ ]]	for extracting parts of expressions
(* *)	to begin and end comments

Types of paired delimiters

A.1.5   Lists

In the previous subsection we introduced lists. *Mathematica* uses lists extensively, and there are many ways to form and manipulate lists. Lists are used in many *Mathematica* commands, and we consider them in more depth here.

As we said earlier, a list has a head of `List` but is normally shown in the form { $expr_1$, $expr_2$, ..., $expr_n$ }. The `Plot[ ]` command uses a list to specify the domain of the plot. Many other functions in *Mathematica* use lists in this same way to specify the values over which a variable is supposed to range. Sometimes, as in `Sum[i, {i, 1, 5}]`, the variable takes on discrete values. In this example this means that i takes on exactly the values 1, 2, 3, 4, and 5. When a list is used in this way it is called an *iterator*. In other cases, such as `Plot[x^2, {x, 2, 7}]`, the variable is supposed to take on all values in the real interval. (In fact, it really takes on only enough of the values to get the *effect* of taking on all values in the interval.)

Another use of lists is simply to group data. When data are stored in a list we can refer to them as a single entity. We can also do many operations on a list that have the effect of doing those operations on each of the elements individually. This is a very powerful way of manipulating data. Functions that behave in this way are called `Listable`. For example, if `f[ ]` is listable, then `f[{a, b, c}]` gets evaluated to `{f[a], f[b], f[c]}`.

One way to generate a list.	$In[1]:=$ `Range[1, 4]`
	$Out[1]=$ `{1, 2, 3, 4}`
The optional third argument to `Range[ ]` is the increment.	$In[2]:=$ `a = Range[1, 2, .3]`
	$Out[2]=$ `{1, 1.3, 1.6, 1.9}`
A list with three elements.	$In[3]:=$ `v = {1, 2, n}`
	$Out[3]=$ `{1, 2, n}`
Many mathematical functions are `Listable`, i.e., they operate element by element on lists.	$In[4]:=$ `u = x^v - 1`
	$Out[4]=$ $\{-1 + x, -1 + x^2, -1 + x^n\}$
This is differentiation with respect to x. Differentiation is also `Listable`.	$In[5]:=$ `D[u, x]`
	$Out[5]=$ $\{1, 2x, n x^{-1+n}\}$
Lists can be formed with elements specified by a formula using the `Table` function. An optional fourth element of an iterator specifies the increment.	$In[6]:=$ `Table[i^3, {i, 1, 6}]`
	$Out[6]=$ `{1, 8, 27, 64, 125, 216}`
`Table[ ]` can also generate a list of lists. The default starting value of an iterator is 1	$In[7]:=$ `m = Table[i^(j-1), {i, 3},{j, 4}]`
	$Out[7]=$ `{{1, 1, 1, 1}, {1, 2, 4, 8}, {1, 3, 9, 27}}`
We can print out a list of lists in matrix format.	$In[8]:=$ `m // MatrixForm`

$Out[8]//MatrixForm=$
$$\begin{array}{cccc} 1 & 1 & 1 & 1 \\ 1 & 2 & 4 & 8 \\ 1 & 3 & 9 & 27 \end{array}$$

Here we form a list of random elements. The iterator simply specifies the count.	$In[9]:=$ `tab = Table[Random[], {4}]`
	$Out[9]=$ `{0.0560708, 0.6303, 0.359894, 0.871377}`

We can refer to an individual *part* of a list using double brackets and its position.

$In[10]:=$ **tab[[3]]**

$Out[10]=$ 0.359894

Length[ ] gives the number of elements in a list (or any expression).

$In[11]:=$ **Length[tab]**

$Out[11]=$ 4

You can assign values to symbols or expressions that represent lists or parts of lists. When you do this, *Mathematica* first evaluates the right-hand side of an assignment and then assigns the result to the left-hand side. Only certain forms of the left-hand side are allowed. If the left-hand side is a symbol, the assignment is to the unevaluated left-hand side. If the left-hand side is a **Part** of a variable whose value is a list, that part of the list is altered to reflect the assignment.

Start with a simple list.

$In[1]:=$ **b = {1, 2, 3}**

$Out[1]=$ {1, 2, 3}

Set the second part of b to a different value.

$In[2]:=$ **b[[2]] = 17**

$Out[2]=$ 17

$In[3]:=$ **b**

$Out[3]=$ {1, 17, 3}

If there is no such part, it cannot be set.

$In[4]:=$ **b[[4]] = 13**

Part::part: Part 4 of {1, 17, 3} does not exist.

$Out[4]=$ 13

Most programming languages require you to use a temporary variable if you want to swap the values of two variables. In *Mathematica* you can do this without a temporary variable.

Set the values of a and b to be 1 and 2, respectively.

$In[5]:=$ **{a, b} = {1, 2}**

$Out[5]=$ {1, 2}

Swap the values of a and b.

$In[6]:=$ **{a, b} = {b, a}**

$Out[6]=$ {2, 1}

A.1.6 Defining your own functions

Functions are defined in *Mathematica* with rules involving "_" (called *blank*). The left-hand side of the rule specifies the name of the function and the argument(s). The right-hand side of the rule describes what the function does.

Define a function called f with the argument x. Notice the use of ":=".

$In[1]:=$ **f[x_] := x + x^3**

Evaluate $f(5)$.

$In[2]:=$ **f[5]**

$Out[2]=$ 130

There is no rule for a function f[ ] with two arguments, so this evaluates to itself.

```
In[3]:= f[2, 3]
Out[3]= f[2, 3]
```

If the function is to have more than one argument, each of the arguments must be indicated by a labeled blank on the left-hand side of the rule.

Define a function of two variables, the formal parameters being x and d.

```
In[4]:= spike[x_, d_] := 1/(d Sqrt[Pi]) Exp[-(x/d)^2]
```

The expression spike[1, 2] is of the form spike[x_, d_], so the rule was used. Recall that only exact arithmetic is used with integers and rationals, so the result is not very simple.

```
In[5]:= spike[1, 2]
                    1
Out[5]= ─────────────────
            1/4
        2 E    Sqrt[Pi]
```

There is no rule for spike[ ] with one argument.

```
In[6]:= spike[1.]
Out[6]= spike[1.]
```

Examine all information associated with the symbol spike.

```
In[7]:= ?spike
Global`spike
spike[x_, d_] := (1*Exp[-(x/d)^2])/(d*Sqrt[Pi])
```

The basic idea in defining a function is to make a rule that describes how any expression of a specified form is to be evaluated. The form f[x_] indicates any expression with a head of f and one *argument*. The x in front of the "_" serves as a label for the argument. The right-hand side of the rule expresses what the function is supposed to do with the argument but uses only the "x", not the "_". For now, just use ":=" to make the rule. There are cases where you would want to use "=", but we can ignore those cases until later.

If a function is defined as a simple mathematical expression that is differentiable, we can evaluate its derivative at any point.

Earlier we defined the function f[ ]. This is the value of f[x].

```
In[7]:= f[x]
                 3
Out[7]= x + x
```

This is the value of the derivative of f[ ] at x.

```
In[8]:= f'[x]
                  2
Out[8]= 1 + 3 x
```

Another way to get the same result is to differentiate the expression given by evaluating f[x].

```
In[9]:= D[f[x], x]
                  2
Out[9]= 1 + 3 x
```

The "'" (prime) is used to take the derivative of a function. You cannot take the derivative of an expression. You differentiate an expression using the operator D[ ].

```
In[10]:= f[x]'
                   3
Out[10]= (x + x )'
```

We know how to define functions that can be expressed by simple formulas. What about more complicated functions? What about functions that can best be described as an algorithm? In fact, programming in *Mathematica* is, for the most part, just a matter of defining functions, i.e., making rules that describe how certain expressions are to be evaluated. As an example let us see how to define a command to find numerically the derivative of a function at a point. Recall that the definition of the derivative is

$$f'(x) = \lim_{h \to 0} \frac{f(x+h) - f(x)}{h}.$$

We will choose a short sequence of values for h that approach 0 and try to see where the values of the difference quotients are headed. Let us first see how we might do the necessary operations one step at a time. We will numerically evaluate $\sin'(1.)$.

Start with a list of values of h to use.

```
In[1]:= hlist = Table[2^(-i), {i, 0, 12}]
```

$$Out[1]= \{1, \frac{1}{2}, \frac{1}{4}, \frac{1}{8}, \frac{1}{16}, \frac{1}{32}, \frac{1}{64}, \frac{1}{128}, \frac{1}{256}, \frac{1}{512}, \frac{1}{1024},$$

$$\frac{1}{2048}, \frac{1}{4096}\}$$

This is the list of values at which we will evaluate sin.

```
In[2]:= 1. + hlist
```

```
Out[2]= {2., 1.5, 1.25, 1.125, 1.0625, 1.03125, 1.01563,
    1.00781, 1.00391, 1.00195, 1.00098, 1.00049, 1.00024}
```

This is the list of differences in the numerator. Note that this relies on the fact that `Sin[ ]` is listable.

```
In[3]:= Sin[%] - Sin[1.]
```

```
Out[3]= {0.0678264, 0.156024, 0.107514, 0.0607966,
    0.032104, 0.0164709, 0.00833916, 0.00419539,
    0.00210413, 0.00105367, 0.000527238, 0.000263719,
    0.000131885}
```

This is the list of difference quotients.

```
In[4]:= % / hlist
```

```
Out[4]= {0.0678264, 0.312048, 0.430055, 0.486373,
    0.513663, 0.527067, 0.533706, 0.53701, 0.538657,
    0.53948, 0.539891, 0.540097, 0.5402}
```

This is the limit of the sequence of difference quotients in that list as evaluated by a particular algorithm.

```
In[5]:= SequenceLimit[%]
```

```
Out[5]= 0.540302
```

To define a function to do all of this for us, we encapsulate the whole sequence of operations in a `Module`.[4]

---

[4]The function `Module[ ]` was new with Version 2.0 of *Mathematica*. In most cases `Block[ ]` will provide the same functionality, but `Module[ ]` and `Block[ ]` are different, and each has its own purpose.

```
nd[f_, x_] := Module[{i, hlist, data},
                hlist = Table[2^(-i), {i, 0, 12}];
                data = (f[x+hlist] - f[x])/hlist;
                SequenceLimit[data]
            ]
```

Notice that the right-hand side of the rule is a nonatomic expression with a head of `Module`. Its first element is a list of the local variables. It appears that there are three other elements, but if you look again you will see that they are separated by semicolons rather than commas. In fact, there are only two elements, and the second element is a `CompoundExpression` composed of three subexpressions. The last subexpression of the compound expression does not have a semicolon after it, and its value is the value that will be returned. In order for `nd[ ]` to work, the function `f[ ]` must be listable because it has to be evaluated at a list of different values.

Define the function.

```
In[1]:= nd[f_, x_] := Module[{i, hlist, data},
                      hlist = Table[2^(-i), {i, 0, 12}];
                      data = (f[x+hlist] - f[x])/hlist;
                      SequenceLimit[data]
                  ]
```

Numerically find the derivative of sin at 1.

```
In[2]:= nd[Sin, 1.]
Out[2]= 0.540302
```

It did a pretty good job.

```
In[3]:= % - Cos[1.]
                    -14
Out[3]= 3.37508 10
```

We close this subsection by mentioning that function definitions can be saved in a file and read back in later in the session or in a completely new *Mathematica* session.

Save the definition of nd in the file `tmp.m` .

```
In[4]:= Save["tmp.m",nd]
```

Clear the definition of the symbol nd, and read it back in.

```
In[5]:= Clear[nd]; << tmp.m;
```

```
In[6]:= ?nd
Global`nd
nd[f_, x_] :=
   Module[{i, hlist, data},
     hlist = Table[2^(-i), {i, 0, 12}];
      data = (f[x + hlist] - f[x])/hlist;
      SequenceLimit[data]]
```

A.1.7 Getting help

By now you are probably wondering how you will ever remember all of this information about *Mathematica*. There are two answers to this. First of all you *will not* remember it if you do not use it. You cannot learn *Mathematica* by reading about it. It may seem rather trivial, but sitting down with a computer and typing in these examples can be a useful exercise if you are just learning to use *Mathematica*.

The other answer to the problem of remembering so much about *Mathematica* is the on-line help that is available. You should try to remember the names of the functions that you need to use, but you do not need to remember the details of the use of each of them.

We can ask for information about a particular function ...

```
In[1]:= ?Plot

Plot[f, {x, xmin, xmax}] generates a plot of f as a
    function of x from xmin to xmax. Plot[{f1, f2, ...},
    {x, xmin, xmax}] plots several functions fi.
```

or we can ask about all symbols whose names contain a particular combination of letters. The "*" represents any sequence of zero or more characters.

```
In[1]:= ?Plot*

Plot            PlotJoined     PlotRange      Plot3D
PlotColor       PlotLabel      PlotRegion     Plot3Matrix
PlotDivision    PlotPoints     PlotStyle
```

With ?? we get the options and the attributes in addition to the usage message.

```
In[1]:= ??Plot

Plot[f, {x, xmin, xmax}] generates a plot of f as a
    function of x from xmin to xmax. Plot[{f1, f2, ...},
    {x, xmin, xmax}] plots several functions fi.

Attributes[Plot] = {HoldAll, Protected}

Options[Plot] =
  {AspectRatio -> GoldenRatio^(-1), Axes -> Automatic,
   AxesLabel -> None, AxesOrigin -> Automatic,
   AxesStyle -> Automatic, Background -> Automatic,
   ColorOutput -> Automatic, Compiled -> True,
   DefaultColor -> Automatic, Epilog -> {},
   Frame -> False, FrameLabel -> None,
   FrameStyle -> Automatic, FrameTicks -> Automatic,
   GridLines -> None, MaxBend -> 10.,
   PlotDivision -> 20., PlotLabel -> None,
   PlotPoints -> 25, PlotRange -> Automatic,
   PlotRegion -> Automatic, PlotStyle -> Automatic,
   Prolog -> {}, RotateLabel -> True, Ticks -> Automatic,
   DefaultFont :> $DefaultFont,
   DisplayFunction :> $DisplayFunction}
```

A.1.8 Miscellanea

You can think of the character ";" (semicolon) as an expression separator and use it much as you would in many other computer languages, but in reality it joins subexpressions to form a single expression with a head of CompoundExpression. Many commands in *Mathematica* require a certain number of arguments; and if you want to do a bit of computation within an argument, you must separate the subexpressions with semicolons. If you separate them with commas, you form additional arguments. A compound expression is evaluated by evaluating each subexpression in order, and the result is the result of the last subexpression. If you end an expression with a ";", you create a CompoundExpression whose last part is the expression Null. This can be useful if the result of an input command is expected to be very long: If you make the final result Null, it will not be displayed.

When comparing different programs that perform the same task, it is useful to measure the time it takes to evaluate an expression. The function `Timing[ ]` provides this facility. In particular, `Timing[expr]` evaluates to a list consisting of the time it took to evaluate *expr* and the result of that evaluation. By using `Timing[expr;]` you create a `CompoundExpression` that evaluates to `Null`. This is useful if *expr* evaluates to a very large expression; you get the time it took to evaluate it but not the large expression.

Mathematica automatically saves the result of line *n* of a *Mathematica* session in the *indexed variable* `Out[n]`, which is why "`Out[n]=`" is printed to the left of the result. To obtain a prior result, you enter "`Out[n]`". A shorter way to accomplish the same thing is to type "`%n`"; or, if you want the immediately preceding result, just "`%`". You can also obtain a prior input by entering "`In[n]`", but this will reevaluate it. In particular, if any symbol used in the evaluation of `In[n]` has changed since it was first evaluated, the current evaluation may give a different result. `InString[n]` prints the input to line *n* as a string (so it is not evaluated). This can be useful when you want to recall what a prior command was. If you are using a Notebook interface, you can just scroll back and look at each input command.

It is easy to make a typing error or ask *Mathematica* to do something that will take an unexpectedly long time to be evaluated. If this happens, you can interrupt *Mathematica* and get a menu with several choices of what to do. The way to interrupt *Mathematica* varies from one computer system to another. On a UNIX system, type CTRL-C. On a Macintosh computer, choose **Interrupt** from the Action menu or hold down the Command key and type a period. On an MS-DOS system, type CTRL-BREAK.

On machines having a Notebook interface everything is automatically saved in the Notebook, and when you exit *Mathematica* you have the option of saving the Notebook. With a text-based interface, if you want to get a nice-looking transcript of a *Mathematica* session, proceed as follows: Read in the package `Record.m` using the command `<< Utilities`Record`` once you have started a *Mathematica* session. All of your input from then on will be appended to the file `math.record` in the current directory. When you are through, edit the file `math.record`, deleting false starts and inserting `$Echo={"stdout"}` as the first line. (Be careful about using "`%`" because by deleting unwanted input commands you can change what it refers to.) Then run your "program" in batch mode; with UNIX, this can be done with the command `math <math.record >log &`.

Computer problems

1. What are the full forms of "_" and "#"?

2. What is the full form of "`(#1^2  #2^#3)&`"?

3. Let `x = Sqrt[2.]` . What is `x x == 2.` and `x x-2.`?

4. Consider the polynomial

$$4t^8 + 8t^7 + 5t^6 - 6t^5 - 15t^4 - 14t^3 - 6t^2 + 1.$$

(a) Determine the smallest real root that is greater than 1 using `NRoots`. Then, using exact arithmetic (integers and rationals only), confirm rigorously that there is at least one real root between 1.292 and 1.293. *Caution:* Any use of `Reals` will invalidate your proof. Advice: To save typing, store the polynomial in a variable or define it to be a function.

(b) By considering the behavior of derivatives of the polynomial, confirm rigorously that there is exactly one root for $t > 1.1$. Hint: Show that the first derivative is positive at $t = 1.1$ and that the second derivative is positive for all $t > 1$.

5. Use `Table[Random[Integer, {-5, 5}], {8}]  .  (x^Range[0,7])` to generate a random polynomial of degree 7. Use `NRoots[ ]` to find the roots of this polynomial. Does the number of roots agree with the number required by the fundamental theorem of algebra?

6. Express $\sum_{i=3}^{7} f(i)$ and $\prod_{j=-2}^{6} (f(j) - j)$ in *Mathematica* notation using `Sum[ ]` and `Product[ ]`.

A.2   Lesson Two

A.2.1   More on floating-point numbers

In Lesson One we mentioned some obvious differences between the arithmetic in *Mathematica* and that of most calculators. A more subtle difference between the arithmetic of *Mathematica* and that of calculators is that *Mathematica* has two kinds of floating-point numbers. Computer hardware is designed to handle numbers represented in a certain format and is quite fast at doing arithmetic with these numbers. However, such numbers have limited precision. To avoid this restriction *Mathematica* also has "arbitrary-precision numbers" to allow for higher precision and very large numbers. The arithmetic that deals with arbitrary-precision numbers is done in software and is much slower. For many purposes you do not need to worry about this distinction, but you cannot ignore it completely because there are differences that are particularly relevant to numerical analysis.

The function `N[ ]` normally produces a machine number.

```
In[1]:= c = N[Pi]

Out[1]= 3.14159
```

You can use the test `MachineNumberQ[ ]` to test whether a number is a machine number or an arbitrary-precision number.

```
In[2]:= MachineNumberQ[c]

Out[2]= True
```

`N[ ]` will produce an arbitrary-precision number if the result cannot be represented as a machine number. The fact that there are more than 6 digits displayed is a good indication that it is not a machine number. The only sure way to tell is to test it.

```
In[3]:= N[23^456]

Out[3]= 8.869379219848028 10^620
```

```
In[4]:= MachineNumberQ[%]

Out[4]= False
```

N[ ] can be used to give an arbitrary-precision number by giving a second argument to specify how many digits you would like.

```
In[5]:= b = N[Pi, 30]
Out[5]= 3.14159265358979323846264338328
```

Note that there is no guarantee that you will get that many digits. N[ ] merely calculates π to 30 digits and then subtracts. If digits are lost due to cancellation, then you get fewer than what you asked for.

```
In[6]:= N[Pi - 314159265359/100000000000, 30]
                                      -13
Out[6]= -2.0676153735661672 10
```

You can use the function Precision[ ] to see just how many digits a number has.

```
In[7]:= Precision[%]
Out[7]= 17
```

The precision of machine numbers on this computer is 16 digits.

```
In[8]:= $MachinePrecision
Out[8]= 16
```

Since c is a machine number, it has precision $MachinePrecision.

```
In[9]:= Precision[c]
Out[9]= 16
```

Arithmetic with machine numbers results in a machine number (if possible).

```
In[10]:= Precision[c - 314159/100000]
Out[10]= 16
```

We defined b earlier to have 30 digits.

```
In[11]:= Precision[b]
Out[11]= 30
```

Arithmetic with arbitrary-precision numbers results in numbers whose Precision reflects the perceived accuracy of the result. This is the biggest difference between arbitrary-precision numbers and machine numbers.

```
In[12]:= Precision[b - 314159/100000]
Out[12]= 24
```

You can even get greater precision than that with which you started.

```
In[13]:= Precision[10^20 + b]
Out[13]= 50
```

In addition to having two different kinds of floating-point numbers, *Mathematica* uses different kinds of arithmetic. When working with machine numbers, *Mathematica* uses the sort of arithmetic that we study in this book. With arbitrary-precision numbers, however, *Mathematica* adjusts the precision of each result to reflect its perceived accuracy. We prefer not to use this sort of arithmetic for several reasons, and we will compensate for the effect of adjusted precision[5] by simply starting with sufficiently high precision that the result will have the necessary precision. Since N[ ] cannot increase the precision of a number, you cannot use it to get high-precision starting values. The command SetPrecision[ ] can be used to

---

[5]In version 2.1 and later of *Mathematica* you can control the precision by setting the global variables $MinPrecision and $MaxPrecision. The precision of any arbitrary-precision number will always be maintained between these two bounds.

produce an arbitrary-precision number whose precision is any specified value (within certain limits). In fact, `SetPrecision[expr, n]` will give a new expression equal to *expr* in which the precision of each of the (nonzero) numbers is *n* digits.

You should be aware of several rules that are used in any arithmetic that involves machine numbers or arbitrary-precision numbers. The general philosophy is that machine numbers are for speed and their accuracy is unknown. Thus, arithmetic with machine numbers generally results in a machine number unless the result is too large or too small. If the result cannot be represented as a machine number, it is converted to an arbitrary-precision number with `$MachinePrecision` digits. If no machine numbers are involved, arithmetic with arbitrary-precision numbers results in an arbitrary-precision number. This is the case even if the result has fewer than `$MachinePrecision` digits.

You should be aware that the comparison operators in *Mathematica* are inexact. That is, *Mathematica* may say that two numbers are equal when they are in fact only very close.

Start with values for a and b that are very close together. (`$MachineEpsilon` is the difference between 1.0 and the next larger machine number.)

```
In[14]:= a = 1.0; b = 1 + 2.0 $MachineEpsilon
Out[14]= 1.
```

It is clear that b is greater than a.

```
In[15]:= b - a > 0
Out[15]= True
```

Mathematica accepts these values as being equal.

```
In[16]:= a == b
Out[16]= True
```

It also claims that a is not less than b.

```
In[17]:= a < b
Out[17]= False
```

The way to get exact, reliable comparisons is to subtract the two numbers being compared.

A.2.2 Plotting functions and data

Plotting functions with *Mathematica* is fairly simple. You just need to specify three things: the expression to be plotted, the independent variable, and the domain of the independent variable. *Mathematica* will automatically choose a range for the dependent variable, put in the axes and label them, and draw the graph for you. The result of a plot command is what is called a "graphics object." Since one would rarely want to *see* the contents of a graphics object (they are quite large and not very useful), the result is simply printed as "-**Graphics**-". "So," you ask, "what is the use of a plot command?" Well, as a *side effect* of the plot command, *Mathematica* also draws a picture for you. The picture itself is not the result, and you cannot refer to the picture with % or any other way. With the Notebook interface this picture is placed right in the Notebook document. With the text-based interface the picture either pops up in a new window or is drawn on the entire screen and disappears when you continue with the *Mathematica* session. With the Notebook interface the plot gets printed if and when you print the document, or you can print the plot by itself. With the text-based interface, the procedure for printing a plot can vary widely, and you should ask for local assistance. (Typically the *Mathematica* command is `PSPrint[ ]` or there is a special keystroke to get a screen dump.)

   The most important plotting function is `Plot[ ]`, but there are many other ones. In addition, each plotting function has many "knobs" known as "options" that you can adjust to get effects that you want. Here we will only touch on a few of the many different possibilities for producing plots.

Plot $\sin x$ on the interval $x \in [0, 20]$.   *In[1]:=* `Plot[Sin[x], {x, 0, 20}]`

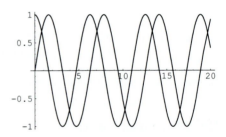

Plot both $\sin x$ and $\cos x$ on the same interval.   *In[2]:=* `Plot[{Sin[x], Cos[x]}, {x, 0, 20}]`

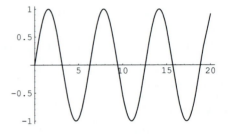

By adjusting the option `PlotStyle` we have made the curve for $\sin x$ dashed and that for $\cos x$ very thick.   *In[3]:=* `Plot[{Sin[x], Cos[x]}, {x, 0, 20},`
`                PlotStyle -> {Dashing[{.02}], Thickness[.007]}]`

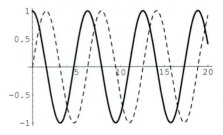

If there are too many wiggles, *Mathematica* does not resolve them all properly. The option `PlotLabel` can be set to a string to label a plot.

In[4]:= `Plot[Sin[x], {x, 0, 300}, PlotLabel -> "Bad Plot"]`

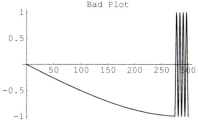

By asking for more sample points we get a better (but slower) plot.

In[5]:= `Plot[Sin[x], {x, 0, 300}, PlotPoints -> 120]`

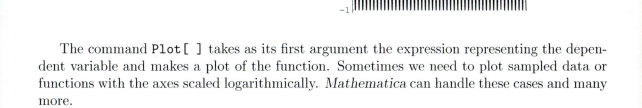

The command `Plot[ ]` takes as its first argument the expression representing the dependent variable and makes a plot of the function. Sometimes we need to plot sampled data or functions with the axes scaled logarithmically. *Mathematica* can handle these cases and many more.

A list of ordered pairs.

In[6]:= `data = {{0,4}, {1,7}, {2,4}, {3,1}, {4,4}}`

Out[6]= `{{0, 4}, {1, 7}, {2, 4}, {3, 1}, {4, 4}}`

We can plot the data as separate points.

In[7]:= `ListPlot[data]`

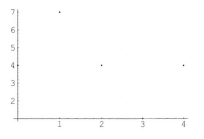

Or we can join the points with straight line segments.

In[8]:= `ListPlot[data, PlotJoined -> True]`

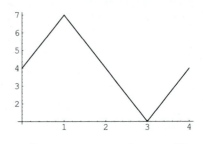

Here is a cubic polynomial that passes through the same set of points.

In[9]:= `Plot[x^3-6x^2+8x+4, {x, 0, 4}]`

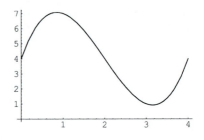

We can redraw two graphs on the same set of axes.

In[10]:= `Show[{%, %%}]`

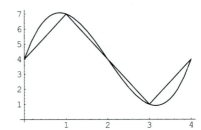

The plotting functions have many options that can be used to control just about anything about the picture. We will have no reason to change most of these options, but we present here a brief example of the use of `GridLines` and `PlotRange`.

Draw coordinate lines and restrict the range of the plot to the interval [0, 1].

In[1]:=
`Plot[Sin[x], {x, 0, 20}, GridLines -> Automatic,`
`                          PlotRange -> {0, 1}]`

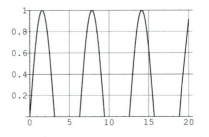

A.2.3 **Symbolic calculations**

In most programming languages variables are declared to be of a certain type and you can assign only values of the declared type to a variable. However, since everything in *Mathematica* is an expression, we can set the value of any symbol to be any expression; we do not have to declare types. We declare local variables in a `Module` or `Block` to localize the symbols so that conflicts with external symbols with the same name do not occur. When *Mathematica* evaluates a symbol, it first looks to see whether that symbol has any rules associated with it. If it does not, then that symbol is its own value. If it does have a rule, then *Mathematica* applies the rule and keeps on evaluating things until no more rules apply. This is the basic model of how *Mathematica* does everything. Unless you understand this idea, you are likely to get very confused about what *Mathematica* is doing.

Set the variable `t1` to be an expression in `x`.

```
In[1]:= t1 = 1 + x^2
           2
Out[1]= 1 + x
```

Set `x` to be 3.

```
In[2]:= x = 3
Out[2]= 3
```

This looks like the rule we made for `t1`, but it is quite different. Since `x` has a value of 3, `t2` gets the value 10.

```
In[3]:= t2 = 1 + x^2
Out[3]= 10
```

The rule for `t1` is still `1 + x^2`, regardless of what `x` is.

```
In[4]:= ?t1
Global`t1
t1 = 1 + x^2
```

The rule for `t2` is simply 10.

```
In[4]:= ?t2
     Global`t2
t2 = 10
```

If we change `x`, the result of evaluating `t1` changes (but not `t1` itself.) However, the value of `t2` is still just 10.

```
In[4]:= x = 2; {t1, t2}
Out[4]= {5, 10}
```

If we clear `x`, then evaluation of `t1` stops at `1 + x^2`.

```
In[5]:= Clear[x]; {t1, t2}
                   2
Out[5]= {1 + x , 10}
```

The above method of evaluating expressions at specific values of a variable does work, but it is easy to make mistakes. Too much is happening in the background that you do not see; if you forget to clear a variable when you should, you can get quite confused. A much better way to do it is to use explicit replacement rules that do not affect the value of the replaced variable.

Evaluate `t1` using 2 for `x`. The expression "`x -> 2`" is a `Rule` and "`t /. x -> 2`" is analogous to the mathematical notation $t|_{x=2}$.

```
In[6]:= t1 /. x -> 2
Out[6]= 5
```

We can replace more than one variable at a time.

$In[7]:=$ `(x - y)^2 /. {x -> 3, y -> 1 - a}`

$Out[7]=$ $(2 + a)^2$

Equations can be created in *Mathematica* by using the **Equal** operator (==), because *Mathematica* leaves expressions alone if they cannot be evaluated any further.

The notation "==" is used to form an equation. Inequalities can be formed with the notation !=, <, >, <=, or >= .

$In[1]:=$ `equ = x^2 + x == 6`

$Out[1]=$ $x + x^2 == 6$

An equation can be **True**, ...

$In[2]:=$ `x = 2; equ`

$Out[2]=$ `True`

False, ...

$In[3]:=$ `x = 3; equ`

$Out[3]=$ `False`

or simply an equation.

$In[4]:=$ `x = .; equ`

$Out[4]=$ $x + x^2 == 6$

The left- and right-hand sides can be obtained as **equ[[1]]** and **equ[[2]]**, respectively. (**equ[[0]]** yields the head **Equal**.)

$In[5]:=$ `{equ[[0]], equ[[1]], equ[[2]]}`

$Out[5]=$ $\{Equal, x + x^2, 6\}$

The function **Solve[ ]** takes equations and returns results in the form of rules.

Start with two equations in two variables.

$In[6]:=$ `eq1 = x^2 + y^2 == 1; eq2 = y == x^2;`

Solve for x and y. The result is a list of solution sets.

$In[7]:=$ `sol = Solve[ {eq1, eq2}, {x, y}]`

$$Out[7]= \{\{y \to \frac{-1 + \mathrm{Sqrt}[5]}{2}, x \to \frac{\mathrm{Sqrt}[-1 + \mathrm{Sqrt}[5]]}{\mathrm{Sqrt}[2]}\},$$
$$\{y \to \frac{-1 + \mathrm{Sqrt}[5]}{2}, x \to -(\frac{\mathrm{Sqrt}[-1 + \mathrm{Sqrt}[5]]}{\mathrm{Sqrt}[2]})\},$$
$$\{y \to \frac{-1 - \mathrm{Sqrt}[5]}{2}, x \to \frac{\mathrm{Sqrt}[-1 - \mathrm{Sqrt}[5]]}{\mathrm{Sqrt}[2]}\},$$
$$\{y \to \frac{-1 - \mathrm{Sqrt}[5]}{2}, x \to -(\frac{\mathrm{Sqrt}[-1 - \mathrm{Sqrt}[5]]}{\mathrm{Sqrt}[2]})\}\}$$

Since each solution is given as a list of replacement rules, we can use `ReplaceAll[ ]` ("/.") to replace the variables in the original equations.

$In[8]:=$ **{eq1, eq2} /. sol**

$Out[8]=$ $\{\{\dfrac{-1 + \text{Sqrt}[5]}{2} + \dfrac{(-1 + \text{Sqrt}[5])^2}{4} == 1, \text{True}\},$

$\{\dfrac{-1 + \text{Sqrt}[5]}{2} + \dfrac{(-1 + \text{Sqrt}[5])^2}{4} == 1, \text{True}\},$

$\{\dfrac{-1 - \text{Sqrt}[5]}{2} + \dfrac{(-1 - \text{Sqrt}[5])^2}{4} == 1, \text{True}\},$

$\{\dfrac{-1 - \text{Sqrt}[5]}{2} + \dfrac{(-1 - \text{Sqrt}[5])^2}{4} == 1, \text{True}\}\}$

Each solution satisfies both equations. `Simplify[ ]` tries several different transformations and returns the result that is the simplest.

$In[9]:=$ **Simplify[%]**

$Out[9]=$ {{True, True}, {True, True}, {True, True}, {True, True}}

We can get the pair of expressions representing a solution by using rules to replace the variables themselves.

$In[10]:=$ **{x, y} /. sol[[2]]**

$Out[10]=$ $\{-(\dfrac{\text{Sqrt}[-1 + \text{Sqrt}[5]]}{\text{Sqrt}[2]}), \dfrac{-1 + \text{Sqrt}[5]}{2}\}$

There are many functions in *Mathematica* that can be used to manipulate symbolic expressions. We present here only a few of them. Others will be mentioned later.

Expand the factored form of a polynomial.

$In[1]:=$ **Expand[(x-1)^2(x + 2y)]**

$Out[1]=$ $x - 2 x^2 + x^3 + 2 y - 4 x y + 2 x^2 y$

Factor a polynomial.

$In[2]:=$ **Factor[%]**

$Out[2]=$ $(-1 + x)^2 (x + 2 y)$

Get the list of coefficients of a polynomial.

$In[3]:=$ **CoefficientList[3x^2 + 4x - 7, x]**

$Out[3]=$ {-7, 4, 3}

Find the derivative of an expression with respect to a variable.

$In[4]:=$ **D[Sin[x^2 + 2c], x]**

$Out[4]=$ $2 x \cos[2 c + x^2]$

Find an antiderivative of an expression with respect to a specified variable.

$In[5]:=$ **Integrate[x Sin[x^2 + y], x]**

$Out[5]=$ $\dfrac{-\cos[x^2 + y]}{2}$

Evaluate a definite integral.

In[6]:= `Integrate[x Sin[x^2], {x, 0, 2}]`

$$Out[6]= \frac{1}{2} - \frac{Cos[4]}{2}$$

Evaluate a sum from 1 to 9 in increments of 2.

In[7]:= `Sum[x^i/i!, {i, 1, 9, 2}]`

$$Out[7]= x + \frac{x^3}{6} + \frac{x^5}{120} + \frac{x^7}{5040} + \frac{x^9}{362880}$$

This expression cannot be simplified by *Mathematica*.

In[8]:= `Sum[1/i^2, {i, 1, Infinity}]`

$$Out[8]= Sum[i^{-2}, \{i, 1, Infinity\}]$$

However, *Mathematica* can evaluate it numerically.

In[9]:= `N[%]`

Out[9]= `1.64493`

A.2.4 Loops and conditionals

Listable functions can often be used to avoid loops. In general it is a good idea to exploit this attribute when it is possible, but problems often arise that are best solved with a loop or a conditional structure. There are many *Mathematica* control structures. A partial list of them includes If, Do, Switch, Condition, Fold, FoldList, Nest, NestList, For, While, FixedPoint, Sum, and Product. We consider some of them here. Most of them return a computed expression when evaluated, but Do, For, and While perform their tasks and return the symbol Null, which represents "nothing." Null is not normally printed in output form.

Do is one type of loop structure in *Mathematica*. Note that t was initialized before the loop was entered.

In[1]:= `t = s; Do[t = k/(1 + t), {k, 3, 5}]; t`

$$Out[1]= \cfrac{5}{1 + \cfrac{4}{1 + \cfrac{3}{1 + s}}}$$

The result of a While[ ] is Null. The printing of intermediate results is only a side effect caused by the Print[ ] command.

In[2]:= `n = 37; While[(n = Ceiling[n/2]) > 1, Print[n]]`

```
19
10
5
3
2
```

The If in *Mathematica* is a bit different from what you might expect. This is because an expression may be True, False, or undecided.

Define a function that is supposed to give the absolute value of its argument for real numbers.

In[1]:= `f[x_] := If[x < 0, -x]`

Well, it works for negative numbers, but it does nothing with positive numbers.

In[2]:= `{f[3.2], f[-5.3]}`

Out[2]= `{Null, 5.3}`

The third argument is for when the first argument is `False`.

```
In[3]:= f[x_] := If[x < 0, -x, x]
```

It still does not know what to do if the argument is not a number.

```
In[4]:= {f[3.2], f[-5.3], f[a]}
Out[4]= {3.2, 5.3, If[a < 0, -a, a]}
```

The fourth argument is for when the first argument is undecided.

```
In[5]:= f[x_] := If[x < 0, -x, x, Abs[x]]
```

Now it does something in each of the three cases. (Of course `Abs[ ]` itself also works in each of the three cases.)

```
In[6]:= {f[3.2], f[-5.3], f[a]}
Out[6]= {3.2, 5.3, Abs[a]}
```

The `Which` construct takes an even number of arguments. It operates by considering each of its odd-numbered parts (i.e., the first, third, fifth, etc.) in turn, and when it encounters one that evaluates to `True` it returns the next (even-numbered) part. Note that even though several of the "tests" may be true, it is the first of these whose corresponding result is returned. One use of `Which[ ]` is to define a function in pieces.

Even though the last test is always `True`, the value −1 is returned only if none of the prior tests evaluates to `True`.

```
In[7]:= Plot[
          Which[ x < 0,           1,
                 x < N[Pi], Cos[x],
                 True,           -1
          ], {x, -2, 5}]
```

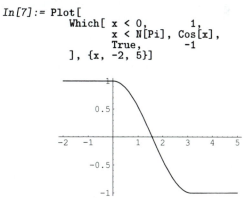

`Break[ ]` and `Return[ ]` can be used to exit from loops. In particular, `Break[ ]` takes no arguments and will cause an exit from the innermost `Do`, `For`, or `While` loop that contains it. Evaluation will continue at the next subexpression after the loop. `Return[expr]` will cause an exit from the function that contains it, and the function will return a value of *expr*.

Define a function using both `Break[ ]` and `Return[ ]`.

```
In[8]:= f[x_] :=
          Module[{i, sum = 0},
                 If[x < 0, Return[x]];
                 Do[ sum = sum + i;
                     If[sum > 20, Break[ ]],
                 {i, x}];
                 sum
          ];
```

Since the argument is negative, it is immediately returned.

```
In[9]:= f[-3]
Out[9]= -3
```

| This is $1 + 2 + 3 + 4$. | *In[10]:=* **f[4]** |
| | *Out[10]=* 10 |

| The loop was exited when **sum** became $1 + 2 + 3 + 4 + 5 + 6$. | *In[11]:=* **f[30]** |
| | *Out[11]=* 21 |

The functions **And[ ]**, **Or[ ]**, and **Xor[ ]** can be used to combine elementary conditions to form more complicated conditions. **And[ ]** and **Or[ ]** can be invoked with the infix notation **&&** and **||**, respectively. In addition to **AtomQ[ ]** and **MachineNumberQ[ ]** there are more than 30 other predicate functions that can be used to form conditions. The names of all of these predicate functions end with the letter "Q", and the functions always return either **True** or **False**. Among them are **NumberQ[ ]**, **EvenQ[ ]**, **IntegerQ[ ]**.

A.2.5 Defining rules
The basic process in *Mathematica* is the evaluation of expressions. This is done by the application of *rules* in a precisely defined fashion until no more rules are applicable. Many rules are built in, and you can define others.

| Define b[1] . | *In[1]:=* **b[1] = 11** |
| | *Out[1]=* 11 |

| Define b[3] . | *In[2]:=* **b[3] = 13** |
| | *Out[2]=* 13 |

| The value of b itself is unaffected. | *In[3]:=* **b** |
| | *Out[3]=* b |

The definitions of b[1] and b[3] are associated with b.	*In[4]:=* **?b**
	Global`b
	b[1] = 11
	b[3] = 13

| b[2], b[4], and b[5] have no value other than themselves. | *In[4]:=* **Table[b[i], {i, 5}]** |
| | *Out[4]=* {11, b[2], 13, b[4], b[5]} |

| The argument gets evaluated, but nothing more happens. | *In[5]:=* **f[7-4]** |
| | *Out[5]=* f[3] |

| Here is a definition for the expression f[x]. | *In[6]:=* **f[x] = Sin[w]** |
| | *Out[6]=* Sin[w] |

| Here is a rule for f with an arbitrary argument. | *In[7]:=* **f[x_] := x^2-3** |

When more than one rule applies, the more specific rules are tried before the more general ones. Thus, the rule for `f[x]` is tried before the rule for `f[ ]`, and the result is `Sin[w]`

```
In[8]:= f[x]
Out[8]= Sin[w]
```

We have no special rule for `f[y]`, so the more general rule is used.

```
In[9]:= f[y]

Out[9]= -3 + y
              2
```

The head of `f[x]` gets evaluated to 23 before any other rules are checked. There is no rule for `23[4]`

```
In[10]:= f = 23; f[4]
Out[10]= 23[4]
```

Mathematica allows functions to be defined recursively; but if the recursion never bottoms out, it will stop when `$RecursionLimit` is reached.

Define a value at which to stop.

```
In[1]:= fac[1] = 1
Out[1]= 1
```

Define the recursion relation.

```
In[2]:= fac[n_] := n fac[n-1]
```

We have defined the factorial function for the positive integers.

```
In[3]:= fac[7] == 7!
Out[3]= True
```

Recursion stops when it gets down to `fac[1]` or when it hits `$RecursionLimit`. Here it got down to `fac[1.]` but continued on because `fac[1.]` is not the same as `fac[1]`.

```
In[4]:= fac[13.]
$RecursionLimit::reclim: Recursion depth of 256 exceeded.
$RecursionLimit::reclim: Recursion depth of 256 exceeded.
$RecursionLimit::reclim: Recursion depth of 256 exceeded.
General::stop:
    Further output of $RecursionLimit::reclim
         will be suppressed during this calculation.
Out[4]= 0. Hold[fac[Hold[-234. - 1] - 1]]

        Hold[Hold[-234. - 1]]
```

Now it works because it stops at `fac[1.]`.

```
In[5]:= fac[1.] = 1.; fac[13.]

Out[5]= 6.22702 10
                    9
```

A.2.6 Replacing subexpressions

Mathematica uses rules for evaluating expressions. This concept is fundamental to understanding the way *Mathematica* works. These rules are associated with symbols, and they are used in the evaluation process as they apply. This evaluation is automatic; the only control you have over it is through the ability to define and erase the rules and the ability to ask for specific expressions to be evaluated. There is a way to manipulate expressions that allows you much more control over what happens. This involves replacement of subexpressions by other expressions using "/." (`ReplaceAll[ ]`) and "->" (`Rule[ ]`). This was briefly mentioned earlier in this lesson, but we explore it further here.

Start with an expression involving the symbol x. Assign this expression to the symbol y.	`In[1]:= y = 3x^3 - 4x^2 + 2x - 7`
	
	`Out[1]= -7 + 2 x - 4 x$^2$ + 3 x$^3$`

Evaluate y and replace every occurrence of x in the result by the number 3.	`In[2]:= y /. x -> 3` `Out[2]= 44`

It is sometimes convenient to use this substitution mechanism to evaluate expressions as above, but it has other uses too. One important use arises when you want to simplify an expression. This involves the use of `Rules` for replacing all expressions of a particular form rather than a specific expression. As with defining functions, a class of expressions is indicated by using "_".

Start with an expression.	`In[3]:= Log[a] + Log[b]` `Out[3]= Log[a] + Log[b]`

Replace the sum of logarithms by the logarithm of the product.	`In[4]:= % /. Log[x_] + Log[y_] -> Log[x y]`
	
	`Out[4]= Log[a (-7 + 2 a - 4 a$^2$ + 3 a$^3$)]`

You can use a rule to go the other way too.	`In[5]:= % /. Log[x_ y_] -> Log[x] + Log[y]`
	
	`Out[5]= Log[a] + Log[-7 + 2 a - 4 a$^2$ + 3 a$^3$]`

A.2.7 Attributes of symbols

Evaluation can be controlled in several ways. Certain attributes have a very significant effect on evaluation. Here we consider some of these attributes. Use the function `SetAttributes[ ]` to add one or more attributes to a symbol. Use `ClearAttributes[ ]` to remove attributes from a symbol.

We saw the attribute `Listable` in Section A.1.5. If a function f has the attribute `Listable`, then `f[{a, b}]` will be evaluated as `{f[a], f[b]}`. Nearly all of the built-in mathematical functions have the attribute `Listable`.

Using the ordinary rules of evaluation, the result is just f[{a, b, c}].	`In[1]:= f[{a, b, c}]` `Out[1]= f[{a, b, c}]`

Make f Listable.	`In[2]:= SetAttributes[f, Listable]`

Examine what attributes f has.	`In[3]:= Attributes[f]` `Out[3]= {Listable}`

Now f gets mapped over the elements of a list.	`In[4]:= f[{a, b, c}]` `Out[4]= {f[a], f[b], f[c]}`

The attribute `Orderless` causes the arguments of a function to be arranged in sorted order as one of the first steps in the evaluation process.

Add the attribute `Orderless`.	`In[5]:= SetAttributes[f, Orderless]`
The attribute `Listable` is still there.	`In[6]:= Attributes[f]`
	`Out[6]= {Listable, Orderless}`
The arguments get sorted.	`In[7]:= f[c, a, d, b]`
	`Out[7]= f[a, b, c, d]`

Another common attribute is `Protected`. If a function is `Protected`, it cannot be changed (e.g., you cannot add rules) without first `Unprotecting` it. This is to prevent you from accidentally changing a function in such a way that it no longer works properly. Of course, you can still break a protected function, you just have to be more deliberate about it.

There are 16 different attributes that any symbol can have. They are `Constant`, `Flat`, `HoldAll`, `HoldFirst`, `HoldRest`, `Listable`, `Locked`, `OneIdentity`, `Orderless`, `Protected`, `ReadProtected`, `Temporary`, `Stub`, `NProtectedFirst`, `NProtectedRest`, `NProtectedAll`. Consult the *Mathematica* manual for further explanation of what they do.

A.2.8   The evaluation process

We have said that *Mathematica* works by evaluating expressions, i.e., applying rules until no rules are applicable. The basic structure of the evaluation process for an expression is as follows:

procedure evaluate *expr*
    if *expr* is a number or a string or a symbol with no value
        then leave it unchanged
    else if *expr* is a symbol with a value
        then replace it by its value
    else (∗ recursive step ∗)
        evaluate the head and each of the elements of *expr* in order;
        apply any applicable rules to the result
    end if
end procedure

To apply a rule, take the right-hand side of that rule, replace formal by actual arguments, evaluate that expression, and replace the old expression by the result. Note that the evauation procedure is recursive: to evaluate an expression we must first evaluate each of its parts, and whenever a rule is applied, the right-hand side of that rule is first evaluated. Note that user-defined rules always take precedence over built-in rules. The above description glosses over many details and ignores exceptions to the standard evaluation process. In Lesson Three we give a detailed description of the steps in the evaluation process.

A.2.9 Using external packages

There are well over 100 external packages that come with *Mathematica*. These packages define many more functions and greatly extend the things that *Mathematica* can do. We will have cause to use about half a dozen of these packages. To use a package, simply start up *Mathematica* in the usual way and read in a package as a command. The syntax for doing this is << *packagename* or Get["*packagename*"]. Once the package has been read in, any functions that were defined in the package become available for use.

Read in the package
NumericalMath`ComputerArithmetic`.
The notation means that the package is in
the directory NumericalMath and the name
of the file is ComputerArithmetic.m.

```
In[1]:= << NumericalMath`ComputerArithmetic`
```

Once the package has been read in,
everything defined in the package becomes
available for use. One of the functions is
SetArithmetic[ ], which is used to define
the parameters of the arithmetic you want
to use.

```
In[2]:= ?SetArithmetic
```
SetArithmetic[dig] evaluates certain global constants used in the package ComputerArithmetic.m to make the arithmetic work properly with dig digits precision. The value of dig must be an integer between 1 and 10, inclusive, and the default value is 4. SetArithmetic[dig, base] causes the arithmetic to be dig digits in base base. The value of base must be an integer between 2 and 16, and the default is 10. Changing the arithmetic and attempting to refer to ComputerNumbers that were defined prior to the change can lead to unpredictable results.

Here we have set the arithmetic to be 5 bits
in base 2, with a rounding rule of
round-to-even.

```
In[2]:= SetArithmetic[5, 2, RoundingRule -> RoundToEven]

Out[2]= {5, 2, RoundingRule -> RoundToEven,
    ExponentRange -> {-50, 50}, MixedMode -> False,
    IdealDivide -> False}
```

The closest approximation to Pi that exists
in the arithmetic we have defined.

```
In[3]:= ComputerNumber[Pi]

Out[3]= 11.001
                2
```

You can do computer arithmetic with these
numbers.

```
In[4]:= % + %

Out[4]= 110.01
               2
```

One thing you need to be careful not to do is attempt to refer to a function defined in a package *before* that package has been read in. If you do, you will create a symbol that will hide or "shadow" the real function; and even after you read in the package *Mathematica* will think you want the undefined function when you refer to it. Fortunately this problem is easily fixed: if you Remove the symbol, *Mathematica* will likewise remove the one you do not want, allowing the one you do want to become visible.

Consider the following example involving a package NumericalMath`Microscope`, which defines a function called Microscope.

Mathematica does not know about the function `Microscope[ ]` because the package has not been read in yet. Referring to `Microscope` causes *Mathematica* to create a symbol `Microscope` in the context `Global`.

```
In[5]:= Microscope[x^(3/2), {x, 1}]

Out[5]= Microscope[x^(3/2), {x, 1}]
```

Read in the package. Notice the warning message regarding a possible conflict. There are now two different symbols called `Microscope`: `NumericalMath`Microscope`Microscope` and `Global`Microscope`.

```
In[6]:= << NumericalMath`Microscope`

Microscope::shdw:
    Warning: Symbol Microscope
      appears in multiple contexts
    {NumericalMath`Microscope`, Global`}
      ; definitions in context NumericalMath`Microscope`
      may shadow or be shadowed by other definitions.
```

Mathematica can find no rules that apply to this expression because `Microscope` in the context `NumericalMath`Microscope` is shadowed by `Microscope` in the context `Global`.

```
In[7]:= Microscope[x^(3/2), {x, 1}]

Out[7]= Microscope[x^(3/2), {x, 1}]
```

This removes the symbol `Global`Microscope`, allowing the other one to become visible.

```
In[8]:= Remove[Microscope]
```

Now the function `Microscope[ ]` is accessible.

```
In[9]:= Microscope[x^(3/2), {x, 1}]
```

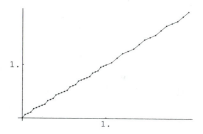

Note that the `Global` symbol `Microscope` was created by a simple reference to it. There were no rules associated with it. Its mere existence is what caused the problem. `Remove[ ]` causes it to be completely removed, as if it had never existed.

A.2.10 Miscellanea

The file `init.m` holds commands that are to be executed by *Mathematica* at the beginning of a session before the first prompt appears. *Mathematica* looks for this file in the directories specified by the global variable `$Path`. It looks in each directory in turn, and the first `init.m` it finds, it uses. There is a default `init.m`, but you can create your own and place it where it will be found before the default one. You can add lines such as `<< Utilities`Record`` to your `init.m` file. You may also choose to redefine some defaults for various functions. One example might be to include `SetOptions[ Plot3D, PlotPoints -> 50 ]` if the default `PlotPoints -> 25` is not adequate. Another way you might want to customize *Mathematica*

in your init.m is with SetOptions[Plot, AxesLabel -> {"x","y"}, PlotRange -> All].
It is an easy matter to over-ride these defaults in individual plots where the defaults are not
appropriate.

Computer problems

1. Let f[x_] := Exp[-x x]. Try to determine its integral with Integrate using limits
   -Infinity to Infinity. Also try numerically with NIntegrate using limits $\pm\infty$, then
   ± 1000, ± 100, and ± 10.

2. Plot $f(x)$, as defined in the preceding problem, for $-10 \leq x \leq 10$.

3. Plot $\tan x$ and $\tanh x$, $-10 \leq x \leq 10$, on the same graph. From the plot you should
   be able to see five roots of $\tan x - \tanh x = 0$. Using a *Mathematica* comment, state
   approximate values of the roots.

4. Plot $|\sin x|$ for $1 \leq x \leq 4$.

5. We can store code in a variable by using := as in

$$\text{it := (y = (y + x/y)/2)}$$

We will execute it for symbolic values. Set y = 1 and Clear[x] . The idea is that
we are considering an iteration for the square root of an arbitrary number x but with
an initial guess of 1. (Advice: It is a good idea to use Clear[ ] to clear the values of
variables that you are through with. This prevents unintended results that can occur if
the variable is later used purely as a symbol.) Execute the iteration three times to get
an expression in x. Simplify this. Then Plot this for x ranging from 0 to 4. You can
use a variable or % to capture this expression for these last two operations. Compare
this plot with that of Sqrt[x] over the same range.

A.3   Lesson Three

A.3.1   Using pure functions

In Lesson One we saw one way to define functions. Here we consider an alternative way with
pure functions. Pure functions have their own special uses, but before we see those uses, let
us understand how they work. A pure function is simply an expression that describes how the
argument(s) get mapped to the value of the function. In the expression for the pure function,
"#" (or *slot*) represents the argument to the function and the expression itself describes the
mapping involved.

Define a function that maps anything to its   In[1]:= f = Function[#^2]
square. The special form for this expression
is #^2.   Out[1]= #1^2 &

We can use f just like we would any other function. The argument gets substituted for every occurrence of #, and this then gets evaluated.

```
In[2]:= f[3]
Out[2]= 9
```

The important thing about pure functions is that they do not have to be given a name. To use a function, just make it the head of an expression.

```
In[3]:= #^2&[x+y]
            2
Out[3]= (x + y)
```

You can also have a pure function of several variables. To do so you need to number the #'s.

```
In[4]:= Function[#1^2 + #2^3][u, v]
           2    3
Out[4]= u  + v
```

Graph of the functions 1& and #& .

```
In[5]:= Plot[{1&[x], #&[x]}, {x, -2, 2}]
```

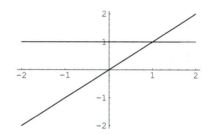

Note that there is no "#" in the expression 1&[3]. The pure function 1& applied to any argument(s) will always evaluate to 1; the argument does not need to fit into a slot.

You never have to use pure functions. You can always define a function and use it when you need it, but there are times when you need to specify a function that will be used once and never again. There are several reasons you might not want to define a function first: it is inconvenient, it clutters up the workspace of *Mathematica* to have unnecessary functions defined, and it is a burden on the memory of both the writer and the reader of the code to have to remember what different functions do.

Pure functions have some rather specialized uses. One such use is described in the next subsection.

A.3.2 More on patterns and rules

In Lesson One we used the notation f[x_] to define functions. The "_" is called a *pattern*, and the "x" is a label for any expression that the pattern will represent. Patterns are an important part of *Mathematica*. Here we explain a little about them.

A pattern in *Mathematica* is defined to be a set of expressions. The set of all expressions is denoted by _, which in full form is Blank[ ]. The pattern _^_ contains, or matches, all expressions having a head Power and exactly two elements. This would include a^b but not c a^b. The pattern _ + _ matches all expressions that are the sum of two elements. By the associativity of addition, the sum of more than two elements can still be seen as the sum of two elements, so it also matches all expressions having a head of Plus and more than two elements.

Define a rule for expressions of the form `f[_ + _]`.	`In[1]:= f[x_ + y_] := {x, y}`

The expression 2x + 3y - z matches the pattern _ + _ as the sum of 2x and 3y - z. There are other possibilities, but *Mathematica* uses the first match it finds.	`In[2]:= f[2x + 3y - z]` `Out[2]= {2 x, 3 y - z}`

There are several ways to restrict patterns so that they match only in certain cases. The simplest way is to require that the head of the matched expression be something in particular. This is done by specifying the desired head immediately after the "_".

Define a function that gives the expanded form of a polynomial raised to an *integer* power.	`In[3]:= pow[p_, n_Integer] := Expand[p^n]`

The result gets expanded.	`In[4]:= pow[x+3, 3]` `Out[4]= 27 + 27 x + 9 x$^2$ + x$^3$`

The pattern does not match because 5/3 has a head of `Rational` rather than `Integer`.	`In[5]:= pow[x+3, 5/3]` `Out[5]= pow[3 + x, $\frac{5}{3}$]`

You can also use patterns with alternative heads as in `f[x_Integer | x_Rational]` to match any rational number. (Mathematically speaking, integers are also rational numbers, but in *Mathematica* the head of an integer is `Integer`, not `Rational`.) When you use such an alternative pattern you must be careful to use the same label for both alternatives.

Define a function for all rational numbers.	`In[6]:= f[x_Integer	x_Rational] := -N[x]`

`f[ ]` is evaluated for non-floating-point numbers.	`In[7]:= {f[23], f[2/3], f[3.7]}` `Out[7]= {-23., -0.666667, f[3.7]}`

Sometimes we do not want to look for a specific head but rather to apply a test to decide whether a "_" should match an expression. The way to do this is to specify the test immediately after "_?". The test must return `True` to match.

This defines the maximum norm of a vector.	`In[8]:= norm[v_?VectorQ] := Max[Abs[v]]`

It works for a vector.	`In[9]:= norm[{2, -3}]` `Out[9]= 3`

It is not defined for matrices and other things that are not vectors.	`In[10]:= norm[{{1, 2}, {3, 4}}]` `Out[10]= norm[{{1, 2}, {3, 4}}]`

Sometimes the test you want to apply does not already exist as a named function. For example, you may want to test whether an expression is a polynomial in the variable x. No such test exists, but there is a function that tests whether an expression is a polynomial in a specified variable. You could define a test to do what you want, but there is a more convenient way using a pure function.

This test restricts the pattern to being a polynomial in the variable x. Note the use of a pure function in the pattern test.

```
In[11]:= zeros[poly_?(PolynomialQ[#, x]&)] :=
             Roots[poly == 0, x]
```

The test gives `True`, and the pattern matches.

```
In[12]:= zeros[x^2 - (a+b)x + a b]
Out[12]= x == a || x == b
```

`Sin[x]` is not a polynomial in x so the pattern does not match.

```
In[13]:= zeros[Sin[x]]
Out[13]= zeros[Sin[x]]
```

Sometimes the test you want to use to restrict the use of a rule involves a relationship between two or more of the arguments. In such cases you cannot simply use a pattern-matching test on those arguments, but you can make the rule conditional and reject it even if the pattern itself does match.

Here the pattern will match anything of the form `f[_, _]`, but the rule `f[x_, y_] := y - x` will be applied only if y is greater than x. The "/;" is the notation for a `Condition`.

```
In[14]:= f[x_, y_] := y - x /; y > x
```

The rule is applied only to the first subexpression.

```
In[15]:= {f[4, 7], f[5, 1]}
Out[15]= {3, f[5, 1]}
```

For efficiency reasons you should usually use tests on a pattern rather than apply conditions to a rule when you have a choice of either method.

We mentioned in Lesson Two that in addition to evaluation rules, which get associated with symbols, you can use "/." and "//." to apply `Rules` as you choose. Patterns play an equally important role in `Rules`.

Define a rule to simplify the difference of sines.

```
In[1]:= sinrule = Sin[x_] - Sin[y_] -> 2*Cos[(x+y)/2]*
            Sin[(x-y)/2]
```

$$Out[1]= \text{Sin}[x\_] - \text{Sin}[y\_] \rightarrow 2 \text{ Cos}[\frac{x + y}{2}] \text{ Sin}[\frac{x - y}{2}]$$

The rule works as expected.

```
In[2]:= Sin[a+h] - Sin[a] /. sinrule
```

$$Out[2]= 2 \text{ Cos}[\frac{2 a + h}{2}] \text{ Sin}[\frac{h}{2}]$$

One could use such rules to rearrange algebraic expressions for a computer program. Restricted patterns can also be used with replacement `Rules`.

Start with a list of various expressions.

$In[1]:=$ list = {7, 2/3, 3.4, f[x]}

$Out[1]=$ {7, $\frac{2}{3}$, 3.4, f[x]}

Square the elements that have a head of Integer or f.

$In[2]:=$ list /. x_Integer | x_f -> x^2

$Out[2]=$ {49, $\frac{2}{3}$, 3.4, f[x]^2}

Change every symbol to a.

$In[3]:=$ list /. _Symbol -> a

$Out[3]=$ a[7, $\frac{2}{3}$, 3.4, a[a]]

This does not change anything because the right-hand side of the Rule, N[x], gets evaluated to x before the rule is applied.

$In[4]:=$ list /. x_?NumberQ -> N[x]

$Out[4]=$ {7, $\frac{2}{3}$, 3.4, f[x]}

Using ":>" (RuleDelayed) causes N[x] to be evaluated only after the x has a numerical value.

$In[5]:=$ list /. x_?NumberQ :> N[x]

$Out[5]=$ {7., 0.666667, 3.4, f[x]}

A.3.3 How evaluation works

The general idea in evaluation is to keep applying rules until none of the rules apply. This will cause problems if you define a rule such as x := x + 1 and then try to evaluate x. To evaluate x, *Mathematica* applies the rule for x and evaluates the right-hand side, which requires the evaluation of x: there is no end to the recursion until $RecursionLimit is encountered. There are identifiable steps in the evaluation process. We examine some of them here.

Before we describe the evaluation process, we need to understand a bit more about expressions and rules. Any expression in *Mathematica* can be thought of as an inverted tree. The parts of the expression form the branches of the tree, and the atoms of the expression are the leaves of the tree. For example, the expression a x^2 + f[b, y, z] is shown as an inverted tree in Figure A.1. *Mathematica* itself can produce crude drawings of trees, but except for very simple trees the screen is often too narrow and the output must be broken over several lines.

$In[1]:=$ TreeForm[a x^c + b]

$Out[1]//TreeForm=$ Plus[b, |]
                              Times[a, |]
                                        Power[x, c]

Every rule in *Mathematica* must be associated with some symbol, and the symbol to which a rule is associated must appear in that rule. The symbol must appear in one of several places in the rule, and rules are classified according to where the symbol appears. The most common type of rule is one in which the symbol appears as the head of the left-hand side of the rule.

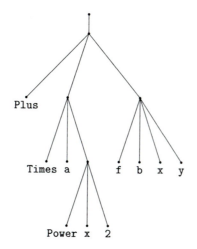

Figure A.1: Tree representation of `a x^2 + f[b, y, z]`

You typically define functions with this type of rule. You can also associate a rule with one of the elements (or the head of one of the elements) of its left-hand side.

Normally rules are associated with the head of the left-hand side.

```
In[2]:= f[g[2]] := 1
```

This rule is associated with f.

```
In[3]:= ?f
Global`f
f[g[2]] := 1
```

We can explicitly specify that a rule should be associated with the head of an argument of the left-hand side.

```
In[3]:= g /: f[g[5]] := 3
```

This rule is associated with g. Notice the notation "^:=". We could have given the rule using this notation instead of preceding the rule with "g /:".

```
In[4]:= ?g
Global`g
f[g[5]] ^:= 3
```

The first and third elements were evaluated using different types of rules. There is no rule at all for `f[g[3]]`.

```
In[4]:= {f[g[2]], f[g[3]], f[g[5]]}

Out[4]= {1, f[g[3]], 3}
```

We can now explain the evaluation process. You are not expected to remember all of this, and you may never even need it, but it is here for your reference if and when you do need it. The basic steps in standard evaluation of an expression are

1. If the expression is a number or a string, leave it unchanged.

2. If the expression is a symbol, apply any applicable rules. If no rule applies, leave it unchanged.

3. Completely evaluate the head of the expression (using recursion if necessary).

4. Completely evaluate each of the elements in the expression in order (using recursion if necessary). Note: There are exceptions to this. See the discussion below regarding `Hold` and its relatives.

5. Apply general rules associated with certain attributes that the head may have. (For example, if the head has the attribute `Orderless`, then sort the elements.)

6. Apply any user-defined rules associated with the elements or heads of the elements.

7. Apply any built-in rules associated with the elements or heads of the elements.

8. Apply any user-defined rules associated with the head or the head of the head of the expression.

9. Apply any built-in rules associated with the head or the head of the head of the expression.

In general the choice of which type of rule to use (assuming you have a choice) should be decided by which symbol is likely to be encountered most frequently. Generally speaking it is a bad idea to associate a rule with one of the four arithmetic operations because they are encountered very frequently. If every time you want to use `Plus[ ]`, *Mathematica* has to go off and check whether any of the rules associated with `Plus` happen to match the expression being evaluated, then evaluation will be very slow. In addition, you are not allowed to associate rules with `N` and certain other functions. For further details you should consult the *Mathematica* manual.

$$In[1]:= a = 7; \ b = 1; \ c = 2;$$

Turn on tracing of all rule applications.

$$In[2]:= On[]$$
$$On::trace: \ On[] \ \longrightarrow \ Null.$$

We can see exactly how the evaluation proceeds.

$$In[3]:= e = a \ x{\wedge}c + b$$
$$a::trace: \ a \ \longrightarrow \ 7.$$
$$c::trace: \ c \ \longrightarrow \ 2.$$
$$Power::trace: \ x^c \ \longrightarrow \ x^2 .$$
$$Times::trace: \ a \ x^c \ \longrightarrow \ 7 \ x^2 .$$
$$b::trace: \ b \ \longrightarrow \ 1.$$
$$Plus::trace: \ a \ x^c + b \ \longrightarrow \ 7 \ x^2 + 1.$$
$$Plus::trace: \ 7 \ x^2 + 1 \ \longrightarrow \ 1 + 7 \ x^2 .$$
$$Set::trace: \ e = a \ x^c + b \ \longrightarrow \ e = 1 + 7 \ x^2 .$$
$$Set::trace: \ e = 1 + 7 \ x^2 \ \longrightarrow \ 1 + 7 \ x^2 .$$
$$Out[3]= 1 + 7 \ x^2$$

Turn off tracing.	*In[4]:= Off[]*
Trace all applications of rules associated with **Power**.	*In[5]:= On[Power]*
Now we see only one rule being used.	*In[6]:= e = a x^c + b*

$$\text{Power::trace: } x^c \longrightarrow x^2.$$

$$Out[6]= 1 + 7\ x^2$$

Turn off tracing.	*In[7]:= Off[Power]*
Turn on tracing for **f**, and make two rules for it.	*In[8]:= On[f]; f[3, 4] := f34; f[4, 3] := f43;*
Both rules work.	*In[9]:= {f[3, 4], f[4, 3]}*

```
f::trace: f[3, 4] --> f34.
f::trace: f[4, 3] --> f43.
```

$$Out[9]= \{f34, f43\}$$

Make **f** orderless.	*In[10]:= SetAttributes[f, Orderless]*
Since **f** is **Orderless**, its elements get sorted before any rules are applied. Notice that the first element of the list gets completely evaluated before evaluation begins on the second element.	*In[11]:= {f[3, 4], f[4, 3]}*

```
f::trace: f[3, 4] --> f34.
f::trace: f[4, 3] --> f[3, 4].
f::trace: f[3, 4] --> f34.
```

$$Out[11]= \{f34, f34\}$$

In addition to tracing the evaluation process as we have done above, there are many tracing functions in *Mathematica* that return lists of partially evaluated expressions that you can manipulate. For further details you should consult the *Mathematica* manual.

There are some variations to the standard evaluation process, most notably those associated with **Hold** and its relatives. The simplest case of nonstandard evaluation occurs whenever you assign a value to a symbol such as in a = b. This expression has the full form **Set[a, b]**.

Give **b** and **c** values.	*In[1]:= b = 5; c = 2;*
Now turn tracing on so we can watch what happens.	*In[2]:= On[]*

```
On::trace: On[] --> Null.
```

Notice that **b** got evaluated, but **c** did not.	*In[3]:= c = b*

```
b::trace: b --> 5.
Set::trace: c = b --> c = 5.
Set::trace: c = 5 --> 5.
```

$$Out[3]= 5$$

In standard evaluation *both* c and b would get evaluated before any rules for Set would be applied. The reason c is not evaluated is that Set has the attribute HoldFirst. This means that when an expression involving Set is evaluated the first element is not evaluated. If it were evaluated, then in the above example *Mathematica* would try to assign the value of b to the number 2. But 2 is always supposed to be 2, not something else! Below we change Set to behave differently. *This is only for demonstration purposes. It is not recommended except to deliberately cause strange effects in Mathematica.*

Change Set[ ].

```
In[4]:= (Off[]; Unprotect[Set];
              SetAttributes[Set, HoldAll];)
```

Now c gets the value of the unevaluated b. The result 5 comes from evaluating b *after* the Set operation has occurred.

```
In[5]:= c = b
Out[5]= 5
```

The rule is simply c = b, and whatever value b happens to have *at the time you evaluate* c is what you will get for c.

```
In[6]:= ?c
Global`c
c = b
```

The head Hold can be used to prevent evaluation of any expression, but there are three attributes with similar effect that functions can have. If a function has one of the attributes HoldAll, HoldFirst, or HoldRest, all of the arguments, the first argument, or all but the first argument, respectively, remain unevaluated as evaluation proceeds. The various plotting functions are all HoldAll. This means that you cannot do things like Plot[{f[x], D[f[x], x]}, {x, 0, 3}] to plot a function and its derivative on the same graph. The reason is that the D[f[x], x] remains unevaluated until x gets assigned a numerical value, say 1.1. Then it tries to evaluate D[f[1.1], 1.1], but this makes no sense. The way to get around the problem is to use Plot[Evaluate[{f[x], D[f[x], x]}], {x, 0, 3}]. If Evaluate[ ] appears as the head of an argument, that argument will be evaluated regardless of any "hold" attribute.

We cannot plot a derivative in this way.

```
In[1]:= Plot[{Sin[x], D[Sin[x], x]}, {x, 0, 10}]
```

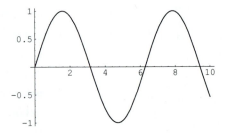

If you specifically request evaluation of something that would otherwise be held, then it does get evaluated.

In[2]:= Plot[Evaluate[{Sin[x], D[Sin[x], x]}], {x, 0, 10}]

There are many functions in *Mathematica* that have one of the three "hold" attributes. These functions have one of these attributes for specific reasons, and the attributes are generally appropriate. When such an attribute is not appropriate, you should use Evaluate[ ] rather than change the attribute.

A.3.4 The function N[ ]

As we have said before, there are two ways to use N[ ]: N[*expr*] and N[*expr*, *prec*]. In the first way machine numbers are used in the evaluation. In the second way machine numbers are used if *prec* is less than or equal to $MachinePrecision, otherwise arbitrary-precision numbers are used except that any machine numbers that may already be in the expression are left as machine numbers. You should also be aware of the way in which N[ ] deals with expressions. Just as there are specific steps used in the evaluation of an expression, so too the evaluation of N[*expr*] and N[*expr*, *prec*] follow specific rules. For example, N[Pi] gives the machine number approximation to π because there is a built-in rule associated with the symbol Pi. The standard evaluation of N[*expr*] or N[*expr*, *prec*] is as follows:

1. The argument(s) of N are first evaluated in the usual way.

2. If *expr* is a string, the result is that string.

3. If *expr* is the integer 0, the result is the integer 0.

4. If *expr* is any other number, the result is an approximation to that number to *prec* digits (or the nearest machine number if *prec* is not used or is not greater than $MachinePrecision) except that N[ ] never increases the precision of any number.

5. If *expr* is a symbol and there is a rule associated with that symbol for N of it, that rule is used. User-defined rules take precedence.

6. If *expr* is a symbol and there is no rule for N of it, the result is that symbol.

7. If *expr* is a nonatomic expression and there is a rule associated with the head or the head of the head of *expr* for N of it, that rule is used. User-defined rules take precedence.

8. If *expr* is a nonatomic expression and there is no rule for N of it, N is applied (recursively) to the head and each of the elements of *expr*.

You are not permitted to associate rules for numerical evaluation with N. You can, however, associate them with the first argument or the head of the first argument of N. For example, suppose b represents the unique real number such that $b = \cos b$. You can use this defining equation to simplify expressions involving b, but sometimes it would be simplest to just apply N[ ] to an expression involving b and be able to get a numerical result.

Define a rule for evaluating b numerically.

```
In[1]:= b /: N[b, prec_] :=
          Module[{x},
              x /. FindRoot[x == Cos[x], {x, 1},
                      WorkingPrecision -> prec,
                      AccuracyGoal -> prec - 5]
          ]
```

We can now numerically evaluate any expression involving b because N[ ] is recursive.

```
In[2]:= N[Log[Sin[b] + 3], 25]
Out[2]= 1.301175382192254175264164
```

There are times when N[ ] should be prevented from converting certain numbers to their Real equivalent. The way to achieve this is to use one of the three attributes NProtectedFirst, NProtectedRest, and NProtectedAll. These attributes are reminiscent of the various Hold attributes, but N-protection is used to control N[ ] rather than evaluation.

Start with some rules for x[1] and x[2].

```
In[3]:= sol = Solve[{x[1]^2 + x[2]^2 == 1,
                   x[2] == x[1]^2}, {x[1], x[2]}]
```

$$Out[3]= \left\{\left\{x[2] \rightarrow \frac{-1 + \text{Sqrt}[5]}{2},\right.\right.$$

$$\left. x[1] \rightarrow \frac{\text{Sqrt}[-1 + \text{Sqrt}[5]]}{\text{Sqrt}[2]}\right\},$$

$$\left\{x[2] \rightarrow \frac{-1 + \text{Sqrt}[5]}{2}, \; x[1] \rightarrow -\left(\frac{\text{Sqrt}[-1 + \text{Sqrt}[5]]}{\text{Sqrt}[2]}\right)\right\},$$

$$\left\{x[2] \rightarrow \frac{-1 - \text{Sqrt}[5]}{2}, \; x[1] \rightarrow \frac{\text{Sqrt}[-1 - \text{Sqrt}[5]]}{\text{Sqrt}[2]}\right\},$$

$$\left.\left\{x[2] \rightarrow \frac{-1 - \text{Sqrt}[5]}{2}, \; x[1] \rightarrow -\left(\frac{\text{Sqrt}[-1 - \text{Sqrt}[5]]}{\text{Sqrt}[2]}\right)\right\}\right\}$$

N[ ] goes in and converts x[1] and x[2] to x[1.] and x[2.]. These rules are now useless.

```
In[4]:= N[sol]
Out[4]= {{x[2.] -> 0.618034, x[1.] -> 0.786151},
         {x[2.] -> 0.618034, x[1.] -> -0.786151},
         {x[2.] -> -1.61803, x[1.] -> 0. + 1.27202 I},
         {x[2.] -> -1.61803, x[1.] -> 0. - 1.27202 I}}
```

Fix it so N[ ] is not permitted inside expressions with a head of x.

```
In[5]:= SetAttributes[x, NProtectedAll]
```

These rules can be used to replace the variables `x[1]` and `x[2]` with numerical values.

```
In[6]:= N[sol]
Out[6]= {{x[2] -> 0.618034, x[1] -> 0.786151},
         {x[2] -> 0.618034, x[1] -> -0.786151},
         {x[2] -> -1.61803, x[1] -> 0. + 1.27202 I},
         {x[2] -> -1.61803, x[1] -> 0. - 1.27202 I}}
```

A.3.5 Delayed evaluation

You may have noticed that `In[n]` is always followed by a ":=" while `Out[n]` is always followed by a "=". There is an important distinction between the two symbols := (`SetDelayed[ ]`) and = (`Set[ ]`). We have said that := should be used for defining functions and = should be used for setting the value of a variable. These simple rules will nearly always have the intended effect, but there are cases where the other symbol should be used instead. In order to always choose the better symbol, we need to understand just what they do. Both symbols cause a rule to be made and associated with either the head of the left-hand side or an otherwise specified symbol (which must appear in a head of one of the elements of the nonatomic expression on the left-hand side). The main difference is that with = the right-hand side is evaluated immediately and the rule that is formed involves the result of that evaluation. With := the right-hand side is left unevaluated and the rule is saved exactly as you typed it (possibly subject to some reformatting). The other difference is that the result of forming a rule with = is the value of the right-hand side, while the result of forming a rule with := is `Null`, a symbol meaning that result was "nothing."

Form two similar rules for b and c.

```
In[1]:= b := 4^6 - 13; c = 4^6 - 13;
```

The rule for b involves an unevaluated expression. Whenever b gets evaluated, that expression will have to be reevaluated, making it slower than necesary.

```
In[2]:= ?b
Global`b
b := 4^6 - 13
```

The rule for c involves a completely evaluated expression. Whenever c gets evaluated, the rule quickly returns the number.

```
In[2]:= ?c
    Global`c
c = 4083
```

Give values to w and z.

```
In[2]:= w = 2; z = 3;
```

Make two rules for x and y.

```
In[3]:= x = w + 3z; y := w + 3z;
```

x has the value 11.

```
In[4]:= ?x
Global`x
x = 11
```

y has the value w + 3z.

```
In[4]:= ?y
    Global`y
y := w + 3*z
```

x and y evaluate to the same thing.

```
In[4]:= {x, y}
Out[4]= {11, 11}
```

If we change w, the evaluation of y changes but not that of x.

```
In[5]:= w = Tan[t]; {x, y}
Out[5]= {11, 9 + Tan[t]}
```

If we clear w and z, y can only evaluate to the right-hand side of the rule.

```
In[6]:= Clear[w, z]; {x, y}
Out[6]= {11, w + 3 z}
```

Initialize n and define a symbol inc that has the side effect of incrementing n each time it is evaluated. Notice the delayed evaluation for inc.

```
In[7]:= n = 0; inc := (n = n + 1)
```

Each time inc is called, n gets incremented.

```
In[8]:= Table[inc, {4}]
Out[8]= {1, 2, 3, 4}
```

The value of n really did change.

```
In[9]:= n
Out[9]= 4
```

Define a function that is supposed to be the derivative of the sin function.

```
In[10]:= f[t_] := D[Sin[t], t]
```

It works for symbolic arguments.

```
In[11]:= f[t]
Out[11]= Cos[t]
```

It does not work for numbers.

```
In[12]:= f[2]
General::ivar: 2 is not a valid variable.
Out[12]= D[Sin[2], 2]
```

Here we evaluate the derivative right when the rule is formed.

```
In[13]:= f[t_] = D[Sin[t], t]
Out[13]= Cos[t]
```

Now it works for both numbers and symbols.

```
In[14]:= {f[2], f[t]}
Out[14]= {Cos[2], Cos[t]}
```

If you try

```
fac[0] = 1
fac[n_] = n fac[n-1]
```

without delayed assignment, what happens is the following: The first line makes the rule `fac[0] = 1`, associates it with `fac`, and returns the value of the right-hand side: 1. The second line makes the rule `fac[n_] = n fac[n-1]` (no problem with evaluating the right-hand side because the rule is not yet in place), associates it with `fac`, and attempts to evaluate the result again because now a rule is applicable. However, now there is a problem because it thinks it can evaluate `n fac[n-1]` as `n (n-1) fac[n-2]`, `n (n-1) fac[n-2]` as `n (n-1) (n-2) fac[n-3]`, etc. This continues until the recursion limit is reached. One gets the desired effect (the rule is formed) but also a lot of annoying output.

A.3.6 Miscellanea

If a function is not listable and you want to evaluate it at a list of values, you can `Map` it over that list.

Map `f` over the list `{a, b, c, d}`.

```
In[1]:= Map[f, {a, b, c, d}]
Out[1]= {f[a], f[b], f[c], f[d]}
```

The notation "/@" is a special form for `Map`.

```
In[2]:= f /@ {a, b, c, d}
Out[2]= {f[a], f[b], f[c], f[d]}
```

If you want to change the head of an expression to something else, you can use `Apply`.

Change the head to g.

```
In[3]:= Apply[g, f[a,b,c]]
Out[3]= g[a, b, c]
```

The notation "@@" is a special form for `Apply`.

```
In[4]:= g @@ f[a, b, c]
Out[4]= g[a, b, c]
```

When software fails to work properly for whatever reason, it should detect that failure and issue a message to the user explaining what it thinks the problem may be. It is reasonably convenient to do this in *Mathematica* once a problem is detected, but, of course, detecting all possible problems is not an easy task.

Define an error message named int::nsym. The "`1`" identifies a place into which an expression is to be inserted when the message is issued.

```
In[1]:= int::nsym = "The expression `1` is not symbol."
Out[1]= The expression `1` is not symbol.
```

Define an error message named int::napp.

```
In[2]:= int::napp = "The symbol `1` does not appear in the
        integrand `2`."
Out[2]= The symbol `1` does not appear in the integrand\
        `2`.
```

Define a function `int[ ]` that catches certain errors.

```
In[3]:= int[f_, x_, a_, b_] :=
           Module[{},
             If[Head[x] =!= Symbol,
               Message[int::nsym, x]; Return[]
             ];
             If[FreeQ[f, x], Message[int::napp, x, f]];
             Integrate[f, {x, a, b}]
           ]
```

A list of the messages associated with `int`.

```
In[4]:= Messages[int]
Out[4]= {Literal[int::napp] :>

         The symbol `1` does not appear in the integrand `2`.,
         Literal[int::nsym] :> The expression `1` is not symbol.}
```

This catches one type of problem and exits.

```
In[5]:= int[f, 2, 3, 6]
int::nsym: The expression 2 is not symbol.
```

This catches another potential problem, but proceeds anyway.

```
In[6]:= int[f, x, 3, 6]
int::napp: The symbol x does not appear in the integrand f

Out[6]= 3 f
```

This turns off the error message `int::napp`. You can turn a message back on using `On[ ]`.

```
In[7]:= Off[int::napp]
```

Now the error message does not appear.

```
In[8]:= int[f, x, 3, 6]
Out[8]= 3 f
```

Computer problems

1. What will the rule

   ```
   x_?NumberQ :> If[Precision[x] === Infinity, "infprec", "finprec"]
   ```

   do if it is used with "/."? How will the behavior be different if the head is changed from `RuleDelayed` to `Rule`?

2. Explain what happens in the following:

   ```
   x = 7; {x-1, x, x+1} /. x -> 5
   ```

3. Find a single, simple `Rule` that will convert any real (i.e., `Integer`, `Rational`, or `Real`) number to the string `"real"` when used with `ReplaceAll[ ]`.

4. Suppose `expr` is some expression involving the variable `x` and you want to define a function `f[x_]` to give the derivative of `expr` with respect to `x` at any value of `x`. Why will

$$f[x_-] := D[expr, x]$$

not work? What slight alteration is needed to make it work properly?

5. In this problem we examine how we can form *Mathematica* rules to do error analysis using intervals.

(a) Enter the rule r/: r[a_, b_] + r[c_, d_] := r[a+c, b+d] . Define a rule for Times[-1, r[a_, b_]]. To test your rules, set rx = r[-4, -2], ry = r[-3, 2], and rz = r[5, 6] and evaluate -ry, rz - rx, and rz - rx - ry. It may be helpful for debugging to trace the application of your rules by typing On[r] or On[ ]. There is also an Off[ ].

(b) Define a rule for r[a_, b_] r[c_, d_]. Be careful: A range may be negative, positive, or both. The functions Min and Max may be useful. Complicated logic is unnecessary for this or the other parts of this problem. To test your rule, use rx, ry, and rz from above, and evaluate rx ry and rx rz.

(c) Define a rule for Power[r[a_, b_], -1]. The reciprocal of a range containing 0 is not defined (unless ∞ is allowed, and even then it is not a range), so in such a case return the range unevaluated. To do this, define a Conditional rule:

$$r/: \text{Power}[r[a_-, b_-], -1] := whatever /; logical\ expression$$

that will be applied only when the logical expression evaluates to True. To test your rule, use rx, ry, and rz from above, and evaluate rz/rx, ry/rz, and rz/ry.

(d) Extend your definition for Times[-1, r[a_, b_]] to include multiplication by an arbitrary integer scalar. That is, define a rule for Times[s_Integer, r[a_, b_]]. Test your rule with 3 rx, -5 ry, and 0 rz.

(e) Extend your definition for Power[r[a_, b_], -1] to include raising a range to an arbitrary integer power. That is, define a rule for Power[r[a_, b_], n_Integer]. Be careful: A positive even power of a range may have a minimum that is independent of the endpoints of the range. Give an example that shows that a range times itself is not the same as the square of that range. Test your rule using rx^-2, ry^-3, rx^2, and ry^4.

Appendix B
Review of Basic Mathematics

The study of mathematics, perhaps more than any other discipline, requires that the student master prerequisite material before attempting to go on. Failure to do so in some disciplines may lead to less thorough understanding of the current material, but in mathematics it will almost certainly lead to little or no understanding of the current material. While this effect can be disguised or even delayed a bit by replacing comprehension with memorization, the end result is still the same: a very limited ability to make any use of the mathematics so "learned." Moreover, the learning process is much less enjoyable if it is approached as a memorization chore rather than an adventure in which pieces of knowledge fit beautifully together and reinforce each other. With this in mind we present here a review of intermediate-level mathematics: mathematics that we assume as a prerequisite for the material in this book but that you may be less than fully proficient at.

B.1 Sets and Logic

B.1.1 Sets

We do not rigorously define a set but use the informal idea that a set is a collection of objects called the **elements** of the set. We write $a \in A$ to indicate that a is an element of A. A set with no elements is called the **empty set**.

There are two important ways to describe sets. The first way is simply to list the elements between the delimiters $\{$ and $\}$ as in $\{a, b, c\}$. Explicitly listing the elements becomes a problem for sets with more than a few elements, so the alternative is to give a description of the elements as in $\{n \mid n$ is an integer greater than $1, n$ cannot be factored$\}$, which is the set of prime numbers.

There are certain sets that we use repeatedly. In particular, we use the set of **natural numbers**: $\mathbf{N} = \{1, 2, 3, \dots\}$, the set of **integers**: $\mathbf{Z} = \{\dots, -2, -1, 0, 1, 2, \dots\}$, the set of **rational numbers**, i.e., the ratio of two integers (excluding division by zero): $\mathbf{Q} = \{m/n \mid m, n \in \mathbf{Z}, m \neq 0\}$, the set of **real numbers**: $\mathbf{R} = \{x \mid x$ has a (possibly infinite) decimal representation$\}$, and the set of **complex numbers**: $\mathbf{C} = \{x + iy \mid x, y \in \mathbf{R}\}$. The set of **imaginary numbers** is the set $\{x + iy \mid x, y \in \mathbf{R}, y \neq 0\}$.

When dealing with sets we often want to refer to only a part of a set. A set B is said to be a **subset** of a set A if every element of B is also in A. We write this as $B \subseteq A$. Note that

B could be the empty set, A itself, or a set containing some elements of A and not others. Note that the sets we named above are nested subsets in the order $\mathbf{N} \subseteq \mathbf{Z} \subseteq \mathbf{Q} \subseteq \mathbf{R} \subseteq \mathbf{C}$.

An important type of subset of $\mathbf{R}$ is an *interval*. The set of numbers x between a and b, inclusive, i.e., $\{x \mid x \in \mathbf{R}, a \leq x \leq b\}$ is written $[a, b]$. Of course, this makes sense only if $a \leq b$. If we want the set that does not include the endpoint(s) a and/or b, we turn the appropriate bracket(s) around: $]a, b[$ is the interval between a and b but does not include either a or b. If an interval includes its endpoints, it is called **closed**. If it does not include its endpoints, it is called **open**. If it includes one endpoint but not the other, it is **half-open** or **half-closed**.

One type of open interval that is important for calculus is an ε-**neighborhood**. An ε-neighborhood of a point x, written $N_\varepsilon(x)$, is an open interval $]x - \varepsilon, x + \varepsilon[$.

B.1.2 Logic

The terms "and" and "or" refer to logical operators. If p and q are logical propositions, then the **conjunction** p and q (written as $p \wedge q$) is true if both p and q are true, otherwise (i.e., if neither of them is true or if only one of them is true) $p \wedge q$ is false. On the other hand, the **disjunction** p or q (written as $p \vee q$) is true if at least one of them is true. If neither of them is true, then $p \vee q$ is false as well. Conjunction and disjunction are commutative operations. That is, $p \vee q = q \vee p$ and $p \wedge q = q \wedge p$.

The operator "not" negates the truth of a proposition. Thus "not true" is "false" and "not false" is "true". Symbolically we write $\neg p$ for the negation of p. De Morgan's laws for logic say that negation of a conjunction is the disjunction of the negation of its operands and the negation of a disjunction is the conjunction of the negation of its operands. Symbolically this is $\neg(p \wedge q) = \neg p \vee \neg q$ and $\neg(p \vee q) = \neg p \wedge \neg q$.

The **implication** "if p then q" is a statement about the truth of q on the condition that p is true. If p is not true then it says nothing at all about q. Thus "if $x > 10$ then $x > 5$" is true, but it says nothing about where x may be relative to either 5 or 10. There are three cases to consider:

- $x \leq 5$ in which case both $x > 10$ and $x > 5$ are false,

- $5 < x \leq 10$ in which case $x > 10$ is false and $x > 5$ true, and

- $x > 10$ in which case both $x > 10$ and $x > 5$ are true.

Note that it is not possible to have the fourth case: $x > 10$ is true and $x > 5$ is false. This is exactly why the implication "if $x > 10$ then $x > 5$" itself is true. Symbolically we write "if p then q" as $\neg p \vee q$. The negation of the implication $\neg p \vee q$ is $p \wedge \neg q$.

The **contrapositive** of the implication "if p then q" is "if $\neg q$ then $\neg p$". The contrapositive of an implication is equivalent to the implication itself. That is, the contrapositive of an implication is true if and only if the implication is true. Contraposition is the basis for indirect proofs.

B.2 Advanced Algebra

B.2.1 Absolute values

Definition B.1 *The **absolute value** of a number x is x if $x \geq 0$ and $-x$ otherwise. The absolute value of x is written $|x|$.*

The only number with an absolute value of 0 is the number 0. All other numbers have a positive absolute value.

The absolute value is important when considering size and distance. Sometimes we are concerned with the size or magnitude of a quantity without reference to its sign. The distance between two numbers x and y is given by $|x - y|$.

In the case of explicit numbers such as $+3.2$ or -4.5, the absolute value gives the number without the sign. That is, $|+3.2| = 3.2$ and $|-4.5| = 4.5$. While this is in fact true, it is not at all central to the understanding of what absolute values are all about. The fundamental idea behind absolute value is that of measuring size or distance.

B.2.2 Inequalities

A property of the real numbers is that any two of them, say x and y, can be compared and the result will be exactly one of the following three possibilities: x and y can be the same number, x can be to the left of y on the real number line, or x can be to the right of y on the real number line. We say x is **less than** y (written as $x < y$) if x is to the left of y, x is **equal to** y (written as $x = y$) if x is the same as y, and x is **greater than** y (written as $x > y$) if x is to the right of y. In addition we sometimes want to combine two of these three possibilities. Thus we have $x < y \vee x = y$, $x < y \vee x > y$, $x > y \vee x = y$, which are written as $x \leq y$, $x \neq y$, and $x \geq y$, respectively.

An important use of inequalities is in conjunction with absolute values. We often want to be able to say that the difference between an approximate result $\tilde{x}$ and the correct result x is less than some small number ε. We write this as $|\tilde{x} - x| < \varepsilon$. In this same vein, we may know that $\tilde{x}$ and x are both close to some third number y, but we do not know just how close $\tilde{x}$ is to x. The **triangle inequality** allows us to at least find a value that is not less than the difference between $\tilde{x}$ and x. In particular, it says that $|(\tilde{x} - y) + (y - x)| \leq |(\tilde{x} - y)| + |(y - x)|$. Thus if we can show that $|(\tilde{x} - y)| + |(y - x)| < \varepsilon$, we will also have that $|(\tilde{x} - x)| < \varepsilon$.

B.2.3 Functions and inverses

Definition B.2 *A **function** f from a set A (called the **domain**) to a set B, $f : A \rightarrow B$, is a set of ordered pairs (a, b), $a \in A$ and $b \in B$, such that each element in A appears as the first coordinate in exactly one ordered pair. The elements of B that appear as the second coordinate in at least one ordered pair form a subset of B that is called the **range** of f.*

Another name for a function is a **mapping**, and we say that f maps x to $f(x)$.

The use of set notation to define a function is rather cumbersome, and mathematicians often abbreviate things considerably. For example, consider the function $f = \{(x, x^2) \mid x \in \mathbf{R}\}$. We have the set of real numbers as the domain and the set of nonnegative reals as the range. The negative reals are not in the range because the second coordinate of each of the ordered pairs is the square of a real number and cannot be negative. When it is clear from the context what the domain of a function is and there is a simple formula relating the first and second coordinates of the ordered pairs, we will often use that formula to describe the function. Thus we might simply say $f(x) = x^2$ or $f = x \mapsto x^2$ to describe the above function. In this notation x is called the **argument** of the function f.

A function is said to be **increasing** if whenever $x_1 < x_2$, we also have $f(x_1) < f(x_2)$. The functions $x \mapsto \sqrt{x}$ and $3x + x^5$ are increasing functions. A function is said to be **decreasing** if whenever $x_1 < x_2$, $f(x_1) > f(x_2)$. Many functions are neither increasing nor decreasing, although they may increase or decrease on a restricted domain. The function $x \mapsto x^2$ is increasing for $x > 0$ and decreasing for $x < 0$. Increasing and decreasing functions have an important property: they are **one-to-one**. A function is said to be one-to-one if every element in its domain gets mapped to a unique value, i.e., whenever $f(x_1) = f(x_2)$ we have $x_1 = x_2$. When a function is one-to-one, we can exploit the one-to-one correspondence between elements in the domain and the range to define a new function that maps elements in the other direction.

Definition B.3 *The* **inverse function** *of $f(x) = y$ is $f^{-1}(y) = x$.*

Notice the notational relationship between $f(x) = y$ and $f^{-1}(y) = x$: The name of the function has changed from f to f^{-1} and the roles of x and y have been switched. The graphs of a function and its inverse are related by a reflection in the line $y = x$ as shown in Figure B.1.

Note the convenience of the notation f^{-1}. We can write things like $f^{-1}(f(x)) = x$ and $f(f^{-1}(y)) = y$: the f and f^{-1} "cancel" each other. Also, given $y = f(x)$ we can "divide"

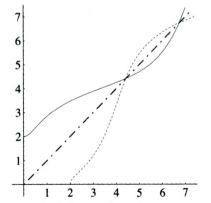

Figure B.1: A function (solid curve) and its inverse (dashed curve)

both sides of the equation by f and get $f^{-1}(y) = x$. This is certainly not related to division at all, but it is a convenient notation.

Although many of the functions we encounter will be neither increasing nor decreasing, most will be one or the other on restricted domains. For example, if we consider $x \mapsto x^2$ on the interval $[1, 2]$, we get an increasing function. This will allow us to talk about the inverse of a function locally when a global inverse would be problematic.

There are many different ways to classify functions; we saw *increasing* and *decreasing* functions above. Two other important classes are the **even** and **odd** functions. A function f is even if for all x in the domain $f(-x) = f(x)$. Likewise, f is odd if $f(-x) = -f(x)$. The names "even" and "odd" come about because of the behavior of the functions $f(x) = x^n$, $n \in \mathbf{N}$: f is even or odd as n is even or odd. Graphically, even functions are symmetric about the vertical axis; odd functions are unchanged under rotation by $180°$ about the origin. Note that most functions, e.g., $x \mapsto x + x^2$, are neither even nor odd.

B.2.4 Elementary functions

The most basic functions of mathematics are the four arithmetic operations. They are functions from the set of ordered pairs of complex numbers to the set of complex numbers (with, of course, division by 0 being excluded).

The next most important function is exponentiation. Just as multiplication on the integers can be seen as repeated addition, exponentiation on the integers can be seen as repeated multiplication. Thus $a \times a \times a$ is usually written as a^3 and we have that $a^m \times a^n = a^{m+n}$. Because multiplication is repeated addition, we have that $(a^m)^n = a^{(mn)}$. With negative integer exponents we simply take the reciprocal, i.e., $a^{-m} = 1/a^m$ (assuming $a \neq 0$).

When we generalize this idea to exponents that are not integers, it gets a little more complicated because we cannot multiply a by itself $3\frac{1}{2}$ times. There is, however, only one sensible way to define what fractional exponents should mean. For example, we would like $(2^{\frac{1}{2}})^2$ to be 2^1, so we define $2^{\frac{1}{2}} = \sqrt{2}$. If the base a is a positive real number, the rules for integer exponents are also true for real exponents. However, for negative bases these rules no longer hold. For example, $((-1)^2)^{\frac{1}{2}} = 1$ while $(-1)^{(2)(\frac{1}{2})} = -1$.

There is one base for exponentiation that is particularly important. That base is called e and has the value $2.7182818\cdots$. The function $x \mapsto e^x$ is so important that it is given a special name: the exponential function, or exp.

The inverse of an exponential function is a logarithmic function. That is, if $a > 1$ and $y = a^x$, then $x = \log_a y$. Other ways to say this are $\log_a(a^x) = x$ and $a^{\log_a y} = y$. When we use the base e for logarithms we call it the natural logarithm and use the notation ln, i.e., $\ln x \equiv \log_e x$. For our purposes we will only find it useful to consider positive real bases and usually only bases greater than 1. Moreover, we will restrict the domain of our logarithmic functions to the positive reals. With these restrictions we have the following pairs

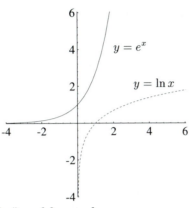

Figure B.2: Plot of e^x and $\ln x = \log_e x$

of exponential and logarithmic rules:

$$a^x a^y = a^{x+y}, \qquad\qquad (a^x)^y = a^{xy}, \qquad\qquad (a^x)^z = a^{xz},$$
$$\log_a(uv) = \log_a u + \log_a v, \qquad \log_a u^y = y \log_a u, \qquad \log_a v = \log_a u \ \log_u v.$$

The identity $\log_a v = \log_a u \ \log_u v$ is often written as $\log_u v = (\log_a v)/(\log_a u)$ and is used to change the base of logarithms.

Other important elementary functions are the (circular) trigonometric functions: sine (sin), cosine (cos), tangent (tan), cosecant (csc), secant (sec), and cotangent (cot).

Given a real number t, let (x, y) be the point on the unit circle whose distance measured along the circumference of the circle in the counterclockwise direction from the point $(1, 0)$ is t. See Figure B.3. Then $\cos t = x$ and $\sin t = y$. Moreover, if division by 0 does not occur,

$$\tan t = \frac{\sin t}{\cos t}, \qquad \sec t = \frac{1}{\cos t}, \qquad \csc t = \frac{1}{\sin t}, \qquad \cot = \frac{\cos t}{\sin t}.$$

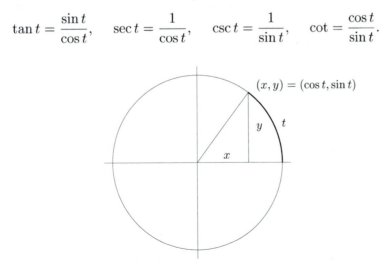

Figure B.3: Unit circle for the trigonometric functions

There are many identities relating these functions. The most fundamental identity is $\sin^2 t + \cos^2 t = 1$. Each of the functions f is related to its complementary function co-f by the relations co-$f(t) = f(\pi/2 - t)$. Thus $\cos t = \sin(\pi/2 - t)$ and $\tan t = \cot(\pi/2 - t)$. The functions $\cos t$ and $\sec t$ are even functions, while the other four are odd functions. Two other identities are useful to remember:

$$\sin(s + t) = \sin s \, \cos t + \cos s \, \sin t$$
$$\cos(s + t) = \cos s \, \cos t - \sin s \, \sin t$$

From these identities, nearly all of the many other identities can be derived without a great deal of difficulty.

The six hyperbolic trigonometric functions are $\sinh t$, $\cosh t$, $\tanh t$, $\operatorname{csch} t$, $\operatorname{sech} t$, and $\coth t$. These can be defined in a way that is somewhat analogous to the definition of the circular trigonometric functions, with the unit circle being replaced by the unit hyperbola $x^2 - y^2 = 1$. This is the reason for the name hyperbolic trigonometric functions, but those definitions are not particularly useful. A better way to define them is in terms of the exponential function:

$$\sinh t = \frac{e^t - e^{-t}}{2}, \quad \cosh t = \frac{e^t + e^{-t}}{2}, \quad \tanh t = \frac{e^t - e^{-t}}{e^t + e^{-t}}$$

with

$$\operatorname{csch} t = \frac{1}{\sinh t}, \quad \operatorname{sech} t = \frac{1}{\cosh t}, \quad \coth t = \frac{1}{\tanh t}$$

whenever division by zero is not a problem.

B.2.5 Fundamental theorem of algebra

The **degree** of a polynomial is the highest power to which the variable is raised. A **root** of a function $f(x)$ is a value x such that $f(x) = 0$. Another term for root is **zero**, and a function is said to **vanish** when it evaluates to 0.

The fundamental theorem of algebra concerns the roots of polynomial functions.

Theorem B.4 (Fundamental theorem of algebra) *Every polynomial of degree n in a single variable x with coefficients $c_j \in \mathbf{C}$, i.e.,*

$$c_0 + c_1 x + c_2 x^2 + \cdots + c_n x^n$$

where $c_n \neq 0$, has exactly n roots.

If the n roots are $\rho_1, \rho_2, \ldots, \rho_n$, then the polynomial can be factored and written in the form

$$c_n(x - \rho_1)(x - \rho_2) \cdots (x - \rho_n).$$

This does not mean that the roots are all **distinct** or different. For example, the polynomial x^2 has two roots, namely $x = 0$ and $x = 0$. The zero gets counted twice because the factor $(x - 0)$ appears twice in the factored form.

B.2.6 Summation and product notation

There are many times when we need to add several numbers such as $a_1 + a_2 + a_3 + a_4$ or $b_0 + b_1 + \cdots + b_n$. Because this is so common, mathematicians have developed a convenient notation for it. The notation involves the Greek letter Σ (sigma) for sum. The above sums are written in this notation as

$$\sum_{i=1}^{4} a_i \qquad \text{and} \qquad \sum_{i=0}^{n} b_i$$

The **index** i is a dummy variable, that is, it is simply part of the notation and is used to keep track of which terms are included in the sum. The range of the index is defined by the numbers below and above the Σ.

A similar notation exists for products, the difference being that the Greek letter Π (pi) is used instead of Σ. Thus

$$\prod_{i=1}^{5} (x - i) = (x - 1)(x - 2)(x - 3)(x - 4)(x - 5).$$

B.3 Calculus

B.3.1 Limits

Consider the following sequence of numbers: 1, 1, 2, 3, 5, 8, 13, ..., where each number after the second one is given by the sum of the previous two. This particular sequence of numbers has many interesting properties, but let us just look at the ratios of successive numbers: $1/1$, $2/1$, $3/2$, $5/3$, $8/5$, $13/8$, ... A question arises as to the behavior of this sequence of numbers. In particular, if we take the millionth number in this sequence, can we say anything about it without actually calculating it? One thing we might do is look at the decimal expansions of these numbers so that they are easier to compare.

$$
\begin{aligned}
1/1 &= 1.000000000000 \cdots \\
2/1 &= 2.000000000000 \cdots \\
3/2 &= 1.500000000000 \cdots \\
5/3 &= 1.666666666667 \cdots \\
8/5 &= 1.600000000000 \cdots \\
13/8 &= 1.625000000000 \cdots \\
21/13 &= 1.615384615385 \cdots \\
34/21 &= 1.619047619048 \cdots \\
&\ \ \vdots
\end{aligned}
$$

$$
\begin{aligned}
28657/17711 &= 1.618033990176\cdots \\
46368/28657 &= 1.618033988205\cdots \\
75025/46368 &= 1.618033988958\cdots \\
121393/75025 &= 1.618033988670\cdots \\
196418/121393 &= 1.618033988780\cdots \\
&\;\;\vdots
\end{aligned}
$$

It appears that these numbers are rapidly approaching a limiting value, and we would expect the millionth number in this sequence to be close to 1.6180339887. In fact, the numbers get closer and closer to the number $1.61803398874989484820458683436563 8\cdots$. The phrase "closer and closer" is not precise enough for mathematics. Instead we make a definition as follows:

Definition B.5 *We say that a sequence of numbers a_1, a_2, a_3, ... converges to the limit l and write*

$$
\lim_{n \to \infty} a_n = l,
$$

if for every $\varepsilon > 0$ there is a number N_ε such that $|a_n - l| < \varepsilon$ for all $n > N_\varepsilon$.

What this says in plain English is that for the example above, no matter how close we want to get to the number $1.61803398874989484820458683436563 8\cdots$, say within $\varepsilon = 10^{-30}$, if we go far enough out in the sequence we will eventually reach a point where *every* number in the sequence from then on will be within ε of the limiting value. Moreover, if we change our minds and decide that we want to get within $\varepsilon = 10^{-60}$, or even 10^{-6000}, there will be some point beyond which every number in the sequence is within ε of the limit $1.61803398\cdots$.

Sometimes a function cannot be evaluated at some point because the formula for the function gives some indeterminate form such as $0/0$. For example, the function $x \mapsto \sin x/x$ cannot be evaluated at $x = 0$. It can, however, be evaluated at points arbitrarily close to 0. If the values of the function get arbitrarily close to some value as the argument gets arbitrarily close to the point where the function becomes indeterminate, we say that the limit exists.

Definition B.6 *We say that the **limit** of $f(x)$ as x approaches a is l and write*

$$
\lim_{x \to a} f(x) = l,
$$

if for every $\varepsilon > 0$ there is a corresponding δ_ε such that $|f(x) - l| < \varepsilon$ whenever $|a - x| < \delta_\varepsilon$ and $x \neq a$.

For example, we have

$$
\begin{aligned}
(\sin 0.1)/0.1 &= 0.998334166468281523068141984\cdots \\
(\sin 0.01)/0.01 &= 0.999983333416666468254243826\cdots
\end{aligned}
$$

$$(\sin 0.001)/0.001 \;=\; 0.99999983333341666666468253\cdots$$
$$(\sin 0.0001)/0.0001 \;=\; 0.999999998333333334166666666\cdots$$
$$(\sin 0.00001)/0.00001 \;=\; 0.9999999999983333333333416666\cdots$$
$$(\sin 0.000001)/0.000001 \;=\; 0.99999999999998333333333333341\cdots$$
$$(\sin 0.0000001)/0.0000001 \;=\; 0.999999999999999833333333333333\cdots$$
$$(\sin 0.00000001)/0.00000001 \;=\; 0.99999999999999999833333333333\cdots$$
$$(\sin 0.000000001)/0.000000001 \;=\; 0.99999999999999999983333333333\cdots$$
$$(\sin 0.0000000001)/0.0000000001 \;=\; 0.9999999999999999999998333333\cdots$$
$$(\sin 0.00000000001)/0.00000000001 \;=\; 0.9999999999999999999999983333\cdots$$
$$(\sin 0.000000000001)/0.000000000001 \;=\; 0.99999999999999999999999999833\cdots$$

$$\vdots$$

Certainly this proves nothing, but it would appear that the limit of $\sin x/x$ as x approaches 0 is 1. In particular, it appears that for $\varepsilon = 10^{-2n}$ a δ that works is $\delta = 10^{-n}$. For example, if we want to get $|\sin x/x - 1| < 10^{-50}$ we should choose $|x| < 10^{-25}$. As with limits of sequences, no matter how small the ε is chosen we can always choose an appropriate δ.

B.3.2   Power series

Consider evaluating $1/(1-x)$ for some small x without using division. We can rearrange the expression to be

$$\frac{1}{1-x} = \frac{1-x+x}{1-x} = 1 + x\frac{1}{1-x}.$$

This still does not avoid the division, but it gives us an expression for $1/(1-x)$ involving itself. Using this relationship and substituting recursively for $1/(1-x)$, we get

$$\frac{1}{1-x} \;=\; 1 + x(1 + x(1 + x(1 + x(1 + \cdots))))$$
$$=\; 1 + x + x^2 + x^3 + x^4 + x^5 + \cdots.$$

Note what happens for $x = 0.1$:

$$\frac{1}{0.9} = 1 + 0.1 + 0.01 + 0.001 + 0.0001 + \cdots = 1.1111\cdots.$$

Any expression such as $1 + x + x^2 + x^3 + \cdots$ that involves an infinite sum of powers of some variable is called a *power series*. Power series are useful because they allow us to work with many functions as if they were polynomials of infinite degree.

If the coefficients in a power series are related in a nice way, we can sometimes turn it back into a simple expression. For example, consider

$$y = 1 + 2x + 3x^2 + 4x^3 + 5x^4 + 6x^5 + \cdots.$$

If we multiply both sides of this expression by x, we get

$$xy = x + 2x^2 + 3x^3 + 4x^4 + 5x^5 + 6x^6 + \cdots.$$

Taking the difference between these two power series we get

$$(1 - x)y = 1 + x + x^2 + x^3 + x^4 + x^5 + x^6 + \cdots,$$

which we know from above is $1/(1 - x)$. Thus we must have that

$$y = \frac{1}{(1 - x)^2}.$$

One common power series that you should know is

$$e^x = 1 + x + \frac{x^2}{2!} + \frac{x^3}{3!} + \frac{x^4}{4!} + \cdots.$$

B.3.3 Continuity
One important class of functions is the set of continuous functions. Informally we can think of these as functions whose graphs can be drawn without any breaks.

Definition B.7 *A function $f(x)$ is said to be* **continuous** *at $x = c$ if*

$$\lim_{x \to c} f(x) = f(c).$$

We will be concerned almost exclusively with functions that are continuous.

B.3.4 Intermediate-value theorem
Theorem B.8 (Intermediate-value theorem) *If $f(x)$ is a continuous function on the interval $[a, b]$ and $f(a) \neq f(b)$, then for every number y between $f(a)$ and $f(b)$ there exists a number x where $x \in [a, b]$ and $f(x) = y$.*

Note that the theorem does not say how to find x or even that there is only one such value. There may be many different values for x that give $f(x) = y$.

One important use of this theorem is that of finding a root of $f(x)$. In particular, if $f(a)$ and $f(b)$ are on opposite sides of 0 and $f(x)$ is continuous, then there must be a root of $f(x)$ between a and b. In fact, the proof of this theorem is closely related to one rootfinding algorithm.

B.3.5 Derivatives

One of the most important uses of limits is to define a derivative.

Definition B.9 *The* **derivative** *of $f(x)$ at $x = a$ is defined to be*

$$f'(a) = \lim_{h \to 0} \frac{f(a+h) - f(a)}{h}.$$

If the limit does not exist, then the derivative does not exist. As alternative notation we have

$$f'(x) = \frac{d}{dx} f(x).$$

There are many rules for finding the derivative of a function defined by a formula that involves elementary functions. While these are useful to know, it is the above definition that is crucial. Many times we will not have a formula for the function we are trying to find the derivative of and we will have to come back to the definition to derive anything. The process of finding a derivative is called **differentiation**.

B.3.6 Antiderivatives and definite integrals

The differentiation operator can be thought of as a mapping from differentiable functions to functions. The inverse of differentiation is antidifferentiation, and the result is an antiderivative. The problem is, antidifferentiation does not yield a unique result: the derivatives of $2x^2 - 3$ and $2x^2 + 5$ are both $4x$. In fact, any constant can be added to an antiderivative and we just get another antiderivative. Fortunately, for most purposes the arbitrary constant is not important as long as we use *the same constant everywhere* for any particular antiderivative.

We can think of the definite integral

$$\int_a^b f(x)\, dx$$

as the area bounded by the lines $x = a$, $x = b$, the x-axis, and the curve $\{(x, f(x)) \mid x \in [a, b]\}$. (See Figure B.4.) However, a definition needs to say what is meant by "area" even if it does not give a practical way to evaluate it.

Definition B.10 *If $f(x)$ is continuous on the interval $[a, b]$, then the* **definite integral of** $f(x)$ **over** $[a, b]$ *is*

$$\int_a^b f(x)\, dx = \lim_{n \to \infty} \frac{b-a}{n} \sum_{i=1}^n f\left(a + \frac{b-a}{n}\left(i - \frac{1}{2}\right)\right).$$

There are many ways to define the definite integral that involve more general partitions of the interval; but if the integral exists, all definitions result in the same value. What we have in this definition is the n-fold midpoint rule, which we study in detail in Chapter 7.

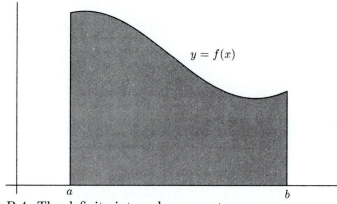

Figure B.4: The definite integral represents area.

B.3.7 Fundamental theorem of calculus

Although antiderivatives and definite integrals appear to be very different ideas, the fundamental theorem of calculus shows that they are intimately related.

Theorem B.11 (Fundamental theorem of calculus) *Suppose that $f(x)$ is a continuous function on the closed interval $[a, b]$ and that $F(x)$ is some antiderivative of $f(x)$. Then*

$$\int_a^b f(x)\,dx = F(b) - F(a).$$

B.3.8 Mean-value theorem

If someone drove 140 miles in 2 hours on a 65-mile-per-hour highway, it is clear that they exceeded the speed limit. We know that their *average* speed was 70 miles per hour, but we do not know what their *instantaneous* speed was at any time. The mean-value theorem tells us that at some time during those 2 hours their speed was 70 miles per hour, hence they exceeded the speed limit.

Theorem B.12 (Mean-value theorem) *If $f(x)$ is continuous on the closed interval $[a, b]$ and differentiable on the open interval $]a, b[$, then there exists some $\xi \in]a, b[$ such that*

$$f'(\xi) = \frac{f(b) - f(a)}{b - a}.$$

B.3.9 Table of derivatives

$$\frac{d}{dx}(a) = 0 \qquad\qquad\qquad \frac{d}{dx}(au) = a\frac{du}{dx}$$

$$\frac{d}{dx}(x^a) = ax^{a-1} \qquad\qquad \frac{d}{dx}(u^a) = au^{a-1}\frac{du}{dx}$$

$$\frac{d}{dx}(uv) = u\frac{dv}{dx} + v\frac{du}{dx}$$

$$\frac{d}{dx}\left(\frac{u}{v}\right) = \frac{v\dfrac{du}{dx} - u\dfrac{dv}{dx}}{v^2}$$

$$\frac{d}{dx}(f(x)) = f'(x)$$

$$\frac{d}{dx}(f(g(x))) = f'(g(x))g'(x)$$

$$\frac{d}{dx}(e^x) = e^x$$

$$\frac{d}{dx}(\ln x) = \frac{1}{x}$$

$$\frac{d}{dx}(\sin x) = \cos x$$

$$\frac{d}{dx}(\cos x) = -\sin x$$

$$\frac{d}{dx}(\tan x) = \sec^2 x$$

$$\frac{d}{dx}(\cot x) = -\csc^2 x$$

$$\frac{d}{dx}(\sec x) = \sec x \tan x$$

$$\frac{d}{dx}(\csc x) = \csc x \cot x$$

$$\frac{d}{dx}(\sinh x) = \cosh x$$

$$\frac{d}{dx}(\cosh x) = \sinh x$$

$$\frac{d}{dx}(\tanh x) = \operatorname{sech}^2 x$$

$$\frac{d}{dx}(\coth x) = -\operatorname{csch}^2 x$$

$$\frac{d}{dx}(\operatorname{sech} x) = -\operatorname{sech} x \tanh x$$

$$\frac{d}{dx}(\operatorname{csch} x) = -\operatorname{csch} x \coth x$$

$$\frac{d}{dx}(\sin^{-1} x) = \frac{1}{\sqrt{1-x^2}}$$

$$\frac{d}{dx}(\sinh^{-1} x) = \frac{1}{\sqrt{x^2+1}}$$

$$\frac{d}{dx}(\cos^{-1} x) = -\frac{1}{\sqrt{1-x^2}}$$

$$\frac{d}{dx}(\cos^{-1} x) = \frac{1}{\sqrt{x^2-1}}$$

$$\frac{d}{dx}(\tan^{-1} x) = \frac{1}{1+x^2}$$

$$\frac{d}{dx}(\tanh^{-1} x) = \frac{1}{1-x^2}$$

$$\frac{d}{dx}\int_u^v f(t)\,dt = f(v)\frac{dv}{dx} - f(u)\frac{du}{dx}$$

B.3.10   Table of antiderivatives

$$\int a\,dx = ax$$

$$\int au\,dx = a\int u\,dx$$

$$\int (u+v)\,dx = \int u\,dx + \int v\,dx$$

$$\int u\frac{dv}{dx}\,dx = uv - \int v\frac{du}{dx}\,dx$$

$$\int x^a \, dx = \frac{x^{a+1}}{a+1} \quad (a \neq -1)$$

$$\int \frac{dx}{x} = \ln x$$

$$\int a^x \, dx = \frac{a^x}{\ln a}$$

$$\int \frac{dx}{a^2 + x^2} = \frac{1}{a} \tan^{-1} \frac{x}{a}$$

$$\int \frac{dx}{a^2 - x^2} = \frac{1}{a} \tanh^{-1} \frac{x}{a}$$

$$\int \frac{dx}{x^2 - a^2} = -\frac{1}{a} \coth^{-1} \frac{x}{a}$$

B.4 Probability and Statistics

We will not have a great need for probability and statistics, but we do need to be familiar with a few basic terms. To this end let us consider an experiment with a single fair die. The probability of getting any of 1, 2, 3, 4, 5, or 6 is 1/6. We get each of these probabilities by knowing that there are six equally likely results. However, this is a very idealized experiment. In real life we can rarely analyze random events sufficiently to know their probability distributions. In most cases we have to repeat the experiment many times and try to determine the probability distribution from the relative frequency of each of the possible outcomes. If we throw a die 100 000 times, we may end up with 16 329 ones, 16 372 twos, 16 797 threes, 16 881 fours, 16 732 fives, and 16 889 sixes. (In fact, these numbers were generated by using *Mathematica* to simulate 100 000 throws of a die.) Note that we did not get even two of these counts to agree. The closest two were the counts for the 4's and the 6's, which differ by only 8. In fact, it would have been surprising if two of them had agreed. We would have been even more surprised if all 100 000 rolls had been 3's. Probability can explain why we should be surprised at such events. It tells us just how improbable such events might be.

B.4.1 Measures of location and dispersion

The two most important parameters of a probability distribution are its mean μ and standard deviation σ. The mean tells us the expected value of a random variable. The variance tells us the expected square of the difference between a random variable and the mean. The standard deviation is the square root of the variance. If the standard deviation is small, we can expect a random variable to be close to the mean. In the above example these are

$$\mu = \tfrac{1}{6}(1) + \tfrac{1}{6}(2) + \tfrac{1}{6}(3) + \tfrac{1}{6}(4) + \tfrac{1}{6}(5) + \tfrac{1}{6}(6) = \tfrac{7}{2}$$

$$\sigma = \sqrt{\tfrac{1}{6}(1 - \tfrac{7}{2})^2 + \tfrac{1}{6}(2 - \tfrac{7}{2})^2 + \tfrac{1}{6}(3 - \tfrac{7}{2})^2 + \tfrac{1}{6}(4 - \tfrac{7}{2})^2 + \tfrac{1}{6}(5 - \tfrac{7}{2})^2 + \tfrac{1}{6}(6 - \tfrac{7}{2})^2}$$

$$= \frac{\sqrt{105}}{6} \approx 1.70783.$$

In general, these values are given by the following definitions.

Definition B.13 *The* **mean** *of a random variable with a probability distribution* $p(x_i)$ *is*

$$\mu = \sum_i p(x_i)x_i,$$

and the **variance** *is*

$$\sigma^2 = \sum_i p(x_i)(x_i - \mu)^2.$$

The **standard deviation** *is the square root of the variance.*

If the random variable can take on values in an interval rather than just discrete values, the sums get changed to integrals.

Definition B.14 *The* **mean** *of a random variable with a probability density function* $f(t)$ *is*

$$\mu = \int_{-\infty}^{\infty} f(t)t\, dt$$

and the **variance** *is*

$$\sigma^2 = \int_{-\infty}^{\infty} f(t)(t - \mu)^2\, dt.$$

The mean μ and standard deviation σ are properties of the probability distribution or density function itself. Usually we do not know their values but must estimate them by sampling the distribution. Intuitively, our confidence in the accuracy of these estimates increases with the size of the sample.

References

Numerical Methods References

K.E. Atkinson, *Elementary Numerical Analysis*, Wiley, 1985.

G. Dahlquist and Å. Björck, tr. N. Anderson, *Numerical Methods*, Prentice-Hall, Englewood Cliffs, N.J., 1974.

G.E. Forsythe, M.A. Malcolm, and C.B. Moler, *Computer Methods for Mathematical Computations*, Prentice-Hall, Englewood Cliffs, N.J., 1977.

G.H. Golub and J.M. Ortega, *Scientific Computing and Differential Equations*, Academic Press, San Diego, CA, 1992.

D. Kahaner, C. Moler, and S. Nash, *Numerical Methods and Software*, Prentice-Hall, Englewood Cliffs, N.J., 1989.

A. Ralston and P. Rabinowitz, *Introduction to Numerical Analysis*, second edition, McGraw-Hill, New York, 1978.

Mathematica References

N. Blachman, *Mathematica: A Practical Approach*, Prentice-Hall, Englewood Cliffs, N.J., 1992.

S. Wolfram, *Mathematica: A System for Doing Mathematics by Computer*, second edition, Addison-Wesley, Redwood City, Calif., 1991.

Index

For information about *Mathematica* consult the separate *Mathematica* index, which follows this index.

Mathematica **Index**